8/03

3000 800054 59011
St. Louis Community College

Meramec Library
St. Louis Community College
11333 Big Bend Blvd.
Kirkwood, MO 63122-5799
314-984-7797

WITHDRAWN

D0082698

St. Louis Community College
at Meramec
Library

Tricolor and Crescent

Tricolor and Crescent

France and the Islamic World

WILLIAM E. WATSON

Perspectives on the Twentieth Century
Edward R. Beauchamp
Series Adviser

Westport, Connecticut
London

Library of Congress Cataloging-in-Publication Data

Watson, William E.
   Tricolor and crescent: France and the Islamic world/William
   E. Watson.
      p.   cm.—(Perspectives on the twentieth century, ISSN 1538-9626)
   Includes bibliographical references and index.
   ISBN 0-275-97470-7 (alk. paper)
   1. Islamic countries—Relations—France. 2. France—Relations—Islamic countries.
I. Title. II. Series.
DS35.74.F7 W38 2003
325'.3440961—dc21   2002030336

British Library Cataloguing in Publication Data is available.

Copyright © 2003 by William E. Watson

All rights reserved. No portion of this book may be
reproduced, by any process or technique, without the
express written consent of the publisher.

Library of Congress Catalog Card Number: 2002030336
ISBN: 0-275-97470-7
ISSN: 1538-9626

First published in 2003

Praeger Publishers, 88 Post Road West, Westport, CT 06881
An imprint of Greenwood Publishing Group, Inc.
www.praeger.com

Printed in the United States of America

The paper used in this book complies with the
Permanent Paper Standard issued by the National
Information Standards Organization (Z39.48-1984).

10 9 8 7 6 5 4 3 2 1

Contents

Photo essay follows chapter 3.

Series Foreword

Whoever first coined the phrase, "When the siècle hit the fin," described the twentieth century perfectly! The past century was arguably a century of intellectual, physical, and emotional violence unparalleled in world history. As Haynes Johnson of the *Washington Post* has pointed out in his *The Best of Times* (2001), "since the first century, 149 million people have died in major wars; 111 million of those deaths occurred in the twentieth century. War deaths per population soared from 3.2 deaths per 1,000 in the sixteenth century to 44.4 per 1,000 in the twentieth."[1] Giving parameters to the twentieth century, however, is no easy task. Did it begin in 1900 or 1901? Was it, as in historian Eric Hobsbawm's words, a "short twentieth century" that did not begin until 1917 and end in 1991?[2] Or was it more accurately the "long twentieth century," as Giovanni Arrighi argued in *The Long Twentieth Century: Money, Power, and the Origins of Our Times*?[3] Strong cases can be made for all of these constructs and it is each reader's prerogative to come to his or her own conclusion.

Whatever the conclusion, however, there is a short list of people, events, and intellectual currents found in the period between the nineteenth and twenty-first centuries that is, indeed, impressive in scope. There is little doubt that the hopes represented by the Paris Exhibition of 1900 represented the mood of the time—a time of optimism, even utopian expectations, in much of the so-called civilized world (which was the only world that counted in those days). Many saw the fruits of the Industrial Revolution, the application of science and technology to everyday life, as having the potential to greatly enhance life, at least in the West.

In addition to the theme of progress, the power of nationalism in conflicts—not only over territory, but also economic advantage and intellectual dominance—came to characterize the last century. It was truly a
century of war, from the "little" wars of the Balkans and colonial conflicts
of the early 1900s to the "Great" War of 1914–1918 that resulted in
unprecedented conflict over the remainder of the century.

Every century has its "great" as well as "infamous" individuals, most
often men, although that too would begin to change as the century drew
to a close. Great political figures such as Lenin, Trotsky, Stalin, Hitler, Mussolini, Churchill, the two Roosevelts, de Gaulle, Adenauer, Mahatma
Gandhi, Mao Tse-tung, Ho Chi Minh, and others were joined in the last
part of the century by tough competent women like Golda Meir, Indira
Gandhi, Margaret Thatcher, and scores of others who took the reins of
power for the first time.

A quick listing of some major events of the century includes World War
I, the Russian Revolution, the rise of Fascism, the Great Depression of the
1930s, the abdication of Edward VIII, Pearl Harbor and World War II, the
unleashing of atomic bombs on Hiroshima and Nagasaki, the long
Indochina War, the Cold War, the rise of nationalism (with an increase in
nation-states from about fifty to almost two hundred), the establishment
of Israel, the triumph of the free market, an increasingly strident battle
between religious fanaticism and secular preferences, and on and on. At
the same time that these events occurred, there was a great creative flour-
ishing of mass entertainment (especially television and the Internet), not
to mention important literary, dramatic, cinematic, and musical contributions of all kinds.

These elements incorporate some of the subject matter of this new series
focusing on "Perspectives on the Twentieth Century," which strives to
illuminate the last century. The editor actively seeks out manuscripts that
deal with virtually any subject and with any part of our planet, bringing a
better understanding of the twentieth century to readers. He is especially
interested in subjects on "small" as well as "large" events and trends,
including the role of sports in various societies, the impact of popular
music on the social fabric, the contribution of film studies to our understanding of the twentieth century, and so on. The success of this series is
largely dependent on the creativity and imagination of its authors.

Edward R. Beauchamp

Acknowledgments

I wish to extend my thanks to the following individuals: Dr. Edward Beauchamp of the University of Hawaii and Dr. Heather Ruland Staines of Praeger Publishers, for their editorial expertise and patience; my fellow educator, Meredith Borger, for reading the first half of the manuscript and offering her suggestions; my colleagues in the Immaculata University History Department: Dr. John Hill, Professor John Ahtes, and my assistants, Anna Besch, Stefanie Spizzirro, and Maura O'Leary, for their valuable assistance and encouragement; Daniele Beaulieu and Helen Beaulieu for their generous help with the Legion; my wife Debra, for her patience, and my children Laura, William, Jr., and Margaret, to whom this volume is dedicated.

Introduction

France has had the longest sustained contact with Islam and Muslim populations of almost any Western nation. Spain, Italy, and Russia have likewise had extensive contact with Islam, but an important part of that experience has included extended periods of Muslim occupation of parts of the Iberian and Italian peninsulas (as well as the Mediterranean islands) and of the Russian steppe lands. France, alone among the Western nations having sustained contact with Islam, has never been fully conquered by Muslim arms during the lengthy period of cross-cultural contact and conflict.

France's experience with Islam and Muslims stretches back 1,400 years. In the eighth century, Arab and Berber Muslim armies carried the Islamic faith, Arabic language, culture, and caliphal government into the Frankish Kingdom. Muslim armies had already successfully transported Islam and Muslim colonizing populations into the entire southern and eastern rim of the Mediterranean basin (an area that remains Islamic to this day). The responses of French leaders to the threats posed to the integrity of French lands and French culture by Muslims led to the defeat of Muslim armies on French soil (e.g., Charles Martel's victory at Tours-Poitiers in 732), and also to three distinct periods of French overseas expansion against Muslims—in the period of the crusades (circa 1100–1300, which campaigns were mainly manned by French-speaking knights); during the Napoleonic period (1798–1800, when Napoleon's Army of the Orient conquered Egypt and part of Syria); and in the era of the New Imperialism (circa 1800–1900, when a French Islamic Empire was created). Arab populations were so impressed by the military vigor of the French that the word *Franj* (Frank) entered the Arabic language as "European" or "Westerner," and a host of adjectives and nouns remain in modern standard Arabic as a consequence of this early period of military contact.

France was first among the Western nations to acquire trade capitulations from the much-feared "Invincible Turk," and in the nineteenth century, French governments used a variety of excuses to justify the conquest of a significant portion of the world's Muslim populations, including the need to eliminate Barbary piracy, the desire to spread France's "civilizing mission," and the interest in expanding French overseas markets. By 1900, France ruled almost all of the Saharan African Muslim populations, and half of the Sudanic African Muslim populations, as well as other smaller Muslim communities dispersed throughout the globe, as distant as the Chams of Indochina.

The modern French Empire was essentially an empire of Muslims controlled by France—a French Islamic Empire. An outgrowth of the empire, the academic phenomenon of Oriental studies was pioneered by the French, as a consequence of the sustained curiosity about the Islamic enemy. France was unique among the Western nations in being able to put trained Arabists into the field to help administer the empire (from the Arab Bureaus and the SAS (Section Administrative Specialiseé) of Algeria, to the career of the great Orientalist Louis Massignon in the Middle East before and during World War I).

The twentieth century saw the expansion of French influence in the Islamic world, with the introduction of League of Nations mandates into Syria and Lebanon—areas once called *Outremer* by the French crusaders of previous centuries. French soldiers found there were Arabs who remained in contact with their crusader forebears—the Maronite Catholics, Arabs who came to prefer to speak French rather than Arabic. Given this long and important experience of contact with Islam and Muslim populations, French governments of the twentieth century believed that they knew better than their Western colleagues how to administer colonial government over Muslim subjects. French politicians of both the Left and the Right spoke of France's "rights" in Syria and the Sahara, which derived from France's unique history. Successive French regimes would try to hold onto their inherited colonial empire longer than many of their Western counterparts. The crisis of empire even brought about the dramatic downfall of the Fourth French Republic and the rise of the Fifth Republic.

Despite an ungraceful end to the French Islamic Empire in the 1950s and early 1960s, France's experience of empire imparted significant knowledge of Islam and of Muslim populations in two regards—the ability to continue to exercise decisive foreign policy within the Islamic world (for example, in the Sahara), and the capacity to infiltrate radical Islamic terrorist organizations. Despite the presence of Muslim terrorist organizations like the "Roubaix Gang" and *al-Qa-ida* on French soil, French intelligence agencies have managed to stave off September 11–type attacks on French targets. Much can be learned from the history of French contacts with Islam.

1

Three Legacies: Charles Martel, the Crusades, and Napoleon

THE ARAB CONQUEST OF SOUTHERN FRANCE

The initial Arab drive to expand Islam carried Muslim armies and Muslim colonists into Europe in the first half of the eighth century. Three waves of Arab and Berber expansion reached the Kingdom of the Franks following the Arab-Berber Muslim victory over the Visigothic Kingdom in Spain in 711. Spain and Portugal were incorporated into the *dar al-Islam* (literally, the house of Islam) as the province of al-Andalus by the Umayyad Caliphate in the second decade of the eighth century.[1]

The Andalusi Muslims expanded north of the Pyrenees to eliminate the last pockets of Visigothic resistance in the vicinity of Narbonne, Carcassonne, and Nîmes.[2] A Muslim strike force captured Narbonne in 719, and Arab and Berber soldiers and administrators settled down. They constructed a mosque attached to the local Church of St.-Rustique, which lent a sense of permanence to their forty-year presence there.[3] The city was referred to as *'Arbuna* in medieval Arabic geographical literature, and it served as the base for more far-reaching Muslim raids into Aquitaine and the Rhône valley (to Avignon, Lyon, and Autun). In these activities, the last remnants of the Visigothic presence in the Languedoc region were extinguished.

Although the Muslims were stopped at Toulouse in 721 by Duke Eudo of Aquitaine, they were active in the Rhône valley, and in particular the tributary Ardèche region, leaving behind many place names attesting to their short-lived military presence in the area (for example, Rieu Mouren, Roquemaure, Rochemaure, Morelle, and Sarrasinière).[4] The purpose of this activity seems to have been to probe the region to discern the extent of

Eudo's holdings and to find monasteries and towns that could serve as new sources of plunder.

A second wave of expansion into the Frankish lands occurred in the fall of 732 when Andalusi amir 'Abd ar-Rahman al-Ghafiqi sought to eliminate Duke Eudo as a strategic threat to his northern borders. This time, the Muslims decisively defeated the Aquitanians at Bordeaux, and Eudo barely managed to escape north into the Frankish heartland.[5] 'Abd ar-Rahman pursued him, but Eudo was able to warn the Merovingian *major domus* (master of the palace) Charles, who was the principal Frankish warlord and the kingdom's treasurer. Charles gathered together his mainly infantry levies and prepared for a defensive stand against the then largely unknown "infidels" advancing from the south. As 'Abd ar-Rahman crossed the borders of the Frankish Kingdom proper, he was probably unaware that he had gone from one polity to another, but he indeed knew of the wealth of the shrines of St. Hilary at Poitiers and St. Martin at Tours, which he intended to sack. The Merovingian infantry army, however, proved to be too strong for the mounted Andalusi forces in the resulting Battle of Tours-Poitiers (October 25, 732), as the Arab-Berber cavalry units were driven back repeatedly by an impenetrable Frankish infantry square. 'Abd ar-Rahman himself was struck down in combat.[6]

The battle has figured prominently in French historiography, and has served for many centuries to define France as an unbeaten country in the struggle between "Cross and Crescent," standing in stark contrast to other European countries such as neighboring Spain and distant Russia, which had to endure much longer, more culturally and politically devastating episodes of contact with Islam. The importance of the battle has been magnified in the centuries since Frankish monastic chroniclers first stated that Charles had won the battle *Christo auxiliante* (with Christ's help).[7] Charles subsequently received the title of *Martellus* (the hammer) for beating the Muslims back at Tours-Poitiers, and he provided the name of the future Frankish Carolingian dynasty (from *Carolus*—Charles in Latin). In 1869, a time of great French success against Muslim forces abroad, François Guizot and Madame Guizot de Witt stated of the Battle of Tours-Poitiers:

It was a struggle between East and West, South and North, Asia and Europe, the Gospel and the Koran; and we now say, on a general consideration of events, peoples, and ages, that the civilization of the world depended on it.[8]

Strong and increasingly mobile Frankish forces under Charles Martel eliminated the Andalusi Muslim presence in the Rhône valley through the 730s, but it was Charles's son Pepin III ("the Short") who managed to take Narbonne in 759. The city fell due to a combination of Umayyad neglect and local Languedocian Christian disaffection with Islamic rule (the city's Christians rose up to aid the Frankish assault in 759). Pepin's son Charlemagne (r. 768–814) extended the prior Frankish policy of resistance to the Muslims into campaigns against the Muslims within the Iberian peninsula. His purpose was the liberation of Hispanic Catholics from Islamic rule, and he came to realize that he could exploit the unstable political environment of northern al-Andalus to the advantage of the Frankish Kingdom. In a series of campaigns lasting from 777 to 795, his forces conquered to the Ebro River. The success of Frankish arms in this theater, however, was probably not as great as he had hoped. Charlemagne desired to expand the frontiers of Catholic culture in many areas simultaneously—in Saxony (772–804); in Slavic central and eastern Europe (789–812); in the Avar Khanate in Hungary (791–796), as well as in Islamic al-Andalus. Frankish manpower and material resources were strained too thinly on too many fronts to score an overwhelming victory over the Muslims, with perhaps 3,000 cavalry and between 6,000 and 10,000 infantry available for the campaign. The Frankish epic *Song of Roland*, however, focused exclusively on the Andalusi theater of the expanding frontiers of Western Christendom.[9] Islam, after all, provided an ideology that challenged Catholic universalism to a degree that Germanic, Slavic, or Avar paganism could not do.

The Frankish realm and the Islamic world intersected, however, in the emerging Muslim-dominated global economy of the ninth century.[10] Charlemagne traded Frankish finished products with Baltic Slav merchants for Arab *dirhams*, which were universally prized for their high silver content. Addionally, the Arab-controlled slave and fur trades of northeastern Europe passed through the Frankish Kingdom en route to al-Andalus. When Frankish political unity and military power began to deteriorate in the mid-ninth century, Umayyad piracy began to be directed against the Christian areas of the central and eastern Mediterranean Sea. The once-unified land of the Franks remained divided for about five centuries into the Paris-based Kingdom of France in the north, and numerous feudal duchies and principalities that in turn were subdivided by the customary military-aristocratic "ties of dependence."

Provence was particularly vulnerable to Muslim piracy in the late 880s because the local ruler, Louis, was preoccupied in Italy. A band of Andalusi Muslim brigands established a base on the Côte d'Azur in 888 called Fraxinetum by the Europeans (after the Latin word for ash tree, present in abundance there) and *jabal al-Qilal* by the Arabs (Arabic for the Mountain of Peaks).[11] The Umayyad court in Córdova sent a force of about a hundred men to garrison the fort and the nearby manor house, which they also captured. For ninety years the Muslims attacked the important monasteries of Provence and the Alpine region, advancing as far north as St. Gall in Switzerland. They acquired plunder as well as hostages to hold for ransom. Among their hostages was the popular and influential Abbot Mayeul of Cluny (later canonized), who dared engage in a religious disputation with the Muslims and, according to his hagiography, defeated his Muslim persecutors in a war of words.[12]

The Muslims established seasonal operational bases throughout the Alpine region, and a variety of Provençal place names attest to their presence, including the Massif des Maures mountain range: Ramatuelle (named after the Arabic phrase rahmat Allahu, meaning the blessings of Allah); Les Maurras; and La Londe les Maures.[13] After both Burgundian and Byzantine military operations failed to capture Fraxinetum, the Saxon army of Holy Roman Emperor Otto the Great prepared to march south to expel the Muslims. A coalition of local aristocrats led by William of Arles, however, assembled and finally succeeded in eliminating the Muslim base in 972 (fearing a Saxon presence almost as much as they despised the Muslims).

SOURCES OF KNOWLEDGE

Muslim geographers of the Classical School of Islamic Geography in Abbasid Baghdad documented the Frankish realm in ninth-century trade networks, as well as hostile encounters between the Muslims and Christians that occurred regularly along the rough frontiers of al-Andalus.[14] The Arabs attached a greater significance to their confrontation with the Franks than with any other European people except perhaps the Byzantine Greeks. The word *Franj* entered the Arabic language in the eighth century with the meaning of "Franks" (and later, "Frenchmen") in particular, and of "Europeans" in general. The impact of the Franks has persisted into modern standard Arabic (*Fusha*): the verb *tafarnaja* (root = f-r-n-j) means "to become Europeanized"; the adjective *mutafarnij* means "Europeanized"; *al-ifranj* means "the Europeans"; and *ifranja* and *bilad al-ifranj* mean "Europe."

Throughout the former Frankish realm, the French could naturally derive some important facts regarding Muslim intentions in the Christian world from the frequent Muslim military campaigns against them—including the knowledge that their churches and monasteries were considered legitimate targets by most Muslim military commanders. They also knew of the existence of Christian communities behind a kind of medieval Islamic "Iron Curtain," and understood that their coreligionists were placed in an inferior position by the circumstances of their conquest by the Muslims. If the plight of the Copts in Egypt, the Nestorians in Mesopotamia, or the Armenians in the Caucasus and Anatolia were only vaguely understood by them, they could not help but view the case of the Hispanic Christians (the *Mozarabs*) in al-Andalus as uncomfortably proximate to them, and therefore relevant to their experience of frontline contact with Islam. The list of *Mozarab* martyrs to Islamic law for proclaiming Christ to a Muslim audience was indeed a long one and was known by the French. The fate of the *Mozarabs* in al-Andalus was a possible foreshadowing of what might await the French in the event that Islamic arms would prevail in the next Muslim incursion across the Pyrenees.

The French, especially the monks at Cluny in Burgundy, were eager to acquire knowledge of the enemy to the south.[15] Many earlier Byzantine Greek texts on Islam were translated into Latin by the Cluniacs in the ninth and tenth centuries. Cluniac abbot Peter the Venerable (1122–1156) sponsored a Latin translation of the *Our'an* and wrote an influential anti-Islamic polemic titled *Book against the Abominable Heresy or Sect of the Saracens*.[16] On the popular level, Frankish fears of Islam were manifested in the *Chansons de Geste*, which tended to depict the Muslims as perpetrators of atrocities and worshipers of an evil trinity (*Mahound, Termagant*, and *Appolyon*).[17] Popular fears of Islam were also manifested in military actions against the Muslims. Southern French knights fought in Spain on behalf of Spanish Christians regularly from the early 1060s, and French knights would be the most numerous group to participate in the crusade movement to Palestine and Syria.[18] Abbot Peter the Venerable was also a strong proponent of the use of warfare against Islam, and he corresponded with St. Bernard of Clairvaux regarding the probable inability to sway Muslims (despite the presumed success of St. Mayeul at Fraxinetum). St. Bernard preached avidly on the benefits of warfare against Islam, and wrote that "a Christian glories in the death of a pagan because Christ is glorified."[19]

THE CRUSADES

The French-Muslim conflict was taken to a new theater in the late eleventh century in the form of the crusades. The new battleground was *Outremer*, "the land beyond the sea," that is, Palestine and Syria (and later, Egypt and Tunisia as well). Historians have discerned several precursors and preconditions of the crusades: attempts by the Church to regulate warfare in the Peace of God and Truce of God movements; an emphasis on the efficacy of pilgrimage; and the Cluniac and Gregorian reforms and liturgical renewal.[20] Considerable intellectual justification was provided by Catholic thinkers to the sense of universalism and triumphalism that came to prevail in the Catholic West in the eleventh century. The immediate precedents for Catholic military operations against Islam were the Frankish campaigns of the Carolingians, the ongoing Spanish Reconquista (in which the French participated), and the Norman-French conquest of Islamic Sicily (circa 1060–1090). In these theaters, French-speaking Catholic warriors drove out Muslim overlords from European lands that had retained majority-Christian populations. The crusades, however, sought to eliminate Islamic control and establish Catholic Christian dominion in parts of the world that had by then become majority-Muslim areas.[21]

The crusades were in fact European colonial ventures in which a minority colonial population of mainly French-speaking knights and their followers was sustained within hostile territory by the presence of garrison forces provided by the home territories (primarily the Parisian-based Kingdom of France and the northern and southern French duchies and principalities of post-Carolingian France).[22] The first call for crusaders in 1095 by Pope Urban II was made in Clermont in southern France to a predominantly French-speaking audience. The appeal included very specific historical references to prior Frankish successes against Islam in the more detailed version recorded by Robert of Reims, monk of Marmoutier-Lez-Tours, and sometime abbot of St.-Remi (see documents).[23]

The inciting incident for the First Crusade was an appeal for Western Catholic mercenaries by Alexius I Comnenus to help the Orthodox Byzantines in the fight against the Seljuk Turks in Asia Minor. The participants in the First Crusade did not view themselves as mercenaries in the employ of the Byzantine emperor. Instead, they regarded themselves as *peregrini* (pilgrims) who were undertaking an armed pilgrimage to liberate the places in Palestine associated with the life of Christ.[24] Many decades later a formal rite evolved in which soldiers were "signed with the cross" and liturgically transformed into crusaders. Some of the *peregrini* had sold or mortgaged their estates out of a sense of idealism, and there were some landless younger sons who sought land and glory abroad.

There were eight major expeditions and perhaps two dozen smaller operations from Western Europe to the Middle East in the era of the crusades (1099–1270).[25] Strategies varied over the centuries. Four campaigns went to Palestine; two went to Egypt; one went to Tunisia; and one was diverted to Constantinople. Unique among these campaigns, the First Crusade (1095–1099) succeeded in establishing a grouping of feudal states in *Outremer* that lasted for almost 200 years. The First Crusade consisted of contingents from the Ile-de-France, Champagne, Orleans, Lorraine, Aquitaine, Normandy, Flanders, and Norman southern Italy, with their combined forces totaling 7,000 knights.

At the time of their arrival in Palestine, the crusaders found the regional Muslim powers (the Seljuks and Fatimids) at odds and unable to offer a unified resistance. The crusaders achieved a spectacular series of victories in Asia Minor and Syria beginning in 1097. The Aquitanian leader, Raymond of St. Gilles, arrived outside Jerusalem in June 1099 with the main body of knights and initiated a siege. Although numerically inferior to the Muslim defenders of the city, and even though they received word of an approaching Fatimid relief column, the crusader knights possessed supreme confidence that they would win in what they regarded as a holy endeavor. They engaged in public penances (such as a barefooted procession around the city) and listened to sermons by their chaplains to purify themselves for the impending assault. They also began constructing siege engines including catapults, a battering ram, and protective siege towers. Genoese and English ships arrived in Jaffa at the right time with much-needed supplies. Finally, on July 15, 1099, the crusaders captured Jerusalem by storm. They massacred the city's Muslim population and transformed the mosques into Catholic churches.[26]

CRUSADER SETTLEMENT IN *OUTREMER*

Four colonial crusader states were established, stretching south from the county of Edessa, to the principality of Antioch, the county of Tripoli, and finally, in the south, the Kingdom of Jerusalem. These states were originally garrisoned by only 600 soldiers (half of whom were knights), as most of the original crusaders returned to France following their victories and the fulfillment of their vows. There followed, however, a steady stream of colonists from Europe. By 1140, there were about 140,000 European colonial settlers (mainly French) in *Outremer* protected by about 2,000 knights and 5,000 sergeants.[27] The military forces of the four crusader states occasionally combined under the command of the king of Jerusalem, but they were never as united as political or military necessity might have dictated. The crusaders were unable to capture strategically important Syrian cities such as Damascus, Homs, Hama, or Aleppo, which, stretching southward, hemmed them in close to the coast and formed a barrier to further expansion eastward. By means of their own castles and forts, which contained elements of Western, Byzantine, and Islamic defensive engineering, as well as natural and man-made obstructions, their relatively small garrisons maintained a degree of security within their four states in *Outremer* for almost ninety years. Some castles were garrisoned with only a dozen or so knights.[28]

Fulcher of Chartres, a priest who had attended the Council of Clermont, and had marched to *Outremer* with the First Crusade, wrote that the settlers quickly became orientalized:

One who was once a citizen of Reims or Chartres now has been made a citizen of Tyre or of Antioch. We have already forgotten the places of our birth....Some have taken wives not merely of their own people, but Syrians, or Armenians, or even Saracens who have received the grace of baptism....Different languages, now made common, become known to both races, and faith unites those whose forbears [*sic*] were strangers.[29]

The crusaders' insistence on the supremacy of Catholicism over Orthodoxy cost them the allegiance of many native Christians, but they found support from two groups that converted from Orthodoxy to Catholicism and formed the first Uniate churches (which maintained their own hierarchy and ritual). These were the Maronites who lived in the county of Tripoli, and submitted to Rome in 1181, and a group of Cilician Armenians who submitted in 1198. Such Uniates intermarried with the crusader settlers and adopted elements of crusader culture such as the French language. In the case of the Maronites, this created an enclave of unique Franco-Arab culture within the Islamic Middle East that has survived to this day in Lebanon. Franciscan and Dominican missions based in Acre made efforts to convert the Jacobite and Nestorian communities to Catholicism, but with little success (notable exceptions being an individual Jacobite patriarch and a Nestorian archbishop).

Two Catholic crusader monastic orders provided a military advantage to the crusader states even though the crusaders had no material advantage over their Muslim adversaries. Members of the Hospitallers (formed in 1110) and the Templars (formed in 1118) took the same vows as monks, but their labor included doing combat with the infidel.[30] They possessed a superior training and discipline that gave them an advantage in battle, as they had a reputation for fighting with fanatical intensity. France and England were the most successful recruiting grounds for members of the orders, and it was in those countries that the orders had their largest churches in Europe. The Templars became particularly strong, controlling about 9,000 castles and manors by the thirteenth century (including the important Safita Castle in *Outremer*). Eventually, as the Muslims pushed the crusaders out of *Outremer*, the two groups moved westward—the Hospitallers to Cyprus (1291), Rhodes (1310), and Malta (1530), and the Templars to France, where they were eliminated brutally by King Philip IV ("the Fair") in 1307–1312 because he feared their power and wanted their resources for himself. By the early 1400s, the Hospitallers were organized into eight "tongues" or "nations," three of which were French—"France," "Auvergne," and "Provence" (the others being "England," "Italy," "Germany," "Aragón" "Catalonia," and "Castile-León"). The grand master was chosen by a monastic chapter-general, and could come from any "tongue." Several important positions, however, were restricted to Frenchmen: France provided the chief hospitaller; Auvergne provided the marshal; and Provence provided the grand commander. Their small but effecive fleet of war galleys operated successfully against Muslim positions throughout the Mediterranean through the seventeenth century.[31]

The Ayyubid Kurdish leader Saladin (Salah ad-Din) unified the Islamic Middle East from his base in Egypt in the 1170s and 1180s, and then sought to expel the crusaders from the region.[32] Saladin was especially angered by a crusader operation to the vicinity of Mecca in Arabia launched by a consummate crusader, Reynaud of Châtillon (the lord of Transjordan). The crusader settler army under Guy of Lusignon, king of Jerusalem, was decisively defeated by Saladin at the Horns of Hattin (July 14, 1187), and although Jerusalem fell thereafter, the crusaders tenuously held onto a coastal strip in central Palestine and Syria for about a hundred years longer.

THE CAPETIANS AND ST. LOUIS

Following the First Crusade, three kings of France undertook four subsequent crusade operations—to Palestine, Egypt, and Tunisia. King Louis VII went on the Second Crusade (1144–1149), which unsuccessfully besieged Damascus. His son, Philip II Augustus, went on the Third Crusade (1187–1192) and helped capture Acre before becoming ill and returning home—leaving Richard the Lion Heart of England to battle Saladin to a draw. Philip's grandson, the saintly Louis IX (1226–1270), conceived and executed the last two conventional crusade campaigns.[33] The Seventh Crusade (1248–1254) sailed to Egypt, but failed on the Nile during the march to Cairo. Louis was actually captured by the Muslims, but was released upon payment of a huge ransom. He then spent four years in *Outremer*, refortifying Acre, Caesaria, Jaffa, and Sidon, and establishing a "French regiment" of a hundred knights in Acre, all at his own expense.

Among Louis's troops was Jean de Joinville, seneschal of Champagne, whose ancestors had participated in the Second, Third, Fourth, and Fifth Crusades, and were, in the words of Jonathan Riley-Smith, "a line of men obsessed with the crusading." Joinville penned one of the most vivid accounts of medieval warfare and the terrors of capture in his *Vie de Saint Louis* (see Section III documents).[34] Louis believed that his campaign to Egypt had failed because of his own sinfulness. When he returned to France, he engaged in a series of penances, and strove to live a life of simplicity. He had earlier taken strides to impose his vision of a Catholic moral order on France. His assistant and confessor, Geoffrey de Beaulieu, explained that Louis led the Eighth Crusade to Tunisia in 1270 because the current Hafsid ruler there (Abu 'Abd Allah Muhammad al-Muntasir) had sent an embassy to Paris in 1269 regarding the possibility of his conversion to Catholicism.[35] After setting up a base near the ancient site of Carthage, disease broke out in the French camp. First his son John Tristan died, and then Louis himself on August 25, 1270. He supposedly sighed, "Jerusalem, Jerusalem," before his death. The campaign returned to France, and Pope Boniface VIII canonized Louis in 1297. The classic era of the crusades ended with Louis, and the last vestiges of the crusader states were wiped out by the Egyptian Mamluks in the summer of 1291 (see documents).[36]

THE VALOIS-OTTOMAN ENTENTE

The classic era of the crusades occurred during the Capetian dynasty of French kings (987–1328), when France was politically disunited, but Parisian culture and language had begun to dominate northern France. During much of that time the English monarchy held a vast amount of land in France, a consequence of two English dynasties having their origins in France (the Normans and the Angevins) and holding onto their ancestral lands. The main achievement of the succeeding Valois dynasty (1328–1589) was the final victory over the English forces in the Hundred Years' War in 1453 and the political unification of the country. French absolute monarchs through the Bourbon dynasty (1589–1789) struggled to overcome lingering regional cultural and political diversity. Linguistic unity would not be achieved until the imposition of the French public education system after 1870 (at which time one-fourth of the country still spoke no French at all, and another fourth spoke it as a second tongue).

In the Valois period, there were a number of smaller crusade-like operations undertaken by Europeans in which French forces participated, including campaigns to the Asia Minor coast (1334); Smyrna (1344); Alexandria (1365); Mahdia (1390); Nikopolis (1396); Constantinople (1399); the coast of Palestine and Lebanon (1403); and Jerba Island (1560).[37] But the Valois regime itself undertook a departure from the Islamic policy of the Capetians. Valois monarchs participated in an alliance with the Ottoman Turkish Empire in eastern Europe, directed against the Hapsburg monarchy, which ruled the Holy Roman Empire and Spain. Valois interest in the Turks dates to the 1480s, when Ottoman prince Jem, younger brother of Sultan Bayazid II, fled to France in September 1482, after a failed attempt to wrest the throne from his brother. The Hospitallers handed Jem over to the papacy, which sought to exploit his wealth and use his supporters against Bayazid. Jem was captured by Valois king Charles VIII in January 1495, and died in French captivity, possibly poisoned at Bayazid's urging.[38]

King Francis I (1515–1547) pursued an entente with the Turks that was directed against the rival Hapsburgs.[39] This was despite the fact that three different popes urged Francis to go on crusade following the example of his Capetian ancestors (Leo X in 1516; Adrian VI in 1522; and Clement VII in 1524). Francis's forces were defeated by Holy Roman Emperor Charles V, and for a time he was held captive by Charles. Francis was forced to surrender Valois lands in Spain and Italy. In 1535, Francis suggested to Ottoman sultan Sulayman the Magnificent (1520–1566) that French and Turkish forces launch a combined operation against the Hapsburgs.[40] This offer led to the first Turkish "capitulations" with a Western power (February 1536), in which a "Community of Franks" was established in Istanbul, as a new form of Ottoman-sanctioned *millet* (a non-Muslim national subgrouping within the Turkish Empire).[41]

French merchants acquired unique access to the Turkish economy throughout the Middle East, as they were permitted to trade and travel freely in the Ottoman Empire and still be subject to French law in many cases (they were given access to French consular advice in cases involving Turkish subjects and their testimony weighed equally with that of a Turkish subject). The Ottomans were obliged to protect Catholic merchants and pilgrims in their Middle Eastern domains. Most importantly to Francis, the "capitulation" gave the French a privileged position in emerging East-West trade in the Mediterranean, with their merchants paying low customs duties and having a monopoly of access to internal Turkish markets.[42] He especially wanted to gain an advantage over Venice and Genoa, which possessed the last remaining Western outposts in the eastern Mediterranean. There was also a secret anti-Hapsburg military alliance concluded between Francis and Sulayman. The Ottomans believed they could use trade as an inducement to certain Western powers to ally with them and thus weaken the ability of the West to block their advances in the Danube and the Mediterranean.[43]

The military alliance, however, proved to be more difficult to sustain than the economic cooperation. In 1534, Turkish naval forces sailed west against Hapsburg positions because of a specific request for help by Francis. The Ottomans first attacked the Italian coast and then sailed to southern France, where Francis's representatives welcomed the Turkish ships. Feeling increasing pressure to break from the alliance with the Muslim enemy, Francis changed his position, and directed that his representatives not cooperate with the Turks. Under the infamous pirate "Barbarossa," the Turks occupied Toulon in early August 1543, and forced local French authorities to assist them in an unsuccessful siege of Hapsburg-controlled Nice (August 20–September 8). The Turks returned east embittered by the experience, and there followed both a Valois-Hapsburg treaty and a Hapsburg-Ottoman treaty that fundamentally altered the status quo of the previous eight years.

Although England (in 1590) and even the Hapsburgs (in 1615) received limited capitulations from the sultan, Valois king Charles IX (1560–1574) renewed the French advantages in the capitulations of 1569, gaining free passage for French ships within Ottoman waters, and requiring other Western ships to fly the French flag to enjoy similar privileges.[44] France was allowed to collect fees from Western merchants entering Ottoman territory.[45] Charles supported Ottoman intrigues in Poland and Transylvania in the early 1570s by backing pro-Turkish claimants to the throne. Relations between the Valois and Ottomans soured temporarily in 1669 due to French support for the Venetians in Crete, during the reign of the great "Sun King," Louis XIV (1643–1715). Louis, however, still despised the Hapsburgs more than the Turks, and he sent French troops into the Spanish Netherlands to distract the Hapsburgs when the Turks unsuccessfully besieged Vienna in 1683.[46] French forces were also deployed on Louis's orders across the Rhine to Bavaria in 1689 when the Hapsburg army fought the Turks in Bosnia.

A curious case study in Bourbon-Ottoman relations is the story of Count Claude-Alexandre de Bonneval (1675–1747), a military engineer who served under Louis XIV.[47] After a falling-out with the king, the count went to the Ottoman court to offer his services to Sultan Mahmud I (1739–1754).

Patronized by Grand Vizier Topol Osman Pasha, the count converted to Islam and took the name of Ahmad. He revived a defunct bombardier corps, and attempted to modernize the whole Turkish military structure. The count brought in three other Frenchmen to assist him, each of whom also converted to Islam. Conservative Ottoman commanders resisted the plans for modernization because they feared and distrusted the Westernization that they believed was creeping into the Ottoman military infrastructure through Ahmad's influence. But the count and his colleagues did modernize the Ottoman imperial cannon foundry, powder works, and musket factory, and under their influence a new Turkish military engineering school was opened. Their influence lessened when Topol Osman Pasha fell from power, but the precedent for Westernization under a French pattern within the Islamic world was set.

NAPOLEON AND EGYPT

Like many other Western nations, France was transformed in the eighteenth and nineteenth centuries by an overwhelming combination of factors—the egalitarian ideology of the Enlightenment, the technological power unleashed by the Industrial Revolution, and the flood of geographical and sociological knowledge brought back to Europe by overseas explorers. The French Revolution of 1789, which toppled the Bourbon monarchy and created a republic, seemed at first to be the embodiment of the political ideal of the French *philosophes* of the Enlightenment. It was also the product of an interconnecting series of events including long-term exploitation of peasants by landowners; the example of the American Revolution, and French participation in that war (to exact revenge for France's loss in the Seven Years' War); the bankruptcy of the Bourbon regime as a consequence of that participation; and the call for new taxes by the monarchy in 1789 to remedy the country's financial problems.

After the Revolution descended into Maximilien Robespierre's "Reign of Terror" in 1793, more conservative elements finally prevailed, and Robespierre himself was guillotined. The rule of the five-man Directory (1794–1799) provided the setting for the rise of the remarkable Corsican artillery officer, Napoleon Bonaparte. Fascinated by Rousseau's *Social Contract*, Napoleon supported the Revolution and aided the regime by winning over Corsica to the republican cause. In 1793 he helped lift the English-Neapolitan siege of Toulon, and his military abilities were noticed by Agustin Robespierre, who managed to get him promoted to general. Recalled to Paris, Napoleon began his ascent to power when he crushed the opponents of the Directory with "a whiff of grapeshot" in October 1795. There, his innovative thinking in both tactical and strategic matters won him the loyalty of many military men. Although his campaigns were initially launched to preserve the revolutionary regime against its monarchical opponents, Napoleon plotted the conquest of foreign lands and the creation of a personal empire. His soldiers were driven by a spirit of nationalism and personal loyalty to their commander to expand the borders of the empire.

Napoleon's first significant campaign success occurred in northern Italy in 1796–1797, when he managed to push out an Austrian army. After his forces took Switzerland in 1798, Napoleon prepared for a campaign to Egypt. He wanted to harm British trade in the Middle East, thereby enhancing the trade dominance enjoyed by France since the days of the Ottoman capitulations, but he also dreamed of marching on either Constantinople or India (and for the latter possibility, he planned to link up with a Muslim opponent of the British dominance in India, Tippoo Sahib).[48] Napoleon's Egyptian campaign would not prove as successful as the later operations that won for him a mastery of Western Europe. The Egyptian experience, however, provided valuable lessons in strategy, logistics, and battlefield tactics for officers who in time achieved smashing victories over their European opponents and won an empire at Marengo, Austerlitz, Jena, and Wagram.

The 30,000 to 40,000 troops in Napoleon's Army of Italy were renamed the Army of the Orient and were transported by some 400 ships to the island of Malta, which was to be the staging area for the operation. When the French troops landed, they found 322 Hospitaller knights who might have defended the island. The order's property in France had been seized by the revolutionary regime in 1792, and there was no ideological affinity for the Revolution as was held by brother knights. The majority of the knights were French, but fifty were too old to fight. In addition, the available gunpowder had gotten wet, and the order's handful of gunships was no match for the massive Napoleonic armada that descended on the island on June 13, 1798. Napoleon seized the order's treasure, which had been accumulated in countless campaigns in *Outremer*, but lost it all in battle with the British two months later. A few brother knights, however, were captivated by the prospect of doing combat in the East with their countrymen and enlisted in the Army of the Orient.[49]

In the proclamation Napoleon made to his troops before Alexandria, the general revealed an understanding of Islam that was more the product of the centuries of the Valois-Ottoman entente than of the crusades (see Document IV).[50] The Mamluks had no clue of Napoleon's intentions and his landings on Marabout beach on the Nile delta on July 1, 1798, were unopposed. On the next day, the French forces under Generals Menou, Kléber, and Bon successfully stormed Alexandria. Napoleon issued a proclamation at Alexandria intended to try to win over both the Egyptian Muslim population and the Ottomans:

Peoples of Egypt, you will be told that I have come to destroy your religion: do not believe it! Answer that I have come to restore your rights and punish the usurpers, and that, more than the Mamluks, I respect God, his Prophet and the Koran....Is it not we who have been through the centuries the friends of the Sultan?[51]

He attended public celebrations of Muhammad's birthday, and tried (unsuccessfully) to obtain a *fatwa* from the imams of al-Azhar in Cairo that it did not violate Qur'anic law if the population swore allegiance to him.[52] While he was in Egypt, Napoleon queried the Directory several times as to whether Foreign Minister Charles Maurice de Talleyrand was going to negotiate with the Ottomans in Constantinople (he declined to do so). The Ottomans declared war on France on September 9. The French did not waste any time in Alexandria, like the Fifth and Seventh crusades had centuries earlier, and Napoleon sent out four divisions (18,000 men) toward Cairo on July 3–6, with more to follow in the weeks to come.[53]

Napoleon faced superior numbers in Egypt, but the French troops had an advantage in training and equipment. Overwhelming French victories occurred at Shubra Khit and Embaba (the so-called Battle of the Pyramids), and Napoleon entered Cairo on July 22. After British naval forces sank his Egyptian fleet on August 1–2, Napoleon stepped up his strategy and marched into Palestine in spring 1799, to head off a potential overland invasion of Egypt by Turkish and British forces. In Palestine, the French again scored huge victories, now over Turkish armies—at Cana, Lake Tiberias, and Mount Tabor (where Kléber and 2,000 French held off 35,000 Turks until Napoleon arrived with artillery and scattered the Ottomans on April 16, 1799).[54] In the Holy Land, many French troops experienced a kind of Catholic religious revival, after a few years of official animosity directed toward the Catholic church by the republican regime.[55] The French made contact again with Maronite communities, and Napoleon's troops were welcomed by the Catholic minority in Palestine as though they were a new crusader army. After a prolonged French siege of Acre failed in May, however, in which the Turks were assisted by the British, Napoleon decided to return to Egypt.

A large Turkish invasion force was beaten back at Abukir Bay in July, but Napoleon felt it was politically necessary to return to France on August 18.[56] He became first consul later that year. Napoleon left Kléber in charge of the French occupation forces and an increasingly disgruntled Muslim citizenry. French soldiers became the targets of individual Muslim assassins, and Kléber himself was assassinated in June 1800. He was succeeded by Jacques Menou, a French officer who had converted to Islam and now called himself Abdallah.[57] Menou, however, lacked credibility in the eyes of his men, who believed he had converted to Islam to marry a Muslim woman whom he was fond of. The Muslim population as a whole thought he had converted for political reasons only. But Menou used his position to transform Egypt (at least temporarily) into his own vision of a modern Franco-Islamic state, by imposing his unique interpretation of

Islamic jurisprudence (which was more like French law) in criminal cases and inheritance laws; by creating a central registry of births and deaths; by starting the first Arabic language newspaper; and by undertaking urban renewal in some of Cairo's older and more congested neighborhoods.[58]

The arrival of a British expeditionary force in Egypt, however, in March 1801, foreshortened Menou's experiment. After losing two decisive battles to the British in March at Abukir Bay and Canopus, the 13,000 Frenchmen in Cairo surrendered. Menou held out in Alexandria with 7,000 men until September, when he, too, surrendered (they were all repatriated by the British that fall). Menou's experiment at a French-Islamic republican regime and Napoleon's dream of an eastern empire ended in 1801 at British, not Muslim, hands. His Arabic-language newspaper spurred the subsequent creation of similar journals throughout the Arab Middle East. It is difficult to determine what kind of impact a prolonged Napoleonic presence would have had on Egypt. The citizenry as a whole came to think of his occupation troops simply as a new group of infidel interlopers, although perhaps less so than the crusaders of many centuries before. One unfortunate side effect of the crusades in Egypt had been the ruthless persecution of the Coptic Christian community by the Muslim establishment, following the expulsion of the crusaders.

This did not happen in the aftermath of Napoleon's invasion. At St. Helena, toward the end of his life, Napoleon wrote about his campaign in comparison to that of Alexander the Great (in which Alexander restored the old religion of Egypt, after years of persecution by unpopular Persian occupation forces):

What I like about Alexander the Great is not his campaigns...but his political methods....It was most politic of him to go to Amon; it was thus he conquered Egypt. If I had stayed in the Orient, I probably would have founded an empire like Alexander's by going on pilgrimage to Mecca.[59]

CONCLUSION

French policy toward Islam from 700 to 1800 became more complex as the forms of contact became more varied. Modern France inherited three legacies from the past with regard to Islam. The first of these was a siege mentality and a sense of superiority over Islam, gained from the battlefield victories of Charles Martel, Pepin, and Charlemagne over Muslims in France and Spain in the eighth and ninth centuries. Umayyad Arab forces had conquered Christian territories from Byzantine North Africa to Visigothic Spain, and the ability of the Franks to stop them within France, and take the war against Islam into al-Andalus, imparted a special status to the Frankish warriors.

The second legacy derived from the crusade experience of warring with Islam in the Arab Middle East. The Frankish siege mentality and sense of

superiority over Islam was conveyed across the generations to the Capetian heirs of the Franks. The Capetians and their colleagues in the surrounding duchies and principalities of France played a leading role in the
crusades in the eleventh through the thirteenth centuries, campaigning
against various Muslim powers in Palestine, Syria, Egypt, and Tunisia.
French settlers also played a leading role in the creation of the crusader
states in *Outremer*. The crusader belief in the superiority of Catholic Christian culture over Islamic culture derived in large part from the earlier
experiences of Frankish successes over Andalusi Muslims in the eighth,
ninth, and tenth centuries. In the sixteenth and seventeenth centuries the
Valois dynasty, heir of the Capetians, was virtually unique among Christian powers in its ability to negotiate on seemingly equal terms with the
Ottoman Turks, who were the scourge of Christendom for three centuries.

The third legacy was a belief in the ability of France to transform the
Islamic world, not by crusader conquest, but by Enlightenment-era
reforms promulgated by a secular administration and army. Republican
France under Napoleon was the first European regime to attempt to
impose a post-crusade Western system within the Islamic world in Egypt
in the late eighteenth and early nineteenth centuries.

2

The Sahara and the Legion

THE BARBARY PIRATES

Piracy and hostage taking were integral components of the Christian-Muslim conflict in the Mediterranean world as far back as St. Mayeul. France, Spain, Italy, and the Mediterranean islands were principal targets of Muslim maritime brigands based in North Africa. Napoleon's conquests put a temporary halt to such activities, as Muslim powers in the Maghrib made peace with him in 1800, despite Ottoman insistence on their support against the French in Egypt. North Africa had four main "Barbary pirate" states—the sultanate of Morocco, and the three Ottoman "regencies" (Maghribi proxies of the Turks) in the *pashalik* of Algiers, the Husaynid *beylik* in Tunis, and the Qaramanlid *beylik* in Tripoli. During the heyday of the Barbary pirates in the sixteenth and seventeenth centuries, Morocco typically held 10,000 European slaves; Algiers, 25,000; Tunis, 7,000; and Tripoli, 1,500.[1]

The ransom business was very profitable, but there were always many unredeemed slaves who served in galleys and in the harem, and did heavy manual labor. The Moroccan sultan Mulay Isma'il (1672–1727) was the most depraved Barbary pirate leader. He kept his victims in underground grain storage pits and put on public spectacles in which Christian captives were tortured to death. He bragged that 600 Frenchmen were killed on his orders, 127 of whom he killed with his own hands.[2] The mainly French redemptionist Order of the Trinitarians, based at Cerfroy and at St. Maturin's in Paris, worked since 1198 to redeem Christian hostages held in North Africa (and St. Louis chose his chaplains exclusively from their ranks).[3] While the Valois-Ottoman entente was in effect, it was possible to exert pressure on the Turks. In 1605, for example, the French minister to the Ottoman court, De Breves, managed to get all French prisoners in Tunis freed. But the Ottomans exerted no influence on Morocco.

Several Western powers attempted to stop the Barbary pirates over the centuries—Spain (1502–1520); the United States (1801–1809); and Britain (1816). While Napoleon was in power, the regencies, at least, feared his power enough to cause a decline in the trade.[4] In 1803, Napoleon forced Tunis to free a thousand Christians they had taken from San Pietro in 1798. After the fall of Napoleon, however, the trade increased again.

France experienced a Bourbon restoration after Napoleon's downfall, which lasted until 1848. The regime was a constitutional monarchy with a two-tiered parliament (a royally appointed Chamber of Peers and a popularly elected Chamber of Deputies). Although King Charles X (1824–1830) was an archconservative who was unpopular with the middle class, he found a popular cause in an emerging Algerian crisis. While the slave trade provided the context for French hostility toward the Maghrib, nationalism and other economic issues lay behind the decision to commit French forces to the conquest of Algeria. France had purchased grain from the dey of Algiers in the Republican and Napoleonic imperial periods. A complicated financial dispute emerged between the French government, the dey, and Algerian Jewish merchant families (the Bakris and Bushnaqs) who had negotiated a grain deal in 1805 with Napoleon.[5] Napoleon refused to pay the Bakris and Bushnaqs because he felt they had inflated their prices, and they were hard pressed to repay a debt they owed to the dey. Although the French government agreed to pay 7 million francs in 1819 to settle the Napoleonic debt, it was half of what the Bakris and Bushnaqs demanded, and the dey got nothing.

Dey Hussein complained that the French government and the Jews were conspiring to deprive him of his money, and he struck French consul Pierre Deval in the face with a fly swatter during an audience over the money in April 1827.[6] The French press tried to stir the country to war to avenge the insult, and War Minister Clermont-Tonnerre pressed (unsuccessfully) for a campaign to Algiers.[7] The new prime minister in 1828, Count Gay de Martignac, was too heavily involved in the Greek war of independence from the Turks to give much attention to Algeria, and he did not wish to upset France's uneasy allies in that theater—Britain and Russia. Martignac undertook diplomacy, however, to resolve the ongoing conflict: he sent Captain La Bretonniere to negotiate with Dey Hussein on the ship *Provence*. Hussein, urged on by the British (who wanted to prevent French dominance in North Africa) refused to speak to La Bretonniere, and shelled his ship eighty times on August 3, 1829.[8] News of the latest outrage reached Paris just as Martignac was leaving office. Direct French involvement in Algeria was the work of his replacement, the ultraroyalist Prince Auguste Jules Armand Marie de Polignac, whose brief and tumultuous career as prime minister would leave France the legacy of an African empire that lasted for over a century.

Polignac did not have the confidence of the Chamber of Deputies, which censured the king for ignoring it, but the king responded by dissolving the chamber in March 1830 (King Charles's ongoing disputes with his opponents would eventually force both him and Polignac from office later that year, after the conquest of Algiers was completed). Now, even southern French merchants who did legitimate trade with Algeria were compelled to support the cause of French intervention. The king and his backers in the upper house and in the army saw the annexation of Algiers as a means to augment the royal power, while the French commercial houses with North African markets came to believe that annexation best served their interests, as well. For both the political conservatives and the commercial groups in France, nationalistic motives combined with economic motives and superseded any remnant crusade mentality or Napoleonic "civilizing mission." The pasha of Egypt, Muhammad Ali, offered to help the French, asking for 20 million francs and four warships to aid in his proposed trek across the Libyan desert. King Charles himself did not want any French ships to be under the command of a Muslim ruler; he wanted direct French involvement. On January 31, 1830, the Council of Ministers decided in favor of war.

Admiral Duperre accepted leadership of the expedition reluctantly, but he was hesitant to sail for Algeria before the spring of 1831. King Charles, however, compelled the expedition to assemble in only three months. All told, 103 warships and 350 transports gathered in Toulon to ferry across the Mediterranean a force of 37,000 soldiers and eighty-three pieces of artillery. War Minister (and General) Bourmont was placed in command of the expeditionary forces, and his attitude regarding the efficacy of the campaign was decidedly different from that of Admiral Duperre. Bourmont believed that the prestige of the army was at stake and he planned to wage an aggressive campaign.[9] Polignac wrote on March 12: "Our aim is humanitarian. We are seeking, in addition to satisfaction for our grievances, the abolition of the enslavement of Christians, the destruction of piracy, and the end of humiliating tributes that the European states are having to pay to the Regency."[10] The prime minister also promised France's allies that it would consult with them concerning the future status of Algeria. While Russia agreed to the plan, Britain did not, and Polignac replied to the protests of the British ambassador Lord Stuart with the remark: "France doesn't give a damn about England."[11] The liberal opponents of Charles's government sought to stop the expedition by protesting that the money for the campaign was appropriated without the consent of the chambers of the French parliament. The *Journal de Debats*, for example, wrote of the appropriation: "There's the real insult that France must feel, much more than the slap of a barbarian on the cheek of a foolhardy man."[12] The liberal press went so far as publishing confidential information about the size of the French forces and the intended landing sites in Algeria to try to stop the fleet from sailing, but the dey was not apprised of this information and all he could do was await the French arrival.

THE FRENCH CONQUEST

The French expeditionary forces set sail for Algeria from May 25 to May 27, 1830. Duperre was overly cautious, and turned back from the Algerian coast on May 30 because he believed "the winds seemed contrary." The French fleet waited at Palma de Mallorca for ten days until the winds changed, and again set sail (but Duperre inexplicably left the artillery behind at Mallorca for another two weeks).[13] Duperre wanted to wait yet again after arriving off the Algerian coast, but Bourmont forced the landing of his forces on June 14 in Sidi Ferruch Bay, about twelve miles to the west of Algiers. It took four days for them to disembark, and a sudden storm on the night of June 15 threatened to swamp the entire fleet (there were some 27,000 sailors on board the ships). The French had smaller numbers available to them (and no artillery) compared to Dey Hussein, but their commanders, supplies, and training were far superior. Hussein waited until all French forces were ashore before he attacked with between 50,000 and 60,000 men commanded by his son-in-law, Agha Ibrahim. The dey's forces charged the French positions repeatedly on June 19, and were stopped by the volleys of massed French small-arms fire. The French infantry then advanced and captured the dey's artillery as well as Ibrahim's encampment on the plateau of Staouelli. With the arrival of their artillery on June 24, the French advanced to the outskirts of Algiers. On June 29, the French finished a trench in front of a position they called Fort Empereur, which held a commanding view of the city below. On the morning of July 4, the French artillery blasted Fort Empereur to rubble, and the dazed Muslim defenders abandoned the position.[14] Dey Hussein knew his position was untenable in the face of such overwhelming firepower, and he capitulated a few hours later (see documents). Bourmont allowed him to keep his property and permitted him and the Turkish soldiers under him to retire anywhere beyond Algiers. The inhabitants were allowed to maintain their religion, property, and freedom. Only 415 French soldiers had been killed in the conquest, with 2,160 injured. Forty-eight million francs were found in the dey's treasury, more than were needed to finance the entire campaign. Bourmont proclaimed to his troops: "Twenty days were all that were required for the destruction of a state whose existence had harassed Europe for over three centuries."[15]

Back in France, King Charles took the public acclaim for the campaign as a sign of support for his domestic policies. Archbishop Quelen of Paris called for *Te Deums* to commemorate the victory, and added: "Three weeks were enough to reduce the superb Muslims to the weakness of a child. Thus may the enemies of our Lord and King be treated always and everywhere."[16] The elections that Charles had called in May had not gone as he had wished, and the chamber was filled with his opponents. Nevertheless, his decision to retain control of Algiers on July 20 was met with general support within the country and opposition abroad (he had told the British ambassador: "In taking Algiers, I considered only France's dignity, in keeping it or returning it, I shall consider only her interests").[17] But domestic support for Charles's government was collapsing. On July 26 the king's "July Ordinances"—calling for rigid control of the press, the ability to dissolve the Chamber of Deputies, and changes in the electoral system to favor the royalists—were met by protests and revolution. Ironically, Charles went into exile in Britain.

The new king, Louis-Philippe (1830–1848), the so-called Citizen-King, had bourgeois inclinations and was opposed to ideas of military adventurism, yet he was just as inclined to hold onto Algeria as Charles had been. On March 10, 1831, he created the Foreign Legion. Comprised of many men from Napoleon's former officer corps and recruits from Spain, Italy, Switzerland, Belgium, the Netherlands, and Poland, the Legion would be charged with holding onto the conquered territory and eventually expanding the French base of power there. Five battalions were raised and sent to Algeria by September 1831, commanded by Colonel Stoffel, who was a veteran of Napoleon's Spanish campaigns. After the fall of Algiers, Bourmont's troops stormed Oran and Bône, and pushed inland as far as Blida in the Lesser Atlas foothills.[18] Bourmont was replaced after the July 1830 Revolution by General Clauzel, who was appointed France's governor-general of Algeria.[19] Clauzel arrived in September and prepared to hold the coastal areas and foster European colonization in the cities that he believed the French could retain.[20] He offered control of the city of Constantine to the bey of Tunis, but was shortly recalled by the government for overstepping his authority. Thereafter, the French position in Algeria almost became untenable with the commencement of a jihad directed at their presence in the Maghrib.

'ABD AL-QADIR

Maghribi opposition to the French presence coalesced in 1832 under 'Abd al-Qadir, a man whose family had connections with the local *Qadiri* order of Muslim mystics and who, although he was only twenty-four years old, had already gone on the *Hajj* to Mecca twice.[21] His stated intention was the creation of an Islamic state based on the *sharia*, and he despised the remnant Turkish garrisons in Algeria as much as he hated the French, due to the corruption of their former administration.[22] 'Abd al-Qadir accordingly began a siege of the remote Turkish garrison posted at Tlemsen in the Atlas range near Morocco. The French commander at Oran, General Desmichel, negotiated with him, but a French force that challenged him in the field (commanded by General Trezel) was beaten at Macta in July 1835.[23] Clauzel was reappointed as governor-general that August because the government felt it needed his experience in the widening crisis.[24] Clauzel immediately took the initiative by pushing 'Abd al-Qadir's forces out of their base at Mascara, and lifting the siege of Turkish forces at Tlemsen. Clauzel was charged now with the conquest of Constantine, although the government did not provide adequate funds for a large-scale operation. He linked up with a local Muslim opponent of the city's unpopular bey, and attacked Constantine with only 7,000 men. His effort failed, and in February 1837, he was replaced by General Damremont.[25]

Meanwhile, General Thomas Bugeaud (also a veteran of Napoleon's army) held the line against 'Abd al-Qadir's forces in the west.[26] But the government's primary concern was the capture of Constantine, and Bugeaud had to make a hasty treaty with 'Abd al-Qadir at the Tafnah River in late May 1837.[27] He relinquished to 'Abd al-Qadir control of Mascara and most of Oran province. Damremont thus led 12,000 men against Constantine in late September, and the French bombardment began on October 6. Damremont, however, was killed in the early operations and General Valleé took over.[28] French forces broke into the city in early October and desperate fighting in the streets went on until Valleé bombarded the fort into submission on October 13.[29] The French subsequently built Philippeville on the coast to serve as a harbor for Constantine, which is situated inland in the Atlases. French troops from Algiers took Blida in the Atlas foothills around this time, as well, but 'Abd al-Qadir was also expanding his base of power while the French were consolidating their hold on the coast.

'Abd al-Qadir placed his own governors in towns within the French area that had been established in the treaty with General Bugeaud (in Laghwat, Majjanah, and Ziban), and moved into the Sahara in November 1838. Ibn Salim, 'Abd al-Qadir's governor at Medea (south of Blida), threatened Algiers anew in the spring of 1840, until General Valleé beat 'Abd al-Qadir at Shiffa in mid-May, and occupied Medea. Bugeaud, now marshal of the army, was appointed governor-general of Algeria by late 1840, and marched out from Medea in force against 'Abd al-Qadir.[30] He wanted to force a decisive battle, which he believed his men were capable of winning. He found the Muslims in early May 1841, and won an engagement near Mascara (resulting in the retaking of that city), but he could not capture 'Abd al-Qadir. On May 18, Bugeaud took Taghdemt, 'Abd al-Qadir's new capital, and also destroyed the nearby fort that had been constructed by 'Abd al-Qadir's father.[31] In the spring of 1842, Bugeaud retook Tlemsen and captured Sebdu, the last city held by 'Abd al-Qadir's forces.[32] The Muslim leader then led his followers (numbering some 50,000 individuals) into the desert to evade the French.

In mid-May 1842, French forces under the duke of Aumale began pursuing 'Abd al-Qadir in the desert. A decisive battle finally occurred on May 16, resulting in a complete French victory—they took 4,000 Muslim warriors captive, together with many members of aristocratic Berber and Bedouin Arab families who had supported 'Abd al-Qadir, and the Muslim leader's entire treasury. 'Abd al-Qadir's bodyguard, however, was willing to defend him to the last man and he was able to flee into Morocco. The French tried to force the Moroccan sultan to extradite 'Abd al-Qadir in 1843, but to no avail—even if the sultan wished to cooperate with the French (which he did not), he might anger his subjects by an alliance with the infidels. Thus, the French responded in force in August 1844 by a two-pronged assault on the sultanate of Morocco: on August 6, the duke of Joinville (whose ancestors were prominent crusaders) attacked the Moroccan coast by sea, bombarding Tangier and capturing Mogador; and Bugeaud himself with 6,000 men destroyed a force of 65,000 undisciplined Moroccans at Isli on August 14.[33] A Franco-Moroccan peace treaty was signed at Tangier on September 10, and although the sultan was now prepared to cooperate with the French, the backcountry Berber tribes (only loosely controlled by the sultan) hid 'Abd al-Qadir and provided him with a new less-numerous, but highly mobile, base of support. The Convention of Lalla Maghnia fixed the Moroccan-Algerian boundary along the coast in March 1845, but the interior was largely a no-man's land characterized by vast, open stretches of desert and by the peaks of the Atlas Mountains.

'Abd al-Qadir harried the French through the winter of 1845–1846, but Bugeaud assembled eighteen flying columns against him, and the Muslims were beaten several times in Algeria before returning to Morocco in the spring of 1846. Bugeaud then compelled the sultan to march against 'Abd al-Qadir in order to force him across the border toward French forces awaiting him in Algeria.[34] This tactic worked in late December 1847, when the Moroccans forced 'Abd al-Qadir across the Muluya River (within modern-day Morocco), where he was encircled by French forces under General Christophe Lamoriciere and was forced to surrender on December 23.[35] The French government promised to send 'Abd al-Qadir to Acre or Alexandria, as he indicated that he wished to undertake yet another *Hajj*. Instead, he was taken to Toulon and held at Amboise until he was freed in 1852 and moved to the Ottoman Empire (living at Brusa, Istanbul, and finally Damascus, where he died in 1883).[36]

THE COLONIAL ESTABLISHMENT

The French initiated colonization policies in Algeria even before the defeat of 'Abd al-Qadir. By 1841, there were 37,374 European colonists, or *colons*, to about 3 million *indigènes*, or native Muslim Maghribis. The *colons* were sometimes referred to as *pieds noirs* (black feet), a term with derisive connotations in Paris that originated from either the black shoes worn by the soldiers who fought in Algeria or from the belief that the *colons* had been "Africanized" by their colonial experience. Many Maghribis found themselves dispossessed of their lands by the *colons*. Marshal Bugeaud remarked that such policies were necessary: "Wherever the water supply is good and the land fertile, there we must place colonists without bothering about the previous owners."[37] The central government in Paris was generally opposed to the idea of dispossession early on because of the security issues that such policies raised, but it went on anyway. Native Muslims left the more fertile coastal areas and fled into the desert, only returning decades later as laborers on French farms. There was also a great deal of destruction that attended the French conquest. Again, Marshal Bugeaud believed it was all necessary: "We have burned a great deal and destroyed a great deal. It may be that I shall be called a barbarian, but I have the conviction that I have done something useful for my country."[38]

Europeans settled in Algeria for the economic or social opportunities the colony offered them that they did not have at home.[39] Spaniards predominated in Oran, while Italians, Sicilians, and Maltese settled in the eastern provinces. An interesting irony of the early days of the colony was that the French colonists feared a "foreign peril," that their French language and culture was imperiled by the presence of so many non-Frenchmen in Algeria. In 1895, however, the government solved the problem by enacting legislation that made the children of resident foreigners into French citizens. The *colons* had a reputation for being unruly, and the authority of several of Bugeaud's successors was challenged by them. The colony's governor-generals were replaced as governments changed in Paris, and the *colons* consistently voiced their opinions about prospective changes in the regime.

Marshal Bugeaud resigned but was recalled to France to lead the French Army after his colonial victories, and found himself involved in the revolution that ended the monarchy of Louis-Philippe in February 1848.[40] The liberal opposition in France had galvanized due to the successes of liberal causes in Switzerland and elsewhere and in sympathy with the anti-Hapsburg movement in Italy. An anti-monarchical revolt broke out in the capital when the government broke up a banquet of the twelfth *arrondissement* of Paris. Shots were fired at the Foreign Ministry, and soldiers fired into a crowd, killing fifty bystanders. Bugeaud was told to withdraw his forces to the Tuilleries, and he resigned in protest. Louis-Philippe fled the country, and the Second French Republic was proclaimed in late February. A four-year presidency and three-year legislature voted by universal male suffrage were created; the death penalty and slavery were abolished; and a ten-hour workday was mandated in Paris. The presidential election was set for December of that year.

General Cavaignac, Louis-Philippe's last governor-general in Algeria, told the incoming governor-general appointed by the Republican regime, General Changarnier, that the *colons* did not want him, and turned his ship back at the harbor in May 1848. Changarnier was reappointed that May and landed in Algiers just in time to save General Cavaignac from a mob of enraged *colons* who had surrounded his palace. The French presidential election of 1848 saw a landslide victory for Louis Napoleon Bonaparte, nephew of Napoleon I and the only nationally recognizable name on the ballot. He wanted to change the Republic's constitution in 1851 to allow him to run for a second term, and when the Assembly refused, he dissolved it. He subsequently got a national referendum to give him presidential powers for ten years (an astounding 92 percent of the population voted for it), and in 1852 a national plebiscite made him hereditary emperor. He ruled as Napoleon III (Napoleon's son had previously died). Such was the lingering power of the Bonaparte name in France. Napoleon III, however, did grant workers the right to form unions and to strike. He rebuilt Paris, and restricted but did not abolish the Assembly (thereby creating a constitutional monarchy). During his reign the French also conquered the rest of Algeria. The emperor declared Algeria to be "an Arab kingdom, a European colony and a French camp," and pronounced that "this is forever French."[41]

In 1857 a Berber "prophetess" arose in Kabyle country (located to the east of Algiers) named Lallah Zaynab. She initiated a new regional jihad against the French by uniting her own Yenni tribe with other neighboring Berber tribes.[42] The latest governor-general, Count Jacques de Randon, led some 30,000 French troops against her and finally captured her, but another Berber revolt erupted farther to the south, led by the Uled Sidi clan. The French had previously relied upon this clan to keep local order for them in the southern reaches of Algeria, but in February 1864 tribal leader Si Sliman began a revolt against French rule. The garrison forces stationed at Tiaret rode out under their commander, Beaupretre, but were betrayed by their native cavalry auxiliaries and were ambushed and wiped out to the last man. In the final hand-to-hand combat, the dying Beaupretre shot Si Sliman and killed him. Si Sliman's brother Muhammad and another tribal leader, Si Lazrag, then assumed leadership of the jihad, but were hampered by inadequate manpower and resources.[43] They were both killed shortly and the remaining small bands of rebels went farther south into the Sahara or fled westward into Morocco. Such Berber resistance finally ended in 1884.

Napoleon III's policies in Algeria angered both the *colons* and the Muslim *indigènes*. His government confiscated lands held by Muslims in the Mitija area for colonization purposes (some 500,000 acres), leaving only

30,000 acres for the Muslim natives.[44] As a consequence of the Berber revolts, he wanted to create new lines of settlement to be used for defensive purposes. The emperor established a new ministry in Paris that was responsible for ensuring the dominance of French cultural elements in the colony, but quickly changed his mind and returned such issues to the prerogative of the governor-general. In 1865 the emperor issued an imperial decree stating that the Muslim *indigènes* were French subjects. The *colons* reacted very violently against the decree, believing that their interests were going to be submerged under those of the Muslim majority.

Utter chaos broke out in the colony after the defeat of French forces in the Franco-Prussian War and the abdication of Napoleon III in 1871. In France, the abdication paved the way for the Third Republic (1871–1940), which was governed by a two-chamber parliament and a council of ministers led by a prime minister. Radical Communards in Paris took control and executed the archbishop. The army finally restored order at a cost of 20,000 dead. Within Algeria, mobs turned away the new Republic's governor-general, General Walsin-Esterhazy, and a *colon* named Vuillermoz telegrammed Paris and declared that "the population of Algiers and the National Guard in a spontaneous and irresistible movement have put an end to the military government."[45] The government took six months to restore order among the *colons* in the colony. The Muslims, meanwhile, hoped to gain their freedom in 1871 with the fall of the Second Empire. Many of them were aghast at the Third Republic's granting of citizenship to Jews in October of that year. This act was partly responsible for the revolt of the Muslim *indigènes* under the aristocratic Muzraqi in the Kabyle area, who stated that he "would not serve a Jew."[46] His revolt lingered into 1872, even after he was killed and his brother Bu Ma'za and others took over.[47] The government finally crushed this revolt, as well, and confiscated 11 million acres of land from the Muslims as a penalty, in addition to imposing an indemnity of over 36 million francs. The land was granted to the *colons*, and the money was specifically used to settle in new *colons* from Alsace.[48]

By 1870, there were 200,000 *colons* in the colony. Algiers, Constantine, and Oran were organized as *départments* of France, administered under prefects who were dependent on the governor-general and the Ministry of the Interior. The three *départments* elected senators and deputies to the National Assembly in Paris. At first, only French citizens were entitled to vote, but later all inhabitants could do so under a double electoral system in which the vote of the outnumbered *colons* carried equal weight with the Muslim majority (by 1946, Algerians sent eight senators and fifteen deputies to the Assembly). On the local level, the communities with a European majority or near-majority had a *colon* mayor and a three-fifths *colon* majority guaranteed on the municipal council (*communes de pleine exercice*). In the towns that were overwhelmingly Muslim, a European administrator oversaw a number of Muslim *qa'ids* (*communes mixtes*). The Muslim *indigènes* were allowed to maintain Islamic law in the Muslim majority areas of the colony (except Constantine), but they were technically "subjects" and not "citizens" of France. Very elaborate procedures were established for a Muslim to become a French citizen, and by 1936, only 2,500 had bothered to do so (despite the obvious rise in colonial status that such a decision entailed).

The Muslims' political interests were essentially ignored and the dual system put in place caused lingering resentment. They had had no say in the previous government of the Ottoman Turks either, but the new French regime was more intrusive on a daily level, and of course the French were non-Muslims. Some Muslim individuals and groups chose to collaborate with the French for reasons of personal advancement. A muffled undercurrent of resentment prevailed among the colony's Muslim majority, as they watched the *colons'* prosperity increase while their own level of poverty rose.

THE LEGION AND THE SAHARA

Ever present in the colony were the regiments of the Foreign Legion, posted in forts in cities along the coast and in the remote desert interior. Legion headquarters was established in 1843 at Sidi-bel-Abbès (sixty miles south of Oran). The Legion underwent many changes in the years 1830 to 1870. It was originally called the "Foreign Regiment," and was at first wholly an infantry force. The soldiers operated out of Sidi-bel-Abbès as a flying column, engaging in firefights with the enemy as required, but also literally building the infrastructure of the colony.[49] It constructed roads, rail lines, mines, and quarries, as well as forts, markets, and schools. The town council of Sidi-bel-Abbès was originally comprised entirely of the personnel of the Legion. Serving as an instrument of the foreign policy of the various French governments of the nineteenth century, the Legion served in a Spanish civil war on behalf of the *Cristinos* against the *Carlists* (1835–1837), during which time artillery, cavalry, and sapper units were added to its ranks. The Old Legion was so decimated in Spain, however, that a New Legion was raised for the pacification of the Algerian interior. The Legion also served in the Crimean War (1854–1855), in Italy against the Hapsburgs (1859), and in Mexico on behalf of Emperor Maximilian, puppet of Napoleon III (1863–1867). In 1875 its name was officially changed to the "Foreign Legion," and by 1900 Sidi-bel-Abbès was a large French colonial town of 40,000 people.

The French increasingly became involved in the neighboring *beylik* of Tunis in the 1870s, when the Berbers of the Algerian interior were being pacified. The bey borrowed heavily from European nations, and in 1869 he allowed France, Italy, and Britain to take over his finances because he was unable to repay his debt. Italy vied with France over concessions in Tunisia such as the railroads and the telegraph lines that were being set up in the country from 1879 to 1881. French forces crossed from Algeria into Tunisia in 1881 in a punitive campaign against the Krumir tribe of Bedouin Arabs.[50] The French, however, also went into Tunis and disarmed the bey (allowing him to reside in his palace as a puppet). In the Treaty of Bardo (May 12, 1881), the bey accepted the presence of French diplomatic and military personnel in a French protectorate.[51] Southern Tunisia was acquired (1881–1883), ostensibly in the suppression of anti-French campaigns waged by the Berber Bu Amama into Algeria. A French resident-general took control of Tunisian affairs officially in the Convention of Marsa (June 8, 1883), and the protectorate came under the administration of the French Ministry of Foreign Affairs and later, the Ministry of the Colonies.[52] Turkish, Italian, and British protests were ignored by the French, while Bismarck of Germany approved of the move in order to create a more stable regional balance of power.[53] Prime Minister Jules Ferry (1880–1881 and 1883–1885) made a series of speeches to the Assembly in Paris during the first half of the 1880s, explaining the necessity of empire. He articulated the need for overseas markets and coaling stations, as well as the superiority of the French "civilizing mission" in the world, and the prestige that came from possession of an overseas domain (which France deserved, as one of the "great powers").

The French came to view the entire Sahara west and south of Libya and Egypt as their domain. In the mid-1890s, deputy François Deloncle proclaimed: "We shall counter the English dream summed up in the formula 'From Cape to Cairo,' we shall counter with the French dream 'From the Atlantic to the Red Sea.' "[54] Deloncle represented a good many French politicians, both conservatives and liberals, who believed that it was their duty to defend the territories conquered by the previous generations of Frenchmen. Their beliefs were a far cry from the crusades and also from Napoleonic ideas of global conquest on the basis of alleged Enlightenment principles. These men not only firmed up the already-existing French positions in material and diplomatic terms, but they also found ample opportunities for France to expand further on the basis of self-defense against the jihads of several Muslim leaders who arose to challenge their presence within the Sahara. The western borders of their North African realm were firmed up in March 1899 by the Anglo-French Convention, which established fixed borders in Tripolitania-Libya as the middle ground between Algeria and Egypt. From 1900 to 1903, the French occupied several oases in southwestern Algeria (Igli, Gourara, Timmimun, and Tuat), that had been claimed previously by the sultans of Morocco, but over which the Moroccans were unable to exert their authority.[55]

A French position was established on the west coast of Africa in 1626 called St. Louis de Senegal, located on the Senegal River.[56] Frenchman

Paul Imbert became one of the first Europeans to visit Timbuktu in the middle of Niger in 1618. Although control of St. Louis was yielded to the English on two occasions (1763 and 1817), the French reacquired control of the town and began expanding inland along the river, establishing forts along the route. In 1849, they established a protectorate in Guinea, farther in the interior.[57] Protectorates became the norm for many European colonial powers in the second half of the nineteenth century (Tunisia and Guinea are but two examples from the French). There was no colonization within the protectorate, but rather, a small corps of European administrators and soldiers ran the possession with the assistance of local elites. Prime Minister Jules Ferry and Professor Pierre Paul Leroy-Beaulieu were the strongest advocates of the protectorate and the attending theory of "association" (reliance on local elites) over "assimilation," which is what some had advocated in the colonization of Algeria (to no effect among the Muslim *indigènes*).[58] Elaborate theories of empire began to be articulated by French administrators and political scientists by the end of the nineteenth century to explain the peculiar nature of government in different areas of the empire—subjection, assimilation, and association, which, as M. M. Knight argued in 1933, were "elements or factors in policy, present in varying degrees and combinations in the same colonies at the same time."[59] Gabriel Charmes, a journalist for the *Journel des Debats*, traveled extensively throughout the Ottoman Empire, Egypt, and Morocco in the 1870s and 1880s, and influenced French public opinion by promoting French economic involvement in the Islamic world in numerous articles.[60]

The French presence in much of West Africa in the nineteenth century resembled the kind of French colonial dominion that existed in southern Algeria—garrison forces (usually natives, however) established in frontier outposts and a few soldiers and European administrators located in the towns. A succession of jihads were launched against the French in the Sahara and Sudan in the second half of the nineteenth century, in reaction to the extension of French influence farther into the African interior south of Algeria. The first of these began in the Tukulor region along the Senegal River in the 1850s, and was led by al-Hajj 'Umar.[61] The Tukulor state arose in the 1770s, and al-Hajj 'Umar exploited the French presence along the Senegal coast as justification for expanding his control over an area as far east as Lake Chad. He made a temporary peace with the French in 1860 so that he could turn his attention to conquering the central Sudanic lands and imposing his version of Islamic law over his subject populations. The French governor of the Sudan (*Commandant Superieur*), Colonel Louis Archinard, was based in Mali and campaigned against Al-Hajj 'Umar and the Tukulor throughout most of the 1850s and 1860s, managing to reduce Tukulor resistance after al-Hajj 'Umar's untimely death in 1864.[62]

Another anti-French jihad was proclaimed by the Mandinka imam Samori, in the 1860s.[63] Based in the Guinea Highlands, Samori proclaimed

himself to be the *mahdi* and established a strict Islamic state. He eluded the
French for decades, and his anti-French policies served as the pretext for
further French expansion around Guinea. A French base was established
at Porto Novo on the Dahomey coast in 1863, and in two decades French
forces began expanding inland from that direction toward the Niger
River.[64] The French conquest of the upper Niger valley began in 1883, and
was completed five years later, with the establishment of a fort at
Bamako.[65] A French protectorate was established over the Ivory Coast in
1889, and two wars had to be waged in Dahomey (1890 and 1892) before
the area could be organized as a colony in 1894.[66] Samori established a
peace with France in 1866 and used the opportunity to consolidate his
holdings. He proclaimed the creation of a secular state, and guaranteed
toleration of other religions. He also recruited African soldiers who had
fled from French or British service, and built up his army with the technical expertise that the defectors brought with them.[67] Not surprisingly, hostilities resumed in the early 1890s.[68]

Archinard initiated a major offensive against Samori in 1891, but a rash
attack on the Muslim leader's capital at Bissangudu was easily beaten
off.[69] He was recalled to France, and his successor captured the town in the
following year. The government realized, however, that Archinard's
extensive expertise in the region was needed to subdue Samori, and he
was returned to his post in 1893.[70] Archinard's forces captured the fabled
cities of Jenne and Timbuktu in 1893, and beat a coalition of Tuareg tribesmen. Further campaigns against Samori were undertaken in 1894–1895 by
Major Parfait-Louis Monteil, and in 1895 the various French West African
colonies were reorganized under a single governor-general.[71] Samori's
resources were finally exhausted and he was captured by French forces in
late September 1898.

He was exiled to Gabon, where he died in 1900 in French captivity. In
1904 all of French West Africa was unified, with the colonial capital being
placed at Dakar in Senegal. The final areas to be subdued, according to the
vision of Deloncle, were the largely uninhabited wastelands of Mauritania
(conquered by General Henri Gouraud in 1908–1909), the eastern Sudan,
and Morocco. In the last two areas, French interests almost precipitated a
world war prior to 1914.

Morocco had been in a state of internal turmoil since the reign of the
despotic Mulay Isma'il (d. 1727). A number of cities broke away from central authority in the eighteenth century (including Fez, Rabat, and Sallee),
and many Berber tribes of the interior simply ignored the dictates of the
sultan.[72] The black African military force created by Mulay Isma'il also
began wielding power in its own right, placing pliable sultans on the
throne as it suited them. The internal chaos of the country was the cause
of Bugeaud's difficulty in dealing with 'Abd al-Qadir effectively in the
1840s. Spain gradually acquired control of the northern coast in the eigh-

teenth and nineteenth centuries, while the French exerted influence unofficially in the south, where the border was porous. While both Spain and France had lost North American empires by this time (France in the eighteenth century and Spain in the nineteenth century), France's new empire in North Africa and Southeast Asia was not matched by Spain, which saw the remnants of its old empire fade in the Spanish-American War of 1898. France came to view control of Morocco as vital to its imperial interests in North Africa.

French and British interests came into conflict over the Sudan. At the same time that the French were campaigning against Samori in the Western Sudan, Anglo-Egyptian forces were preparing for a massive campaign against the successor of Muhammad Ahmad, who had proclaimed himself *mahdi* at Omdurman in the upper Nile valley in 1881. The French had an interest in Egypt and the Nile valley after Napoleon, and had promoted the construction of the Suez Canal in 1869 (a French engineer, Ferdinand de Lesseps, designed the canal). The British, however, saw control of the canal as essential for their eastern empire. The canal would dramatically shorten the time entailed in travel to India, Hong Kong, Singapore, Australia, and New Zealand. The British obtained the controlling shares in the Suez Canal in 1876. When traditionalist Muslims under Colonel Arabi Pasha threatened Western domination of the canal, the French sent an expeditionary force to Alexandria in 1882, but quickly withdrew out of fear of the reaction of other Western powers. Consequently, it was British forces rather than French ones that defeated Arabi Pasha at Tel el-Kabir in September 1882.[73]

The British came to view control of the entire Nile valley as essential for the security of the Suez Canal, and in 1874, Charles Gordon was sent to Khartoum to "modernize" the province of Equitoria (Nilotic Sudan) and abolish the slave trade there. The creation of Muhammad Ahmad's Mahdist state in 1881, however, shortly led to the proclamation of jihad by him and his followers against the Westernized Anglo-Egyptian regime. The killing of Gordon in 1885 by Mahdist forces added the element of revenge to the British motivations for expanding south along the Nile, and a two-pronged offensive—British forces under Kitchener and Egyptian forces under MacDonald—finally succeeded in taking the Mahdist capital of Omdurman in September 1898.[74] Shortly after that, British and French expansionist drives in the Sudan collided at a place called Fashoda.

FASHODA

Official French policy in the mid-1890s came to resemble Deloncle's statement that the French should counter Britain's "Cairo to the Cape" drive with an "Atlantic to the Red Sea" drive. Jean-Baptiste Marchand, an officer who had served under Archinard in the Tukulor campaigns, and a member of the pro-colonization *Comité de l'Afrique français* proposed the idea of a race to the Nile in 1895. He did not envision a war against the Mahdists, but perhaps an alliance with them: "We must not lose sight of the fact that Muslims ought to be, whatever the price, our friends in the Nile region, our allies."[75] Although he fought against Muslims engaged in an anti-French jihad in the Western Sudan, Marchand respected the Islamic religion and his Muslim opponents. He even wore Arab-style dress on occasion.[76]

After a long wait caused by changes in governmental ministries at home, Captain Marchand received a commission to go to the Nile in June 1896. Foreign Minister Gabriel Hanotaux told him: "Go to Fashoda. France is going to fire her pistol."[77] Setting off from Gabon in West Africa, Marchand sought to counter British claims in the upper Nile by reaching an abandoned fort at Fashoda and holding it with a small force of men, thereby preventing the British from cutting off French access to the Red Sea. The mission was not conducted in a clandestine manner, however, and *Le Temps* even included a notice about the precise aims of French diplomacy in the Sudan on June 25:

Captain Marchand, who is to take command of the military forces supporting us in the Upper Ubangi, leaves from Marseilles tomorrow. These forces are intended simply to occupy those posts in the Mbonu valley that were returned to us nineteen months ago by the Congo Free State. Under no circumstances is this to be construed as an operation against the Dervishes.[78]

The Belgians had no real claim in the area and no capability of extending their power there, but the mention of the prior Franco-Belgian diplomacy was presented as a means of legitimizing the French claim on an area that was one of the few remaining native areas in the Sudan beyond the Mahdist state and the dwindling realm of Samori in the west. The French hoped that at the least, the Mahdists would continue to occupy the British while Marchand slipped through to the Nile. In the most optimistic scenario, they envisioned that they could forge an alliance with the Mahdists.

The French also arranged secretly with the Ethiopian emperor Menelik II to support Ethiopian claims to the right bank of the Nile in return for Ethiopian recognition of French claims to the left bank. Two Frenchmen journeyed with an Ethiopian expedition along the Sobat River to the right bank of the Nile in June 1898. Marchand traveled eastward along the Mbonu River, and reached the left bank on July 10 at Fashoda (modern Kodok).[79] He had a small force intended for stealthy, rapid movement, which would not attract the attention of the British while it moved eastward.[80] The British were then occupied in the final campaign against the Mahdists, and on September 2, they completely defeated the Mahdist forces at Omdurman.[81] The British were aware of French interest in the upper Nile, and General Kitchener quickly pushed farther south after the battle, arriving at Fashoda on September 18 with overwhelming force.[82] A major diplomatic crisis ensued for over a month, as Marchand refused Kitchener's repeated orders to evacuate on behalf of prior Egyptian claims.[83] War loomed, as both countries made veiled and not-so-veiled threats. The French government, however, soon became preoccupied in the Dreyfus Affair (1898–1906).[84]

The Dreyfus Affair stemmed from the charge of treason alleged against Jewish French army officer Alfred Dreyfus. The convoluted case, which dragged on for years, pitted royalists, Catholic leaders, and the army against pro-republican reformers. Dreyfus's ultimate vindication paved the way for laws that established a more rigid separation of church and state in France (Dreyfus was entirely exonerated and promoted in 1906). The beginnings of the affair caused such a sensation within France in 1898 that foreign policy issues, including the Atlantic to the Red Sea dream, were relegated to the periphery. Although the Muslim *indigènes* of the Sahara might not be able to hope for liberation in the new climate, neither could French imperialists gather enough domestic support to lay claim to the upper Nile. Marchand was ordered by his government to evacuate Fashoda on November 3, 1898, and his forces withdrew in mid-December. In March 1899, the French formally renounced all claims to territory in the Nilotic Sudan in return for the right to acquire any unclaimed lands west of the Nile valley in east-central Sudan.

MOROCCO

While Marchand was formulating his plan to go to the Nile, French officials also scrutinized developments in Morocco, the remaining block of territory west of Egypt that was not under the French flag. Sultan 'Abd al-Aziz came to the throne in 1894 at age thirteen and was overshadowed by his various advisors and by European representatives for several years. The French took advantage of the unstable situation and took strategic oases that had formerly been claimed by Morocco located deep in the interior of the Sahara (Igli, Gourara, Timmimun, Tidikelt, and Tuat) in the period 1900–1903. These areas more directly linked the French presence in the western Sudan and the Algerian Sahara. In mid-December 1900 a secret agreement was drawn up between France and Italy that granted France the right to dominate Morocco without Italian opposition, while the Italians were granted the same powers in Libya without French opposition. French control of the Algerian-Moroccan frontier was ensured in July 1901 by a diplomatic agreement with the sultan. Britain provided France with the same kind of assurances in Morocco as had been granted by Italy in the April 1904 *Entente Cordiale*. The French, however, recognized Spanish control of a narrow block of territory on Morocco's northern coast that October.

Meanwhile, the country continued to dissolve—a pretender to the throne ('Umar Zarhuni) threatened the sultan, and brigands (like Raisuli) captured foreigners for ransom.[85] Diplomat Saint-René Taillandier arrived in Fez on a mission in January 1905 to request that the sultan accept France's proposals for reform, but his mission ended without any success in February. German emperor Wilhelm II made a trip to Tangier in March, in a show of German interest in the region.[86] The apparent divergence of French and German interests in Morocco precipitated the First Moroccan Crisis, which might have led to war among the self-proclaimed "great powers" of Europe. In June, the "great powers" assembled in a conference at Algeciras in Morocco to discuss the various ideas of reform.[87] The conference was held from January to April of 1906, and in the end France and Spain were charged with overseeing reform in Morocco, but the country technically remained independent under the sultan. The Algeciras Conference, however, had succeeded in driving a wedge between the "great powers," with Britain and Italy supporting the dominance of France and Germany supporting Spain. Thus, 'Abd al-Aziz deftly preserved the quasi-independence of his country at a time when most of the African continent was being unceremoniously swallowed up in the "Scramble for Africa." Spain, however, was in such a weakened state from its loss to the United States in the Spanish-American War (1898)—ceding its remaining American and Pacific colonies—that it could not hope to compete with France on equal terms in Morocco.

Despite Algeciras, internal order continued to deteriorate in Morocco over the year 1906–1907, and anti-foreign riots broke out. Morocco had not been a very cohesive state since the time of Mulay Isma'il several centuries earlier, but anti-Western slave raiding on the high seas, encouraged by the sultan, was now superseded by attacks on foreigners visiting or working in the country, undertaken by local warlords. The "great powers" exclusively consisted of Western countries, and the current sultan's position was therefore quite precarious. In the summer of 1907 the French used the murder of a French citizen (Dr. Emile Mauchamp) as the pretext for sending military forces into the country. They took Udja in the northwest in July, and Casablanca and the surrounding region on the Atlantic coast in August.[88] That summer, a civil war also broke out, after 'Abd al-Hafiz, brother of the sultan, was proclaimed to be the new sultan by his followers at Marrakesh. The civil war lasted a year, until in August 1908, 'Abd al-Aziz was finally beaten at Marrakesh and deposed.

'Abd al-Hafiz was recognized one month later by Germany, and then the other "great powers" followed suit after he pledged support of the Act of Algeciras, in which the conference participants had established the framework for Moroccan reform. The ongoing Franco-German conflict over Morocco, however, escalated for the next three years—beginning with the 1908 Casablanca Affair (involving German deserters from the Foreign Legion, an issue eventually adjudicated by the Hague international court). A Franco-German Agreement in 1909 entailed German recognition of France's supreme position in Moroccan affairs, in return for economic concessions granted to Germany within the country. In the 1910 Franco-Moroccan Agreement, the French evacuated Udja, and the sultan reiterated his assent for domestic reforms. A rash of anti-foreign outbursts in Morocco in 1911 brought about the Second Moroccan Crisis, threatening war between the "great powers." The French occupied Fez in May when Berber rebel groups threatened Europeans in the area. A German gunboat arrived at Agadir on the Atlantic coast in July, and the French protested vigorously the German presence there. Another Franco-German Agreement that November confirmed the French position of superiority in Morocco, but this time included French concessions to Germany in the area of the French Congo, near German Cameroon (Kamerun).

The French position in Morocco became an official protectorate in March 1912 when 'Abd al-Hafiz accepted French overlordship (although he still technically reigned as sultan).[89] In May, General Louis H. G. Lyautey arrived as resident-general, and he employed the Foreign Legion to great effect in restoring order to several areas in the interior (he had previously served in Indochina, Madagascar, and Algeria).[90] 'Abd al-Hafiz, however, did not wish to serve as a puppet of the French, and abdicated in August. He was succeeded by Sultan Yusuf. A Franco-Spanish Agreement in November further clarified the Spanish zone in the north, and established Tangier as an international city.[91] The outbreak of World War I would see French attentions drawn to Europe, and many small Berber groups took advantage of the opportunity to rebel against French authority. Lyautey was charged with holding onto the coast and only a few inland areas, but instead with two infantry regiments and only two cavalry companies, he pacified some troublesome inland areas. Ironically, the units under him were mainly composed of Germans, Austrians, Bulgarians, and Turks—whose national colleagues in Europe comprised the Central Powers with whom France was at war (1914–1918). Lyautey's men fought Berber guerrilla bands in the remote Rif mountains from 1921 to 1926, when the last foe of note, 'Abd al-Krim (who commanded 100,000 poorly trained Berbers), was defeated by the Legion in conjunction with Spanish forces.[92] 'Abd al-Krim was exiled to Marseilles, and then to Mauritius, meeting a fate similar to that of 'Abd al-Qadir and Samori before him. By 1926, the French had conquered virtually the entire realm of the former Barbary pirates and had a trans-Saharan empire, which, if not exactly the fulfillment of Deloncle's Atlantic to the Red Sea dream, was nevertheless an empire larger than that of Napoleon. Altogether, by 1926, France had control of about 40 percent of all the colonial territories and an equal percentage of the colonial populations throughout the world.

CONCLUSION

The Maghrib continued to be a focal point of French strategic interest for over five centuries after St. Louis had died in the attempt to subjugate a portion of it at Tunis in 1270. The Ottoman Turkish Empire, with whom the Valois regime had established an *entente*, came to employ the Maghribi Muslim pirates (known in the West as the Barbary pirates) as proxies in their perennial struggle with Western Christendom. French citizens, as well as French shipping, sustained a great many casualties as a consequence of that policy. The Restoration Bourbon government, however, used the personal insult sustained by a French diplomat at the hands of an Ottoman functionary to help solidify public opinion in favor of an invasion that was overwhelmingly successful. French territorial ambitions in north and central Africa were spurred on by the fear of jihad emanating from behind the Muslim lines, and by 1926, France and its Foreign Legion had conquered a swath of territory extending from the Atlantic coast across the Sahara toward the Nile valley.

Prior Franco-Muslim conflicts in the Mediterranean, together with economic dreams and a desire to recapture the fleeting imperial glory of the Napoleonic era, shaped the pro-imperial attitudes of the French government, the press, and the population in favor of continued conquests against Muslim populations adjacent to the areas of initial conquest along the Algerian coast. As the mercenaries of the Legion were more expendable than a citizen army, the battle casualties sustained in France's conquests in the Sahara were never an issue in domestic politics (and France never sustained an imperial defeat in the Sahara comparable to the Zulu defeat of a British column at Isandlwana in South Africa in 1879, or to the Ethiopian defeat of the Italians at Adowa in 1896). The global balance of power was altered by the sequence of events that began in Algeria in 1830. France had one of the largest empires in the world, almost equal with that of Britain in scope. Many of France's colonial subjects were Muslims, and most of them were in northern and western Africa.[93]

3

France, the Muslims, and the Eastern Mediterranean through World War I

BACKGROUND: FRANCE AND OTTOMAN TURKEY

France's interest in the affairs of the eastern Mediterranean intensified through the nineteenth century, until by 1920, it had reacquired control of a large part of the former *Outremer* as a consequence of World War I. The roots of post-crusade French involvement in the area, however, date back far before the twentieth century.[1] Modern French interest in the Arab Middle East in general rose with the decline of the Ottoman Empire, the "Sick Man of Europe." In 1740, the Bourbon king Louis XV (1715–1774) requested and received a capitulation from the Ottomans extending the privileges of the Catholic church over the Christian shrines sacred to both the Catholic and Orthodox traditions.[2] In reaction to the capitulation, the Russians began agitating for a reversal of the decision, and incrementally, local Turkish officials granted limited rulings favoring the Orthodox monks over the Catholics. The rising tension between the two Christian communities provided the background for a wider conflict, as France and Russia used what came to be called the "Shrines Conflict" as an opportunity to extend their influence in the region.[3]

The Greek Revolt in 1821, however, provided a brief opportunity for superpower cooperation. France and Britain backed the revolt for romantic reasons (Classical Greece as the source of Western civilization), and Russia did so as well (Byzantine Greece as the source of Russian Orthodox civilization).[4] For Restoration Bourbon France, the benefits of the old *entente* were superceded by the need to secure France's share of economic and political dominance in the Arab Middle East. Allied intervention took the form of a combined fleet of twenty-six ships, including ten ships-of-the-line, led by the British vice-admiral Sir Edward Coderington. The French contingent of six ships was led by Rear Admiral Gauthier de Rigny.[5]

Assembling at Zante, off the Peloponnese, in September 1827, the allies sailed into Navarino harbor to treat with Turkish naval commander Ibrahim Pasha (who had sixty-five Turkish and Egyptian ships, but only three ships-of-the-line). After preliminary negotiations regarding an armistice already agreed to by the Greeks, tensions rose due to the unexpected arrival of a British-led Greek naval contingent and Turkish plundering of the nearby Greek town of Pylos. Firing started unexpectedly on October 20. In fierce and confused fighting at close range, which lasted less than an hour, the allies' superior fire power destroyed much of the Turkish-Egyptian fleet (and many Turkish commanders set their ships on fire in the hopes of burning any allied vessel that came near). The French ship *Sirene* lost her mizzen mast when the Turkish ship *Irania* exploded, and the only Turkish ship to strike its colors was forced to do so by the French aboard the *Trident*. The battle's losses were 43 Frenchmen, 75 Britons, 59 Russians, and several hundred Turks and Egyptians. Coderington was relieved of his command by his government for exceeding his authority, but Gauthier de Rigny was promoted to vice-admiral and granted a title by King Charles X.[6]

THE CRIMEAN WAR

In the Treaty of Adrianople (1829), Greece and Serbia gained their independence, which initiated a century-long process of Ottoman dissolution.[7] It also gave the Russian navy access to the Black Sea, and provided autonomy to Moldavia and Wallachia. The next French military activity in the region, however, was on the side of Ottoman Turkey and Britain against Russia in the Crimean War (1854–1856).[8] Both France and Britain suspected Russian intentions at the conclusion of the Treaty of Unkiar-Skelessi in 1833, and anti-Russian propaganda began to spread in Paris and London.[9] Fearing that a "secret clause" in the treaty would give the Russians an unfair advantage in the region, the French and British agreed to help the Turks in the event of an attack by Russia in the Straits Convention in 1841.[10] The "Shrines Conflict" in the 1850s in Palestine between Catholic monks (supported by Emperor Napoleon III) and Orthodox monks (supported by Tsar Nicholas I) provided the background of the Crimean War.[11] France and Britain both saw the potential for commercial and imperial opportunities in the Mediterranean, but there were also leaders in France who still referred to their country as "the eldest daughter of the Church," and who had a nostalgia for *Outremer*. Napoleon III's ambassador to the Ottoman Empire, Marquis Charles Jean de Lavalette, demanded that the Turks restore all Catholic privileges as agreed to in 1740, and he threatened the use of a French fleet to force the issue.[12]

The Catholic monks specifically wanted to gain control of the keys to the main door of the Church of the Nativity in Bethlehem, and of the manger area (demanding also a silver star there bearing the French imperial arms). The Turks gave in, but the Russians soon forced them to reverse their decision, sending troops into Moldavia and Wallachia.[13] The Turks feared Russia more than distant France, and so declared war on Russia, in October 1853. The war's inciting incident for France and Britain was the Russian destruction of the Turkish Black Sea fleet in Sinope Bay in November.[14] The principal theater of the war was the long siege of the Russian Black Sea naval base at Sevastopol in the Crimean peninsula, although fighting also occurred in the Caucasus, the Baltic, and the Kamchatka peninsula.[15] The allies fielded 57,000 troops, with command held jointly by French field marshal Saint-Arnaud and aged British field marshal (and veteran of the Napoleonic wars) Lord Raglan, who consistently called the enemy "the French." A third of the French and half of the British were using new rifles, while only about one-twentieth of the Russians had modern rifles. The allies consequently possessed a decided technological advantage. French forces played an important role in the battles at Alma, Kamiesch, Inkermann, Tchernaya River, and the Malakoff during the campaign. The Russians lost a great deal in the resulting Treaty of Paris (1856), including access to the Dardanelles and guardianship of the Christians in the Ottoman Empire. French prestige in the eastern Mediterranean was greatly enhanced by the Russian defeat.

FRENCH INFLUENCE IN LEBANON PRIOR TO WORLD WAR I

France solidified trade concessions along the Lebanese coast, which it had secured in the 1830s from Pasha Bashir II (a former Druze who converted to Maronite-rite Catholicism). The Maronites came under heavy French influence again, as during the days of *Outremer*. The Orthodox Christians in the area favored the influence of Russia, while the Druze were cultivated by the British, and the Muslims looked directly to the Ottoman overlords of the region for guidance. Animosity between the Maronites and Druze erupted into violence in 1860, and some 14,000 Maronites were massacred by the Druze in Mount Lebanon, and by Muslims in Damascus.[16] Many Maronites were saved by the timely intervention of the exiled Algerian leader 'Abd al-Qadir. French armed forces intervened, but the Turks had already put down the disorder.

In 1861, the Turks declared Lebanon to be a *sanjak*, an autonomous area of the Ottoman Empire led by a Christian governor based at Deir al-Qamr. The *sanjak* encompassed 1,600 square miles, but excluded Beirut (the third biggest port in the Ottoman Empire), Tripoli, Sidon, and Tyre.[17] The Ottoman *Sublime Porte* confirmed the governor after consultation with the

European "great powers." The population of the *sanjak* was perhaps 250,000, and the region was allowed a separate customs service from the rest of Syria. No Turkish soldiers were allowed to enter the *sanjak*, and the Maronites residing there were excluded from compulsory military service until 1909. The police were composed mainly of Maronites, and their commander was always a Maronite. *Sanjak* law was modeled after Turkish law in 1879, with commercial cases being heard in Beirut. In 1912, the law was amended so that commercial cases were heard in Mount Lebanon. The *sanjak* started publishing an annual budget in 1912 to ensure fiscal responsibility. Despite the high degree of freedom enjoyed by the *sanjak's* residents, compared to other areas in the Ottoman Empire, the Maronites were not pleased at their subordinate status within an Islamic state, and sought still more autonomy. Recurring problems stemmed from the Maronites' request for access to Lebanese coastal ports (denied by the Turks), and police demands for higher salaries. Most Maronites refused to participate in national parliamentary elections.

France began investing heavily in the development of the physical infrastructure of Lebanon and Syria in the mid-1800s. Much of the language of Ottoman business was in French. French-language books and newspapers circulated widely in Syria and Lebanon.[18] France made substantial loans to the Ottoman government, and both French and British interests controlled the Imperial Ottoman Bank.[19] Numerous French experts were hired by the Turkish government in the nineteenth century. French officers administered the Ottoman public debt and the *Régie des Tabacs*. French agents oversaw the manufacture of cigarettes from local tobacco, and local wine for export. French capital and businesses built the main roads in the region (Beirut to Damascus, and Beirut to Tyre), as well as the main railroad lines Beirut-Rayaq-Damascus-Muzayrib, and Jaffa to Jerusalem). In the Ottoman *Régie Générale*, which maintained the rail lines, there were numerous French managers, engineers, and financial experts. French companies received the contracts for the construction of the regional gas and electric systems, as well as for the coastal lights and port development.[20] France did more shipping to Ottoman ports than did any other country, and was the biggest importer of Syrian goods (including silk, dried fruit, and wool). A deal was made in 1913 in which France was granted the opportunity to modernize Haifa, Jaffa, and Tripoli. The French began modernizing Alexandretta, a venture that, however, was completed by Germany. French operatives cultivated the local silk industry and set up chemical factories. France and Britain were also the biggest exporters of goods into Syria and Lebanon.[21] The Maronites and other Christian *millets* were heavily involved in the trade with France (including also the Armenians, Jacobites, Nestorians, Greek Catholics, and Greek Orthodox).

Education in the region was heavily influenced by France and the French language. Both Christian and Muslim intellectuals in Lebanon and

Syria spoke French.[22] This is an aspect of what has been called France's "civilizing mission." Despite the secularization of France in the nineteenth and twentieth centuries, Catholicism was a crucial factor in France's "civilizing mission" abroad. There were about two dozen Catholic missionary orders active in Lebanon and Syria, overseeing missions and schools. Among the male orders active in education in the region were the Benedictines, Carmelites, Capuchins, Franciscans, Dominicans, Jesuits, Lazarists, Marists, Salesians, Trappists, and White Fathers. Among the female orders were the sisters of Besancon, Charity, the Holy Family, Notre Dame de Douleurs, St. Francis, and St. Vincent de Paul. By the outbreak of World War I, over half of the children in Lebanon and Syria who attended school went to French mission schools, and were taught by French monks and nuns.[23]

Several Arab reformist political organizations emerged in Paris before World War I. They were dominated by Maronites, who were of course the segment of the Ottoman population most heavily influenced by French culture and history. One such organization was the Ottoman League, formed in 1908, which overtly sought the creation of a new regime in Istanbul. This organization and a few others like it, frequently composed of a few dozen to a few hundred members, were the precursors of the modern Arab nationalist movement. The Arab nationalist movement looked back to the time of Arab unity in the Umayyad period. While modern French politics came to influence Arab subjects of the sultan, French interest in Islam and Arab culture had a longer pedigree.

FRENCH "ORIENTALISM" THROUGH WORLD WAR I

Within the French colonial administrative apparatus were Arab Bureaus staffed with Arabists, who served to mediate problems between Muslim subjects and the government. The French had an advantage over many of their European rivals in their colonial administration, for French scholars had already pioneered the field of Islamic studies. The expertise of French Orientalists greatly enhanced the ability of the colonial government to gauge the varieties of problems that arose in Algeria and other Islamic parts of the French Empire in the era of the New Imperialism of the nineteenth century. But while these scholars served as mediators between the conquered populations and the government, and were consulted by the regime, French governmental policy toward the Muslims was not built upon any appreciation for, or sympathy of, the Muslims, which the French Arabists themselves may have felt.

The study of the Arabic language and culture already had a venerable lineage in France, dating back as far as the time of the Cluniacs. The first vernacular translation of the Qur'an from Arabic into a European language was made by André du Ryer into French in 1647, and King Louis

XIV founded one of the earliest European schools for training interpreters in Arabic and other "Oriental" languages in 1700. Two Maronite scholars active in Paris in the 1620s and 1630s (Gabriel Sionita and Abraham Ecchelensis) had utilized Arabic sources in their research, and their work encouraged Pierre Vattier, a professor at the College de France, to translate Arabic texts in history, medicine, philosophy, and poetry into French in the 1650s.[24] Barthelemy d'Herbelot produced a dictionary of Arabic, Persian, and Turkish terminology titled *Bibliothèque orientale* (published posthumously in 1697), which remained a standard reference work in Europe for over a century. D'Herbelot paved the way for many other French scholars, including Antoine Galland (1646–1715), who first translated *The Thousand and One Nights* into a European language (French), and who wrote the preface for d'Herbelot's *Bibliothèque*.[25]

The scholar who is generally considered to be the founder of "Oriental Studies"—in the non-pejorative sense of the term—is Baron Antoine-Isaac Silvestre de Sacy (1757–1838), who mastered Arabic, Syriac, Chaldaean, and Hebrew.[26] De Sacy began his career teaching Arabic at the School of Living Oriental Languages in 1769 (he rose to be director of the school in 1824), became a professor at the College de France in 1806, and was the first president of the Société asiatique in 1822.[27] His many publications include the *Grammaire arabe*, published in 1810, and the *Chrestomathie arabe* (published in 1806 and 1827). In addition to his academic career, however, de Sacy was influential in shaping governmental policy toward the Muslim world. As a member of Napoleon's Institut de France in 1802, he was responsible for assessing the current state of knowledge of the "Orient," and thus was responsible for subsequently shaping the directions in which the field would expand.[28] He also began a tradition of Orientalist influence on French national policy toward the Islamic world. De Sacy was responsible for translating Napoleon's proclamations into Arabic, and delved into the possibility of inciting the Turkic Muslims of Central Asia against Russia.[29] With the conquest of Algeria in 1830, de Sacy was again charged with translating the decrees of the government into Arabic.[30] From then on, he served as a consultant to the French Ministry of Foreign Affairs and the Ministry of War with regard to the Islamic world. De Sacy trained virtually an entire generation of Arabists, and in the nineteenth century his disciples could be found in all the older and newer centers of Islamic studies in Europe, such as Leiden and Berlin.[31]

The term "Orientalist" appeared in France for the first time in 1799, and the 1838 *Dictionnaire de L'Academie Française* included an entry titled "Orientalisme." Much has been written about the connection between the rise of European empires in the nineteenth century and the rise of "Oriental studies" in Europe. Edward Said's powerful attack on Western attitudes toward Islam, titled *Orientalism* (1978), emphasizes the connection between the colonial domination of the Middle East by the Western powers and the attitudes of Western superiority that he alleges were present in the writings of the "Orientalist" scholars whose opinions increasingly shaped Western policy in the Middle East:

In the depths of this Oriental stage stands a prodigious cultural repertoire whose individual items evoke a fabulously rich world: the Sphinx, Cleopatra, Eden, Troy, Sodom and Gomorrah, Astarte, Isis and Osiris, Sheba, Babylon, the Genii, the Magi, Nineveh, Prester John, Mahomet, and dozens more; settings, in some cases names only, half-imagined, half-known; monsters, devils, heroes; terrors, pleasures, desires. The European imagination was nourished extensively from this repertoire.[32]

David Levering Lewis characterized French colonial administrators as follows: "As a rule French officers were more excited than their British peers about what they found in Africa or Asia, more prone to conceptualizing the meaning of their experiences, and more determined to improve what was there."[33] While there were a good many romantics and dilettante Arabists serving in the French colonial administration, there were also some truly brilliant scholars, such as Louis Massignon (1882–1962), a scholar who possessed the enthusiasm of the romantic for the people and cities of the Islamic Middle East.[34] Massignon studied Arabic literature in Paris, then traveled to Algeria, Cairo, and Iraq (where he participated in an archaeological excavation and where he was arrested and imprisoned by Turkish authorities in 1908 for espionage).[35] While in Turkish custody he had a conversion experience of a sort (over realization of the "horror of myself"), and was drawn into Islamic mysticism.[36] His doctoral dissertation was completed in 1914 on the Sufi mystic al-Hussein Ibn Mansur al-Hallaj, who was executed by the 'Abbasids for teaching that Islamic rituals were less important than inner sanctity. It was published in 1922, the thousandth anniversary of the martyrdom of al-Hallaj.[37]

Massignon entered French military and diplomatic service during World War I, and his skills were employed on the Southeastern Front, first at the Dardanelles and Macedonia, and then as assistant political officer attached to the mission of Georges Picot, France's high commissioner for the Allied-occupied territories in Palestine and Syria.[38] These areas had been taken by British forces from Egypt under General Edmund H. H. Allenby and by Arab forces under Colonel Thomas Edward Lawrence, the famed "Lawrence of Arabia."[39] Massignon met Lawrence in 1917. They shared a similar sentimental attachment to the Arab people and to the desert: "I have a nostalgia for the desert, this perfect serene sea, balanced in its very immensity by the daily passage of the sun … it is there that I was truly born."[40] Albert Hourani, however, in *Islam in European Thought*, distinguished between Lawrence's vision of the desert as a primordial location where a man might master himself in isolation from the distractions of civilization ("the Arab East to me is always an empty place") and Massignon's vision of a location "filled with human beings, past and present."[41] Massignon quoted Lawrence as once saying to him: "You love the Arabs more than I do."[42] This affection for the Arab people drove Massignon to criticize French colonial policies in Algeria and Morocco on more than one occasion. Massignon the mystic became a Greek-rite Catholic priest in later life.

FRANCE AND THE GREAT WAR

The decline of the Ottoman Turkish Empire lay behind the outbreak of World War I (1914–1918), and in a sense, the wider world war emanated out of a century of Balkan wars between the Balkan Christian subjects (Orthodox and Catholic) and their Muslim overlords.[43] French interests in the Ottoman Empire were already well established by this time, but the Hohenzollern German Empire and the Hapsburg Austrian Empire were beginning to be intrigued by the possibilities of investment in the Arab Middle East.[44] The Germans, with Turkish support, began construction of a Berlin-Baghdad rail line that they hoped would presage German supremacy in the Orient.[45] The Ottomans granted Deutsche Bank a ninety-nine-year commission on the projected railway in 1903, and by 1914, Germany had assumed the lead among developers and investors of the Turkish rail system. Although France controlled about 60 percent of the Ottoman public debt (to Germany's 24 percent), French trade with Ottoman Turkey dropped precipitously from 1900 to 1914. By the start of World War I, France fell down to fifth place among countries doing commerce with the Ottomans. The outbreak of the war in 1914 would provide France with the hope of reasserting its interests in the Middle East.[46]

In 1904 France and Britain agreed to the *Entente Cordiale*, in which any French claims on Egypt stemming from the Fashoda Crisis period were dropped, in return for British recognition of French claims on Morocco.[47] France then entered into the Triple Entente with both Britain and Russia, out of a common fear of German intentions. France had been subjected to a humiliating defeat by Prussia in 1870, and French leaders believed the Hohenzollern Empire (which was born out of the old Kingdom of Prussia) sought to isolate and weaken France. British and German interests collided in southern Africa in the Boer War (1899–1902), while Russia was suspicious of German interests in the Baltic Sea, where it had been supreme since the days of Tsar Peter the Great. Russia supported Serb claims in the Balkans in Bosnia and Albania, while Germany backed Austria's claims in the region.[48] Competition between the two front-line powers of Serbia and Austria led to an international crisis, and the Serb-backed "Black Hand" terrorist organization caused the war's inciting incident on June 28, 1914, the assassination of the Hapsburg heir, Archduke Franz Ferdinand.[49]

With the declarations of war that followed a month later, the Triple Entente powers faced the Central Powers, consisting of Germany, Austria, Turkey, and Bulgaria. By war's end, most of the world had lined up with the Entente as the Allies. Much of the important combat occurred in northeastern France and northwestern Russia, and the Balkans became a backwater of the war. The German Von Schlieffen Plan called for an invasion of France, followed by a campaign against Russia.[50] German forces pushed through Belgium in 1914 along the left bank of the Meuse, and drove through between Liege and Namur. After the French and the British Expeditionary Force stopped the German advance at the Marne River in September 1914, however, the Western Front became bogged down in four years of trench warfare, which was characterized by battles of attrition rather than movement. In 1916 alone there were two attrition battles that cost a million casualties each—the French-German battle at Verdun and the British-German battle on the Somme. The Somme had been planned originally as a battle of movement, but both sides lacked sufficient mobility because of the unique conditions of the trenches.

The war provided opportunities for the "great powers" to envision their dominance, following the ruin of the Turkish Empire.[51] France and Russia in particular seemed eager to stake their claims in the region, and intense negotiations between the Allied powers began in 1915 in advance of the anticipated collapse of Turkish power. France, along with all the "great powers," sought commercial supremacy in the eastern Mediterranean. Unlike the other powers, however, France had something to regain in the region—the preeminence it had possessed in the days of the Valois-Ottoman *entente*. France also had never lost interest in the lands of the former *Outremer*, and had a desire to regain direct influence within Syria and Lebanon. Russian Foreign Minister Sergei Sazanov spoke to the Russian Duma in February 1915 of the Russian need for control of the Dardanelles and the city of Constantinople, calling it "Russian access to the open sea."[52] The Russians, historically supportive of Greece, wanted the British and French to keep Greek forces out of any potential invasion of Constantinople, so as to preempt the longstanding Greek claims on that city.[53] France and Britain tended to prefer that Constantinople become a neutral city, with no fortifications allowed there.

Foreign Minister Sazanov wrote to the French and British governments on March 4, 1915, that Russia wanted control of the left bank of the Bosphorus, the Sea of Marmara, and the Dardanelles, and suggested that Russia would back French and British claims elsewhere in the Turkish imperial domains in return for their support of Russia's claims on the straits.[54] Ten days later, the French ambassador to Russia, Paleologue, informed the Romanov government that France sought the annexation of Syria, including the Gulf of Alexandretta and Cilicia as far as the Taurus Mountains in Anatolia.[55] He included an addendum the following day that France's interpretation of the borders of "Syria" encompassed Palestine.[56] Sazanov needed to discuss the status of the holy sites with the tsar, and upon consultation, Tsar Nicholas II consented to the French claims on March 16. The tsar's government got the assurances it sought from France and Britain later in March and April 1915.[57] Reeling from the staggering losses sustained by the Imperial Army in the war, discredited by the Rasputin Scandal, and undermined by a host of revolutionary elements, the Romanov dynasty was overthrown in the February-March 1917 revolution. The succeeding provisional government of Alexander Kerensky, however, was not interested in control of the straits and dropped the demands that had been made by the tsar's government. By that time it was apparent that Britain and France had become the chief arbiters of the fate of Ottoman Turkey.

THE MIDDLE EASTERN THEATER OF WAR AND DIPLOMACY

The Ottoman Empire declared war on France, Russia, and Britain on October 29, 1914, and German officers went east to assist in the war effort. The Turkish Fourth Army, under Jemal Pasha, was headquartered in Damascus, and was responsible for the region of Syria. Later in the war, it was commanded by German generals—Marshal von Falkenhayn, architect of Verdun (1917–1918), and from March 1918 on, General von Sanders (who led Turkish defenders against a British amphibious assault at Gallipoli in 1915). With the great drain of manpower felt by France on the Western Front, the French Army could not afford to employ military personnel in significant numbers in campaigns elsewhere.

The Arab Middle East, however, remained a strategically important location for French planners. A French "Naval Division of the Levant" sailed into the eastern Mediterranean, and remained there throughout the war.[58] Some French units joined the British and Anzac forces in the ill-fated Gallipoli campaign (1915–1916), and French ships repulsed a Turkish attempt led by Jemal Pasha on the Suez Canal in February 1915.[59] Syrians joined the Foreign Legion during the war, and the French began training Arabs in 1918 in a "Legion d'Orient."[60] When the British suggested an Allied landing at Alexandretta, France insisted on command of the operation, but it never occurred because French personnel were needed at home against the Germans.[61] Consequently, most of the Allied success in the Middle East was directed by Britain—Colonel Lawrence's desert campaigns with the Arabs against Turkish railroads and towns from the Hijaz to Syria, and General Allenby's march out from Egypt into Palestine in 1917–1918.[62] In all almost a million British troops participated in the Middle Eastern theater. Jerusalem surrendered to the British on December 9, 1917, and in the fall of 1918, Allenby's men pushed the Turks out of Syria and Lebanon—Damascus surrendered on October 1, Beirut on October 8, and Aleppo on October 26.[63]

French forces, however, did participate in Allenby's campaign. A French brigade, called the *Détachement français de Palestine-Syrie*, was attached to the Fifty-fourth (East Anglian) Division in Allenby's army.[64] The *Détachement* was commanded by Colonel de Piepappe, and although it was a relatively small unit (about 1,500 men), it nevertheless fought with distinction in the combat at Tulkaram and Nablus on September 19–21, 1918. When the British Twenty-first Corps entered Beirut on October 8, 1918, most of the French *Détachement* also entered, along with fresh French troops shipped in for the occasion.[65] A small French detachment accompanied Faysal's Arab army, and France established a military mission under Colonel Bremond at Jidda in the Arabian peninsula, near the British mission.[66] The French government also sent large quantities of ammunition for the Allied campaign in the Middle East. Georges Picot was assigned as the high commissioner of France in the Levant in April 1917, and his task was to push for French claims in the region.

BRITISH DIPLOMACY, FRENCH COMPLACENCY

In early 1915, the British high commissioner in Cairo, Sir Henry McMahon, indicated to Arab leaders that, in return for Arab support against the Turks, the British would back an independent Arab state in the Arabian peninsula after the defeat of Turkish forces. *Sharif* Hussein Ibn 'Ali of Mecca corresponded with McMahon in 1915–1916, and twice sent his son Amir Faysal north to link up with Syrian secret pan-Arab societies including *Fatat*, which had begun agitating for Arab independence.[67] Many Syrian Arabs feared the insertion of French forces into the region in the event of a Turkish military collapse, and pushed for independence. Some important Syrian Arabs supported the "Damascus Protocol," in June 1915, which called for an alliance with Britain against the Turks, in return for British support for an independent Arab caliphate, whose borders would stretch north from the Arabian peninsula into Syria.[68] Britain would receive economic benefits in trade with the new Arab state.[69]

In the exchanges between McMahon and the *sharif*, the British high commissioner at first did not sanction the borders of the proposed state that would extend northward to Syria. But by late October 1915, he finally agreed to most of the borders, with two exceptions: (1) the coastal region west of Damascus, Homs, Hama, and Aleppo (i.e., Lebanon) because the region was "not purely Arab" (following an argument put forth by the Maronites), and because it was an area vital to the "interests of her ally, France"; and (2) Baghdad and Basra, where the British themselves had interests.[70] McMahon later claimed that Palestine was not included in the deal, but the British Foreign Office documents in the Westermann Papers (documents held at Stanford University's Hoover Institution, and not opened until 1964) indicate otherwise.[71] The *sharif* disagreed over the details of the excepted areas, but felt they could be worked out later with the high commissioner.[72] McMahon's second note stated clearly that Britain backed the creation of an Arab state: "Subject to the above modifications...Great Britain is prepared to recognise and uphold the independence of the Arabs in all those regions within the frontiers proposed by the Sharif of Mecca."[73]

Turkish authorities found documents in the French consulates in Beirut and Damascus that had been left behind by the French consul-general Georges Picot that indicated the extent of the discontent of local Arabs with the Ottoman regime. In July 1915, fifty-eight leading Syrian Arabs were charged with treason and condemned to death on account of the documents.[74] Many of them were abroad, but eleven were publicly executed that August in Beirut. Another twenty-two were executed in May 1916. The executions galvanized Arab public opinion from Syria south to the Arabian peninsula. A general Arab revolt against the Turks broke out in the Hijaz in June 1916.[75] Turkish forces were pushed out of Mecca, and the *sharif* proclaimed himself "King of the Arab Countries." The Allies recognized him specifically as monarch of the Hijaz region. Faysal led Arab forces with Lawrence in the Arab Army of the North, and in the course of the war captured several Syrian cities, which forced the surrender of Turkish forces in northern Syria.

The British revealed the McMahon-Hussein correspondence to the French in October 1915, and a conference between the two powers was arranged. Georges Picot and Sir Mark Sykes of Britain agreed in February 1916 to a secret partition of the Ottoman Empire, in which certain areas were to be under the "direct or indirect administration" of France and Britain.[76] France was to get much of Syria and the Lebanese coast directly, including Beirut, Tripoli, Tyre, Sidon, Alexandretta, and Latakia. The French area also extended into Asia Minor, including the cities of Adana, Mersin, and Sivas. The British were to get most of Iraq, including Baghdad, Karbala, and Basra, as well as part of the Palestinian coast, including Haifa and Acre.[77] The two countries also agreed on the creation of areas intended to be under independent Arab control (but under French and British "influence"). The so-called French A Zone consisted of a great deal of the Syrian interior, including Damascus, Homs, Hama, and Aleppo, as well as Mosul in northern Mesopotamia while the British agreed to a band that ran northeast from Aqaba and Amman to Kirkuk, and was primarily uninhabited desert terrain.[78] A portion of Palestine, including Jerusalem, was to be under an undefined international administration. The document, in its final form, referred to "the limits of an Arab state," which was to be "under the suzerainty of an Arab chief," but more of the document pertains to French and British commerce in the Middle East, and the construction of future rail lines connecting certain cities with each other to facilitate Anglo-French trade, than to the precise limits of a future Arab state. Britain and France, however, were to be "the protectors of the Arab state," and they agreed on the independence of the Arabian peninsula, and on preventing its acquisition by a third party. Fearful perhaps of the military capabilities of their Arab allies, they also agreed to consider "measures to control the importation of arms into the Arab territories." Russia was to be apprised of the agreement, and the British suggested that Japan be similarly informed.[79]

At the same time that British colonial officials from Egypt were negotiating with the *sharif*, other British colonial officials from India were negotiating with Arab tribal leader Ibn Sa'ud about the fate of the central and eastern Arabian peninsula.[80] The British government came to back the independence of Ibn Sa'ud in that part of the peninsula, even though he had no popular backing outside the peninsula as did the *sharif*. The future of the Arabian peninsula was further complicated due to the existence of other, separate, British treaties with Arab tribal leaders in Kuwait, Bahrain, Qatar, and Oman. None of these areas were included in the Hussein or Ibn Sa'ud agreements.

In November 1917, the Bolsheviks (who had just overthrown the provisional government) found documents referring to the Sykes-Picot agreement, and handed them over to the Turks, who in turn revealed them to the Arabs to try to break the British-Arab alliance in the Middle East.[81] McMahon had been succeeded as British high commissioner in Cairo by Sir Reginald Wingate, and *Sharif* Hussein quickly demanded an explanation from the British government. Wingate told the *sharif* that the documents represented very early discussions between the Allies that were not valid anymore because Imperial Russia (and its short-lived democratic successor state) had dropped out of the conflict, and the Arab forces' military success had established a "new situation."

CONSEQUENCES FOR THE ARABS

Other Syrian and Lebanese Arabs were recruited into the Turkish Army, where prevailing conditions were poor. The Turkish forces were generally poorly equipped and badly supplied with food. Atrocities were regularly perpetrated on Arab civilians whose loyalties were suspected by the Turks, or who had become a liability. Civilians were killed as a matter of policy when Turkish forces retreated from a village following an Allied advance. Some 150,000 Syrian and Lebanese Arab soldiers recruited by the Turks died in Ottoman military service during the war. Conditions became so unbearable that Arab desertion rates increased in 1917 to about 50 percent of the total Arab troops available to the Turks.

Another terrible consequence of the war emerged in 1916, when famine and epidemics (malaria and typhus in particular) emerged among the civilians living in Lebanon and Syria, accounting for perhaps a half-million non-combatant casualties by 1919 (out of a total prewar regional population of 4 million). Hardest hit were the Maronite Christians living in Mount Lebanon, who believed (as did French military personnel in the region) that the Turks had engineered it because the Ottomans suspected Maronite loyalties.[82] As many as a third of the Maronite population in Mount Lebanon perished. The Turks blamed it on the Allied economic blockade in the eastern Mediterranean. Many wealthy citizens fled from the cities, and the population of Beirut dropped by more than one-half by the middle of 1916 to a mere 75,000 people. Poor harvests, loss of men to the Turkish conscription (ages seventeen to fifty-five), and the lack of imports due to the blockade all contributed to the mounting loss of life. Maronite archbishop Joseph Darien persuaded the French consul in Egypt to request an invasion by Franco-British forces to end the famine in May 1916.[83] Foreign Minister Aristide Briand, however, replied that an invasion would result in a Turkish massacre of the Maronites. Evidence already existed of large-scale Turkish atrocities on the Armenian population in Asia Minor and northern Mesopotamia, and of brutal treatment of Armenians in Damascus.[84] A subsequent request to end the blockade was rebuffed, on the grounds that the anti-Turkish Arab revolt would widen if famine conditions worsened. Although there is evidence that low-level French officials wished to intervene, the French government acquiesced to the policy of its ally, Britain.[85]

The British Balfour Declaration, which stated British support for "the establishment in Palestine of a national homeland for the Jewish people" (November 2, 1917), further complicated the future of the Arab territories that were being conquered from the Turks. The declaration was issued by the British foreign secretary to Lord Rothschild, a leading British Jew, before the Sykes-Picot agreement was made public by the Bolsheviks.[86] The Zionist movement was founded by Theodor Herzel, a Viennese Jewish journalist who became convinced of the necessity of a Jewish state while covering the trial of Alfred Dreyfus in France. The First Zionist World Congress in 1894 preferred to use the term "home" rather than "state," allegedly so that the Arab inhabitants would not perceive Jewish migration as a threat to their rights. Herzel approached Ottoman sultan Abdul Hamid and tried to broker a deal wherein a Jewish financial syndicate would assume the foreign Ottoman debt, in return for allowing Jewish settlement in Palestine.[87] Although the sultan refused the offer, he did allow some Jewish settlement in Palestine.[88] On Herzel's death, the leadership of the movement fell to a naturalized British subject, Chaim Weizmann. Weizmann's efforts at getting British support for the Zionist cause led to the Balfour Declaration in 1917.

AFRICAN *TIRAILLEURS* ON THE WESTERN FRONT

When war broke out in 1914, most of the Foreign Legion left Algeria for battlefields in France—except the German and Austrian troops who remained behind to pacify Morocco—and the legion lost 4,116 officers and men on the Western Front. France entered the war with forty-seven divisions, composed of about 777,000 French troops and 46,000 colonial troops. Many of the colonial troops were Muslims from West Africa, who served in the *Tirailleurs Senegalais*. This was a unit established in 1857 by the governor-general of West Africa, Louis Faidherbe.[89] Personnel were obtained originally by the *rachet* system (from the French *acheter*, "to buy"), whereby African slaves held by fellow Africans were purchased by the French government and trained to be soldiers in the service of France. Later, the French had a great deal of success in recruitment, as many Africans saw military service as a way of personal advancement in the French Empire. The principal tribal groups who entered *Tirailleur* service included the Bambara, Tukulor, and Mande. They garrisoned forts throughout West Africa as far north as Morocco. Many important French military leaders in World War I, including Marshal Joseph Joffre himself, had served as officers in the *Tirailleurs*. One of the main advocates of *Tirailleur* force was General Charles Mangin, who wrote an influential book titled *La Force Noire* (1910), which argued that black Africans were ideally suited for war.[90] Although his theories were based on racist pseudo-science, he had a wide audience, and recruitment of the West Africans intensified during the war.

Many *Tirailleur* regiments were sent to the Western Front in the opening weeks of the war, while some continued to garrison posts throughout the French Empire. The force of almost 30,000 *Tirailleurs* was augmented through the war years—over 30,000 more were added in 1915; 51,000 in 1916; and 60,000 in 1917. The government offered various inducements for service, including a 200-franc sign-on bonus in 1915, and an array of offers in 1918 including tax exemptions and guaranteed veterans' employment upon return from service. While many French colonial administrators in West Africa feared that increased governmental calls for recruits might lead to civil unrest in the empire, the Senegalese deputy in the French National Assembly, Blaise Daigne, was able to raise more than the number of troops that the government had hoped for, in his position as commissioner general for recruitment. Some units of *Tirailleurs* guarded prisoners and did the kind of conventional support work expected of colonial troops. But a significant number of them saw combat in campaigns including those at the User and Somme rivers, at St.-Mihiel, and in the war's final Meuse-Argonne offensive.

The Germans accused them of atrocities, and British and American officers tended to regard them as less than professional, but the French felt the exigencies of the war necessitated their presence. In all, some 212,000 Africans were recruited, with 163,000 seeing service on the Western Front. Thirty thousand of them died in the service of France during the war, out of a total number of 1.3 million French casualties sustained throughout the conflict. Many of the French African troops experienced significant social and economic advancement in their home territory as a result of their experiences in the war in France, and the colonial government utilized them as part of a loyal colonial infrastructure—providing them with jobs and opening veterans clubs for them.

THE QUESTION OF ALGERIAN SOLDIERS

Some French officers thought about the possibility of raising native Maghribi Muslim forces in large numbers to serve France. Colonel Paul-Louis Azan's experiences in colonial service in North Africa led him to believe that a policy of assimilation in Algeria would do harm to Muslims individually and to Maghribi society and culture in general. He advocated the creation of two separate societies in a 1903 book called *Recherche d'une Solution de la question indigène en Algérie*. He argued also for the raising of large numbers of Algerian troops in World War I, and as James J. Cooke has shown, the idea met huge opposition from the *colons* and their backers in the Assembly.[91]

Algerian soldiers were recruited and did serve honorably on the Western Front, but in lesser numbers than Azan had hoped for. The subsequent effort to grant the Maghrib Muslim veterans citizenship in a way that would not alter their standing in Qur'anic law (in the so-called Jonnart Laws of 1919) was also stifled by the *colons*. *Colon* deputy Eugene Étienne of Oran was one of the principal opponents of Azan's ideas. Azan continued to push his idea through the 1920s, and wrote in a book called *L'Armée indigène nord-Africaine* that Maghribis were naturally superior fighters, and that such a native force politically loyal to France would be able to block the Muslims from a possible future of assimilation efforts that might harm Maghribi society and cause problems in the empire.[92] Marshal Lyautey backed him, but in the end, Azan's ideas were suppressed, and met the fate of other reforms proposed to help the Muslim *indigènes*.[93] *Colon* political power effectively eliminated any possibility of substantial change in French North Africa.

THE END OF THE GREAT WAR IN THE MIDDLE EAST

British and Arab military victories over Turkish forces mounted until on October 30, 1918, the Turkish Army surrendered and signed the Mudros Armistice.[94] French prime minister Clemenceau pushed for a French representative to be present on the island of Mudros, but the British prime minister David Lloyd George rejected the idea. British admiral Calthorpe formally accepted the Turkish surrender.[95] The Central Powers collapsed entirely that fall in Europe in the face of the Allied Meuse-Argonne Offensive. Revolution overtook Germany, Austria, and Turkey, and the centuries-old Hohenzollern, Hapsburg, and Ottoman Empires disintegrated. The French Third Republic survived a supreme test, but the extremely high casualty rate on the Western Front in Europe—62 percent of French effectives—cost the government and the army the confidence of many survivors.

No final determinations were made about the Turkish Arab territories in the Paris Peace Conference at the conclusion of World War I, or in the final Treaty of Versailles, signed in June 1919. Faysal went to Paris in 1919 to try to reach an accord with France about the status of Syria, but the French government was not interested in negotiating with him about its "historic claims." Faysal also attended the Paris Peace Conference and urged the union of Syria and Mesopotamia with the Hijaz, but to no avail.[96] On September 19, 1918, the French and British Foreign Ministries met in London to decide on policies for the Occupied Enemy Territories Administrations (OETA) in Syria-Palestine.[97] Three administrative areas were agreed to—each intended to be influenced by one of the three Allied forces in Syria—Britain, France, and the Arabs. OETA South, including the cities of Acre, Nablus, and Jerusalem, constituted the British area. Britain also administered Iraq, Kuwait, Bahrain, and Qatar. France had OETA North, consisting of the coastal strip from Alexandretta to halfway between Beirut and Tyre. Colonel de Piepappe of the *Détachement français* was installed as OETA North administrator.[98] A former Turkish Army officer of Syrian Arab extraction (and a supporter of Faysal), 'Ali Ridha al-Rikabi, was made administrator of OETA East. He had British and French liaison officers at his side.[99]

Arab forces entered Damascus on October 1, 1918, and Colonel Lawrence made Rikabi governor on behalf of Faysal. British forces entered the next day, with a small French detachment led by Captain Pisani. Descendants of the famed Algerian leader 'Abd al-Qadir (the *Jaza'iri* faction) led a revolt against both the Westerners and Faysal on October 1 and 2, but were crushed.[100] They had incorrectly assumed their lineage would connote leadership in the new situation. After the departure of the Turkish governor from Beirut, a small Arab force under Shukri Pasha al-Ayyubi entered that city in the name of Faysal, and appointed Habib Pasha Sa'd as "Governor of the Lebanon." This pleased neither the Maronites nor the French. The British Twenty-first Corps entered Beirut on October 8, together with most of the *Détachement français*, as well as fresh French troops debarked from ships that entered the harbor.[101] Allenby soon ordered the removal of Faysal's troops and flag from Beirut and established French officers there, as well as in Tyre and Sidon. The British established Colonel de Piepappe as military governor of Beirut. None of these latter developments pleased the Arabs.

In a January 8, 1918, address to Congress, American president Woodrow Wilson outlined what he regarded as the legitimate aims of the Allied peace that would follow the conclusion of the war. His Fourteen Points referred to specific areas of international tension, and stressed the need for national self-determination. Point XII addressed the Ottoman Empire and specified that "other nationalities which are now under Turkish rule should be assured an undoubted security of life and an absolutely unmolested opportunity of autonomous development."[102] The British Foreign Office issued a statement through its embassy in Washington, D.C., on November 8, 1918, intended to clarify the purposes of Britain and France in the Middle East for an American audience familiar with the spirit of the Fourteen Points. Stressing the culpability of "Germany's ambitions" at the start of the war in the Middle East, and of the Turkish role in "discords" between native populations, the Foreign Office claimed that

the aim of France and Britain...is the complete and final liberation of the peoples so long oppressed by the Turks and the establishment of governments and administrations that shall derive their authority from the free exercise of the initiative and choice of the indigenous populations....Far from wishing to impose this or that system upon the populations of those regions, France and Great Britain have no other concern than to ensure by their support and their active assistance the normal working of the governments and institutions which the populations shall have freely adopted.[103]

French foreign minister Stephen Pichon spoke in a somewhat different tone about France's interests in the Ottoman Empire before the Chamber of Deputies that December 29: "We have in their empire incontestable rights to safeguard; we have them in Syria, the Lebanon, in Cilicia, and Palestine."[104] Clemenceau told American president Wilson that if France did not take possession of Syria, it was tantamount to a "national humiliation, as the desertion of a soldier from the battlefield."

Clemenceau visited Lloyd George in London in December 1918 and made a deal with the British because the French occupation forces were having trouble policing Syria, and Britain had an abundant supply of troops at hand in the Middle East. Clemenceau conceded French backing of British control of Mosul and Palestine, and Britain eventually agreed to granting France a 25 percent share of Mesopotamian oil (in the April 1919 Long-Berenger Agreement).[105] France also received British backing of France's territorial claims against Germany within Europe, including French control of Alsace-Lorraine and the Saar, as well as the occupation of the Rhineland by French troops. President Wilson insisted on sending an international commission led by Oberlin College president Charles R. Crane to the Arab-Turkish areas to investigate the wishes of the Arab populace.[106] Clemenceau and Lloyd George were not pleased with the prospect of Americans or others facilitating local criticism of French and British policies in the region, and both France and Britain refused to send representatives. The commission arrived at Jaffa in June 1919, and visited Palestine, Syria, and Lebanon, and interviewed representatives of the region's various communities. The commission's report was issued on August 28, 1919, and in its conclusion recommended the creation of a constitutional monarchy in Syria (under an American mandate), and a separate British mandate in Iraq.[107] The report included ample evidence of the Maronites' desire for a French presence in Lebanon:

From Tyre to Tripoli they mostly followed a rigid formula which calls for a Greater Lebanon, absolutely independent of the rest of Syria, and under France; the supporters of this view showed no response to the idea of Syrian national unity, and apparently wish to become French citizens at an early moment. Others desire the unity of Syria under the French Mandate, preferring ordinarily that the Lebanon district should be enlarged and given a high degree of autonomy. In the Lebanon proper the majority is probably sincerely for a French, as opposed to a British mandate. . . . The French policy of "colonization" shows its fruits in many inhabitants of this area, as well as of Beirut and other parts of Syria, who feel that they know French better than Arabic, and who are apt to hold themselves as of a distinctly higher order of civilization than the people of the interior.[108]

The report also indicated that most of the Muslims throughout the region were opposed to the creation of both French and British mandates.

The Allied governments eventually agreed at the Paris Peace Conference to the creation of mandates—temporary custodianships—over the Arab lands. Article 22 of the Treaty of Versailles (1919) states that "peoples not yet able to stand by themselves under the strenuous conditions of the modern world" needed "tutelage" in government on behalf of the League of Nations. The treaty states specifically that

certain communities formerly belonging to the Turkish Empire have reached a stage of development where their existence as independent nations can be provisionally recognised subject to the rendering of administrative advice and assistance by a Mandatory until such time as they are able to stand alone. The wishes of the these communities must be a principal consideration in the selection of the Mandatory.[109]

This is contained in the first section of the treaty, which outlines the Covenant of the League of Nations. France received as mandates Lebanon and Syria, while Britain got Palestine, Transjordan, Iraq, and Kuwait. Most Arabs were not pleased with the establishment of the mandates, and the Turks were appalled at the huge loss of territory. Turkey, however, was soon to face the nationalist revolt of a one-time officer stationed in the

Arab Middle Eastern theater of war, Mustafa Kemal (Ataturk), and a formal treaty with the Allies would not be signed until 1923.

Syrian Arab leaders met in a congress in March 1920, and proclaimed that Amir Faysal was now king of Syria.[110] The French high commissioner for Syria, General Henri Gourand, demanded that Faysal accept the French mandate, as well as the French occupation of Aleppo, the introduction of French paper currency throughout the country, the reduction of the Syrian Army, and the punishment of those Arabs who had publicly protested the French presence. Realizing that his Arab army was poorly equipped to do battle with a Western army, Faysal accepted the French ultimatum, but war soon broke out anyway. The French sent in colonial forces composed of other Muslims from the empire—Algerians, Moroccans, and Senegalese—and easily defeated Faysal's army in the Battle of Maysalun on July 24, 1920.[111] The French Army entered Damascus, and Faysal fled (ironically) to British territory.[112] General Gourand divided the region up into five areas: Greater Lebanon (which was largely Maronite and pro-French, although it had no history of being a territorial subdivision in the past); the 'Alawite Muslim seacoast north of Tripoli (Latakia); Aleppo; Damascus; and Druze lands to the south of Damascus (Jabal Druze). The League of Nations officially sanctioned the French mandate in July 1922—after the French had defeated Faysal.

The French military administrators in the mandate clearly favored the Maronites, and the heavy-handed nature of the French administration with regard to the Muslims and the Druze led to a major revolt, which lasted from 1925 to 1928. The revolt began in the Druze areas over reforms introduced by the French commander, Captain Carbillet, which were opposed by the Druze, and the subsequent arrest of most Druze leaders at a banquet to which High Commissioner General Maurice Sarrail had lured them.[113] The revolt spread to all the cities of the mandate, and the new high commissioner, General Maurice Gamelin, needed tanks and airplanes to crush it. Syria would remain an unruly section of the empire until its independence in 1946.

CONCLUSION

France's interest in the Arab lands of the eastern Mediterranean dates back to the age of the crusades, when mainly French knights heeded the call for the First Crusade. Successive French regimes displayed an interest in the economic and strategic value of the region through the Bourbon-Ottoman *entente* and Napoleon's Egyptian-Syrian campaign. As the Turkish Empire began to decline in the nineteenth century, French policy was geared toward securing France's share of any possible imperial spoils in this region of historical importance. French commercial development in Syria and Lebanon followed the allied victory in the Crimean War (on behalf of Turkey and against Russian claims in the region). The evolution of French policy in the eastern Mediterranean, however, was determined by a different set of conditions than those that characterized France's rapid absorption of territory in North Africa and the Sahara in the nineteenth century. But while France lacked an excuse of Barbary piracy as a *casus belli* to intervene in Syria and Lebanon, as it had in Algeria, the plight of the Francophile Maronites served as the moral cause that could mask French economic drives in the region as the Turkish Empire progressed toward collapse. The sultan of Morocco visited Syria before World War I and made the public comment that French occupation of the country was inevitable. Even Britain acquiesced to France in the area, as witnessed in McMahon's statement to *Sharif* Hussein of Mecca in 1915, despite the fact that is was mainly British and Arab arms that had cleared Syria and Lebanon of Turkish forces. Britain needed the backing of France to justify British claims in the Middle East, so Britain supported France's claim to territory in the region.

Given the preconditions for French involvement in the area, no European power contested France's mandate. The establishment of the mandate, however, was executed in such a manner that the Arab leaders who had helped the Allied cause in World War I subsequently felt betrayed by France and the other Western superpowers. The setting up of the mandates and the Treaty of Lausanne with Turkey (1923), which documented the formal secession of the Arab Middle East from Turkish control, will be treated in the next chapter. Despite the history of prior French involvement in Syria and Lebanon, successive French governmental leaders needed to justify their control of the area to a degree that they did not have to in the other areas of the Islamic world then under French control. The Muslims of Algeria and in many regions of the Sahara had been under French occupation for several decades prior to World War I, and the French government had no need to provide any further explanation to the Muslim *indigènes* or the wider world of the French presence there. The *indigènes* of Algeria understood that their aspirations were submerged under the interests of the European colonists, just as the Muslim pan-Arabists of Syria understood the consequences of the favor that the authorities bestowed on the pro-French Maronite Catholics. A centennial history of French Algeria produced in 1930 by Augustan Bernard sums up the basic attitudes of many French administrators toward all of their colonies within the Islamic world:

Now we did not go to Algeria merely to bring order into the native administration or to equip the country and then see it break away, retaining perhaps some gratitude towards us. No, our ultimate aim was always, as it still is, to found an overseas France where our language and our civilization would live again through ever-closer cooperation of the natives with France—in other words, by their being made Frenchmen.[114]

Charles Martel and the Battle of Tours (732).

St. Louis arriving in Egypt (1249).

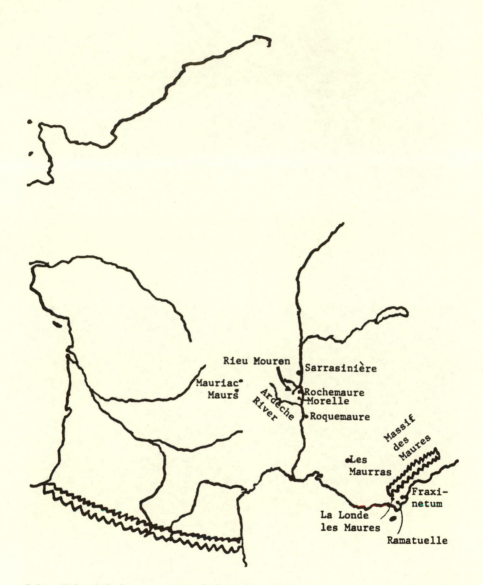

Select "Islamic" place names in southern Francia.

Napoleon in Egypt (1798).

Capture of 'Abd al-Qadir (1847).

ASIA

Morocco   Algeria

Tripoli

EGYPT

Rio de
Oro

French West A.

Anglo-
Egyptian
Sudan

Eritrea

Brit.
Somaliland

L. Chad

Senegal

Gambia

Niger

Nigeria

Abyssinia

Ital.
Somalild.

Portu.
Guinea

Sierra
Leone

Liberia

Gold Coast

Togo

Cameroons

Spanish
Guinea

French

Congo

Equat. A.

Uganda

Brit. East A.

Belgian
Congo

German
East A.

Zanzibar (Brit.)

Congo

AFRICA
1914

British .....
French ......
German ....
Portuguese ..
Belgian .....
Spanish ....
Italian ....

Portuguese
West A.

Rhodesia

Portug.
East A.

Zambesi

Mada-
gascar

German
S.-West A.

Walfish Bay (Brit.)

Bechuana

Limpopo

Orange R.

Union of S.A.

J.F.H.

The Marchand Expedition (1898).

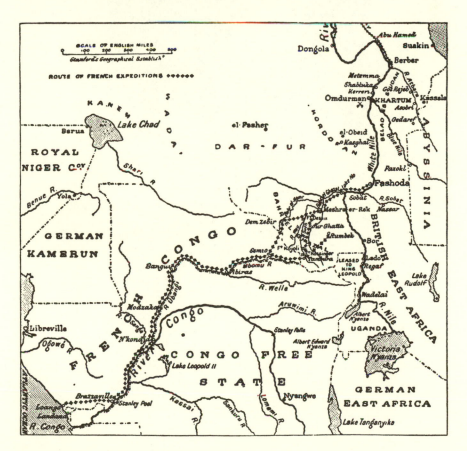

Map of the Marchand Expedition (1898).

Prince Faysal. He led the Arab Army of the North
with British Colonel T. E. Lawrence against the
Turks in World War I, and attended the Paris
Peace Conference at the end of the war. His supporters in Syria proclaimed him King of Syria in
1918, until they were defeated by French colonial
forces (ironically composed of Muslims from
elsewhere—Algeria, Morocco, and Senegal) in the
Battle of Maysalun on July 24, 1920. Faysal subsequently became King of Iraq. (Reproduced from
the Collections of the Library of Congress)

General Charles de Gaulle. Leading Free French troops to victory alongside Anglo-American forces in World War II, de Gaulle subsequently became the head of the Provisional Government and of the Fourth Republic, 1944–1946. After leaving politics, he was swept back into power by the army and the *colon* revolutionaries in Algeria in 1958, and ruled again until 1969. Brought back by many who believed he would save the last large portion of the French Empire—Algeria—he decided that it was in the best interests of France to jettison the colony. His decision to make peace with the FLN and grant Algerian independence on terms favorable to the FLN led to another revolt of some of the top colonial generals and *colons,* which almost toppled the Fifth Republic. In the end, the Evian Accords led to the exodus of about a million European colonists from Algeria back to France. (Reproduced from the Collections of the Library of Congress)

Ahmed Ben Bella (leader of the FLN Algerian independence movement and the first president of independent Algeria) meeting with U.S. President John Kennedy in Washington. Kennedy's criticism of French policies in Algeria and the general U.S. support for the Algerian revolution helped the FLN considerably. Ironically, as the FLN moved toward the socialist camp, Ben Bella flew to Cuba and agreed with Fidel Castro in his opposition to "American imperialism." (Reproduced from the Collections of the Library of Congress)

French Colonization
in the Islamic World
through the Interwar Years

THE NEW EMPIRE

The empire of France consisted of over 80 million people residing in northern, western, and central Africa, Madagascar, the Arab Middle East, Indochina, New Caledonia, Guyana, and a few other outlying parts of the French *imperium*. Collectively, the French Empire constituted about 40 percent of all the colonial areas and all the colonial populations held in the world.[1] The empire was France's main trading partner in the interwar years, and Edward Peter Fitzgerald has shown that in the 1930s, France's colonial regime accounted for between 20 percent and almost 30 percent of French exports, and between 12 percent and 28 percent of French imports.[2] The artificially high prices paid for goods by both the mother country and the colonies, according to Fitzgerald, "eroded aggregate consumer demand," by generating "internationally uncompetitive prices."[3] Few domestic observers at the time in France, however, doubted that the empire was in fact completely beneficial to the mother country.

On the hundredth anniversary of the conquest of Algeria, France put on a huge colonial exhibition, chaired by the old colonial hero General Lyautey (then seventy-seven years old).[4] Opening on May 6, 1931, the exhibition attempted to demonstrate to the French home population, and the wider world, the various economic and cultural possibilities that existed within the empire. Native troops, colonial civilians wearing colorful costumes, authentic wildlife, and samples of colonial art and architecture were all put on display. The exhibition showed the empire to France, while out in the empire, France was transplanting elements of France into the native societies that constituted the empire's population.[5] As colonization proceeded in Islamic areas of the empire, colonial administrators oversaw the creation of modern European quarters side by side with traditional Arab cities, which Gwendolyn Wright has argued was intended "to make colonialism more popular among Europeans and more tolerable to the colonized peoples."[6]

The economic aspects of modernization primarily benefited the mother country and the colonial elites more than the natives. Discriminatory work codes were conceived in the 1920s and 1930s, and France introduced paid conscription into those parts of the empire that the colonial establishment wanted to improve. The Maghrib and areas of tropical western and central Africa saw a substantial part of these projects, including the Abidjan-Ferkessedegou rail line. Such projects incurred many human casualties in the name of progress (up to 10 percent of native workers lost was not uncommon). There was an uneven modernization taking place in the empire, however, as some areas received more official interest and more large-scale investment from French business interests.

By the time the French colonial administration took over in Syria and Lebanon, the French presence in North Africa was already ninety years old. A distinct minority settler colony had been created in French North Africa, comparable to the crusader states of a thousand years before (or, more recently, to the Scots in Ulster or the Boers in South Africa). Both Syria-Lebanon and North Africa shared a common historical lineage of French interest stretching back to the age of the crusades, and by 1925, a good many Frenchmen (and Maronites, and possibly many *colons*, as well) believed that the empire finally had been created that had been a thousand years in coming. Indeed, many of the French, Italian, Maltese, and Spanish *colons* in Algeria emphasized that their common colonial world was comparable to that of the Romans at Hippo Regius.[7]

The actual colonial situation in Syria-Lebanon, however, was vastly different from the situation in French North Africa. The establishment of the French title to the eastern Mediterranean area was complicated by post–World War I "great power" diplomacy, and the technically temporary nature of the mandate precluded the kind of intensive colonial recruitment that brought tens of thousands of *colons* each decade into Algeria, as well as many to Tunisia and Morocco. In Syria-Lebanon, the Catholic Arab Maronites served a similar function of promoting Western culture in an alien Islamic environment as did the *colons* of Algeria.[8]

The French title to Syria-Lebanon derived directly from the San Remo Conference of April 1920, when the "great powers" decided that France would have the mandate for the region. This was based on the precedent of the Sykes-Picot Agreement. The other Western powers felt a great sympathy for France, due to the fact that much of the war's destruction had been experienced by French forces and French material resources, and this accounts for the hard line taken by the Allies against Germany at the Versailles Peace Conference. The Treaty of Sèvres (August 10, 1920), signed by Sultan Muhammad VI at Constantinople, eliminated the Ottoman Turkish Empire, and removed many non-Turkish areas from Turkish control—the Arab areas, already slated to go under mandate (Syria-Lebanon, Mesopotamia-Kuwait, and Palestine), as well as most of European Turkey, Armenia, the Hijaz, and Kurdistan.[9] The Straits Zone was to be under international administration; Eastern Thrace and the Aegean Islands were ceded to Greece (due to their mainly Greek populations); and Smyrna (Izmir) was placed under temporary Greek administration until a plebiscite determined permanent sovereignty. Italy got Rhodes and the Dodecanese Islands. The Turkish economy was dominated by the "great powers," so as to help finance the various transitions.

According to the Treaty of Sèvres, the self-proclaimed "great powers"— "the British Empire, France [interestingly, not the French Empire], Italy, and Japan"—provisionally recognized Syria and Mesopotamia "as independent States subject to the rendering of administrative advice and assistance by a Mandatory until such time as they are able to stand alone." This "rendering of administrative advice and assistance" was the legal basis for the French colonial presence in Syria-Lebanon. It seems hard to imagine that a French parallel society ever could have been created there to mirror the settler colonial society of Algeria. Mustafa Kemal ("Ataturk") had commenced his nationalist revolt against the sultan, however, and from his new capital at Ankara in the Anatolian interior rejected the Sèvres Treaty a week after the treaty was signed.[10]

Ataturk defeated a Greek invasion force, overthrew the Ottoman sultan, and negotiated a separate peace treaty with the Soviet Union. The Sèvres Treaty was renegotiated in 1922–1923 by the Allies, Ataturk, and the Soviet Union at Lausanne, Switzerland. The resulting Treaty of Lausanne provided for Turkish control over a few areas ceded at Sèvres, including the Straits Zone (but it had to remain demilitarized nevertheless), Eastern Thrace, Smryna (Izmir), some Aegean islands, and a strip along the Syrian border.[11] The mandate areas stood as in the Sèvres Treaty, although the Turks desired a great slice of northern Syria. In 1939, France finally ceded to Turkey the northern Syrian province of Antioch-Alexandretta, which was inhabited almost entirely by Arabs and had only a minuscule Turkish minority.[12] This was done to appease a potential ally in a climate of increasing hostility within Europe that was caused by the rise of the Third Reich in Germany. Many Syrians were angered at the loss of Arab people and ancient Arab cities to the Turks. They felt even more betrayed by the French Mandate, which many believed should have withdrawn long before. The area henceforth became the Turkish province of Hatay.[13]

French policy in Syria-Lebanon was based on maintaining and strengthening the French presence in the area, rather than on rendering "administrative advice and assistance" to the Arab Muslims. The French negotiators at Versailles had placed an emphasis on the need of France to provide relief efforts to the civilian population in the region. It can be argued, however, that French favoritism of the Maronites resulted in such aid being disproportionately disseminated to the pro-French Catholic areas in Lebanon. The Maronites had desired French intervention before, during, and after World War I on their behalf against the Muslims. But there would even be Maronites who tired of the French presence within two decades of the mandate's establishment.

General Henri Gourand was instrumental in maintaining and strengthening the French presence in Syria-Lebanon.[14] He removed Faysal and his supporters from the equation, with a force of almost 13,000 colonial troops in the Army of the Levant. Gourand had been a colonial administrator in Morocco, and served on the front in World War I (where he lost an arm). He now oversaw the establishment of a French colonial infrastructure throughout Syria-Lebanon. The Army of the Levant was composed of French officers and troops from North Africa, Senegal, and Madagascar. The force was expanded in 1921 to almost 70,000 men because of the Arab revolt in northern Syria (which was supported by Ataturk and Prince Abdullah of Transjordan). There were also about 3,500 French police (Sûreté Génerale) dispersed throughout the mandate.[15] Gourand relied heavily on native leaders to serve as intermediaries between the common people and the mandatory regime. He made personal alliances with religious leaders from both the Christian and Muslim communities (but especially the Maronites), with many Arab tribal shaykhs, and various rural landowners. He rewarded certain loyal Arab leaders by spending money on public works projects that modernized the area where their authority prevailed.[16]

Gourand's High Commission, headquartered in Beirut at the Grand Serail, was led by both military and civilian personnel, and contained departments of finance, justice, public health, customs, public works, agriculture, posts and telegraphs, and education.[17] The public works efforts of Gourand's regime, however, were hampered by a lack of adequate funds. Relief efforts were made to alleviate the civilian population from periodic epidemics and starvation scares. This was layered on top of the existing private French social services network, which had been established in the 1800s. The French administration worked with French Catholic clerics to lay the foundation for the mandatory relief effort, including that of the Jesuit and naval officer Father de Martinprey, who set up soup kitchens throughout northern Lebanon, and Father Remy, a Capuchin and sergeant in the French intelligence service, who established shelters for Arab orphans.[18] The Red Cross soon established itself in the mandates, along with the "Drop of Milk" society, which offered sterilized milk and other assistance to poor Arabs. Fifteen thousand tons of food were distributed by the mandate government in 1919–1920 alone, and the government even borrowed camels from the British to carry relief supplies to remote settlements. In addition to helping the Arabs, the French provided assistance to tens of thousands of Armenian and Greek Christian refugees who followed French forces into Syria upon their withdrawal from southern Anatolia.

In addition to the money expended in relief operations, the cost of the colonial administration was also borne by the French treasury. Between 400 and 600 civilian bureaucrats worked in the mandates, along with tens of thousands of colonial officers and troops. Some 13,000 Arab bureaucrats were dispersed throughout the mandates to serve the function of intermediaries between the regime and the population. They held the mandates' infrastructure together along critical lines of communication and transportation. The Muslims complained that Lebanese Christians got more than their share of the civil service jobs, which fact derived from both overt favoritism and disproportionate French language training of the Maronites compared to the Muslims. There were so many opportunities for Maronites in the mandate that a demographic shift occurred, in which numerous Maronites moved from Mount Lebanon into Beirut from the 1920s through the 1940s. More money was spent on education by the mandatory regime within Lebanon than in Syria, and there were more private schools in Lebanon than in Syria. In general, Gourand's administration (1919–1922) was especially susceptible to pro-Maronite policies.

A Representative Council was established for Lebanon alone in 1922.[19] The council's thirty members were elected by their religious constituents, who voted along the lines determined by a census in 1921. Lebanon also received a constitution. Many Muslims, however, felt disenfranchised by the pro-Maronite policies of Gourand. There was an attempt on the general's life in May 1921, and the pro-French director of the interior, As'ad Bey Khurshid, was assassinated in April 1922, during the visit of the Crane Commission.[20] The Muslims disliked the administrative subdivision of Lebanon by France, which kept various sects separate (and thereby, the French asserted, kept the peace).

Within the mandates, General Gourand relied on the advice of prominent pro-imperialist Robert de Caix (publisher of a journal titled *L'Asie française*).[21] De Caix pushed for French-only firms to take over the operation of a number of businesses in the region. He helped form a lobbying group of French business and educational interests called "The Economic Union of Syria" to push for the privatization of many public sector industries within the mandate.[22] These activities would benefit French firms, especially those from the city of Lyon, where businessmen were particularly interested in investing in Syrian-Lebanese ventures. Gourand pushed vigorously for the French government to send him more funds, but postwar domestic exigencies and political opposition prevented the kind of colonial assistance that de Caix and the general desired. Gourand resigned as high commissioner in August 1922 because he did not get the governmental support he believed he needed to promote his vision of a Syrian-Lebanese colony. His replacement, General Maxime Weygand (1923–1924), was somewhat more republican in sympathy and bluntly told the Lyon Chamber of Commerce that "I cannot call Syria a colony."[23]

THE NEW ALGERIA

There was no French settlement in the Syrian-Lebanese Mandates, unlike in North Africa where, by World War I, more resident *colons* were born in Algeria than had immigrated from Europe, and where 60 percent of the settlers lived in urban settings. The city of Algiers was then 80 percent European, while Casablanca was about 30 percent European. By World War I there had been created in Algeria a distinct colonial Catholic settler society located within the Islamic world.[24] This was not the case in the rest of French North Africa or in French West Africa, where French Foreign Legion and *Tirailleur* garrisons served as adequate guarantors of French authority in a frontier environment. In the coastal area inhabited by the European *colons*, the settlers outnumbered the Muslim *indigènes* by two to one. At the start of the twentieth century, the French, Italian, Maltese, and Spanish colonists in Algeria were in the midst of a "melting pot" experience that fused the primarily southern European Catholics into a new people self-consciously "Algerian."[25]

While many French business ventures predated the mandate in Syria, the official position of the mandatory government (after Gourand) was that Syria and Lebanon were not colonies on a par with Algeria, where French economic projects had proceeded apace since the 1840s. French economic development, collectively called *mise en valeur*, began in Algeria before the Muslims were entirely subdued.[26] Much of the early French development derived from the pioneering work of a mining engineer named Henri Fournel.[27] Fournel undertook a series of geological explorations within the new colony in the 1840s, in the company of an armed escort. He was able to acquire information on the location of various mineral deposits from the local Arabs, because he himself was fluent in Arabic (he was also a dilettante ethnologist and historian). Fournel scoured the countryside for any geological evidence and untapped veins or preexisting mines.[28] His maps charted the location of strains of iron ore that would shortly be exploited by French entrepreneurs.

The creation of colonial industries and agriculture in Algeria, however, was hampered by a shortage of European labor. This was due to both frontier insecurity and a high rate of death due to epidemic diseases including typhus, cholera, and malaria in the first decade of French rule in Algeria. Malaria was largely eradicated by the use of quinine, which in Algeria was pioneered by Dr. François Maillot.[29] But there were enough similarities with the economy of the northern shores of the Mediterranean that a steady stream of *colons* arrived. The wine grape industry, for example, attracted many European agriculturalists, as did the olive groves and citrus fruit farms. By World War I, about one-half of the land Europeans held in Algeria was used for vineyards.

The Bône area was the center of the colonial iron ore industry. Three-fourths of all Algerian iron ore was harvested in mines located near that city, which were built in the 1840s through the 1860s. The mine that overshadowed the rest was Mokta el-Hadid, owned by the Talabot family.[30] It outproduced all the others, and served as an instrumental precondition for the development of the port of Bône and regional rail lines. Constantine province, where Bône was located, was also where three-fourths of all forest concessions were granted in Algeria. The French harvested vast quantities of cork oaks for use in making bottle corks.[31] General Randon's road from Bône to the Edough forest in 1842 brought security to the frontier and prosperity to French cork oak entrepreneurs.

The French military and civilian administrators of Algeria played a dominant role in the colony's economic evolution. Governor-General Bertrand Clauzel (1835–1836) previously had helped to create a firm soon after the conquest to acquire and exploit Algerian land for various agricultural schemes. He continued to undertake investments while governor-general, and this set a precedent for future colonial politicians to enrich themselves by virtue of their position.

General Monck d'Uzer, the military commander of Bône, acquired a great deal of land for himself within the city, and as a consequence of his powerful connections, got the city of Bône exempted from an 1832 French law barring land transactions between the settlers and the Muslim *indigènes*.[32] His corruption, however, was legendary, and he was relieved of command. He soon returned to Algeria as a private citizen and managed to convince the colonial authorities to build a new village outside of Bône called Duzerville, where he owned most of the land and continued to enrich himself.[33] General Randon, who commanded the Bône area from 1841 to 1847 (and was governor-general in the 1850s) contributed to the development of the Bône-area colonial infrastructure as well by building a new town called Colonne Randon. Another interesting case is Jerome Bertagna, who started a company that profited from the French conquest of Tunisia (1881), serving as the official supplier for the French Army there. He acquired a great deal of land and was elected mayor of Bône in 1888.[34]

Land was crucial to economic power in Algeria. Several important landholding entrepreneurs helped shape the colonial economy of Algeria. Charles de Lesseps (brother of the builder of the Suez Canal) got 7,000 acres of forest land, and François-Marc Lavie (a flour mill magnate) got land in Constantine, Bône, and Heliopolis.[35] Although the *colons* held only

30 percent of the agricultural land in Algeria, the modern methods of irrigation they introduced made that land far more fruitful than the 70 percent of the land in the hands of the Muslim *indigènes*. The Muslims tended to grow grains, figs, and dates, in contrast to the wine grapes and citrus fruits grown by the European *colons* for export.

The Marquis de Bassano built a blast furnace in Algeria in 1846 in the Bône region to process iron ore within the colony rather than ship it overseas.[36] Bassano's endeavor failed, but the venture indicated the extent of French colonial economic interest in Algeria. By contrast, only British colonies like Canada and Australia, filled with European colonists, saw similar developments in colonial economy. No colonial entrepreneurs were more important than the Talabot family.[37] The Talabots held an economic empire stretching across the Mediterranean from Europe to Algeria with companies in banking, shipping, construction, and railroad lines. The Talabots also owned the massive Mokta el-Hadid iron mine and had an important role in the development of the port of Bône and local rail lines.[38] Family patriarch Paulin was instrumental in forming the *Société Generale Algérienne* (SGA) in 1865.[39] This organization promoted various economic initiatives in the colony and founded five villages there to spur colonization. The SGA was granted 100,000 hectares of land in Algeria for development (at minimal cost) in return for a 100 million-franc loan to Emperor Napoleon III, which the emperor spent on public works within Algeria.[40] Napoleon III visited Algeria twice in the 1860s, and the press made much of his 1865 visit to the Mokta el-Hadid mine. The SGA suffered from changing fortunes in Constantine province and a large loan made to *Khedive* Ismail of Egypt, who was removed by Britain before the loan was paid off. It reformed as the *Compagnie Algérienne* in 1877 and continued to grow.[41]

The colony of Algeria held a comparatively greater importance to French policymakers than neighboring protectorates such as Tunisia or Morocco. A controversy emerged at the turn of the twentieth century over the construction of a regional Maghribi rail line when some proponents called for Bône to be the hub, while others promoted Bizerte in Tunisia.[42] The controversy was resolved just before World War I when Prime Minister Clemenceau threw his political weight behind Bône, a truly colonial settlement, rather than the protectorate Bizerte (Clemenceau's brother worked for a firm in Bône).[43] A useful analogy to the French colonial economic experience in Algeria is the case of the American exploitation along the Western frontier, essentially in the same time period, where there existed overlapping frontiers—a fur-trapping frontier, then a mining frontier, and so on, that evolved with the conquest of Indian tribal areas.

As the French administration in Lebanon favored the Maronites and other Christian denominations over the Muslims, the colonial administration in Algeria favored the *colons* over the Muslim *indigènes*. It ultimately came to favor the Berbers over the Arabs in Algeria, as well. An idea emerged in the years following the conquest among French soldiers and policymakers, called the "Kabyle Myth," that the Kabyle Berbers who lived in the mountains were a kindred Mediterranean people, superior to the "alien" Arabs who lived on the plains. They were allegedly superior in anthropological and sociological terms. This Social Darwinian concept emerged as a consequence of pseudo-scientific analysis like that proposed by Mangin regarding the *Tirailleurs*. In practical terms, the French merely exploited a preexisting cultural and linguistic schism dating from the time of the Arab conquest in the eighth century, and continuing through the present day. It was characteristic, however, also of "divide and conquer" policies followed by other Europeans in the age of New Imperialism in the nineteenth and twentieth centuries, and comparable to British favor shown to Sikhs and Gurkhas in India. The Islamic Ottoman Empire had followed a similar policy toward Western Christian powers from the sixteenth through the eighteenth centuries, of which France itself had of course been the recipient of the sultan's favors.

MUSLIM RESISTANCE IN THE MANDATES

The "pacification" of dissident Arab groups in Syria in the mid-1920s prepared the ground for Muslim dissatisfaction with French control in the mandates. This was evidenced in the popular support of Faysal and of the northern Syrian revolt of Ibrahim Hananu, as well as the assassination attempt on Gourand in 1921.[44] Gourand's successors faced growing Muslim discontent from the 1920s, manifest in armed uprisings, and through the 1930s, it was signaled by the formation of political parties and attending labor strife. The most serious armed revolt was that of the Druze in 1925. It resulted from the reforms of Captain Carbillet within the Jabal Druze area, including massive construction projects that used conscript labor.[45] The French paid low wages to the conscripts, but the work was resented nonetheless. The Jabal Druze area had been isolated for centuries, and Druze clan leaders resented the encroachment of French power through the modern infrastructure Carbillet was introducing to their realm. Carbillet had served in West Africa previously, and had actually been asked by Druze leaders to serve as their governor in 1923.[46] Carbillet built new schools and a museum, engineered canals, and established new law courts in Jabal Druze.

Carbillet's plans to revise the system (or custom) of land tenure in the region had the goal of increasing agricultural productivity, but was regarded as a challenge to the status quo of the wealthy Druze landowners. Carbillet also began collecting taxes effectively, which the Ottomans and many previous regimes had been unable to do. French leaders were caught by surprise in July 1925 when armed bands of Druze began attacking French positions. The town of Salkhad was sacked by the Druze on July 18.[47] Two days later Druze forces ambushed and killed a column of 200 French troops who were marching to rescue some downed French pilots. Then, on July 30, a mixed French-Syrian-Madagascan column, commanded by General Michaud, that had been sent to deal with the Druze rebels was attacked at night at Mazra'a. Almost a third of the column was lost in the battle, along with thousands of weapons and a vast quantity of supplies.[48]

There was no single leader of the Druze revolt (although Sultan al-Atrash was a prominent supporter), and the Druze forces mainly consisted of ragged and undisciplined irregular companies.[49] Some Sunni groups in Syria and Lebanon took the occasion to demand independence, and Sunni rebels attacked French outposts and Maronite communities. In early September, General Gamelin became commander of French forces in the mandates.[50] He gradually reduced the Druze in their villages by air attacks as well as by land operations. For their part, the Sunnis were reacting against the favoritism shown by the regime toward their perennial enemies, the Maronites, although they did not necessarily sympathize with the Druze. The Sunnis already knew that the cities in which they formed a majority were receiving fewer perks from the largesse of the mandatory regime compared to the cities that were majority Maronite. The Muslim population in general, both Sunni and Shi'ite, perceived French economic policy as exploitive. Many of them resented the introduction of a new currency in the mandates, the taxes (on property, animals, and vehicles), and labor conscription. The road connecting Damascus, Homs, Hama, and Aleppo, built in 1924–1930, was constructed by conscript labor, although the French did pay low wages to the workers.

The regime imposed customs duties on imports, with the price of most items raised some 15 percent from 11 percent, as under the Ottoman regime, for League of Nations countries (except for food items, which were still at 11 percent). There were several French companies that utilized local Arab labor, but the French invested little in industrial pursuits within the mandates, compared to Algeria. The first factories built with French capital in the mandates appeared in the 1930s (textiles and food plants). Attempts by the French to expand cotton and silk farming in the mandates failed, due to a lack of willing labor. The old Ottoman public debt was utterly unsupported by the contemporary Arab populace, who had not incurred the debt, and it eventually closed down in 1926 leaving its creditors unfulfilled.[51] Muslim workers began organizing in the 1920s. Curiously, old Ottoman laws were still on the books banning the formation of unions. The mandate officials agreed that French labor laws did not apply in Syria and Lebanon, and did not intervene to set up any similar laws in the mandates. The first unions appeared in Beirut (typesetters and shoemakers), and workers began striking in the late 1920s to protest wages, hours, conditions, and larger political issues in cities like Beirut, Damascus, Aleppo, and Homs.[52] There was a general strike in Syria in 1936.

The imposition of the French educational system within the mandates caused a great number of problems in Muslim-majority areas. The secular basis of French education caused much anxiety in the traditionalist Muslim community, whose constituents did not care to hear of the French interpretation of the Rights of Man. Muslims were also aware (and resentful) that Catholic mission schools received subsidies and tended to be of better quality than the schools that the French installed in Muslim areas. There began to be protests in the 1930s by Muslims against the French educational system. These protests helped to galvanize Islamic political movements that sought to end the French presence in Syria.

APPEASEMENT AND RETREAT

General Maurice Sarrail was high commissioner in 1924–1925.[53] During his tenure, attempts were made by the mandatory government to appease the Muslim population. An anticlericalist, he distanced himself from religious leaders, writing, "to avoid giving them the weight they didn't deserve." Sarrail overstepped the bounds of reason, however, when he snubbed Maronite leaders by refusing to attend a banquet in his honor.[54] The Vatican representative protested, and French authorities in Paris recognized that such attitudes undermined the support of the one Arab constituency in the mandates that was pro-French. Sarrail was ordered by Paris to pay his respects to the Maronite patriarch.[55] The general issued a redivision of Lebanese territory in June 1925 that irked the Maronites further, and he perplexed everyone by declaring the end of the previous voting policy of election along religious lines for the proposed, largely figurehead, Lebanese Chamber. Popular pressures forced him to rescind both "reforms."

Too much of an embarrassment, Sarrail was recalled, and he was replaced by Henri de Jouvenal, a civilian whose administration was also rather short-lived (1925–1926).[56] Jouvenal presided over the creation of the "Lebanese Republic" in May 1926.[57] The Representative Council was created, which polled religious and secular leaders of the mandate on their political views. Many Sunnis boycotted the poll, but the other respondents favored representation along religious lines in a republican government. The Representative Council was now renamed the Chamber of Deputies, and it, along with twelve hand-picked "senators" chosen by Jouvenal, elected a new president of the Republic of Lebanon. They elected Charles Dabbas, a Greek Orthodox lawyer who was promoted by Jouvenal as a compromise to appease those who feared Maronite control within the mandate.[58] A prime minister was appointed by the president from the Maronite community, however. This was financier Auguste Abid, who headed a cabinet composed of two Maronites, a Sunni, a Shi'ite, a Druze, a Greek Orthodox, and a Greek Catholic.[59]

There was much factional disputation, however, and many Lebanese Muslims were dissatisfied because they had hoped one day to be unified with their fellow Muslims in Syria. The mandatory government felt compelled to impose two constitutional amendments to reduce factional discord—one to reduce the legislature to one chamber (1927), and one to increase the power of the president (1929).[60] Nevertheless, this was all somewhat premature, because the French had no plans to evacuate the region. In May 1932, the French suspended the Lebanese Constitution. The high commissioner feared that a Muslim (Muhammad al-Jisr) might run for president, which might alter the engineered political status quo that bolstered the French position.[61] Dabbas was allowed to "rule" by decree, presiding over the Council of Seven Directors.

Within Syria, Sunni Muslims created myriad nationalist parties in the 1920s and 1930s. Most of them were small (a few thousand actual members), but they had a wider support among the population than was indicated by membership rolls. The majority of them were openly opposed to the continued existence of the mandate, and agitated for union with Lebanon. They believed that the several Christian groups in Lebanon ought to be subordinate to the Muslim majority in Syria. Consequently, these groups were able to achieve very little in conjunction with French actions. They were responsible, however, for fomenting dissatisfied Muslim students and journalists, and for instigating strikes by Muslim laborers, and they had a hand in the violence directed against the regime by Muslim militants on occasions such as "Martyrs' Day" (in commemoration of the Battle of Maysalun), and a day spent lamenting the Balfour Declaration and the Zionist influx into Palestine.

There were also a few other nationalist parties in Syria that were moderately pro-French, and that advocated a more gradual evolutionary process toward independence. They also tended to be willing to discuss the fate of the Maronites and other Christians in Lebanon in terms other than inflammatory rhetoric. One such party was the Liberal Constitutional party of Subhi Barakat, a man who was able to achieve far greater success in the Syrian mandate than his more radical colleagues.[62]

High Commissioner Henri Ponsot (1926–1933) distrusted the Muslim radicals, but he thought that, ultimately, he could control the pace of Syrian political evolution.[63] He understood that it would be unwise to completely ignore the aspirations of Syrian Muslims indefinitely, or to favor France's Lebanese Mandate too overtly. The function of the mandatory regime was of course to guide the inhabitants of the mandates toward responsible government. To this end, Ponsot organized a Syrian Constituent Assembly in June 1928 to draft a constitution. He packed it, however, with individuals whom he calculated might be more pro-French, such as satisfied rural landowners.[64] There were a number of individuals in the assembly, however, who supported the extreme nationalist goals of the "National Bloc," which advocated more rapid French withdrawal and union with Lebanon. The National Bloc members were able to prevent Ponsot from manipulating the assembly's proceedings, and they got the assembly to elect as the chairman of the committee to draft the constitution the former north Syrian rebel Ibrahim Hananu. After a great deal of wrangling, the assembly came up with a draft constitution in August 1928.

The draft was sufficiently radical in tone regarding the pace of the ultimate French withdrawal and the subject of union with Lebanon. High Commissioner Ponsot felt compelled to inform the assembly that six articles were unacceptable and needed to be removed.[65] Months of debate and protest followed, and finally, it was decided that a treaty would be drawn up between France and Syria that would ensure that the more "radical" provisions of the constitution would be carried out under circumstances acceptable to both sides. In May 1930, another version of the constitution was drafted, in which the two articles most offensive to the French regime were altered.[66] It was scheduled to take effect upon the election of the Chamber of Deputies.

Meanwhile, the treaty was being discussed in Paris, and it would take another two years before it was fully ready. A moderate Muslim majority won the December 1931 elections to the Syrian Chamber of Deputies, but many radical Muslims were angered by the events, and an attack was made on the house of the moderate Subhi Barakat, who was elected president of the chamber.[67] The chamber was responsible for selecting a "government," by choosing a president (who had to be a Muslim), who then appointed a prime minister. The prime minister determined the policies of the "government" and created ministries. Syria's first president was Muhammad 'Ali Bey al-'Abid, and its first prime minister was Haqqi al-Adhm.

There was a great deal of apprehension in Syria regarding the forthcoming treaty with France through the summer and fall of 1932. A late summer strike by silk dyers in Aleppo was infiltrated by communist agitators, and initiated a new round of violent protests directed against the French occupation.[68] When Ponsot returned from consultations in France in October, he made no public comment about the treaty, which so antagonized the nationalists that they boycotted the opening proceedings of the chamber. Subhi Barakat was reelected as chamber president. Ponsot went back to France in late November to continue his work, but there was no interest in Paris in accommodating the Muslim nationalists. A public statement was made by the French that there would henceforth be a distinction made between the Treaty Zone (consisting of most of Syria) and the Mandatory Zone (consisting of Lebanon, Druze territories, and 'Alawite territory).

Most nationalists were not pleased with this, because they desired to absorb Lebanon into a greater Syria. In response, an April 1933 "Manifesto to the Nation" was issued in Damascus that insisted that all of the mandate territory was Syrian territory.[69] When the chamber reconvened, more than half of all the deputies boycotted the proceedings. A general strike and protests were orchestrated by the nationalists in May. Ponsot fell ill in May, and returned to France in early July. When he recovered he was posted to Morocco, not back to Syria. His replacement in Syria was Count Damien de Martel.

Martel's first visit to Damascus from Beirut, in early November 1933, corresponded with the now-annual Balfour Day protests (November 3), and he was greeted by protests. On November 19, the long-awaited treaty was finally published.[70] It stated that the transfer of power from France to Syria was to be a process occurring in gradual stages over four years. The Syrian Republic was subsequently to join the League of Nations. A cooperative arrangement with France was to last for another twenty-five years, in which the republic's foreign policy and military and police infrastructure were to be organized in a collaborative manner by both Syrian and French officials. When it was put before the Chamber on November 20, chaos reigned within the legislature. High Commissioner Martel suspended it on November 22, declaring that it was unable to make a free and constitutional decision about the treaty. He posted troops in the chamber to prevent it from operating clandestinely.[71]

The reality is that Syrian political aspirations were evolving too quickly for the French. The mandates cost France a great deal of money—on physical infrastructure improvements ranging from roads and school buildings to relief assistance rendered to starving populations. This was the essence of *mise en valeur*, the products of France's "civilizing mission." France, on the other hand, could point to its participation in mandatory government as evidence of its standing among the "great powers." This was an obvious example of its historical significance, and was necessary politically, even if the mandates were a drain economically on French resources. Some French concessionary businesses made money in Syria and Lebanon, though certainly not on a scale comparable to French businesses in Algeria. While many Maronites were pleased with France's decisions to stay, many Muslims were dissatisfied, and they failed to understand the peculiar colonial political justifications that the French used to explain the maintenance of the mandatory government. To the Syrians, the status quo for Muslims within the mandates seemed far too similar to that of the colonies of North Africa.

SUB-SAHARAN AFRICA

The rapid political evolution of the Arabs within the Middle Eastern mandates, however, was quite distinct from the kind of political subservience experienced by the Muslims of French North Africa and French

West Africa. No nationalist movements emerged within French Africa before World War II. South of the belt of North African Arab-Berber countries (Algeria, Tunisia, Morocco), other French African colonies covered a quarter of the continent, within administrative regions called French West Africa and French Equatorial Africa. These areas were sparsely populated, containing less than half the population of British Nigeria alone. The first French outpost in West Africa was at St. Louis in Senegal, established in the sixteenth century. Dakar, Senegal, served as the administrative headquarters of French West Africa. By World War I, there were seven colonies in French West Africa: Senegal, Mauritania, French Soudan (Mali), French Guinea, Ivory Coast, and Niger, and Dahomey. French Equatorial Africa, with a capital at Brazzaville (in the French Congo), consisted of four colonies: Gabon, French Congo, Oubangi-Chari (today's Central African Republic), and Tchad (Chad).[72]

From Senegal, French influence diffused throughout West Africa. The Ivory Coast was conquered in the early nineteenth century, and the city of Abidjan was subsequently developed by France. Ivory Coast crops such as cocoa, coffee, bananas, and pineapples became the most important regional exports from French West Africa. A French presence was established along the Guinea coast in the 1860s. France had a sure hold on the southern section of Guinea in 1883, and the interior was taken in 1911. The first French incursions into Niger began in the 1890s; by 1901 the area was organized as a "military territory," but only in 1922 was the formal occupation established.[73]

During World War I, the French Empire expanded into new Islamic areas south of the Sahara. French and British colonial forces converged on the German territories of Kamerun and Togoland in March 1916, and overwhelmed the German garrisons. The French parts of the conquered territories were added (perhaps prematurely) to the existing subdivisions of the French Empire: Togoland was added to French West Africa in August 1916, and Cameroon (German Kamerun) was added to French Equatorial Africa in July 1917. At the end of World War I, the Allied Supreme Council decided that these German territories indeed would be granted as mandates to France and Britain (May 6, 1919). In the following July, the French and British agreed to a treaty that defined more precisely the borders of their neighboring African mandates.[74]

These areas, like the entire southern tier of French West Africa, and the northern edge of French Equatorial Africa, were only partly Islamic. Muslim communities there were interspersed with tribal animist communities. Islam's spread through the Sahara and Sudanic lands (a centuries-old process) ceased within the new French Empire. By contrast, Islam continued to spread in African areas held by the British, because the British preferred to employ Muslim civil servants in that section of their empire. The British felt that Muslims had an advantage because of their religion that superseded existing regional tribal distinctions. In the African sphere of the French Empire, proven loyalty to Mother France was the only advantage for Muslims. Those Africans who had seen *Tirailleur* duty received material advantages as a consequence of their service. Tribal distinctions were somewhat lessened during the time of their service, and the emphasis on the French language and on unit loyalty within *Tirailleur* divisions caused a kind of cultural transformation among individual troops that lasted beyond the terms of their service rendered to the French Empire.[75]

Between the wars, a great number of construction projects were undertaken by the French in their Saharan and sub-Saharan domains, just as in Algeria, Syria, and Lebanon. While few industries were created in these outlying areas of French power, roads and rail lines were established, which linked together vast stretches of desert with the forested lands to the south. In contrast to Algeria (but like Syria and Lebanon), not many Frenchmen settled in French West Africa. There were scattered Foreign Legion garrisons posted throughout the area, and there were some administrators who worked with the governor-general at his headquarters in Dakar. From time to time, it was deemed advisable to reorganize the colonies. For example, in March 1919, it was decided to organize Upper Volta into a separate colony. This was an accommodation that worked when a sufficient layer of the region's physical infrastructure had been modernized, and when there was a fairly sizable settled population. In the peculiar case of Upper Volta, the colony was dismembered in 1932, with part going back to Ivory Coast and part to French Soudan (Mali). In 1947, however, Upper Volta was permanently made into a separate colony.[76]

Native forces, deemed to be sufficiently loyal to France, could police the region. Conscription was introduced into French West Africa in July 1919 to employ native troops in such numbers as to free up specific *Tirailleur* or Foreign Legion units that had been relegated to garrison duty on the frontiers. A partly elective "Superior Council" was established for French West Africa in December 1920 to assist the governor-general.

As French *mise en valeur* encroached upon more remote areas of the once-impenetrable Sahara, more regions were sectioned off as distinct colonies: Mauritania became a colony on January 1, 1921, and Niger became a separate colony on October 13, 1921.[77] Later that month (October 21), Dakar, capital of French West Africa, became an autonomous area. An Anglo-French agreement was made in 1924 to define the borders of French Equatorial Africa and British Sudan. As more and more desert and tropical areas were surveyed, and the indigenous landscape was transformed, the easier it was for the French to superimpose their physical infrastructure on the land.[78] But unlike in Algeria, there were very few Frenchmen working out in the field in French West Africa other than the soldiers and administrators concentrated in Dakar.

The large French-controlled island of Madagascar, off the coast of East Africa, contained a mainly Muslim population in the northern third of the island, particularly along the coastline. Islam had spread down the coast of East Africa to various islands of the Indian Ocean in the later Middle Ages. Here, the creation of the French Empire had largely ended the further expansion of Islam into non-Muslim areas, as on the African mainland. Madagascar had its own governor-general. In May 1924, the French decided to create several councils composed of Europeans and natives to advise the governor-general on economic issues, including the colonial budget and public works. This was in keeping with the spirit of the times and was similar to the kinds of things being done by the French within the Islamic heartland.

ECONOMIC DISASTER

Before the start of World War II, France, the French Empire, and the rest of the world were hard pressed by the economic disaster of the Great Depression. Both Britain and France did in fact benefit from possession of their respective empires in the artificially high prices paid for goods made in the mother country. Investments in the empire quadrupled in the 1930s. Colonial companies still reaped huge profits in part from the low cost of native labor. The colonizing elite also managed to survive the depression more effectively than many of the natives, due to the political representation of the colonists in the assembly, and the connections between the First World economies of Frenchmen in France and Frenchmen residing in the outlying empire.

The Maghrib in particular suffered during the depression. A widespread famine broke out in 1937. The *colon* journalist and future Nobel Prize–winning novelist Albert Camus covered the ravages of the depression-era starvation experienced by the Berbers of the backcountry in Kabylia in vivid newspaper stories written for the fairly comfortable *colons* living close to the coast. Embitterment caused by the failure of relief efforts might have led to a general Muslim revolt had the population not been so weakened, psychologically as well as physically, by the experience of famine.

CONCLUSION

Prior to World War I, France had created a trans-Saharan empire, one of the largest in the world, composed almost entirely of Muslims. Within Algeria, however, a European, primarily Catholic, settler population had taken root. Its inhabitants hearkened back to the Roman settlers of several thousand years before as their model for placing a European culture on top of an indigenous non-European culture. No indigenous independence movements emerged in French Africa prior to World War I. France had the opportunity to acquire other mainly Muslim and partly Muslim areas during and immediately after World War I—Syria, Lebanon, German Kamerun, and Togoland. France was granted temporary control of these areas as mandates, temporary custodianships that were intended to guide the population toward eventual independence.

Nationalist politics emerged unevenly within these territories—very rapidly in Syria (where many native inhabitants felt their aspirations were negated by France), and more slowly throughout French West Africa. Lebanon had the distinction of providing France with a native population loyal to the mother country—the Maronites—owing to connections fostered in the days of the crusades. The Islamic portions of the French Empire thus consisted of territories in vastly different stages of political development. Throughout the empire, however, the French government and French business interests laid the foundations for a modern physical infrastructure of roads, buildings, and rail lines that had not existed prior to the French presence.

The French Empire, like many contemporary colonial empires, was thus characterized by uneven modernization prior to World War II. It is highly significant and not at all coincidental that the bulk of the people residing within the French Empire were Muslims, given the prior history of French contacts with Islam. The Islamic world had been France's primary window on the wider non-Western world during the previous 1,400 years. Whether a region was held as a colony like Algeria or a mandate like Syria, the French were not inclined to relinquish control of the region in the near future. It would take the turmoil of World War II to give rise to unstoppable nationalist movements and accelerate the pace of change within the French Islamic Empire.

World War II, the Arabs, and the Empire

HOPE AND DESPAIR IN THE MANDATES

The frustrations of Muslim nationalists in Syria reached a peak in January 1936, when a National Pact was proclaimed, demanding independence immediately, union with Lebanon, and an end of Zionism in Palestine. The unrest that inevitably attended the pact's proclamation included strikes, shutdowns, and student protests. Jamil Mardam was arrested on January 11 and held for a time.[1] High Commissioner Martel visited Damascus, but could not come to terms with National Bloc leaders. The next month saw escalating violence in Beirut, Hama, Tyre, Sidon, and Tripoli, and the recourse to French colonial troops and armored units to restore order.[2] Martel managed to get leaders of the new (but technically impotent) Syrian Ministry to Beirut for talks in late February, and by March 1, he and they agreed to the core of a new treaty that might finally ameliorate the nationalist cause or at least quell the current unrest.[3]

Hashim al-Atassi and Jamil Mardam arrived in France in early April to discuss the possibility of a lasting treaty with the French government.[4] The talks went badly at first, and just when it seemed that diplomacy would again fail, and give way to violence, the election of the left-wing and anti-colonial government of Leon Blum opened the path for a diplomatic solution. That September an agreement was hammered out between the French government and the Syrian representatives. In an amazing turn of events, France now recognized Syria as an independent state. There would be a three-year preparatory period starting on January 1, 1937, during which French officials merely would provide advice to Syrian officials. Syria would join the League of Nations; it would send attachés to French diplomatic missions in Turkey, Iraq, and Egypt; and it would send its own diplomat to France.

The November 1936 Syrian elections vindicated the tactics of the National Bloc, as its members won all of the important races. Atassi was president again, Mardam was prime minister again, and the cabinet was composed entirely of bloc members. Lebanese developments so closely paralleled those of Syria that between September and November a similar arrangement was formulated for Lebanon.[5]

The Blum administration came to an end in France in June 1937 as a consequence of changing economics brought about by the Great Depression and politics wrought by fears of the Third Reich in Germany. France was affected somewhat later by the depression than other Western countries. Blum's efforts to shorten the working hours and provide paid vacations for French workers failed to help the French economy to revive. Few Arab leaders were concerned with the rise of fascism in Germany, which, in the 1940s, would come to have an impact on them as well as on Europeans. Several Arab parties, however, employed fascistic methods of organization, such as the Syrian League of National Action of Sabri al-Asali (1935) and Pierre Gemayel's Phalange party (1936).[6] The Germans began making overtures to the Arabs in the late 1930s, playing to Arab antipathy toward Zionist immigrants in Palestine. The coming of a conflict with Germany in 1939 caused the French to suspend the Syrian and Lebanese constitutions in the midst of the chaos of global war.[7]

THE ROAD TO WAR

The Nazi party gained in popularity in Weimar Germany in the 1920s due to Adolf Hitler's criticism of the Treaty of Versailles and French control of the Saar and the Rhineland. In the early 1930s, Nazi popularity was due to the party's criticism of the Weimar Republic's insistence on continuing to pay back World War I reparations to France and other Allies in the midst of the Great Depression. Hitler became chancellor in January 1933, and in the following month the Reichstag's Enabling Act essentially ended the Weimar Republic and created the Third Reich. The Nazi party took over the state and dominated German society, and Hitler was free to prepare his plans for global conquest. In the period of appeasement (1933–1939), the Western democracies (including France) did nothing to stop Hitler's remilitarization of Germany because of a number of factors—they feared Soviet communism and thought the Nazi state could provide a buffer against Soviet expansionism. They began to reevaluate the Treaty of Versailles, and thought that perhaps Germany had been punished enough for World War I aggressions. Finally, they believed that the German economy must be allowed to recover if the European and global economies were to recover, even if it meant turning a blind eye to German remilitarization.

World War II erupted in Europe in 1939 with the invasion of Poland by Nazi Germany—and in the Asian-Pacific theater in 1937 with the Japanese invasion of China—and the French Empire was drastically altered by the Axis powers. All three main Axis leaders (Hitler, Mussolini, and Hirohito) dreamed of global conquest at the expense of the Western democracies and Soviet communism. The French and British entrenched their forces in the Maginot Line near the Franco-German border, anticipating a scenario reminiscent of World War I. They were encircled, however, and smashed by Hitler's *blitzkrieg* tactics in May 1940. Some 350,000 British and French troops were evacuated from Dunkirk to Britain in late May and early June, and Paris surrendered on June 13. An armistice was signed on June 21, and France removed itself from the war. Shortly afterward, a pro-Nazi French fascist regime was established at Vichy in the south of France, led by Pierre Laval and the old marshal, Henri Pétain, calling itself État Français.[8]

General Charles de Gaulle, meanwhile, proclaimed himself the leader of the Free French who had been evacuated to Britain. The Vichy regime claimed all of France's overseas territories, including the mandates in Syria and Lebanon. A very few soldiers fled the French mandates to the British mandate in Palestine at this time to join the Free French forces loyal to de Gaulle that were forming there. Many soldiers in the French colonial forces and the Foreign Legion, however, did not view themselves as instruments of Nazi foreign policy. Rather, they served a state that was theoretically coequal to the Third Reich in Axis diplomacy. The French volunteers of the Charlemagne Division of the Waffen S.S. (the 33rd Waffen Grenadier Division), however, were sympathetic to the Nazi cause, joined the Nazi ranks in 1945, and died to the last man in April and May 1945, while defending the Nazi capital of Berlin from the Red Army.[9] After the war, many former Waffen S.S. men of other nationalities joined the Foreign Legion. The specific offer of joining the Legion was made by the Free French forces to most captured German personnel at the end of the war.

WORLD WAR II IN THE ARAB MANDATES

Within the Arab mandates, High Commissioner Martel reached retirement age and was replaced in January 1939 by Gabriel Puaux.[10] Arab radicals began committing acts of anti-French violence in Damascus late that month, and the *Sûreté* feared that it was incited by German operatives. For security reasons, Puaux felt it was necessary to suspend the Syrian constitution in July and the Lebanese constitution in September, at least for the duration of the troubles with Germany.[11] In late August, General Weygand returned to the mandates, not as high commissioner, but as commander in chief, Middle Eastern Theater of Operations.[12] That September, as the Nazi *blitzkrieg* began rolling across Europe, and France and Britain both declared war on Nazi Germany, emergency war measures were put into effect in the mandates. Puaux declared a state of emergency, and the mandatory regime began censoring the press for signs of pro-German sentiment, and made arrests for listening to German propaganda radio broadcasts. The government assumed control of certain local industries deemed to be vital to the war effort, including metals, chemicals, and textiles. Gas masks were distributed in the cities, and air raid shelters were constructed.[13]

Weygand was recalled in mid-May 1940, and was replaced by General Mittelhauser. After the fall of Paris to the Germans on June 14 and the signing of an armistice on June 21, General Mittelhauser told the British commander in Cairo, Field Marshal Archibald Wavell, that the French Army of the Levant would keep on fighting alongside the British.[14] Vichy officials and French military figures in North Africa disagreed with the general. He was recalled as commander in chief, and replaced by Vichy general Fougere. Puaux was also recalled as high commissioner in November 1940, and was replaced by Jean Chaippe.[15] Chiappe's plane, however, was accidentally shot down over the Mediterranean by Italian forces on November 27, and Puaux's actual successor as high commissioner was Vichy general Henri Dentz.[16]

German agents began arriving in the mandates with the express purpose of stirring up Arab sentiments against both British colonial authorities and against Jewish Zionist immigrants from Europe. Arab nationalist leader Rashid Ali rose up against the British in Iraq in March 1941, and made an appeal to Hitler for help.[17] An Italian Armistice Commission also arrived in the mandates in August 1940, following the signing of a Franco-Italian armistice. In May 1941, the Nazis requested the use of French airfields in the mandates for use by *Luftwaffe* planes against British positions in Iraq. Dentz was prepared to cooperate, to a degree, with German war aims in the Middle East, and granted permission to use Palmyra.[18]

The Vichy military commander and vice premier, Admiral Jean Darlan, then weighed in and ordered Dentz to provide any necessary assistance to the German *Luftwaffe* in transit against the British in Iraq. Dentz was also ordered to resist any British intervention in the mandates. By the end of May 1941, about a hundred German planes, as well as twenty Italian planes, had landed in Syria to coordinate bombing from a base the Germans had seized at Mosul, Iraq, near the Syrian-Iraqi border.[19]

To the British, Iraq was a backwater of a greater conflict taking place at that time to the south, in Egypt. What was at stake in these operations was control of the Suez Canal and access to the oil fields of the Middle East (and potentially, those in the southern Soviet Union, as well). The campaign of Italian forces based in Libya, and of the German Afrika Korps under Field Marshal Erwin Rommel, against British positions in Egypt (1941–1942) were the primary prongs of the Axis drive in the Middle East. The so-called Desert War in the vicinity of Egypt had four basic phases: (1) the Italian drive to Egypt, from September 1940 to January 1941; (2) the British counterattack toward Libya, in February 1941; (3) the German drive to Egypt, from April 1941 through the decisive Battle of El-Alamein in November 1942; and (4) the final British drive from Egypt into Libya.[20] Wavell, the commander in chief of the combined British-Commonwealth forces in the Middle East and India, had his headquarters in Cairo, and Britain's primary strategic concerns were there, rather than in Iraq or Syria.[21]

The Afrika Korps was formed by Hitler from the *Wehrmacht* in February 1941, and had better equipment—guns and aiming mechanisms for long-range artillery—and under Rommel, superior morale than their British counterparts. Rommel's victories at Benghazi (January 1942) and Tobruk (June 1942) led to a momentum that took the Afrika Korps to within sixty miles of Alexandria.[22] There was great fear in Cairo and London that Egypt would soon fall to the Nazi *blitzkrieg*. British prime minister Winston Churchill himself visited Egypt in August 1942 to assess the situation, and make crucial appointments. Generals Harold Alexander and Bernard Montgomery took over the British forces, raising British morale, and Churchill sent adequate numbers of planes, tanks, artillery and troops to defeat Rommel's forces at El-Alamein in October and November 1942.[23] The Axis lost at El-Alamein 10,000 dead, 15,000 wounded, and 30,000 POWs to the British, and the entire momentum of the war in North Africa and the Middle East shifted now in favor of the Allies.

The British, however, did view Axis activities in Syria and Iraq as strategically important. Churchill wrote in his history of the war of "the bitter need to forestall the Germans in Syria," and that if German interests prevailed in Syria and Iraq, "Hitler's hand might have reached out very far towards India and beckoned to Japan."[24] Wavell was reluctant to disperse his forces between Egypt and Syria, and was ordered to scrape together any available forces for an invasion of Syria. He was concerned about having inadequate resources to defend Palestine, given the revolt of Rashid Ali in Iraq and the far more pressing demands on his manpower caused by the Afrika Korps. The threat to British positions was eliminated in Iraq in early May 1941, and then all possible British and French forces were mobilized for an invasion of Syria.

British RAF forces bombed the Vichy airfields used by the Germans at Damascus, Palmyra, and Rayaq on May 12. By June, most Axis planes had withdrawn. De Gaulle's representative in Cairo, General Georges Catroux, feared a unilateral move by the British against Vichy positions in Syria.[25] He knew that Wavell preferred an all-out British campaign, for fear of greater Vichy resistance in the face of civil war between the Free French and Vichy units. De Gaulle, meanwhile, had begun plans for a Free French invasion from his base in Brazzaville in April 1941.

OPERATION EXPORTER

In late 1941, General Wavell was compelled to consolidate the British and French plans for an invasion of the Vichy-controlled Arab mandates.

The designated commander of the operation (code named "Exporter") was General Henry Maitland Wilson.[26] General Catroux issued a call for Vichy forces to defect southward toward British territory, but few heeded his call. A few native auxiliary units under Colonel Collet did go south. Some six battalions of Free French forces (over 10,000 men) would be commanded by General Legentilhomme, former governor of French Somaliland, until he was ousted by the Italians in 1940. The British forces included two cruisers and ten destroyers positioned off the Lebanese coast, and British, Australian, and Indian ground units. Altogether, the Anglo-Free French forces numbered about 35,000 men. With RAF squadrons freed up from duty in Iraq, the Allies possessed air superiority. The Vichy-controlled Army of the Levant also numbered about 35,000 men, and was supported by a naval force of two destroyers and three submarines operating off Lebanon.[27]

Operation Exporter began with a drive northward from Palestine early on June 8, 1941. It was accompanied by the dropping of leaflets on the populated areas of the mandates, intended to urge Arab support for the Allies: "France declares you independent by the voice of her sons who are fighting for her Life and the liberty of the world."[28] The British also provided their own assurance of support for Arab independence in the leaflet. There would be no massive Arab revolt on behalf of the Allies, however, as in World War I. The Free French forces would have found such a situation to be unwelcome. Moreover, the nature of the combat and weaponry was different in World War II, so the Arabs who were not enlisted in colonial auxiliary units tended to be bystanders of the huge events swirling around them.

The columns of invading Anglo-Free French forces advanced slowly toward Beirut, Damascus, and Biqa along the coastal roads, making sure to keep close to their superior naval support vessels. Some British units marched eastward from Iraq, as well. Early German and Italian offers of military assistance to Vichy forces were rebuffed, because victory at the cost of a further loss of prestige was not acceptable to the Vichy men. They also believed at this early moment that they could win on their own.[29]

Promoted to *Général d'Armeé*, Dentz was faced with several possible scenarios for resistance and had on hand a number of unsolicited German and Italian advisors (whose advice he tended to ignore). Despite determined Vichy resistance at Matulla and the rail lines at Dar'a, the Allied advance managed to capture most of its objectives, including Dar'a, Tyre, Qunaytara, Kiswa (near Damascus), and Marj'uyun. Vichy forces managed to recapture Marj'uyun, but the Allies subsequently took it back. On June 21, General Legentilhomme and his men entered Damascus. The general had been injured in the fighting, but he remained in the field. Catroux and de Gaulle soon arrived, and entered the city triumphantly. Colonel Collet was installed as Free France's *Delegue* to the Syrian government, which prudently had not taken a political stand in the conflict between different Frenchmen.[30]

The Allied march on Beirut in late June caused Dentz to lose confidence in the ability of his men to stop the invasion. He made a tentative inquiry of Allied terms on June 20 through the American consul-general Van Enghert. When the Allies were within ten miles of Beirut on June 26, Dentz contacted Darlan, asking for permission to request an armistice. Darlan was overly tentative, unsure of precisely what path to take, and did not immediately reply. But as the Allies drove on, Dentz again inquired through Van Enghert of Allied terms on July 8. Allied terms were offered on July 9, but discussion was hindered by Vichy insistence on the withdrawal of British assurances of Syrian independence. The armistice was eventually signed anyway, on July 14, because Dentz's position was no longer tenable.[31]

Vichy representatives refused to accept Free French representatives at the negotiations. They saw the Gaullist forces as power-hungry traitors and rebels who sided with the British because they were prepared to give up a hard-won empire for political gain. This was far from the truth, of course, but Catroux and de Gaulle were infuriated that the British would accept the Vichy surrender without the presence of Free French representatives. The terms specified that Vichy forces could either submit to Free French units or be repatriated to Vichy France. One-fifth of the remaining Vichy forces switched sides (some 2,500 men and 127 officers). Some Vichy civil authorities were retained for practical reasons. Of the colonial functionaries of the mandatory government, one-third returned to Vichy France, one-third swore loyalty to Free France, and one-third stayed on without switching loyalties. Vichy losses (6,350 men and officers) were more than those of the Allies (4,700, of whom 1,300 were Free French). In July and August, 25,000 Vichy men were transported home. Dentz was held in Jerusalem, but was released and sailed home on September 4. He was subsequently tried and condemned to death by the Free French in April 1945. His sentence was commuted, but he died in prison in December 1945.[32]

De Gaulle was not happy at British acquiescence to Vichy sentiment at the bargaining table, and he went to Cairo to complain to General Auchinleck, Wavell's replacement. De Gaulle argued that Vichy arms and control of native auxiliary units should have been handed over to the Free French officers. His demands were confirmed in an Anglo–Free French "Interpretive Agreement," and a July 25 agreement was firm about future Anglo–Free French collaboration in the Middle East. For the remainder of the war, supplies within the mandates were furnished by the Middle East Supply Center in Cairo, which received a great deal of American support.[33]

The campaign had proven decisive in several regards. First of all, Operation Exporter resulted in a rare Allied victory in 1941, a year when major

Axis successes occurred in Europe and the Pacific. Second, it saved a strategically important crossroads from Axis domination. Finally, it proved the validity of a large-scale multinational combined operation, which was employed again to reduce Axis empires. The lessons learned in Syria and Lebanon would be employed in later operations against Nazi Germany. The fears of French civil war would preclude large French participation in the campaigns to liberate North Africa and Normandy.

For the Arabs, the war proved the weakness of the French Empire. French who sided with Germans were defeated by British and French who sided with the British, and both Germany and Britain had promoted Arab independence. But Free French forces were no more disposed to grant independence to the Arabs than were Vichy forces.

OPERATION TORCH

In early July 1940, British naval forces struck French ships at Oran, Algeria, and sank three battleships and one aircraft carrier to prevent them from falling into Vichy hands. Hitler regarded the conquest of the Soviet Union as his primary strategic objective of the war, and placed the bulk of his forces on the Eastern Front starting in June 1941. By 1942, Soviet military and civilian losses to the Germans were so high that Stalin began pressuring Winston Churchill and Franklin Roosevelt for the creation of a second front in the West. He hoped that this would relieve some of the pressure from the Eastern Front. Stalin wanted the second front opened in France, while Churchill formulated a plan to attack in the Mediterranean area, the "soft underbelly" of the Axis. This idea had been the basis for Churchill's World War I plan for the Gallipoli campaign directed against the "back door" of the Central Powers.

Churchill and Roosevelt knew that France would have to be invaded eventually, and the British conceived of an operation code named "Jubilee" essentially as a test for the future invasion. On August 19, 1942, 5,000 Canadian and 1,000 British soldiers landed at Dieppe in a "reconnaissance in force," and were easily beaten back by the Germans at a cost of 3,400 Canadians and 800 British, as well as thirty-four ships. Thus, as a consequence of the seemingly impenetrable nature of Hitler's "Atlantic Wall" defenses in France, Vichy North Africa, the first part of the Axis "soft underbelly," became the target for a large forthcoming Anglo-American drive planned for the fall of 1942.[34]

The campaign was code-named "Torch," and American general Dwight Eisenhower was placed in overall command to relieve any lingering Franco-British tensions (British POWs from Syria-Lebanon were being shipped to Vichy France and the British held General Dentz as hostage until they were returned). The Allies calculated that they would experience less opposition from Vichy forces if an American were in command,

and American ground troops were landed alongside British forces. Most important, they believed opposition would be lessened if there were no Free French forces involved in the invasion. French opinion may not have been particularly disposed toward Britain, but it was fairly pro-American because of the ties forged from French assistance to the American Revolution through American help to France in World War I. The Allies calculated that such sentiment cut across the lines that otherwise distinguished Vichy policy from Free French policy.

The Vichy government had, according to the armistice terms with Germany, 120,000 soldiers stationed in North Africa—55,000 in Morocco, 50,000 in Algeria, and 15,000 in Tunisia. The troops were mainly native infantry led by French officers, but naturally there were also Foreign Legion units there and Zouave units composed of *colons*. Their equipment was obsolete and in short supply. In terms of armor, Vichy forces in North Africa had 140 obsolete tanks and eighty armored cars in Morocco; 110 old tanks and sixty armored cars in Algeria; and twenty armored cars in Tunisia. In addition, however, they had about 500 planes, with five primary airfields in Morocco (but only one with concrete runways—at Port Lyautey), three in Algeria (with an additional five secondary fields), and two in Tunisia. The French fleet in the area consisted of seven destroyers, eight submarines, a cruiser, and a battleship at Casablanca, and several destroyers and submarines at Bizerte and Oran. In addition, there were three cruisers and one large battleship based at Dakar.[35]

Assembled against this Vichy arsenal were hundreds of modern Allied ships, planes, and ground vehicles, together with tens of thousands of Allied troops armed with state-of-the-art equipment and adequate food and medicine. The Vichy regime militarized the government in most of the colonies with the exception of Algeria where the governor-general, Yves Chatel, was a civilian, but his cabinet was led by a vice-admiral, Raymond Fenard. The commissioner-general for North Africa was General Maxime Weygand (recently recalled from Syria), who, like the overall Vichy military commander for North Africa, General Alphonse Juin, was neither pro-Nazi nor pro-British. The Allies were not quite sure of the political leanings of the resident-generals of Morocco (General Auguste Nogues) or Tunisia (Vice-Admiral Jean-Pierre Esteva). The Allies, however, correctly assumed that two important Vichy major generals stationed in the area had pro-Allied leanings—Charles Mast, commander of the Algiers Division, and Emile Bethouart, commander of the Casablanca Division. Significantly, however, information on the planning of Operation Torch was withheld from Free French generals for fear of Vichy intelligence operations that may have infiltrated their ranks. Free French forces would not be called upon to participate, due to fears that a resulting civil war between Vichy and Free French units would stiffen general resistance to the invasion.

The Anglo-American invasion forces assembled in three waves: 24,500 Americans sailed from America to Morocco (with the specific objectives of Port Lyautey, Casablanca, and Safi); 18,000 Americans sailed from Britain to Oran; and a combined Anglo-American force of another 18,000 men sailed from Britain to Algiers. The various prongs of Operation Torch landed on November 8, 1942. The Americans experienced overwhelming success at Casablanca, having to overcome only minimal resistance there (a French counterattack at the casbah of Mahdia, to the north of Casablanca, was easily beaten back). The American forces landing at Oran had to crush a French counterattack at St. Lucien, near La Macta. Anglo-American forces landing in Algiers, however, faced both opposition and chaos as Vichy units seemed unsure of what to do. Major General Mast anticipated the Allied landing site would be near the location of the French landings in 1830, and tried to ensure that his men were not guarding the area in order to avoid hostile fire. Two British destroyers flying American flags were hit by Vichy artillery in Algiers harbor, but overall, there were few casualties for either side at any point in the landings.[36]

Admiral Darlan happened to be in Algeria at the time, visiting his son in a hospital.[37] He began negotiating with American General Mark Clark almost immediately, and after some prevaricating over whether he was legally capable of such diplomacy, he went over to the Allied side and ordered Vichy forces to cease resistance. Darlan faced continuing intrigues from his ranks, however, and he was assassinated on December 24.[38] But within four days of the initial landings, most of the Algerian coast was taken as far as Tunisia. The Germans were compelled to send reinforcements from Sicily into Tunisia. Operation Torch coincided chronologically with the huge Allied victory at El-Alamein, and the Axis would remain on the defensive for the rest of the North African campaign. The overwhelming success of Operation Torch vindicated Churchill's idea of attacking the "soft underbelly" of the Axis first, thereby drawing strength away from the "Atlantic Wall" defenses of the Nazi Empire along the French coast— am important prelude for an invasion of France.

French units in North Africa were rearmed by the Allies after surrender (two infantry divisions and two armored regiments, as well as reconnaissance, anti-tank, and anti-aircraft battalions). The depth of their participation in the Allied drive into Tunisia is indicated by the high number of casualties that they sustained in battles with the German *Wehrmacht* there—over 19,000. This was far in excess of the men whom they lost in Operation Torch, opposing the Anglo-American invasion forces.

Most of the 17 million inhabitants of French North Africa were unaffected by the conflict between the Axis and the Allies. Just over a million inhabitants of the region were *colons*, with about 775,000 residing in Algeria, 175,000 in Morocco, and 110,000 in Tunisia. Some were moderately pro-Vichy and anti-de Gaulle, because the general had of course fled from

France to Britain and was seen by many *colons* as being somewhat unin-terested in their position.[39] Many more were concerned primarily with the restoration of the old order within the colonies. Most Muslim civilians were mere observers of the titanic conflict between the superpowers. However, several factors during the war contributed to the postwar inde-pendence movements in North Africa: the divisions that were apparent among the French during the war; the apparent weakness of the French forces in relation to the Anglo-American forces of Operation Torch; and the huge casualties that the French forces sustained at the hands of the Germans subsequently in Tunisia. Finally, the substantial numbers of colonial forces employed by the Free French in North Africa, and later, in Italy, saw the French imperial system from within, witnessing examples of incompetence and petty rivalries among the officers. They experienced discrimination at the hands of French officers and harassment by *colon* Zouave troops, while in the service of France. Thousands returned to North Africa after the war further embittered by the experience. They were angered that their loyalty to the Free French cause was not rewarded with a measure of independence. The seeds were sown for the postwar Islamic independence movements that would destroy the French Empire.

THE END OF THE MANDATES

The Arabs in the mandates who sought independence from France had seen their hopes raised and then frustrated by the events of 1936–1937. The framework for Syrian and Lebanese independence was established prior to the end of the Blum administration, and was not erased by the vicissitudes of world war. The war's outcome did not alter the prior arrangements regarding independence in the view of either the Arabs or Free France's Allied partners—Britain, the United States, and the Soviet Union. The attitudes of Free French leaders toward the empire did not dif-fer significantly from those of Vichy leaders. Free France and Vichy both regarded the empire as France's patrimony, including the mandates. Many believed the Blum administration had moved too rapidly in Syria and Lebanon. De Gaulle and his representatives sought to maintain con-trol of the empire's mandates, but with support for Syrian and Lebanese independence openly proclaimed by the United States and the Soviet Union, the only superpowers whose global prestige remained intact at the end of the war, it was a foregone conclusion that France would ultimately have to acquiesce to global opinion. De Gaulle, however, equivocated from 1942 to 1945.

The British Middle East Supply Center in Cairo was responsible for supplying the Free French in the mandates after the defeat of Vichy forces.[40] The supply center received substantial funding from the United States, as well. Despite their dependence on their powerful Allies, it seemed that French administrators were now maneuvering to safeguard this vestige of their former superpower status instead of working toward the goal of independence for their mandates. De Gaulle toured the mandates in July and August 1941, and made it clear that immediate independence was not going to be forthcoming. General Catroux served as de Gaulle's administrator in the mandates from 1941 to 1943. The general was prepared to offer the Syrians and Lebanese the same options as in 1936, but al-Atassi refused to discuss such a scenario. *Shaykh* Taj al-Din, however, agreed to participate in the new-old status quo, and a new Syrian government was established with no National Bloc members.[41]

Under such peculiar conditions, Syrian independence was proclaimed on strictly French terms, on September 27, 1941. In Lebanon, the same terms were offered, and accepted, by President Alfred Naqqash. Lebanese independence was proclaimed on November 26, 1941.[42] In 1942, the United States sent a consul-general (George Wadsworth) to the mandates. Saudi Arabia and Egypt recognized Syria, but not Lebanon. Both mandates, however, recognized each other. *Shaykh* Taj al-Din had a hard time in Syria, as both pan-Arab nationalists and Muslim fundamentalists fomented against him and against France. In February 1942, however, some progress occurred in the handing over of Druze and 'Alawite territories by French officials to Syrian control. At British urging, General Catroux set elections for June 1942. Axis victories (under Rommel) in North Africa led Catroux to postpone the elections. De Gaulle visited the mandates again in August and September 1942, and said it was premature to hold elections. He also arrogantly and unrealistically stated that control of the Middle Eastern Military Command should be transferred to France from Britain. The British rebuffed him.[43]

After the British victory over the Germans at El-Alamein in November 1942, Catroux restored the Syrian and Lebanese constitutions, and declared that elections would be allowed in the near future. The Allied leaders Churchill and Roosevelt met for a conference in Casablanca, Morocco, in January 1943. General de Gaulle was invited to join. The results of the conference included an Allied demand for unconditional surrender from the Axis powers; the start of preparations for forthcoming Anglo-American invasions of Sicily and Normandy; the intensification of the strategic bombing campaign over Germany; and a continued emphasis on anti-U-boat operations in the Atlantic. The ambitious de Gaulle resented Allied preferences for General Henri Giraud as commander in chief of the French Army. Even though he and Giraud became co-presidents of the French National Committee for Liberation (in May 1943), he subsequently schemed to oust Giraud from this position and from that of commander in chief.

It was de Gaulle's insistence on maintaining the prewar status quo of French power in the world that most clearly shaped events in Syria and

Lebanon over the next two years. Catroux went to Algiers to receive his next orders in February and March 1943. When he returned to Beirut, though, he announced that power would soon be transferred to the Syrian and Lebanese governments (he specified in three months' time). He was shortly transferred to Algiers as commissioner for Islamic Affairs, and was replaced by Jean Helleu, whose attitudes regarding French power in the Middle East closely resembled those of de Gaulle.[44] Sensing advantages in the change of leadership, the Lebanese Maronite head of state, Eyub Tabet, caused a stir among Lebanese Muslims by moving to enfranchise mainly Maronite Lebanese *emigrés* who had not become citizens elsewhere, a move that would have drastically altered the political balance of power within Lebanon. There was much Muslim unrest, and Tabet had to be removed.[45]

In the elections that followed, Bishara al-Khuri became president of Lebanon, and Shukhri al-Quwalti became president of Syria. In late October 1943, both governments requested a formal ending of the mandates, and their assumption of full powers by alterations of their constitutions. Helleu went to Algiers to consult with his Free French superiors in the French National Committee on October 28. The Lebanese Chamber meanwhile anxiously began making plans to change the constitution unilaterally on November 8. Helleu was infuriated upon his return to Beirut on November 9. Two days later he immoderately ordered the arrest of the Lebanese president, most of his ministers, and some deputies. The republic's constitution was suspended and the chamber was dissolved.[46]

There were immediate and violent responses throughout the country, and Helleu imposed a curfew. A few ministers and deputies met in the mountains and claimed they were starting a government in exile, protected by Druze warriors. Even the Maronite patriarch supported them. Helleu could of course gauge the attitude of de Gaulle, and he was acting in a manner that he believed appropriate for the maintenance of French prestige. The British and other Allies, however, did not agree with the propriety of Helleu's goals or his tactics, and immediate protests were made to the French National Committee. The Allied position was that the Middle East needed to be a theater free from civil unrest, so that troops would not have to be pulled out of more vital theaters to keep the peace there. Helleu's actions were setting the stage for a greater confrontation, which possibly could be exploited by the Axis. De Gaulle felt compelled to shift his position, and he ordered Catroux to Beirut on November 18 to recall Helleu and nullify all of his decrees. Yves Chataigneau took over from Helleu, and from the end of November 1943, the French no longer seriously challenged the Syrian and Lebanese claims to independence.[47]

The French presence lingered, however, for another three years. In 1944, many governmental departments were handed over to the republics, from the post office to the Sûreté, but a lingering problem was the continued

French control of the native auxiliary forces, the *Troupes Spéciales*. General Beynet took over from Chataigneau in February 1944, and the slow and methodical transfer of powers came to cause unrest, especially in Syria.[48] Anti-French demonstrations, caused by the slow pace of change, erupted in Syria in January 1945, and in response the French military held a parade as a show of who still had power in reality in the country. In May, there was a major escalation of the level of violence. De Gaulle sent in Senegalese troops (whom the Syrians detested) to restore order, and French artillery shelled Syrian cities, causing several hundred casualties.[49]

The British intervened, sending troops into Syria and actually escorting French troops to rural military bases away from the cities.[50] When British troops withdrew, they openly handed power over to the Syrians, not the French. On June 21, 1945, Syria and Lebanon announced their intention to dismiss French officials and judges, and their assumption of control over the *Troupes Spéciales*. They had the support of Arabs elsewhere, in the Arab League (formed in Alexandria, Egypt, in October 1944). The new republics were anxious to form their own native military systems, and their new ministries of defense set about the task of creating some of the first modern Arab armies.

Both republics were invited to the United Nations Conference in San Francisco (April–June 1945), and gradually most countries came to recognize their independence over the next year. After the end of World War II, an Anglo-French Agreement on Military Evacuation was signed (December 13, 1945). The French withdrawal lasted until 1946, and Lebanon took longer because of the more numerous French installations located there. French naval forces finally departed Lebanese waters in the fall of 1946, signaling the conclusion of the mandates' agonizingly slow demise.[51]

CONCLUSION

World War I had brought about the creation of the mandates as a curious extension of the French Islamic Empire. The events of World War II in turn caused their demise. Within twenty years from the end of the war, the rest of the French Empire, possessing a very different history, would follow suit. The French experience in World War II was catastrophic—a decisive defeat by Germany; occupation in the north and the setting up of an Axis puppet state; the salvation of the mother country coming from abroad. De Gaulle believed that the status of France in the wider world depended upon the continued possession of each of the various components of the empire, including the mandates.

The Arabs, however, resented the lingering presence of the French in what was supposed to be a temporary situation of limited mandatory control, on behalf of the League of Nations. De Gaulle's ideas of the greatness of France emerged from his conception of history, and Syria and Lebanon had a long history of French influence, stretching back to the crusades. It was crucial to de Gaulle that France not be viewed as a lesser partner among the Allies, and he did not wish to withdraw from the Middle East without a fight. Both the Middle East and North Africa served as major theaters of World War II, and while no one among the Allies disputed rightful ownership of Algeria and the Sahara by France, a different situation prevailed in Syria and Lebanon. De Gaulle did not want to relinquish control of the mandates under circumstances that he believed would bring dishonor to France, and so he tested the limits of the Allied interests in Syria and Lebanon. In 1946, however, France completed its half-hearted departure from mandatory control in the Middle East at the urging of its British, American, and Soviet Allies. Events in the mandates shaped events soon to unfold in the rest of the French Empire.

The Beginning of the End of the French Islamic Empire

THE LIBERATION OF FRANCE

France had been under Nazi occupation since June 1940, and in 1944, Allied invasion forces began the process of liberation. On June 6, Operation Overlord landed the first waves of 132,500 American, British, and Canadian troops in Normandy, breaching Hitler's "Atlantic Wall" defenses.[1] De Gaulle was furious that, as in Operation Torch, there was little Free French participation. Another prong of Allied invasions, called Operation Anvil, landed in Vichy territory on the Mediterranean coast on August 15 and began moving up the Rhône valley. The Allied breakout from the Normandy coast occurred on July 9 at St.-Lo (American) and Caen (British), and the advance on Paris was begun. The French Forces of the Interior (FFI) had been formed for underground resistance, and rose up in Paris as the Allies crossed the Seine.[2] Parisians rioted against German occupation forces on August 24, and on the following day, General de Gaulle and his Free French forces were the first Allied troops allowed to enter the city.[3]

Much effort had been taken to make the composition of the Free French forces more ethnically French. Colonials had played a large role in North Africa, as well as in Free French operations in Italy, alongside American and British troops. De Gaulle insisted, however, that the liberation forces slated for France be from metropolitan France, not the colonies. This decision disappointed colonial troops who had thus far served loyally under the French flag.

Free French soldiers of the First French Army swept north up the Rhône valley with the American Seventh Army in mid-September, and linked up with the American Third Army at Dijon. As most of France was being liberated by American, British, and Free French forces, the Soviets advanced into Romania in late August 1944, into Bulgaria in early September, and into Hungary in early November. After the failure of the last major German advance in the West at the Ardennes in December (the Battle of the Bulge, December 16–25), the Allies surrounded Germany. In 1945 combined American, British, and French forces advanced into Germany from the West, while the Soviets marched into East Prussia, Poland, and the Danube valley. The final drive on Berlin was by Soviet forces in late April and early May, and after Hitler committed suicide, the Germans surrendered first to the Western Allies in Reims, France (May 7), and then to the Soviets in Berlin (May 9).

De Gaulle's diplomacy and his uncompromising attitude of France's importance had succeeded in maneuvering France into a position of global prominence again. France was given one of the four Allied zones of occupation in Germany and France also got a sphere in the German capital of Berlin. The Free French proceeded to set up a provisional government, which in turn would create the Fourth Republic. Vichy leaders were put on trial for treason, and Pétain was sentenced to death on August 15, 1945. His sentence was commuted to life imprisonment. Laval was sentenced to death on October 9, and he was executed on October 15.[4] Elections to the Constituent Assembly were held on October 21, and the results showed a swing to the Left among the French electorate. Communists and Socialists won a good many seats, to the chagrin of de Gaulle's supporters. The assembly, however, voted in de Gaulle as the president of the provisional government on November 16.

De Gaulle formed a Cabinet of National Union on November 21. Over the next two months, however, the general found himself increasingly at odds with the leftists within the government. He was frustrated that he did not receive the kind of deference from his political colleagues that he had been accustomed to receiving from his soldiers. On January 20, 1946, de Gaulle abruptly resigned his post. He subsequently helped organize a non-communist movement called the *Rassemblement du Peuple Français* in April 1947, whose goal was to start a grass-roots consensus for national unity and reform of the political landscape in France. The party made a strong showing in municipal elections held in October 1947.[5]

De Gaulle was replaced as president of the provisional government by Felix Gouin (January–July 1946) and then Georges Bidault (June 1946–January 1947). French voters agreed on a new constitution for the Fourth Republic on October 13, 1946, with a reduction in the powers of the president. The Fourth Republic survived for thirteen years, and reluctantly presided over the dissolution of most of the French Empire.

TUNISIA AND BOURGUIBA

Of the various North African possessions of the French, Tunisia had one of the most unusual arrangements in internal government. The bey of

Tunis had been preserved by the French as a figurehead with two ministers from the time of the French takeover in 1881. His continued presence was intended to placate Muslims by providing an illusion of a cooperative government. The bey's authority was limited to presiding over the colony's Muslims (theoretically), although the French resident-general had the final say in all matters within the colony pertaining to both the Muslims and the European settler population. Most politically conscious Tunisians recognized this arrangement as a sham, and in 1907 the Young Tunisian party was formed. It had little impact.

The French resident-general in Tunis encouraged European settlement in the colony. Eventually, about one-tenth of Tunisia's farmland was in the hands of the European settlers. Italians were far more numerous in the early years than the French, and tended to possess smaller landholdings than the French, who held the larger estates. The French and Italian farms were concentrated in the more fertile areas to the north and east. There were also many European settlers in the cities of the colony, as in neighboring Algeria. About half of the population of Tunis was European. The resident-general presided over the modernization of the Tunisian physical infrastructure, including port reconstruction and expansion, and the extension of the country's rail lines and road networks.

In 1918, the *Destour* (Constitution) party formed. It was clearly a pro-independence movement, and was very active in the 1920s, but less so in the 1930s. Younger members were dissatisfied at the lack of substantive change, and formed an offshoot called the *Neo-Destour* party in the 1930s. The party secretary-general was a provincial lawyer and journalist who had studied at the Sorbonne in Paris, Habib Bourguiba. Bourguiba was not particularly anti-French, and he even had a French wife. But he favored the tactic of confrontational activism, and was deported as a consequence for two years in September 1934. This was the start of a tumultuous career in which the secretary-general would spend a total of eleven years in French prisons. He was freed in 1936, but was arrested again in 1938 with other *Neo-Destour* party leaders.[6]

Growing fears of Axis expansion slowed down the trial proceedings in French Tunisia, and the trial was still pending in 1939 when World War II broke out. In 1940 Bourguiba and the other prisoners were transferred to Vichy France. The Germans saw Bourguiba as a potential asset, and they requested that he be released to their custody in November 1942. They promptly handed him over to the Italians. Mussolini was charged with trying to get a pro-Axis concession from Bourguiba, which might enhance the now-precarious Axis position in North Africa. Mussolini housed Bourguiba and the other *Neo-Destour* leaders sumptuously at the Palazzo Piacentini in Rome. Bourguiba was pressed to make a public statement to the Tunisian people in favor of the Axis.

The Afrika Korps was retreating to Tunisia from Montgomery's British forces, and Vichy forces in Morocco and Algeria had surrendered to the

Anglo-American Allies. Thus, Tunisia was going to be the scene of the Axis' last stand in the North African Theater.[7] Bourguiba, however, was secretly pro-Allied, and after a few months all he said over the radio to the people of Tunisia was to prepare for war and to rally around Bey Moncif. Unable to coax more from him, the Italians allowed Bourguiba and his *Neo-Destour* colleagues to return to Tunisia in March 1943. The Nazis tried to get him to retreat to Germany, but he refused.

From 1943 to 1945 Bourguiba prodded the Free French and the Allies to allow Tunisia to become independent. He had no support or sympathy from de Gaulle. Realizing that he was a marked man in Tunisia, Bourguiba escaped in disguise through the empty stretches of Libya to Egypt, and linked up with the Arab League in Cairo. He spent the next four years touring Arab countries, East Asia, and America, trying to acquire some international support for the cause of Tunisian independence. The Arab League's leaders disapproved of his relatively moderate approach, but publicly backed him as the legitimate Arab leader of Tunisia. Salah Ben Yusuf was left with the task of party organization as secretary-general in Bourguiba's absence (a position he held through 1955). Ben Yusuf gradually became more radicalized than Bourguiba, and he supported the more direct and violent kinds of approaches advocated by the Arab League.

But in 1949, Bourguiba got the opportunity to return to Tunisia without reprisal, signaling at least a temporary change in the French government's colonial attitudes.[8] The Tunisians were allowed to form their own ministry in 1950, and the French began to negotiate with Ben Yusuf. Bourguiba went to Paris that year to discuss Tunisian independence with the French government, but returned to Tunisia having made little progress. French leaders seemed sure of the necessity of reform, but unsure of the proper pace. The government's position thus was remarkably similar to what had been the case six years earlier with regard to Syria and Lebanon.

Tunisia was an area like Syria and Lebanon, with a venerable lineage of French history. It had been the location of St. Louis's last crusade, and the place where he died in 1270. Over 100,000 European colonists lived there (mainly French and Italian). There were sound political reasons for French hesitation to withdraw precipitously from a historical sphere of influence and from a substantial settler population, even if the territory were merely a protectorate, as Tunisia was. Bourguiba was indeed aware of the cause of the French hesitancy, but he was confident that history was on his side now.

In May 1951, the bey instructed his ministers to request of the French the creation of a Tunisian parliament. Bourguiba visited Britain that August, speaking to sympathetic members of the Labour party and even participating in a BBC radio debate.[9] He stated that a model similar to the British Commonwealth would work for the French Empire. The French government was not happy with his public relations successes. Negotiations between the two sides continued into mid-December, when French officials abruptly ended them. A fateful decision had been made in Paris to send into Tunisia a conservative new resident-general charged with the suppression of nationalistic sentiment, Jean de Hautecloque.[10]

In January 1952, Bourguiba and other *Neo-Destour* party leaders were arrested and held at various locations within the protectorate. A few weeks later, the Tunisian ministry officials were arrested. Salah Ben Yusuf, however, managed to escape to Cairo. French settler pressure had a good deal to do with the about-face in policy and the crackdown on nationalist activity. The central government in Paris was actually consulted only after the decision had been made in the field.[11] But because of the perennial instability of the Fourth Republic and the frequent turnovers in government, there were very few moments in the thirteen-year history of the Fourth Republic when one can say that there was a coherent policy in action regarding the various sections of the empire. The French colonial civil order broke down throughout Tunisia in 1953, as supporters of the *Neo-Destour* party organized protests and acts of terror against the French establishment. Armed bands of rebels roamed the hills. This was not an Islamic insurgency, however, but a secular, European-inspired type of independence movement.

France had begun to experience upheavals all over the empire by now, but was trying to hold on to as much as possible. The dramatic events unfolding in French Indochina in the spring and summer of 1954 would have a large impact on the shape of France's global empire. Ho Chi Minh's communist insurgency in Vietnam dated from World War II. Vichy forces handed power over to the Imperial Japanese Army in Indochina in 1940, in keeping with Axis aims of global cooperation. After the Normandy landings in 1944, however, French colonial forces in Indochina went over to de Gaulle and rose up against the Japanese. The Japanese Army reacted with characteristic brutality and crushed the French. When the war was ended, the departing Japanese troops handed power over to Ho's Viet Minh in North Vietnam. Even though Ho's dubious legitimacy derived from the Axis, France did not have much support in North Vietnam. South Vietnam was traditionally more pro-French and more Catholic than the north. Despite receiving substantial support from the United States, in accordance with that country's "containment" policy, France's position in the north continued to erode until Foreign Legion units were encircled and forced to surrender on May 7, 1954. France no longer had the resolve to hold Vietnam, and an armistice was drawn up on July 20. French forces withdrew and Vietnam was partitioned into a communist north and a non-communist south.

The administration now saw Tunisia in the same regard, as expendable. That July, Prime Minister Mendes-France and Marshal Juin flew to Tunis and finally recognized the right of Tunisia to independence. Negotiations got underway in France, and Bourguiba was released and allowed to go to Paris to participate. This time, the negotiations went well, with a liberal regime in power in Paris, thoroughly committed to ending the current colonial arrangements. Tunisian independence proceeded, even as the French regime responded harshly to the simultaneous revolt in Algeria in late January 1955, and after Mendes-France resigned as a consequence of a vote of no-confidence in the government's handling of the unfolding Algerian crisis. Franco-Tunisian conventions were signed on June 3 that allowed for a measure of self-government, but they did not go as far as many *Neo-Destour* party leaders wanted. They felt it was still too provisional of an arrangement. An independence movement was then underway in Morocco, as well, and the Tunisians jealously eyed the quickly unfolding events in the nearby protectorate.

Ben Yusuf returned to Tunisia from Cairo and declared the conventions to be a betrayal of Tunisian national aspirations. The *Neo-Destour* party, though, thought he was too radical, and deposed him as secretary-general. He resorted to campaigns of terrorism and assassination, but was forced to flee back to Egypt. His continued scheming was a source of ongoing tension between Egypt and Tunisia. Finally, on March 20, 1956, the new Franco-Tunisian treaty was signed, in which Tunisia became an independent country.[12] Most French and Italian colonists fled the country *en masse* and went to France. Some French troops, however, stayed on at strategic locations for a few years, for example, at the Bizerte Naval Base. Bourguiba, the national hero, became president of the National Assembly and prime minister. Tunisia joined the United Nations in November 1956. Theoretically, the country was a constitutional monarchy under the bey until 1957, when the bey was overthrown and a republic was proclaimed (July 25). Not surprisingly, Bourguiba became the first president of the Tunisian Republic.

Relations between France and Tunisia were tense through the period of the Algerian revolt, as the Algerian *Front de Liberation Nationale* (FLN) received support from and through Tunisia. French reprisals on Tunisian soil, which harbored FLN operatives, brought harsh criticisms from the chief NATO allies of France, the United States and Britain (as well as from the United Nations). The most obvious such case was the February 1958 French bombing of Saqiyat, Tunisia, home to an FLN support base. The attack resulted in some seventy Tunisian deaths.[13] When Bourguiba demanded French evacuation of Bizerte in 1960, tensions mounted again, and a battle erupted in the summer of 1961, which France handily won, and which also resulted in UN criticism of France.[14] In the new global political climate, France was hard pressed to salvage any of its former colonial prestige.[15]

MOROCCO AND THE SULTAN

The establishment of the French protectorate over Morocco dated to the Treaty of Fez in 1912, which was signed by Sultan Mulay Hafid. The French presence was overseen by a resident-general at first, as in Tunisia (later by a proconsul), the first of whom was the famous General Lyautey.[16] The brutal pacification of Berber tribes in the interior lasted through the 1920s until 1934.[17] Some southern tribal chiefs sided with the French, including the *Glawi* (later, the pasha) of Marrakesh, who was rewarded for his loyalty to the resident-general by being able to rule a "state within the state" at Marrakesh.[18] The French chose to maintain the Filali branch of sultans (formerly *sharifs*) of Morocco as figureheads, in an attempt to appease the Muslim tribesmen. In 1927 France officially chose Muhammad V Ibn Yusuf over his brothers, believing he was less of a threat to French interests than they were.[19] He was no pawn, however. According to the peculiar arrangements decided to by the French, the sultan had to countersign all Moroccan decrees before they became valid. In time, Muhammad V would exercise a kind of veto power in French policies.

A 1930 piece of legislation unofficially called the "Berber Decree" was issued to facilitate the administration of the country.[20] It legally separated the Berber areas (primarily rural districts) from the Arab areas in Morocco. Urban Muslims regarded it as a "divide and rule" tactic (which it was) and also as the first step in an attempt to convert the Berbers to Christianity (which it was not). The same thinking was behind the decree in Morocco as in the decree of the same time period in Algeria, namely, that the Berbers were a Mediterranean people distinct from the Arabs, with whom the French could conduct business more effectively than with the Arabs. Much domestic unrest in Morocco resulted, and Muslims from other areas also protested the decree. But, the French bureaucracy that became entrenched in Morocco could easily sustain such criticism. The all-encompassing system of bureaucracy established by the French in Morocco was comparable to that of Algeria, despite the provisional nature of the protectorate established by treaty in 1912.[21]

The French established local tribal chiefs (*qa'ids*) whom they regarded as particularly loyal to them in authority in the countryside. The educational system fostered by the French in Morocco (which included French and traditional Islamic schools) provided a learning experience that inadvertently fostered the nationalist cause by exposing the brightest students to Western concepts of statehood and to France's own revolutionary history. The French regime modernized Morocco's infrastructure by constructing new roads, ports, and rail lines, as in Algeria and Tunisia. Tangier had a special status as an international city and trading capital. New towns were also built by the French outside the older towns for the European settler population. Several thousand French and Spanish industrial workers, administrators, and some farmers came to Morocco to take advantage of the economic opportunities provided by the French Protectorate.[22]

The regime offered fairly liberal trade policies with the outside world, especially at the port of Casablanca. Muslims came in from the countryside in great numbers to the new cities to work, mainly in menial jobs. Spain still held onto its old outposts of Ceuta and Melilla on Morocco's Mediterranean coast. From 1919 to 1926, Spanish forces subdued Muslim tribesmen in the interior in the "War of Melilla," and a Spanish company began searching for minerals in the Rif Mountains in 1928. There was less obvious ethnic tension between European rulers and Muslim subjects in the Spanish zone, and public education there was in Arabic rather than Spanish.[23]

The 1940s saw the rise of a Western-style (and socialist-oriented) independence movement in French and Spanish Morocco. The rise and fall of the Axis regimes probably hastened the onset of the movement. Vichy forces were stationed in Morocco, as elsewhere in the empire. World War II came to Morocco in dramatic fashion in November 1942, when Patton's prong of Operation Torch landed at Casablanca. American forces overwhelmed the minimal Vichy opposition, and set up bases for the advance eastward, experiencing no opposition from the Arab and Berber Muslims. The February Casablanca Conference between Roosevelt, Churchill, and de Gaulle, held on Moroccan soil, demonstrated to the Muslims how effective was Allied (especially American) power that such a meeting could be held a mere three months after the defeat of Vichy French forces within the protectorate. Roosevelt spoke in private to Sultan Muhammad V during the conference, cultivating American ties to Arab Muslim leaders here as he did elsewhere in the Middle East (with Ibn Sa'ud in Arabia, for example).[24] Moroccans were also aware of contemporary events unfolding in the Syrian-Lebanese Mandates on the eastern end of the Mediterranean.

There was thus a convergence of many factors in the creation of the *Istiqlal* (Independence) party in Morocco before the end of World War II.[25] The independence movement was primarily an urban phenomenon, because many of the rural *qa'ids* sided with the French regime, from whom their authority derived. The movement received support from inside the northern Spanish-controlled areas in Morocco, despite the protests of the French. Spanish colonial authorities believed that Spain's position in North Africa would be enhanced by the weakening of French power in Morocco. The Spanish regime in Morocco in time welcomed Muslim nationalists fleeing from the French protectorate. General Francisco Franco was able to enlist the support of Moroccans in his war against the Republican regime, and launched his assault on Republican forces from Spanish Morocco in 1936. In 1945 the administration of the French territory received a substantial number of the French bureaucrats (many of them disgruntled) who were displaced from their positions within the mandatory governments in Syria and Lebanon. Their governing attitudes had been shaped by the sobering experience of having lost part of an empire to Muslims, and their presence certainly did not help Franco-Arab relations in Morocco.

Sultan Muhammad V expressed a public dissatisfaction with French rule and thereby a sympathy for the nationalist cause in 1944 by refusing to sign a decree of the protectorate. Through the late 1940s, Muhammad was drawn further into the nationalist camp.[26] He refused an official French request for a formal disavowal of the nationalists. The nationalists dominated in particular the cities of Fez and Casablanca by the early 1950s. By that time, younger, more radical men had risen to leadership positions in the *Istiqlal* party. Older, more moderate leaders were by now mainly arrested. The colonial regime had banned the party in a climate of great civil unrest in 1952. Resident-General Guillaume used the loyal *qa'ids* to engineer a tribal insurrection against Sultan Muhammad in 1953 to deprive the independence movement of a valuable asset.[27] Guillaume felt that it was necessary to imply a degree of local dissatisfaction with the sultan rather than to simply depose him. Muhammad V was officially "overthrown" and then exiled to Madagascar. He thus met a fate that seemed similar to that of 'Abd al-Qadir, Ahmad Samudu, and 'Abd al-Krim before him, although his end was vastly different from theirs.

The French administration installed in his place a puppet ruler, Sidi Muhammad Ben Arafa.[28] Muhammad V, however, was still recognized as the legitimate sultan within the Spanish territory, even by the high commissioner of Spain. Terrorist actions were undertaken against the French regime that December, as popular anger swelled as a consequence of Muhammad V's deposition. The rebellion continued through 1954, and was primarily an urban phenomenon, as the rural *qa'ids* kept order in the Muslim countryside for the protectorate.[29] Isolated French farms, though, were exposed to attacks by Muslim marauders. Casablanca was a primary focal point of discontent. The "native" quarters of the cities in general were areas of rebellion, and there were frequent attacks on Europeans who entered them.[30]

Guillaume's successor as high commissioner, Francis LaCoste (a Gaullist), tried to implement a series of reforms to blunt Muslim dissatisfaction, including wage reforms, judicial reforms, and administrative decentralization.[31] The reforms had no effect on the revolt, and there were 300 attacks on Europeans in August 1954. Other measures taken by Proconsul Gilbert Grandval from August to September 1955 were designed to appease the Muslims, but did not have the desired effect.[32] Conservative administrators and European settlers (fearful of the loss of their privileged position) reacted severely against Grandval, as well. On August 2, 1955, Muslim extremist nationalists killed fifty European settlers at Oued-Zem and Ait-Amar.[33] A French paramilitary organization called the *Presence Française* was formed to protect French settlers from the Muslim rebels.[34] The entire territory was becoming a scene of chaos.[35]

The French government now came to regard Morocco as a liability. Prime Minister Edgar Faure would tell the National Assembly that Moroccan independence "cannot be denied, nor broken, and we must divert it towards cooperation with France."[36] A northern Muslim uprising was fueled by Muslims across the Spanish border. The southern forces of the *Glawi* at Marrakesh at first helped the French, but then switched sides and supported the independence movement.[37] Parisian officials, however, had already made up their minds to allow Moroccan independence, and Ben Arafa was persuaded to resign to make way for the triumphal return of Muhammad V.[38] The Tunisian resident-general who had negotiated the peace with the Tunisian nationalists became the resident-general of Morocco in 1955, General Pierre Boyer de Latour.[39]

Negotiations to facilitate the transfer of power got underway in the fall of 1955 at Aix-Les-Bains in France. A formal treaty recognizing Moroccan independence was signed in the spring of 1956.[40] As in Tunisia, an exodus of Europeans occurred. The Moroccans called their new regime the Kingdom of Morocco (while the French called it the Sherifan Empire), and the sultan was now referred to as king.[41] The *Istiqlal* party did not follow through with elaborate political changes and create a republic, as the *Neo-Destourians* would do in Tunisia.[42] Much of the Spanish zone was handed over to Morocco in 1956, but Spain retained (and still retains) Ceuta and Melilla.[43] Tangier's special status was ended shortly after independence, as it was incorporated into a new Moroccan economy.[44] Much of the old French system of administration was retained in the country. The core of the new army, for example, was the old French colonial Berber (*Goum*) regiments, and there were a few Moroccan Muslim officers who had risen in the ranks of the French Army, who now came home to serve in the new Moroccan armed forces. The *Glawi* coincidentally died of natural causes shortly after the granting of independence, and several members of his family were arrested. A number or rural *qa'ids* retained their powers, as it was convenient for the new regime to rely upon them, as had the French Protectorate.

FRANCE, THE ARABS, AND THE COLD WAR

Charles de Gaulle had assured France a place of prominence in the postwar diplomatic arena. France was one of the founding members of the United Nations, French became one of the organization's official languages, and France has remained one of the permanent members of the Security Council. French forces, along with those of the Americans, British, and Soviets, occupied a part of the former Nazi core territory at the close of World War II, and administered one of the four Allied zones in Berlin. France played an important supporting role in most of the early Cold War clashes between the American-dominated West and Soviet-dominated East. French leaders, however, regarded the preservation of the empire as significant as the delicate and volatile American-Soviet Cold

War.[45] As the events of the Cold War unfolded through the 1960s, French leaders recognized that American priorities did not include the maintenance of European (mainly British and French) colonial territories as a major part of Cold War policy.

The American approach, through the Truman, Eisenhower, and Kennedy administrations, was to support the rising tide of Third World nationalism and to try to win over the new governments to the American Cold War position through economic subsidies. The French position was to try to hold onto the empire to maintain the country's global prestige. They felt that the maintenance of the empire was the surest way to guarantee the containment of communism.[46] Generally speaking, the British came to terms with the American position easier than the French. The Marshall Plan, starting in 1947, offered billions of dollars in aid to European countries devastated by World War II.[47] The idea was to rebuild a thoroughly capitalist environment in which neither communism nor fascism could take root in the future. French foreign minister (and sometime prime minister) Georges Bidault helped get general Western European support behind the Marshall Plan. France in time received $2.7 billion in Marshall Plan money from the United States.

France played only a supporting role in the first flash point of the Cold War, the Berlin Airlift (1948–1949). The Soviet blockade of the Western sectors of the city was intended to force their submission into the Soviet orbit.[48] American president Harry Truman stopped Stalin's blockade by Operation Vittles, an American and British airlift made possible by the then-apparent American air superiority. The North Atlantic Treaty Organization (NATO) was formed in 1949 by the Western Allies as a consequence of the Berlin crisis to create a unified military front that might deter any future Soviet threat to Western interests.[49] France was a founding member of NATO, and Article Six of the NATO Treaty explicitly included "the Algerian departments of France" in the mutual defense pact.[50]

France played a more substantial role in the Cold War's next confrontation—the Korean War (1950–1953).[51] Kim il-Sung's North Korea had been established in 1945 by the Soviets after their invasion into the northern part of the peninsula, in one of the closing moments of World War II. Stalin supplied him with some tanks and airplanes, and tentatively approved his plans for the conquest of the American-influenced southern Republic of Korea, which at the time had no tanks or air force of its own. Kim had approached both Stalin and Mao Zedong of the People's Republic of China (PRC) regarding his plans. Stalin agreed to the sending of Soviet troops and equipment (in return for several hundred tons of lead), provided that the United States did not get involved. He was not willing to risk World War III over Korea. Mao, on the other hand, was too involved with trying to absorb Tibet, Sinkiang, and Taiwan to agree to help. But when the war unfolded, and the UN forces that came to South Korea's help were overwhelmingly American units led by American general Douglas MacArthur, Stalin did not send in much assistance (a few fighter planes), but Mao did intervene, fearing an American invasion of the PRC.[52] The UN forces intervened in September 1950, landing at Pusan and Inchon, and they forced the North Korean forces out of South Korea. France created a UN battalion in August 1950, and its 5,030 men saw service at a number of important battles, including Heartbreak Ridge (it had 270 killed, and about a thousand wounded in the war).

France's main overseas concern in the early 1950s was in Indochina (Indochine), where it was losing control of Vietnam in the bloody colonial war against the communist forces of Ho Chi Minh.[53] Despite receiving substantial American military aid, the French were unable to hold the north (or unwilling to make the sacrifices necessary to do so), after the loss at Dien Bien Phu on May 7, 1954.[54] The government of Pierre Mendes-France (June 1954–February 1955) lost no time in agreeing to an armistice and a partition (into a communist north and a non-communist south in July 1954). America had supported France in this colonial undertaking because it clearly fit into the category of containing communism. The French defeat at Dien Bien Phu and subsequent decision to withdraw from Indochina had wide-ranging implications throughout the empire.

That very November, the Algerian war of independence broke out. French leaders resented the subsequent lack of support from the United States in their attempt to hold onto the empire. The culmination of the rift between the two powers was in 1966, when then President de Gaulle actually pulled France out of NATO. Many French military men, such as General Raoul Salan (governor-general of Algeria), sought to link the Algerian FLN with communism in general and the methods of the Viet Minh in particular.[55]

In the month of June 1956, the British evacuated the Suez Canal and the pan-Arab leader Colonel Jamal 'Abd al-Nasser became president of Egypt. Nasser's dream was to unite all Arab countries into a superstate (with himself at its head) and to push out all European influence from the Middle East. As Nasser drew closer to the Soviet Union, the United States and Britain refused to help finance the construction of the Aswan High Dam on the Nile that July. Nasser seized control of the Suez Canal on July 26, and took over the French- and British-owned Suez Canal Company. In seizing the Suez Canal, Nasser planned to use the canal revenues to finance the construction of the Aswan Dam. Nasser actively supported the Algerian independence movement and sought to undermine the somewhat moderate Arab governments of Tunisia and Morocco and replace them with ardently pan-Arab regimes. The French believed that their hold on Algeria would be more secure with Nasser somehow removed from power in Egypt.[56] They believed that the FLN would collapse without

Nasser's support. Both the French and British governments feared that if some action were not taken immediately, Nasser might at any moment shut down the canal and be able to stop the importation of petroleum into Europe.[57]

Although twenty-two countries met in London to discuss the problem in August, little progress was made, and France and Britain referred the crisis to the UN Security Council on September 23. The following month (October 24), under Nasser's aegis, Egypt, Jordan, and Syria created a joint command of their armed forces. The ongoing Arab-Israeli conflict provided an opportunity for France and Britain. Israel was searching for international support for what it regarded as a preemptive strike against hostile Arab neighbors, while France and Britain were searching for a justification for intervention to preserve a degree of their eroding hegemony.

The liberal regime of Mendes-France failed a vote of no-confidence in regard to the handling of the ongoing Algerian crisis (discussed more fully in the next chapter) and on February 5, 1955, he resigned. Then Prime Minister Guy Mollet authorized French participation in a joint operation with the British and Israelis to retake the Suez Canal from Nasser.[58] On October 29, 1956, Israeli troops invaded the Sinai peninsula and seized Egyptian territory. They advanced to control one side of the canal. When Egypt rejected an Anglo-French ultimatum for a cease-fire, London and Paris moved forward with a plan of overwhelming armed intervention. The Anglo-French plan was code named Operation Musketeer, and was prepared on the island of Cyprus. There was some resentment that French commanders (Rear Admiral Lancelot, Major General Beaufre, and Brigadier General Brohon) were assigned to serve as deputies under British officers.[59]

Many of the French units involved in Musketeer came from service in Algeria. Some motorized units departed directly from Algiers, while most went to Marseilles, and then on to Cyprus. French participation was planned by General Maurice Challe (who would come to play an enormously important role in the history of Algeria). Service branches represented in the operation included air force and naval aviation units, mechanized units, and elite paratroopers under General Jacques Massu (who also would play a huge role in Algerian history). Among the paratroopers were both colonial and Foreign Legion regiments. Altogether, French forces were more numerous than their British counterparts.

French warships and French planes taking off from Israeli air bases attacked Egyptian airfields, covering the Israeli advance. French planes also targeted Egyptian naval vessels at Alexandria. French and British ground forces successfully attacked the Canal Zone and Israeli troops seized the Gaza Strip. On November 5, the Anglo-French forces captured Port Said and Port Fuad.[60] The United States, however, did not support this activity and demanded a cease-fire from its NATO allies.[61] It looked to

Eisenhower to be too heavy-handed, and he felt it could serve to drive other Third World (particularly Arab Muslim) populations toward the Soviets. The Soviet Union vigorously protested the allied intervention. The United Nations weighed in on November 7, also demanding a cease-fire. UN peace-keeping troops arrived on November 21 at the Canal Zone, and the Anglo-French forces finally withdrew on December 22.

The failure to secure their objectives at Suez embittered the French and British policymakers. But while the British maneuvered to repair any damage done to Anglo-American relations, France entrenched to hold onto Algeria, despite American disapproval.[62] The British, on the other hand, came to recognize that the remnant colonial empires were expendable and less significant globally than were close relations with the American super-power across the Atlantic.[63] Algerian FLN revolutionaries were spurred to a flurry of terrorist activities directed against the French colonial regime as a consequence of the Anglo-French withdrawal from the Suez.[64]

The FLN's provisional government, the GPRA, sent emissaries to several communist regimes to garner international support for the movement.[65] In December 1958, emissaries led by Ben Khedda (the most Marxist-oriented FLN leader) went to Moscow and Peking on behalf of the FLN's military wing, the *Armeé de Liberation nationale* (ALN). Zhou Enlai thanked the ALN for tying down NATO units.[66] The People's Republic of China promised rather substantial weapons support. The Soviet Union, however, promised nothing. Subsequent missions went abroad in September 1959 and April 1960. North Korea and North Viet-nam were visited in East Asia. Yugoslavia was most sympathetic to the GPRA, because the FLN's style suited that of Tito. The Soviets officially supported the French and Algerian communist parties, and they in turn supported the rights of poor *colon* industrial workers within Algeria. The Soviets also distrusted the Islamic basis of some FLN doctrines and poli-cies, because they feared the revolutionary potential of Islam within their own borders (in Central Asia and the Caucasus). While the Cold War played a role in shaping France's colonial priorities, it was not in the man-ner France desired—a linkage between Algeria and broader Cold War issues—and successive French leaders came to feel betrayed by NATO. The Cold War world turned out to be much more politically complicated than French civilian and military officials had believed.

THE END OF EMPIRE SOUTH OF THE SAHARA

Late in 1944, General de Gaulle organized a conference of sub-Saharan African leaders at Brazzaville, Congo.[67] Representatives of all the territo-ries in French West Africa and French Equatorial Africa were present. De Gaulle offered them social and economic reforms in the near future in return for their loyalty to the cause of Free France in the war. The Brazzaville Conference had the unexpected consequence of serving as the starting point for the dissolution of the French Empire in Africa south of the Sahara. The territories' prospective reforms would have an impact on both Muslim areas and non-Muslim areas. Each territory was to be granted a separate constitution after the war. Territorial assemblies and *Grands Conseiles* were to be elected in each territory via universal suffrage by a two-tiered electoral system of Africans and Europeans (the latter consisting strictly of businessmen and settlers).[68] The quasi-federal structure of French West Africa and French Equatorial Africa were to be maintained.

These plans indicated that ultimately the sub-Saharan African portion of the empire was to become part of a Union of France and its overseas territories.[69] Sub-Saharan Africa was less important strategically to France than the Maghrib, where there was of course a sizable European settlement. The only Europeans in sub-Saharan French Africa were businessmen, bureaucrats, soldiers, and clerics stationed there temporarily. This was in contrast to British Africa, where there were significant numbers of European settlers in Kenya, the Rhodesias, and South Africa. While Britain came to treat each colony separately in regard to issues of independence, France followed a common policy and a common timetable for all its African colonies south of the Sahara. Significantly, France seemed prepared to jettison the sub-Saharan portion of its empire before North Africa, due to the lack of a European presence there, the distance of those colonies from the mother country, and the lack of strategic significance attached to the area.

The Second French Constitution of 1946 incorporated the ideas of the Brazzaville Conference. The transformation of the empire into a union actually began that year with the creation in Paris of the *Assembleé de l'Union française*. In ten years, representatives from the overseas territories would be eligible for election in the French National Assembly and Senate. The two basic approaches taken by sub-Saharan African leaders toward achieving independence from France were: (1) an emphasis on maintaining the larger territorial federations or (2) an emphasis on sovereignty within the smaller territories. The first approach was championed by Ahmed Sékou Touré (a Muslim postal union leader and Marxist in Guinea), while the latter approach was promoted by Félix Houphouet-Boigny (a Catholic medical doctor in Ivory Coast who became close to de Gaulle).[70] Both men helped found an inter-territorial political party called the *Rassemblement Democratique Africain* (RDA) in 1946.[71] The RDA was influenced by the French Communist party early on, and the colonial government opposed it at first. The French regime worked to split the RDA from the communists. The split occurred in 1950, and from then on, the French government worked with the RDA. Within seven years, the party virtually controlled seven of the twelve French sub-Saharan African countries. The differences between the two dominant leaders Sékou Touré and

Houphouet-Boigny remained, however, and continued to drive a rift in the RDA until, in 1958, a definitive separation occurred upon the introduction of de Gaulle's constitution.

Gaston Defferre, the French minister for overseas territories, helped push through the *Loi Cadre* (Enabling Law) in 1956, which gave a measure of self-government to sub-Saharan French Africa.[72] It emphasized territorial, not federal, government, which would result in the eventual creation of twelve independent states rather than two superstate federations. African territorial leaders were now able to serve in the French National Assembly, and Houphouet-Boigny was elected to represent Ivory Coast in 1946 (ten years later, he was a cabinet minister in the French government).[73] The pro-Marxist Sékou Touré was elected as Guinea's deputy to the National Assembly in 1956.

Algeria was where the primary French colonial interest lay, and as the FLN independence movement got underway there in November 1954, events within Algeria came to have an enormous impact on the independence movements in other parts of the French Empire, including sub-Saharan Africa. Tunisian and Moroccan independence also played a role in accelerating events in sub-Saharan Africa. As will be discussed more fully in the next chapter, unrest in Algeria became more pronounced in May 1958, when *colons* and the French Army caused the overthrow of the Fourth Republic in Paris, which they believed was poised to abandon them to the will of the Muslim majority, and brought back to power the old general, Charles de Gaulle. De Gaulle's attitude toward the empire, however, had changed in his twelve-year absence from government. He had come to the conclusion that the empire was expendable. His 1958 constitution reflected the idea that the French Union was going to be jettisoned. De Gaulle believed that changing geopolitical circumstances now necessitated a new arrangement in which the union of France and its overseas territories would evolve into a *Communauté* (Community) in which each separate territory was a republic.[74]

Members had full internal self-government, but foreign affairs, defense, and economic policy was to be handled by *Communauté* ministers collectively. Guinea, under Sékou Touré alone refused to accept this, and French forces, administrators, technicians, and funds withdrew from the country in 1958.[75] Sékou Touré wanted immediate independence from France, and he began making overtures to the Soviet Union and various other communist states for assistance. In 1959, de Gaulle pragmatically came to the conclusion that the *Communauté* could evolve into an entity that could include independent African states. Madagascar did not join the *Communauté*, and became fully independent in 1960.[76] Senegal and French Soudan formed a union called the Mali Federation (under Mobido Keita) and followed the path of Madagascar (although their union lasted only a year, and French Soudan retained the name of Mali).[77]

Houphouet-Boigny was in favor of the *Communauté*. He organized a conference in 1959 at Abidjan to discuss the fate of Algeria and its FLN independence movement. Attending were representatives of Ivory Coast, Senegal, Mauritania, Upper Volta, Dahomey, Niger, Cameroon, Central African Republic, French Congo, and Gabon. The events unfolding in Algeria galvanized many African Muslims behind the FLN, but Houphouet-Boigny negotiated a position that opposed unconditional support of the FLN. The conference met again at Brazzaville, Congo (hereafter, members were referred to as the "Brazzaville Group"), where members agreed on common policies and an interterritorial airline, Air Afrique. Among the group's problems was the status of Moroccan claims on Mauritania, and Moroccan opposition to Mauritania's entry into the United Nations. The Brazzaville Group evolved into the Union of African States and Madagascar (UAM). Houphouet-Boigny also formed a *Conseil d'Entente* (Council of Understanding) between the Ivory Coast, Upper Volta, Dahomey, and Niger to coordinate economic and foreign policy. They agreed on financial and technical issues, as well as the idea of a mutual defense pact with France. The *Entente* countries, as well as Senegal and Mauritania, formed a customs union. Eventually, the Organization of African Unity was formed in 1963 and replaced the Francophone *Conseil* and customs union, linking the French-speaking countries with most other former colonies that received independence in the late 1950s and early 1960s from Europe.

All fifteen sub-Saharan territories administered by France became independent between 1958 and 1960. Guinea was the first, under Sékou Touré in 1958, and the fourteen others became independent in the course of 1960, including the two protectorates (turned UN dependencies)—Cameroon and Togo. Houphouet-Boigny and a host of other non-communist African leaders (Muslims as well as Christians) helped make the transition from empire to independence in sub-Saharan Africa somewhat more easy for France. The areas south of the Sahara were less important to French leaders and the French public because there were few settlers there, and the region lacked a strategic importance. These areas also did not have a lineage of French involvement stretching back centuries, as in other areas in the Islamic world like Algeria.

CONCLUSION

The liberation of France from Nazi control posed several problems. The dissolution of Axis rule in French territories started in the outlying areas of the empire, with colonial troops providing the bulk of the French fighting forces that worked with Anglo-American forces in the endeavor. World War II provided opportunities for the growth of nascent independence movements in Tunisia and Morocco. The tide of Third World independence was encouraged by both of the main Cold War–era superpowers, the United States and the Soviet Union. Both the *Neo-Destour* and *Istiqlal* parties cultivated American and British backing for their goals of independence. France had a great deal to lose in the process of global colonial dissolution, and it sought to stem the tide by trying to link the containment of global communism with the maintenance of the empire.

French society and French politics were exhausted from the experience of World War II. Lacking American support, French politicians and the French public quickly tired of the effort to hold onto a vast empire. Fanned by the success of Ho Chi Minh in Indochina, Arab independence movements in Tunisia and Morocco achieved their goal and French forces withdrew in 1955 after short-lived struggles by the French. Sub-Saharan Africa was of less significance to French leaders than North Africa, and France relinquished control of these areas without a fight. In the end, France spent more money on its colonies after independence in terms of subsidies and technical support, as a percentage of its annual budget, than Britain did. The French Empire in Africa, as in the case of the Middle Eastern Arab mandates, met an awkward, ungraceful end. But the contraction of the French Empire in the 1950s did not mean the end of French influence in the Islamic world. Moreover, France seemed prepared to make a determined last stand in Algeria, to preserve an important remnant of the French Islamic Empire.

7

The Algerian Crisis

ALGERIA AND THE EMPIRE

Algeria was the centerpiece of the French Empire in the Islamic world: conquered earliest, it was the scene of countless examples of French military heroism and both birthplace and headquarters of the Foreign Legion. It was also the location of the largest European settler population of any Western colonial empire in the Islamic world, both in terms of sheer numbers and in terms of the percentage of the settler population compared to the Muslim natives. During Operation Torch in November 1942, Anglo-American forces had invaded in great numbers in Algeria. They chose General Henri Giraud as high commissioner after the assassination of Admiral Darlan that December. De Gaulle's defiance after Dunkirk and his victories over the Axis forces on the periphery in West Africa had also propelled him into the limelight, and in May 1943, he moved his headquarters to Algiers. He is said to have remarked that now France could not lose the war, because it had the Sahara.

Most of the colonies were firmly behind him. As the Allied offensive shifted north, to Hitler's "Atlantic Wall," de Gaulle and his staff went north. French colonial officials resented the lingering presence of Anglo-American forces on Algerian soil for some months after the German surrender at Reims and Berlin. American and British sentiments toward the Arab world were already well known, and French officials believed the Muslim population might become infected by anti-colonial democratic propaganda.[1]

In time, Algeria became the place where many French civil and military leaders drew the proverbial line in the sand and where France attempted to hold on after giving up most other parts of the empire. The purposes of such a policy were to preserve an integral part of France across the Mediterranean, which was represented in the chamber as departments of the French Republic. After the emergence of the FLN revolution, French leaders would attempt to link the Algerian problem with broader Cold War issues. Failing in the effort to obtain NATO backing for its endeavors in the Maghrib, France would experience an insurrection in Algeria on the scale of Indochina. The fate of the Algerian revolution would alter the fate of the republic itself.

ALGERIA'S MUSLIMS THROUGH THE 1940s

The battles of the North African Theater of World War II prevented the rapid onset of a Muslim independence movement in Algeria in the 1940s, but also served to underscore the potential weaknesses of the French colonial regime. Prior to the war, some French officials recognized the scope of the problems and attempted reforms. Three-time governor-general Charles C. Jonnart (1900–1901, 1903–1911, and 1918–1919) moved to grant citizenship to loyal Algerian Muslim veterans of World War I in 1919, but *colon* opposition prevented the so-called Jonnart Laws from moving forward in the assembly.[2] The colony's rural Muslim majority was especially hard pressed during the depression, and a movement of rural Muslims from the countryside into the coastal cities began. In time the Muslim move toward the cities altered the demographics of the colony considerably, and the Muslim birth rate climbed higher than that of the *colons* in the relative ecological safety of the urban environment.[3]

Governor-General Maurice Violette (1925–1927) wanted to imitate certain examples of limited empowerment employed by other European regimes in areas of the Islamic world, including British Egypt and India, and the Soviet republic of Turkestan. He also met opposition while in office from the *colons*, and later wrote a book called *L'Algérie vivra-t-elle* (1931) explaining his vision for the colony.[4] He urged politicians to commemorate the centenary of the conquest of Algeria with a series of liberal reforms for the Muslims.[5] The 1931 French Colonial Exhibition chaired by Lyautey (who was an old friend of Jonnart) captured some of the spirit of Violette's optimism, but Violette knew that prior policies of assimilation or of autonomy advocated by his predecessors would fail in the Maghrib.[6] Furthermore, he was aware that the dual system created under the guise of association policies was patently discriminatory, and might someday lead to dissent. As former governor-general, Violette and Prime Minister Leon Blum tried in 1936 to initiate a bill that would have granted full citizenship to 25,000 Muslims and training in the French language for all Muslim students, with the goal of a form of cultural assimilation that might be acceptable to moderate Muslim leaders. In fact, many Muslim liberals wished it would pass, but hard-line *colons* exerted their influence again on the National Assembly and it ultimately failed. Violette had announced to the assembly:

When the Muslims protest, you are indignant; when they approve, you are suspicious; when they keep quiet, you are fearful. Messieurs, these men have no political nation. They do not even demand their religious nation. All they ask is to be admitted into yours. If you refuse this, beware lest they do not soon create one for themselves.[7]

Contradictory policies fostered by officials with opposing viewpoints harmed the French position, too. Pro-*colon* officials might be followed by officials who were more sympathetic to the Muslims. Alterations in successive regimes provided an image of a colonial policy that lacked a consensus and a clear direction. The "Kabyle Myth" was perpetuated by many officials who, like the *colons,* believed that the role of modern France was comparable to that of Rome in antiquity, and that all efforts should be made to separate the Berbers from the Arabs and to try to Europeanize the Berbers in the colony and downplay the importance of Islam to traditional Berber society. Such was the intent of legislation passed in 1930 that secularized law within the Berber areas (by taking power away from local *qa'ids* and transferring it to local councils that relied on French law).[8]

Several Muslim reform movements emerged in Algeria and among Algerian workers in France in the 1930s. An Islamic traditionalist movement formed in the Constantine area called the *Association des Ulema.* Led by *Shaykh* Abdul-Hamid Ben Badis, it sought to curb the importation and use of alcohol and tobacco in Algeria, as well as stop dancing and sporting events in which Muslims and *colons* might mingle.[9] A liberal movement also emerged in the Constantine area, guided by Ferhat Abbas, whose varied experiences included war veteran, government administrator, pharmacist, and Muslim student activist at Algiers University.[10] Abbas divorced his Muslim wife and married a Frenchwoman. Other secular radicals were especially strong around Tlemsen. They were guided by Messali Hajj, who also married a Frenchwoman, but whose experiences included World War I service, sometime membership in the French Communist party, and the organizing of Algerian workers in the vicinity of Paris.[11] He created the *Parti Progressive Algérien* in 1937, which subsequently mutated into the *Mouvement pour le Triomphe des Libertés Democratiques.* By 1940, there were 100,000 Algerians working in France, and Hajj saw them as the vanguard of change within Algeria proper.[12]

Ferhat Abbas met American president Franklin Roosevelt's personal representative to Algeria, Robert Murphy, in 1942.[13] Abbas requested that the Americans support the extension of the Atlantic Charter principles to Algeria (especially the third principle regarding "the right of all people to choose the form of government under which they will live"). Murphy's response was polite but noncommittal. A delegation of Muslim dignitaries approached Free French general Giraud in the following year regarding the question of reforms in return for their support of de Gaulle, but the general replied: "I don't care about reforms, I want soldiers first."[14] In the aftermath of Operation Torch, Abbas proclaimed a "Manifesto of the Algerian People," demanding a constitution for Algeria, legal equality of Muslims with the *colons*, and Muslim participation in government. When Abbas agreed to print a supplement (at the urging of Hajj's followers) demanding the creation of "an Algerian State," he was arrested. He subsequently recanted and was released. Algerian troops participated in the Allied invasion of Italy in 1943, and contributed to the Allied war effort in a variety of ways (including front-line combat). In the course of the war, de Gaulle also proclaimed at Brazzaville that the goal of the French colonial empire was "to lead each of the colonial peoples to a development that will permit them to administer themselves."

Abbas and Hajj linked up at Sétif in March 1944, and formed yet another organization, the *Amis du Manifeste et de la Liberté*, and although their differences eventually caused a split between them, their temporary union at Sétif became a focal point for the emergence of a violent anti-colonial revolt in May 1945.[15] The recent emergence of the Arab League and the Allied victory over the Axis both served to spur the hopes of the Algerians at this time. Followers of Messali Hajj had planned a large protest march in Sétif and some anti-government sabotage on May 8. When local colonial authorities intervened, some outraged Muslims attacked the police chief, and a Muslim mob formed and became emboldened by the successful assault on such a symbol of authority. The mob massacred all the *colons* it encountered in Sétif. The massacre spread to surrounding towns—Chevreul, Perigotville, Djidjelli, Kerrata, and Guelma. In all, 103 *colons* were killed, and a hundred more were wounded. Dozens of *colon* women were raped by the mob, and many of the corpses, both male and female, were sexually mutilated. The colonial authorities sent in Senegalese military units to restore order, which they accomplished at a cost of between 500 and 600 Algerian Muslim dead. *Colon* vigilantes killed several hundred more Muslims in reprisal. The Tubert Commission, charged by the government with investigating the sequence of events, discerned that the Muslim casualty figures had been underrepresented in reports made by the colonial regime. The Sétif Massacre and subsequent actions by the *colons* set the tone of the Algerian revolution.[16]

AHMED BEN BELLA AND THE FLN

Recruits to the cause of Algerian independence soon included returning veterans of the Seventh Algerian *Tirailleurs* Regiment from the Constantine area, who had seen combat in Europe, and who were angered by the scope of the military and *colon* reprisals inflicted on their fellow Muslims. One such disaffected veteran was Warrant Officer Ahmed Ben Bella, who had fought at Monte Cassino against the Nazis, and had a medal pinned to his chest by de Gaulle himself. Ben Bella refused a commission in the French Army after Sétif, and soon joined Hajj's *Mouvement pour le Triomphe des Libertés Democratiques* (MTLD). Ben Bella had been elected as a Muslim municipal council member, but went underground with an assumed name after a violent incident involving an inherited farm. He created a 4,500-member military offshoot of the MTLD called the *Organisation speciale*.[17] After the government infiltrated this group, however, Ben Bella fled to Tunisia, then to France, and finally to Egypt, where he linked up with other Algerian radicals and where he sought the support of Nasser.

Progressive colonial authorities proposed a statute in 1947 that would have allowed for more Muslim participation in local elections (including enfranchising women), made Arabic an official language, and demilitarized the Sahara.[18] The pro-Muslim reforms were tabled because of *colon* political clout, but a new Algerian Assembly was created with legislative and fiscal powers. The statute that eventually passed essentially maintained settler control of the colony. Following the directives for the creation of the French Union, Algeria technically fit the criteria perfectly to become a union member, but such a move was anathema to the *colons*, who argued effectively to keep the status quo. The military establishment throughout the empire was in sympathy with the Algerian *colons*, as were many politicians who shared the view of Paul Reynaud who (as a former prime minister) told an American audience in New York City in October 1955 that "the settler community had forged the national identity of the country [Algeria] and saved it from economic chaos."[19]

Marcel Edmond Naegelen became governor-general in February 1948, and he staunchly defended *colon* interests for three years.[20] He presided over the elections for the new Algerian Assembly. Widespread *colon* fears of a Muslim takeover of the assembly were based on the MTLD's showing on the local level in 1947. Naegelen's regime consequently rigged the elections so that the Muslims elected were government candidates (derisively called *Beni Oui-Ouis* [yes men]) rather than followers of Messali Hajj or Ferhat Abbas. Many Muslims were arrested simply for electoral participation.[21] Through the mid–1950s, Algerian Muslims could also watch as Tunisian and Moroccan activism led the way to outright political independence. Politically conscious Algerians were also aware of the parallel developments taking place in sub-Saharan African regions. Mendes-France's administration did much to end what was now the costly burden of colonial empire elsewhere. Mendes-France's Socialist interior minister François Mitterand proposed dramatic reforms in Algeria with the support of the liberal mayor of Algiers, Jacques Chevallier. The proposed reforms included the

equalization of political and educational opportunities for the Muslim population. The *colons* resented Mitterand's meddling, and the reform failed.
The episode illustrated, however, that some of the men at the top in Paris
were beginning to view Algeria differently than their predecessors.

On October 10, 1954, just over five months after Ho Chi Minh's victory
at Dien Bien Phu, Ben Bella and other disaffected Algerian Muslims
formed the *Front de Liberation Nationale* (FLN).[22] The FLN's goals were
complete political autonomy, and the withdrawal of French forces and
European settlers from Algeria, with vague references to Islamic principles. Although it did employ Islamic symbols such as the crescent and star
on its uniforms, the FLN was decidedly not a radical Islamic movement
comparable to that of 'Abd al-Qadir a century earlier.[23] While it claimed to
be a non-Western and non-communist alternative, many French military
and political leaders likened it to communism.[24] It owed more in fact to
the French revolutionary model. The FLN evolved a political consciousness that seemed remarkably Stalinistic or Maoistic—that is, it demanded
total loyalty to the party line, and enforced ideological uniformity among
its constituents.[25] It sought assistance from Muslims abroad, especially
from the Arab League in Cairo.[26]

Dissemination of propaganda was controlled by Ramdane Abane. Abane
was instrumental in creating an underground FLN newspaper called *El-
Moudjahid* and a clandestine radio station called *Voix de l'Algérie* (until he
was killed in interparty strife).[27] The FLN opened an information office in
London to spread information and propaganda to attract Western liberals
to the movement. The movement sanctioned violence against both military
and *colon* civilian targets. FLN revolutionary soldiers were sometimes
called *Mujahidin*, as in the days of old (hence, the name of the newspaper),
and sometimes *Maquisards*. Ben Bella's original task was procuring arms for
the FLN operatives.

The FLN revolution was openly proclaimed on a broadcast from Cairo
on November 1, 1954 (All Saints Day), when a series of simultaneously
coordinated attacks were carried out against French positions in the
colony. The broadcast called for the "restoration of the Algerian state, sovereign, democratic, and social, within the framework of the principles of
Islam." The All Saints Day attacks were launched against military and
police facilities, communications centers, public utilities, warehouses, and
the property of wealthy *colons*. The FLN soon began killing off those Muslims whom it deemed to be collaborators. A handful of leftist *colons* joined
the FLN ranks and provided valuable help in the form of safe houses,
medical assistance, and in a few cases, terrorist logistics. A disaffected
Martiniquan psychiatrist, Frantz Fanon, provided valuable propagandis-
tic assistance by trying in various writings (such as *The Wretched of the
Earth*) to universalize the plight of the Algerian Muslims and rationalize
the violence that came to be the norm in FLN campaigns.[28]

The famous *colon* Nobel Prize–winning author Albert Camus virtually single-handedly tried to create a movement for peaceful coexistence between the Muslim and *colon* communities, but failed because mainstream extremism prevailed on both sides in the face of spiraling violence.[29] Many *colons* came to realize it was a matter of survival for them and their colonial world, while many French politicians and military men began to think that the nation's prestige depended on the survival of this last large part of an ever-diminishing empire. Providing protection to French *colon* citizens became the paramount concern for the government.

The global position became fairly complex for France almost from the beginning. The United States and Britain, its NATO allies, refused to see France's Algerian problems as a part of their global Cold War concerns. Egyptian arms smuggling under Nasser began on December 8, 1954, and continued unabated until the FLN victory in 1962. Most other independent Arab countries also helped the FLN, including the recently liberated former French protectorates of Tunisia and Morocco. French troops were stationed along Algeria's borders at various spots to intercept FLN infiltrators and arms shipments from Tunisia and Morocco. French forces were also positioned in the Fezzan region of Libya for the purpose of intercepting arms from Egypt. FLN representatives attended the Third World Conference at Bandung in April 1955 and made many contacts. They met Ho Chi Minh, who assured them that the French could be beaten.[30]

FLN operatives went directly to the Soviet Union and the People's Republic of China for assistance, and found the Chinese more receptive than the Russians. The Soviet position was to support the French Communist party and the Algerian Communist party (neither of which wanted to alienate the *colon* industrial workers). Tito's Yugoslavia was the most supportive outside power, because the FLN's style suited the approach that had been taken by Tito in World War II.

The French saw their hold on Algeria as vital to the Cold War, while the British pursued less direct approaches in the Arab world, by sponsoring the anti-communist Baghdad Pact. U.S. Presidents Eisenhower and Kennedy did not want to alienate potential Arab Muslim allies in the global war against the Soviet Union and its client states.[31] While John F. Kennedy was the chairman of the Senate Foreign Relations Committee's African Subcommittee, he made a speech before the Senate on July 2, 1957, openly supporting the cause of Algerian independence. Many French politicians, soldiers, and *colons* felt betrayed by America.[32]

JACQUES SOUSTELLE AND THE PHILIPPEVILLE MASSACRE

In 1955, the FLN began preparing for violence. Its smaller Committee of Coordination and Enforcement and larger National Council of the Algerian Revolution oversaw strategy and implemented various actions carried out against the colonial regime. The FLN gathered together a great hoard of World War II–era small arms—American, German, and French leftovers—and organized their partisans into several *Wilayas* (military commands) within the colony. *Wilaya 4*, near Algiers, was particularly important. Several tens of thousands of soldiers (of varying abilities) were assembled. Many were stationed in enclaves near the Moroccan and Tunisian borders. Those few FLN members who were abroad were just as vital to the cause, garnering any international Muslim backing for the revolution that they could obtain (they were called "externals," while those operatives within Algeria were "internals").

One of the most important governors-general of Algeria after World War II was a civilian appointed by Mendes-France a few days before his government fell—Jacques Soustelle.[33] Trained as an ethnologist, Soustelle's academic specialty had been Aztec Mexico. He had studied the manner in which the *conquistadores* had merged Hispanic culture with Aztec culture, and as governor-general, he would come to believe the same process of merger might occur in Algeria between French culture and Maghribi Muslim culture. When he was appointed to the post on January 25, 1955, many *colons* instinctively distrusted him. He was close to de Gaulle, and there were fears of a potential backlash against former Vichyite collaborators. There were individuals in Mendes-France's cabinet such as Mitterand who had sought to initiate reforms on behalf of the colony's Muslim population. Soustelle, however, soon won over the *colons*, and they came to regard him as their man. He tried to siphon off support for the FLN among the Muslims by a variety of measures, and he clashed with the Interior Ministry over his ideas of assimilation. Within France, there was a general fear of a Muslim immigrant invasion if the two societies became more intertwined than they already were in Algeria.[34]

The FLN of course did not desire assimilation, either, and in fact sought the removal of all Europeans from Algeria. The group espoused a policy of violence against the settler population in order to achieve its goal (with the idea that the army would not remain in Algeria if the *colons* were unwilling to stay). The first manifestation of the policy of violence was the Philippeville Massacre of August 20, 1955, in which FLN operatives killed thirty-seven ordinary *colons* with sharp implements, inflicting mutilations on the victims. Another thirteen *colons* were mutilated and left for dead.[35]

Soustelle arrived at the scene of the massacre, and was transformed into an even more staunch supporter of the *colon* community by the sight of the carnage.[36] *Colon* vigilante and army units subsequently killed between 1,000 and 5,000 Muslims in reprisal, in the kind of operation that came to be called a *ratonnade* (rat hunt). Both sides in the struggle for Algeria— *colon* and Muslim—came to emphasize what the other side did to their community, rather than try to neutralize the extreme elements within their own ranks. The French military sided with the *colons*, whose social and cultural background mirrored that of the typical enlisted man or Legionnaire. The *colons* liked Soustelle, but disliked the government in general for not being more overtly pro-colonist, and for trying to appease the Muslims by economic or social reforms. Contemporary Parisian leaders had no real sympathy for the *colons*, whose ancestors had been lured to the colony by previous generations of French leaders.

Philippeville initiated a wave of FLN violence that left 1,000 *colons* dead, along with 6,000 Muslims whom they regarded as collaborators, over the next two years. From the Philippeville Massacre onward, there was little possibility of the *colon* and Muslim communities simply coexisting. Over the next several years, the government came to lose control of many areas of the countryside, but it was able to retain the urban areas. The FLN gained control in areas of the Aures Mountains, Kabyle lands, and around Algiers, Oran, and Constantine. Many *colons* fled to the cities. The government believed that Soustelle's attitudes and policies were not helping matters, and over the objections of the *colons*, he was recalled on February 26, 1956. An enormous number of *colons* came out to see Soustelle off, in the kind of departure few previous governors-general had received before, and none would ever receive again.[37]

TERRORISM AND THE BATTLE OF ALGIERS

At the recall of Soustelle, the governor-general position was changed to that of a resident-minister, who was to be responsible to a Council of Ministers. The first resident was Robert LaCoste, a socialist former deputy from Dordogne. His choice was extremely unpopular with the *colons*, but even more disconcerting for them was the appointment of the aged General Catroux, former wartime governor-general, as the military commander-in-chief of the colony. Catroux (then seventy-nine) was seen as a liberal, responsible for selling out the French interests in Syria and Morocco. Amid this climate of discontent, the new prime minister of France, Guy Mollet (February 1, 1956–May 21, 1957), came to Algiers to place a memorial wreath on the Algiers *Monument aux mortes* on February 6, 1956.

There was now coalescing among the extreme elements of the *colon* community a radical group known as "Ultras," who demanded union with France and espoused violence against governmental officials whom they regarded as traitors. Among the "Ultra" leaders were Robert Martel (founder of the *Union Française Nord-Africaine*) and a radical and flamboyant restaurateur named Joseph Ortiz (owner of the *Bar du Forum*).[38] There was talk in *colon* circles of the necessity of assassinating Catroux, like the fate of Admiral Darlan in World War II, despite prior assurances from Catroux that his objective was not to turn Algeria into a "national state" or alter the status of the *colons*.[39] Paratroopers and special security agents were sent in to protect Mollet. In stark contrast to the wildly adoring mob that saw Soustelle off four days earlier, almost no one greeted Mollet on his arrival in Algiers. When he placed the wreath on the monument, however, an angry *colon* mob almost stormed him, demanding the recall of Catroux. Mollet was shocked by the show of dissatisfaction, and promptly got Catroux to resign. This was a huge victory for *colon* "Ultras," and gave them an indication that violent agitation could influence government policy to perserve their status.[40] Their hopes turned to terror that fall, as the FLN initiated the Battle of Algiers.

Having already sanctioned violence against civilians, the FLN stepped up its offensive against the *colons* in September 1956. That month, FLN organizer Saadi Yacef began an urban terror campaign in Algiers, the heart of French Algeria, by employing Muslim teenage girls (and a European renegade, Danièle Minne) to place time bombs in *colon* ice cream parlors, bars, stores, and restaurants to kill any and all Europeans.[41] Thus began the Battle of Algiers, in which the FLN and the French military engaged in savage urban warfare that almost destroyed the infrastructure of the city. French intelligence operatives diverted a plane on October 22 carrying Ben Bella and other FLN leaders that had been en route to a presumably secret meeting in Morocco.[42] Because it resulted in the arrest of Ben Bella and other key FLN leaders, it was regarded by FLN partisans as an act of provocation more significant than the murder of civilians.

An FLN assassin named Ali Amara (or Ali "LaPointe") began plying his trade against high-placed *colon* officials when he killed the popular mayor of Boufarik, Amedee Froger, on December 28.[43] A bomb placed by Yacef's operatives blew up in the cemetery, intending to kill mourners at Froger's funeral. An enraged *colon* mob subsequently killed four Muslims and wounded fifty in the predictable *ratonnade* that resulted. Amid the climate of terror, a number of military leaders felt the government was not effective, and the Faure Conspiracy was hatched against LaCoste.[44] General Jacques Faure outlined the plot to the chief (secretary-general) of the Algiers Prefecture, Paul Teitgen, intending to enlist his support. Teitgen took the information to LaCoste, and then to senior officials in Paris, including Guy Mollet himself. The bizarre and lukewarm reception he got revealed that a kind of atrophy had taken hold of the French government with regard to the Algerian crisis. Faure was only perfunctorily punished.

The army, however, had more decisive plans. On the December 14, the highly decorated General Raoul Salan arrived as commander in chief of French forces in Algeria. He had a long and distinguished career in colonial service in the Far East, and was nicknamed "the Mandarin."[45] A host of talented and vigorous officers arrived in Salan's wake, whom the *colons* regarded as the modern-day equivalents of French crusaders of a bygone era, like Reynaud of Châtillon and Jean de Boucicault. Among the arriving officers was General Jacques Massu, a staunch Gaullist and a consumate professional soldier.[46] He had served under LeClerc from Lake Chad through the Sahara during World War II. His 4,600-strong paratroop division became the spearhead of anti-FLN operations in 1957. Several tireless and adaptable colonels played a huge role in the Battle of Algiers—Colonel Yves Goddard, who had a crucial intelligence network, and Colonel Marcel Bigeard, who had been captured in Vietnam and was subjected to psychological torture by the Viet Minh (and had learned a great deal in the process).[47] Bigeard's 1,200-man Regiment of Colonial Parachutists (RPC) performed legendary feats of infiltration into FLN enclaves. Together, these colonels provided the French with the means to carry out psychological operations against the FLN, which weakened its indigenous support networks. Massu's paratroopers deployed throughout Algiers on January 7, 1957.

Two days later, Prime Minister Mollet addressed the nation and announced that his government would accept an unconditional cease-fire once the FLN accepted the French framework for nationwide elections. The *colons* believed they were going to be abandoned, while the FLN did not want the possibility of diluting or losing their backers in an election with multiple parties. On January 16, a bazooka attack was carried out on General Salan's office.[48] He was not there at the time, but the assault indicated that there were some very dangerous disaffected elements in Algiers with a knowledge of Salan's routine—probably military men in league with *colon* "Ultras."

Toward the end of the month, the FLN stepped up its activities. Yacef's terror bombers killed five *colon* civilians and wounded sixty on January 26. The FLN called for a general strike of Muslim workers to coincide with the opening session of the United Nations in New York. The strike was intended to elicit a violent response from France and thus demonstrate to the world that France was not the progressive, liberal power that it claimed to be (and which indicated that the FLN regarded casualties among its own constituents as acceptable and even desirable in the global propaganda war). The strike began on schedule because the FLN influenced the *Union Générale des Travailleurs Algériens*. But the FLN did not calculate on the effectiveness of Massu's paratroopers, who cut locks on Muslim shops and forced workers back to their jobs. The strike was broken on January 30. France's actions, though, elicited further public sympathy for the FLN from Syria, Jordan, Egypt, and Saudi Arabia at the Arab Summit in Cairo that February.[49]

Yacef's bombers blew up the casino in Algiers on June 9, causing massive carnage, including nine *colons* killed, and eighty-five wounded.[50] A subsequent *colon ratonnade* resulted in five Muslims killed and fifty wounded. Favorite targets of the FLN were the French *képis bleus* (the *Section Administrative Specialiseé*, or SAS). The SAS started in the period after World War II to serve as an intermediary between the Muslim population and the government, much like the Arab Bureaus of the time of General

Bugeaud. There were some 400 detachments, consisting of Arabic specialists interspersed, throughout Algeria, many of whom worked in the remote rural areas of the country. The FLN targeted the *képis bleus* in particular, because the terrorists needed to negate any good will that may have been fostered by the quiet work of well-meaning and anonymous French Arabists.[51] On the other hand, torture was being applied by French forces on captured suspects, and as news of its use began to filter out of Algeria, more criticism was directed against French policies by the international community. The pro-FLN film *The Battle of Algiers*, which circulated around the world, also served the purpose of garnering international support for the FLN's revolutionary cause. In the era of decolonization, the climate of world opinion had changed such that colonial regimes tended to get blamed for colonist reprisals more often than independence movements did for their own bloodletting, and the international press tended to fixate on what the *colons* did in response to FLN attacks more than on the initial violence perpetrated by the FLN. The role of the United States has already been discussed in relation to the Cold War. The July 2, 1957, speech by then Senator John F. Kennedy in favor of Algerian independence was an example to the French of a predictable kind of international backlash, and caused great harm to Franco-American relations.[52] French representatives at the United Nations also did not utilize photos of FLN atrocities sent by the Parisian government to convince their diplomatic colleagues, for fear of a possible international backlash. They seemed to be clinging to a kind of diplomatic etiquette that no longer prevailed in the rest of the world (and certainly not in Algeria).

The Saqiyat Affair occurred in February 1958, in which the French forces bombed a Tunisian border town to stop FLN cross-border operations.[53] France reaped further international condemnation as a consequence. No French politician could afford as yet to discount domestic opinion, which, although it was tiring of Algeria, was not yet convinced that the colony was a liability on the scale of Indochina. French heavy-handed policies and counterintelligence measures, in fact, were paying off quite well. On September 24, Colonel Goddard himself captured Saadi Yacef, and Massu was able to claim a victory in the Battle of Algiers.[54] Mollet's government fell, as did two subsequent prime ministers in short succession—Bourges-Maunory and Gaillard. The weakness of the central government caused an attending drop in international prestige. But the abilities and the resolve of the military officers in Algeria stood in sharp contrast to the apparent weaknesses of the politicians in Paris.

THE ARMY AND THE RETURN OF DE GAULLE

Many of the *colon* leaders became emboldened over the next few months to try to seize the initiative away from the unmemorable Parisians and take control of their own destinies within Algeria. The fall of 1957 and spring of 1958 saw the rise of a coalition of *colon* "Ultra" groups known as the "Group of the Seven," including Martel and Ortiz, who were now joined by a forceful young former paratrooper who had served at Suez and in the Battle of Algiers, Pierre Lagaillarde. Born in France, but raised in Algeria, Lagaillarde formed the *Association Générale des Étudiants d'Algérie*.[55] A *Loi Cadre* for Algeria was enacted in France, which played out much more slowly than in sub-Saharan Africa. The *colons* feared the consequences, and distrusted any move either in Paris or by LaCoste in Algiers. Lagaillarde plotted LaCoste's overthrow when he was away in Paris on business that May.

On May 13, tens of thousands of *colons*, led by Lagaillarde and 500 *colon* commandos marched on the colonial government's headquarters.[56] The "Ultras" broke in and demanded immediate integration with France. Most Parisian officials were uninterested in such a proposition for fear of having to integrate millions of Arab and Berber Muslims into Metropolitan France. But the sheer scale of the demonstration and the fact that many military units failed to intervene, led LaCoste to act cautiously. He gave orders from Paris to the police, instructing them not to shoot on the demonstrators. General Massu intervened, and his actions in Algeria altered the course of modern French history. He formed a Committee of Public Safety in Algeria and appealed for the return to power in the French government of Charles de Gaulle.[57] He and many others believed that only de Gaulle could restore order in the nation and the empire. Massu stated that it was not a coup, but a message of "the will of Algeria to remain French." Outgoing Prime Minister Gaillard gave his approval for General Salan to take over the committee, and on May 14, Salan shouted to an enormous *colon* throng from the balcony at the governor's residence: "Vive la France! Vive l'Algérie française! Vive de Gaulle!"[58] Tens of thousands of loyal Muslims came out to show their support for the committee on May 16, many of whom were aged war veterans, and they had been prompted to do so by the army. The enormous size of the throng (between 20,000 and 60,000 according to Algerian news reports), however, indicated that the FLN did not have the uniform loyalty of the Muslim population. The high drama of the moment came when the Muslims linked arms with the *colon* crowd before the government building.[59]

Former Governor-General Soustelle now desired to return to Algeria, and his friends smuggled him into Switzerland to escape domestic French intelligence, and then flew him to Algeria on May 17. While Salan distrusted Soustelle, the crowd was still on Soustelle's side, and he was put on the Committee of Public Safety as a matter of course.[60] Gaullists within France began pressing the case for the return to power of the old governor-general, but under such unique circumstances, the necessary politics evolved very slowly. On May 19, de Gaulle made the public statement: "I shall hold myself at the disposition of the country," but he held back from more forceful assertions. Massu, meanwhile, prepared Operation Resurrection to bring de Gaulle back sooner rather than later by means of his paratroopers.[61] The operational objectives included Corsica as well as France, and Massu's men took Corsica on May 24 without a shot being fired.[62] When the current prime minister, Pierre Pflimlin, wanted to retake Corsica, he was told by his naval commanders that the fleet was "at sea." Before the rest of Operation Resurrection could be implemented, de Gaulle's partisans began discussing the circumstances for his return, and de Gaulle himself talked to the presidents of the assembly and the senate on May 28. De Gaulle did not want to be viewed as a pawn of the military.

On May 30, de Gaulle agreed to form a new government, and on June 1, he came before the National Assembly for a vote. By a margin of 329 to 244, de Gaulle was voted in as the new prime minister. He would rule by decree for six months, draft a new constitution, and the assembly would not convene for four months. What transpired had virtually no parallel in modern history—and perhaps the only parallel might be found in later imperial Roman history, in which generals were put forward by their legions in remote corners of the empire. The *colons* might have felt that now there was no way that they might meet the sorry fate of the crusader colonists of *Outremer* over 600 years earlier. The Muslims, though, soon realized that they, too, had reason for hope.

"JE VOUS AI COMPRIS"

At first it looked to the *colons* like de Gaulle would solidify their privileged position, while the Muslims could see also that he was concerned about their plight and wished to enhance their material condition.[63] By December 1958, de Gaulle had visited Algeria a total of five times. His first visit was on June 4, when the combined *colon* and Muslim mob went wild with enthusiasm when he spoke from the balcony of the colonial government headquarters in Algiers: "Je vous ai compris" (I have understood you).[64] These words were variously interpreted at the time, and have been subject to a great deal of reinterpretation since then. At Oran, however, before his return to France that very same day, he was much clearer: "Yes, France is here, with her vocation. She is here forever." When he returned to Algiers on July 3, he announced that he would add 15 billion francs to that year's budget for Algeria, for housing, education, and public works. Finding the money, however, was difficult. That October de Gaulle announced what came to be called the "Constantine Plan" (after the city where it was announced).[65] This was to create 400,000 new jobs, new housing for the Muslim population, and free up a quarter of a million hectares of agricultural land for Muslims. Muslims were to be recruited for colonial posts in greater numbers, as well. Less than a third of the money was to come from the central government in Paris, while the rest was to come from within Algeria in various ways (anticipated commercial development and an expected broader tax base). De Gaulle's goal was to siphon off support for the FLN by bettering the material conditions of the Muslim population. Problems emerged in financing the plan, and in the search for enough acceptable Muslim candidates for governmental posts.

The FLN stepped up its political offensive on September 19 by establishing a Provisional Government of the Republic of Algeria (GPRA) from exile.[66] It was declared in French from Cairo by Ferhat Abbas, who had joined the FLN in April 1956, and who became the GPRA's president. Veteran FLN soldier Belkacim Krim and the imprisoned Ahmed Ben Bella were made vice presidents. The idea was to provide an alternative to the French hand of the Parisian government being extended by de Gaulle toward the Muslim population. Elected president of the Fifth Republic on December 21, de Gaulle also began a policy of granting clemency to captured FLN operatives. This policy angered a number of colonial officers, who began grumbling openly about the problems entailed in letting potentially unrepentant FLN revolutionaries back into the Muslim population. Feeling betrayed by some of his officers, and also the necessity of demonstrating his political power over the military in order to make way for his reforms, de Gaulle transferred many of his officers out of Algeria. On December 12, Salan was replaced by General Maurice Challe (Salan became military governor of Paris). The new civilian leader (now titled the delegate-general) was Paul Delouvrier, who was told by de Gaulle, "You are France in Algeria, not the representative of the Algerians in France."[67]

THE ARMY'S LAST STAND AND THE END OF
FRENCH ALGERIA

Although the war was far from over, Salan, Massu, and their predecessors had achieved quite a bit of success against the FLN. Massu had, of course, won the Battle of Algiers in 1957. The SAS enlisted pro-government Muslim irregulars called *Harkis* (about 150,000 served—far more than the number of FLN troops).[68] A checkerboard system of division of the country was devised called *quadrillage* to facilitate the tracking down of FLN units. Physical barriers were put into place along the borders with Morocco and Tunisia to prevent FLN infiltration. French intelligence infiltrated FLN ranks, obtaining information through the widespread use of torture.[69] General Paul Aussaresses led a special unit during the Battle of Algiers that used torture to obtain information that helped to break the FLN in the colonial capital. He revealed in a 2000 book that some 3,000 FLN operatives were killed after being tortured for information, including two FLN leaders, Larbi Ben M'Hidi and Ali Boumendjel.[70] The FLN, for its part, mutilated and killed its captives and rarely distinguished between military personnel and the civilian *colons* it captured. The war was conducted with equal brutality by both sides, as in the days of jihad and the crusades.

By the time Challe took over, a substantial part of the task of stemming the FLN revolutionary tide in Algiers and in other cities had been achieved. It was Challe's responsibility to take the campaign into the interior (particularly Kabylia) and elminate back-country support for the FLN. Challe was a masterful organizer who recognized the need to augment French forces to carry the war into the interior. As it stood in December 1958, there were only about 15,000 paratroopers and Legionnaires available for mobile operations in the interior, roughly the equivalent of the number of FLN military operatives in the ALN.

The Challe Plan called for the enlargement of the loyal Muslim *Harki* units to guide French commando forces in the interior toward ALN positions. The French *Commandos de Chasse* were to be backed up by greater numbers of a *Reserve Générale*. On July 22, 1959, Challe moved to take high ground positions in Kabylia and initiate Operation Binoculars, a massive series of search and destroy missions directed at the ALN. By late October, Challe estimated that about half of the FLN's operatives in Kabylia had been eliminated by his troops (about 3,000 enemy dead).[71] The final phase of the plan, code named Trident, was to be implemented in the spring of 1960, but de Gaulle recalled Challe on April 23, 1960. By then, the president had changed his mind about Algeria.

In January 1959 de Gaulle gradually became convinced that France's Algerian adventure of 130 years should come to an end. He came to believe that it was not politically, economically, or culturally sound to further integrate Algeria and its huge and impoverished Muslim population with France and its more prosperous Catholic European population. In a visit to General Challe's headquarters in Kabylia on August 30, 1959, the president told an assemblage of officers: "We shall not have the Algerians with us, if they do not want that themselves. The era of the European administration of the indigenous peoples has run its course."[72] De Gaulle believed that France would be stronger in the world without Algeria than with it.[73]

In a speech to the nation on September 19, de Gaulle announced: "I deem it necessary that recourse to self-determination be here and now proclaimed." The *colons* were horrified by this, because they were outnumbered by the Muslims eight to one, and their world of relative privilege would disappear if the idea of self-determination for Algeria were taken to its logical conclusion. Most *colons* were not actually wealthy, but they had a wealth of opportunities compared to the Muslim majority. Many military men, who were then risking their lives to keep the FLN from gaining the upper hand in Algeria, were equally horrified by de Gaulle's statement. Challe wrote to de Gaulle's prime minister, Michel

Debre, in September that French soldiers had been and still were dying every day "in order for Algeria to remain French." Delouvrier went to Paris for Challe in October to inquire as to whether the government agreed with Challe's assessment. He returned with a confirmation from de Gaulle's government that this was indeed so.

Colon "Ultras," however, lost no time that fall in organizing for a potential confrontation. Joseph Ortiz predictably was at the helm, telling his die-hard followers that "for us, henceforth, it's either the suitcase or the coffin," according to the government's plan.[74] He began organizing many disparate "Ultra" groups into the *Front Nationale français* (FNF) and began hoarding weapons. Several colonels under Massu made friendly contact with Ortiz. Interestingly, the FLN wanted to keep up the pressure on the *colons*, and stepped up their attacks on civilians in the outlying areas of Algeria and committed atrocities so that no one could forget their goal. In mid-January, General Massu expressed some unfortunate words to a West German journalist that were published on January 18, to the effect that he would not unconditionally obey orders from de Gaulle that would abandon French Algeria to the Muslims. De Gaulle was infuriated and recalled Massu from Algeria and on January 22 sent him to command the French garrison at Metz.[75]

Now Algeria was without the man within the French establishment whom the *colons* felt would protect them from the worst possible scenario. Ortiz's FNF called for a *colon* strike and protest (in support of Massu) on January 24. A revolution was organizing, and Ortiz's friends among the paratrooper colonels assured him the troops would not fire on the "Ultras."[76] Ex-paratrooper Lagaillarde set up a rival headquarters from Ortiz at Algiers University. This began "Barricades Week" in Algiers, when the *colons* tried to influence the Parisian central government as they had in 1958.[77] When the police intervened on January 24 in Algiers, fourteen of them were killed, and twenty-four wounded. As Ortiz had expected (and Lagaillarde had hoped), the paratroopers stood by and did not get involved. Challe and Delouvrier did not want to either shed blood or get captured by "Ultras," so they fled from Algiers to Reghaia, twenty miles east of the city, on January 28.[78] The next day, de Gaulle adressed the nation in his old general's uniform, and reasserted the case for Algerian self-determination.[79] On February 1, army units in Algeria swore loyalty to Delouvrier and the barricades' "Ultra" groups dissolved in a drenching rainstorm. Ortiz fled, while Lagaillarde marched out in uniform defiantly to surrender to the authorities.[80] In November 1960, the "Barricades Trial" saw Lagaillarde sentenced to ten years in prison (but he was able to flee), while Ortiz was sentenced to death *in absentia*. Both received amnesty in 1968, along with others in the Algerian War.

Unbeknownst to his generals, the front-line troops, the *colons*, or most of the FLN, de Gaulle's operatives made contact with FLN leaders in *Wilaya 4* in June 1960. De Gaulle saw the necessity of starting some kind of direct dialogue with the Muslim side of the conflict before civil war might overtake the colony and the republic. It was a subterfuge code-named Operation Tilsit (recalling the 1807 treaty between Napoleon and Tsar Alexander I). Three FLN leaders from *Wilaya 4* were flown to Paris on June 10 to meet with de Gaulle personally—Si Salah, Si Muhammad, and Si Lakhdar.[81] The ice was broken, and de Gaulle suggested direct talks with the GPRA (all three of these FLN leaders were killed prior to independence, two of them by their own side for making contact with the enemy without authorization). On June 14, de Gaulle appealed on national television for the GPRA to come to Paris to discuss "an honorable end to the fighting."[82] French-FLN talks were undertaken at Melun from June 25 to 29. While there was no breakthrough made in the talks, de Gaulle could argue that at least the two sides were now able to negotiate.[83] This was anathema to the *colons*.

When de Gaulle visited Algeria from December 9 to 13, there were not only huge Muslim demonstrations on behalf of the FLN, but also Muslim riots directed against the *colons*, which the police were hard pressed to control. Several *colon* plots against de Gaulle failed to materialize, but the colony essentially began disintegrating even before de Gaulle left.[84] It was apparent to the *colons* that they were being abandoned by the man whom they had hoped would preserve their world, and that de Gaulle was actually propelling forward the process of creating an independent, Muslim-controlled Algeria. Global opinion now was also substantially behind the Muslims.[85] On December 20, the United Nations recognized the right of Algeria to exist as an independent nation. The French public voted resoundingly in favor of Algerian independence on January 8, 1961, and de Gaulle finally stated the obvious on April 1, that it made better financial sense for France to decolonize.[86]

Colon "Ultras" formed the Secret Army Organization (OAS) in January 1961, and for the next year, engaged in terrorist attacks against those Europeans whom they regarded as traitors and against the Muslim population of Algeria.[87] The OAS consequently caused an even further decline in relations between the *colons* and the Muslims, and made it almost inevitable that either migration or partition would have to occur. The army was not in favor of simply handing over Algeria to the Muslims. Too much history and glory of French arms was connected to the colony for the generals and many of the rank and file to accept what seemed to be de Gaulle's ultimate goal of simply giving up, especially after the Challe Plan had almost succeeded so recently. Many soldiers sympathized with the *colons* and were not prepared to abandon them. In addition, many officers were angered at the way de Gaulle had transferred any of their fellow commanders who expressed a divergent opinion about Algeria.

In this atmosphere of treason was born the so-called Generals' Putsch of April 20 to 26, 1961.[88] Four of the top army commanders who had connections to Algeria discussed the idea of a revolution on behalf of French Algeria directed against de Gaulle. The generals involved in the plot included Salan, Zeller, Jouhaud, and Challe. They had numerous front-line colonels supporting them, and about two divisions of soldiers. Salan, Zeller, and Jouhaud favored starting a military revolt in France, as well as in Algeria, while Challe backed the idea of a revolt in Algeria alone. While the generals slipped back into the colony, the current commander in chief, General Gambiez, was arrested by Legionnaires. The generals began organizing their anticipated government—Salan for civil affairs, Challe for military affairs, Zeller for administration, and Jouhaud for information and propaganda. The *colons*, meanwhile, watched, hoping that there might be a reprise of the events of 1958. The current delegate-general, Jean Morin, who had replaced Delouvrier in November 1960 (and served through March 1962), was powerless to stand in the way of the generals.

The generals and the *colons*, however, underestimated de Gaulle's political agility. The president immediately sent his minister for Algeria, Louis Joxe, along with General Jean Olié, to assess the situation within Algeria.[89] Interior Minister Roger Frey promptly arrested General Faure in France, who correctly was suspected of instigating problems within France (he had, in fact, planned the takeover of Paris).[90] There were 1,800 armed paratroopers placed in the forested area near Orleans, and another 400 in the forest near Rambouillet, who were preparing to link up with an armed column and take over Paris.[91] On April 22, police units made contact with the soldiers and managed to convince them to depart. Tanks were positioned outside the National Assembly and other governmental buildings in Paris on April 23 in case the revolt spread.

De Gaulle addressed the nation in dramatic fashion that night and managed to unify and pacify the population as no other leader could have done.[92] On April 24 and 25 the coup fell apart, as army units swore loyalty to de Gaulle and his officers. Those involved in the putsch attempted to flee, but most were arrested, including the top four generals who had organized the plot.[93] The generals were found guilty in subsequent trials, but their sentences were commuted in de Gaulle's amnesty of 1968, along with Lagaillarde, Ortiz, and the others involved in Barricades Week of 1960. With the collapse of the Generals' Putsch, Muslim hopes for independence appeared to have some substance, while *colon* dreams of maintaining their position vanished.

The *colons* knew that their privileged colonial existence could not be sustained without the requisite will to maintain the French presence on the part of the French government. OAS "Delta" hit squads killed hundreds of suspected *colon* traitors and Muslim activists and ordinary civilians in the summer and fall of 1961.[94] Negotiations between the French government and the FLN occurred between May and July at Évian, with no success.[95] But the negotiations led to the beginning of the end of the oldest, largest, and last of the French colonies in the Islamic world. Amid scenes of chaos and hardship, a mass departure of desperate *colons* for France and other European countries began in January 1962, and continued though July. Almost a million European colonists left behind the homes and livelihoods that had been theirs for the past 130 years in that very European enclave set in the midst of Islamic North Africa. Half a million *colon* refugees arrived destitute in France, while others went to Spain and Italy (none, of course, were compensated for their lost property).

OAS executions soared in January and February 1962 (there were over 500 in February alone), and the resulting Muslim animosity hastened the flight of the *colons*.[96] Peace talks resumed at Évian nevertheless that March, and achieved a breakthrough on May 18. Christian Fouchet was appointed by Paris on March 19 to serve as high commissioner for the thankless task of handing over Algeria to the FLN. An era came to an end on July 4, when High Commissioner Fouchet formally handed power over to the FLN government. An FLN Provisional Committee took over immediately, under Chairman Abd al-Rahman Fares, until in September, Ferhat Abbas chaired a National Constituent Assembly that elected Ahmed Ben Bella as the first president of the Republic of Algeria on September 29. The Algerian revolution had cost the French some 18,000 military deaths and 3,000 *colon* deaths (with 7,000 further *colon* injuries). The revolution cost the Muslims at least 200,000 deaths. Some 30,000 Europeans remained behind, including former Algiers mayor Jacques Chevallier. Most of them, however, were destitute, and felt they had no hope of success in France. In a final scene reminiscent of *Outremer* after the fall of Acre, a remnant of die-hard *colons* fired on incoming FLN units, inciting a Muslim rampage through the *colon* neighborhoods in Oran, and many of the Europeans were massacred.[97]

CONCLUSION

A unified Muslim Algeria was the product of both FLN dreams and 130 years of French rule that had unified the country from a collection of Barbary pirate city-states and vast stretches of Sahara. Despite the precipitous withdrawal in 1962, France maintained strong economic ties to Algeria, as it did in other Maghribi and sub-Saharan African territories (spending more money as a percentage of the French annual budget on economic development within the former empire than even Britain did). One hundred thirty years of effort had been expended in establishing that largest of European colonies within the Islamic world. Algeria had been conquered because of Barbary piracy, and colonized in the era of the New Imperialism because of the efforts of the Legion. French Algeria succeeded as a colony because of the ability of France to insert French, Spanish, and

Italian settlers into a region of the western Islamic world and create an extension of the European world there.

The Maghrib had been tied to the northern shores of the Mediterranean in various ways—political, economic, religious—since the days of Rome. Geographically it was more proximate to France than the Middle Eastern Mandates. Given the events of 1830 and the crusader and Napoleonic legacies in North Africa, the series of French rulers from King Charles X to Prime Minister Pierre Pfimlin believed it was historically coherent to adhere to a policy of assimilating Algeria to France. The problem faced by Charles de Gaulle from 1958 to 1962 was that, in the course of 130 years of French domination, the Muslim majority was not assimilated more fully into the French political and cultural landscape. This was in fact impossible, given the millennium of conflict between France and the Islamic world since the time of Charles Martel, and the diametrically opposed claims of supremacy of the West and the Islamic world that gave rise to those numerous wars between Frenchmen and Muslims.

The colonists and most French politicians had of course worked directly against the policy of assimilation over the 130-year period of French Algerian history. De Gaulle was faced by Cold War issues and the failure of France's NATO allies to merge the Algerian conflict into the Soviet-Western confrontation. The tide of Third World liberation movements appeared unstoppable by 1962, as both the United States and the Soviet Union supported the end of European colonial ventures. De Gaulle and many of his supporters recognized that the French home population ceased to measure the country's greatness by the size of the empire. De Gaulle also recognized that the home population would no longer subsidize a costly (and seemingly parasitical) colony overseas, and absorb the loss of soldiers' lives in an attempt to hold onto a territory whose inhabitants (or most of whose inhabitants) had no interest in remaining in the union. Despite the best efforts of the *colons* and the army, French Algeria ended up meeting the same fate as had French *Outremer* some 600 years earlier.

8

The Aftermath of Empire

THE POSTCOLONIAL WORLD

The end of empire was more traumatic for France than Britain because of the casualties incurred in poorly executed efforts to hold on longer than it was politically prudent to do so. France was still one of the primary military and economic powers in the world in 1962 after the withdrawal from Algeria, and it remains one of the top five nuclear and economic powers after the turn of the second millennium. The appeal of empire ceased to hold the popular imagination in France in 1960 as it had a century earlier, and de Gaulle made it clear that colonies were a drain on France's resources, and not an asset as countless pro-imperialists had argued. French leaders had held on so long to the empire because France was enslaved by its past. The legacies of the Carolingians, crusaders, and Napoleonic armies made for a logic of French expansionism into Islamic parts of the world in the era of the New Imperialism. After the end of empire, these legacies and the romance of the past glory of French arms continued to exert an influence stronger than partisan differences between the Left and Right in French politics, and French leaders have continued to have an influence on, and be influenced by, their former Islamic domains.

The Legion is still an active instrument of foreign policy, with an 8,500-man force based in France (at Aubagne, Orange, Laudun, Nimes, Marseilles, and Castelnaudry, and on Corsica), and in French Guyana (the Third Foreign Infantry Regiment), Djibouti (the Thirteenth Demi-Brigade), and Mayotte (the Mayotte Detachment). It has served in important capacities in foreign operations during the 1980s within former parts of the empire, including Chad and Lebanon.

France remained Algeria's biggest trading partner through de Gaulle's tenure (which ended on April 28, 1969) until West Germany edged out France in the mid-1970s. In most other African areas of the former empire, the French language, French educational structures, and French economic ties still prevailed. President Georges Pompidou (1969–1974), de Gaulle's successor, convened a gathering of former French African territories' representatives in 1973. The conference was so successful in fostering useful regional and international dialogue that it has continued to meet biannually and serve as a means of economic, technological, and cultural exchange. The franc is used as a medium of exchange throughout the former sub-Saharan empire, and France has guaranteed the value of the currency in fourteen former colonies.

In the mid-1970s, during the tenure of Valery Giscard d'Estaing (1974–1981), France jettisoned its last two small colonial territories on and off the African continent—the Comoros in 1975 and Djibouti in 1977. The Comoros is a poor and unstable Islamic republic situated on volcanic islands and coral atolls between Mozambique and Madagascar. It was the scene of several coup attempts as late as the 1990s, but France was not particularly interested in assisting its former territory because the country's infrastructure had been poorly developed, and it lacked any strategic significance. Djibouti (former French Somaliland), on the other hand, is a predominantly Christian enclave set in the midst of a Muslim part of Africa, and it possesses the strategically situated port of Djibouti on the mouth of the Red Sea. It receives substantial support from France, and the French fleet maintains a base there, and the Thirteenth Foreign Legion Demi-Brigade is headquartered there.

Giscard d'Estaing visited Algeria in April 1975, making the first visit of a French leader since Algerian independence. By that time, Colonel Houari Boumedienne had overthrown Ben Bella and become head of state. The visit was the start of somewhat more cordial relations between the two countries. Many of the technical elements of the Évian Accords were discarded by Algeria after independence, including guarantees of freedom for the 30,000 *colons* who remained behind. An educational provision, however, was implemented and several thousand French teachers went to help in Algeria, along with tens of thousands of French technicians, whose presence has bettered the lot of the remaining *colons*.

Changes in French foreign policy in the former empire came during the Socialist administration of François Mitterand (1981–1995). Beginning in 1981, alterations were made in what was frequently described as French "paternalism" toward the former empire, and an emphasis was placed on a more equal relationship between each country and France. One of the alleged changes would be an emphasis on tying aid to efforts to foster democracy. Ironically, however, Mitterand's administration became more actively involved in projecting France's power into areas of the former empire than any other French leader since de Gaulle.

Mitterand insisted on French participation in the UN coalition that fought in the Persian Gulf War in 1991 to push Iraqi forces out of Kuwait. In the massive February 24, 1991, assault into Kuwait, the French Sixth Armored Division drove north on the left flank to the town of al-Salman, and assisted in the American-dominated victory over Saddam Hussein's army. The underlying issue in the war was a guarantee of access to Persian Gulf oil, which might have been hampered if Iraq were allowed to annex Kuwait and threaten other friendly Arab Persian Gulf states (such as Saudi Arabia, Bahrain, Qatar, and the United Arab Emirates). French forces joined American, British, Saudi, and Egyptian forces in the critical ground operations that broke the Iraqi army and thereby liberated Kuwait. Other key areas of Mitterand's interest in the Islamic world lay within the borders of the former empire: Chad, Lebanon, and Algeria.

QADHAFI AND CHAD

One of NATO's consistent southern security problems in the 1980s was Mu'ammar al-Qadhafi's regime in Libya. Colonel Qadhafi and other Libyan Army officers overthrew King Idris in 1969, and imposed a form of Islamic law on the country. Qadhafi shortly assumed total control of the country. After expelling 25,000 remaining Italian colonists from the country, Qadhafi became an ally of the Soviet Union and instituted an Islamic People's Republic (*Jamahariyya*). Qadhafi's regime ostensibly followed his Third International Theory, a unique blending of Islam and Marxism, explained in his *Green Book*.[1] He assumed the mantle of pan-Arabism, although he is himself a Berber, in the mid-1970s, and attempted to create separate unions with four countries—Sudan, Tunisia, Chad, and Morocco. He supplied the Palestine Liberation Organization (PLO) with weapons to fight Israel, and dispatched his forces as far afield as Uganda in 1979, to prop up Kakawa Muslim dictator Idi Amin. His actions in Chad were what concerned the Mitterand administration.[2]

Chad had become independent from France in 1960, and the country's internal balance of power consisted of a not-so-seamless linkage of northern Muslims and southern Catholics (tied to France) and animists.[3] Southern Catholics dominated Chadian politics from 1960 to 1979, and the country's first president, François Tombalbaye, was a willing recipient of French "paternalism." French money flowed into the region in the 1960s through the *Organisation Commune de la Region Sahrienne* for various development projects, and in the form of more direct defense assistance. France remained a primary trading partner for most countries of the former empire in sub-Saharan Africa, including Chad.

In the late 1960s, northern Muslims formed an anti-southern coalition called the "Front for the Liberation of Chad," and got the support of King Idris, and then of Qadhafi. The Muslims caused Tombalbaye enough difficulties that two regiments of the Foreign Legion were called upon to assist in their suppression in 1969–1970.[4] France maintained a small garrison in N'Djamena, Chad's capital in the south. One of the problem areas lay along Chad's northern border adjacent to Libya, in the mineral-rich Aouzou Strip. Qadhafi claimed the area for Libya, and in 1973, he sent troops in and seized control of the region.

In 1975, Tombalbaye was overthrown in a coup by a fellow Catholic southerner, General Félix Malloum, who believed the president was not doing a good job of maintaining order.[5] Malloum felt he could placate the Muslims by bringing in a Muslim from the northern Front as his vice president—Hissène Habré. The power arrangements were not what Habré and his backers wanted, and the coalition between Catholics and Muslims fell apart as Habré demanded the placement of more northern Muslims in the government and Arabic used as the national broadcast language, rather than French. Habré's troops in the Front beat Malloum's men in February 1979, and captured N'Djamena. Malloum's partisans, meanwhile, attacked Muslims residing in the south in reprisal. The small French force in Chad did not intervene.

Chadian inter-tribal disputes further complicated the political arena, and the Organization of African Unity (OAU) finally intervened in August 1979. The OAU got the various feuding groups to meet in Lagos, Nigeria, with observers present from ten different countries.[6] Under OAU auspices, a Government of National Unity (GUNT) was formed as a transitional body toward a more representative government. Goukouni Oueddei, a Muslim, was chosen to become president. Disagreements soon fractured the government, and Habré looked for and received support against Oueddei, who was seen as pro-Libyan.[7] The military fragmented into rival bands, and armed groups roamed the country murdering at will their rivals or suspected rivals.[8]

In February 1980, Habré's troops took control of part of N'Djamena, and the capital was the scene of a savage civil war. Oueddei demanded the withdrawal of French forces in May, which he felt would serve only to complicate matters with Habré. After the French complied, he asked for assistance from Qadhafi that October. In November, 4,000 Libyan soldiers invaded Chad, with tanks, jet aircraft, and field artillery. Over the next few months, another 6,000 Libyans arrived, and by December the Libyans had acquired all northern cities and reached N'Djamena.[9] Oueddei and Qadhafi issued a joint statement in January 1981 that, henceforth, there would be "complete unity" between Chad and Libya. The OAU immediately demanded a Libyan withdrawal from Chad, and offered the services of an Inter-African Force (INF) to provide order. Both Oueddei and Qadhafi ignored the OAU.

Soon after France began making overtures to Oueddei in September, Qadhafi began redeploying his troops to the north. About 5,000 INF peacekeepers then arrived in the country. Habré, meanwhile, began receiving French and American assistance, and in June 1982, his forces took all of N'Djamena and caused Oueddei to flee to Cameroon, and then to Libya. Oueddei shortly returned, however, in the midst of a Libyan invasion force of several thousand troops whose purpose was to install him as Qadhafi's proxy. Mitterand chose this juncture, just a little over a year into his term as president, to intervene in Chad.[10] While there was beginning to be a shift in domestic French politics at this time to the right of center (shown in the change in Mitterand's immigration policies), it actually mattered little which party was then in office in Paris. One of de Gaulle's legacies was that the republic's president did not need a consensus to act in certain areas of foreign policy. Mitterand's decision to intervene in Chad was a consequence of his conception of France's unique history and obligations in the world. Chad was within France's continued sphere of influence, and a partner in the one-time union.[11] Qadhafi was not just a threat to Chad, or to NATO's southern sector, but a challenger to France's role in the wider world.

Mitterand authorized the deployment of several Foreign Legion regiments to Chad to restore Habré's authority throughout the country. It was a pragmatic choice to side with Habré, and not to try to bring back one of the southern Catholic generals, because a civil war and a regional interreligious war would have been a possibility. Operation Manta thus started on August 3, 1983, and aerial help began landing in Chad on August 11. Some 3,000 Foreign Legionnaires began arriving in Chad on August 21. NATO countries and Islamic governments watched cautiously to see if Qadhafi would fight. His military units were clearly outclassed by state-of-the-art French equipment and by troops with superior training, mobility, and logistical support. The Legion established a "Red Line" at the 16th Parallel, as a dividing line to keep Qadhafi's forces out of the south. There were a few brief engagements, on the ground and in the air, in early 1984, and the Libyans and their pro-Oueddei allies melted away. A Franco-Libyan Agreement was reached in September 1984, and Libyan forces withdrew. French forces withdrew on December 1, with their mission accomplished as neatly as possible, given the uncertain circumstances of endemic regional tribal and religious conflict. Habré became a staunch ally of the West—as important a consequence of French intervention as driving Libyan forces out of the country.

Qadhafi, however, continued to claim the Aouzou Strip, and within a year he launched another drive to retake it. This time, Qadhafi stayed above the 16th Parallel. Mitterand sent in an 800-man contingent of Legionnaires in 1986 in Operation *Epervier* (Sparrow Hawk), ostensibly to protect French expatriates. French troops stayed south of the 16th Parallel, while Idris Deby led pro-Habré Chadian forces (supplied by France) to push out most Libyan units in 1987. Relations between Libya and Chad were theoretically normalized in 1988, and the two countries submitted the question of ownership of the Aouzou Strip to the World Court. The court decided in 1994 that the strip belonged to Chad, and Libyan forces finally withdrew. Several hundred French troops stayed on in Chad as technical advisors and training staff for Habré's army, and many of Habré's officers went to train in France. In November 1990, Deby overthrew Habré. Local French forces were not concerned, and the Franco-Chadian relationship continued (there were about 1,800 French troops in the country at that time). Chad continued to receive about one-quarter of the French overseas military budget through the late 1990s.[12]

LEBANESE QUAGMIRE

The delicate power-sharing arrangements in Lebanon between Christians and Muslims worked out so painstakingly during the French mandate continued to function for the first three decades after independence.[13] The situation was made much more volatile, however, when the demographic balance shifted toward the Muslims in the 1960s, due to the influx of Palestinian refugees northward, who were fleeing from Israel. To the region's centuries-old rivalries between Christians and Muslims in the coastal area were added Israeli and Syrian strategic interests in power projection.[14] Many Lebanese Muslims still wanted some form of union with Syria, while the *Baath* (Islamic Socialist) regime of Hafez al-Asad in Syria sought to create in Lebanon a proxy state in its struggles with Israel.[15] The Israelis came to employ the Lebanese Forces (LF) Christian militia as their proxy within Lebanon.

Arab-Israeli wars in 1967 and 1973 left Israel in a position of strategic advantage. Employing American military technology, Israel and its proxy held at bay Syrian forces and their Muslim proxies (which utilized Soviet military hardware). The Lebanese Civil War (1975–1990) between the Maronites and the Muslims altered the regional balance of power, as well.[16] Thousands were killed and Beirut was devastated. Maronite President Sulayman Franjieh called on Syria to assist in trying to maintain order in 1976, but the Syrian Army simply sided with the Muslims. In addition to Maronite and Sunni Muslim militias, the Shi'ite *Amal* militia (and later, *Hizbullah*) and the Druze militia fought for supremacy of urban neighborhoods and rural districts.[17] The Israeli-Palestinian conflict spilled over into Lebanon after the PLO set up headquarters in Beirut, and Israeli forces moved into southern Lebanon in July 1981.[18] U.S. Special Envoy Philip Habib, sent by President Ronald Reagan, managed to negotiate a cease-fire on July 24, which lasted for ten months, although PLO attacks on northern Israel continued.

Israel invaded Lebanon in force on June 6, 1982, intending to push the PLO out of Lebanese territory. West Beirut was encircled, and a three-month siege of PLO and Syrian forces commenced in mid-June. PLO Chairman Yassir Arafat vowed to turn Beirut into a Stalingrad, as in the classic urban war battle of the Eastern Front in World War II. In August, however, Habib arranged yet another settlement and facilitated the evacuation of the PLO and Syrian troops from Beirut. A three-nation Multi-National Force (MNF) arrived in Beirut in late August to keep the peace—consisting of French, American, and Italian troops. They left after the evacuation of the PLO and Syrians, but returned again in late September when Lebanese President Bashir Jumayil (Gemayel) was assassinated, and Maronite militiamen massacred Palestinians in reprisal in the Sabra and Sahtilla refugee camps.

Given France's history of mandatory rule, and the lingering conception of France as a "great power" with obligations in the former empire, Mitterand was compelled to participate in the renewed peacekeeping operations. There were now 1,500 French, 1,400 Americans, and eventually, 2,200 Italian troops, in the new MNF deployment in Beirut. Their goal was to keep the warring sides apart, although Israelis were still in Lebanon, which the Muslims resented. Muslim radicals soon altered the current status quo. On April 18, 1983, the U.S. embassy in West Beirut was bombed by disaffected Muslims (with sixty-three killed), and on October 23 the U.S. and MNF headquarters was car-bombed (with 298 killed).

The limited kind of involvement that France, America, and Italy committed to was not adequate to the task at hand, but the strategic difficulties involved in larger-scale operations precluded what was needed to produce peace in Lebanon. The Muslims so despised the Israelis that the mere presence of Israeli soldiers inflamed Muslim tensions. Most Lebanese Muslims preferred the Syrians, as in the days of the mandate. A Lebanese-Israeli-American Accord made in May 1982 was subsequently repudiated by the Lebanese due to Syrian pressure.[19] Through the late 1980s, Lebanon was divided into warring Christian, Muslim, and Druze enclaves.[20] Both Syrian and Israeli forces supported native proxy armies and rival Christian and Muslim prime ministers. Finally, an Arab League Committee composed of Algerian president Benjadid, Moroccan king Hassan, and Saudi king Fahd helped arrange a cease-fire in September 1989. Within two years, the militias dissolved except the Shi'ite *Hizbullah* (supported by Iran). Syrian forces who were still occupying part of the country through the end of 2001 numbered some 25,000 men.

France had backed Maronite strongman Michel Aoun, and he sought protection from Syria in the French Embassy in October 1990 (where he stayed until he fled to France in August 1991). A degree of stability was achieved when the Lebanese Parliament elected Elias Hrawi as president in November 1989. Hrawi visited France in June 1995, and President Jacques Chirac spoke during the visit of a peculiar Lebanese "vocation to be a remarkable example to the world" of religious cooperation.[21] Given the massive political difficulties in Lebanon, France could do nothing more direct to alter the former mandate's situation. The Maronites, however, still looked to France for support, and they resented the Syrian presence, which favored the Muslims. Problems between Maronites and Syrian occupation forces lingered through 2001, when in August of that year some 250 Maronite activists were arrested for protesting the continued Syrian presence.[22] Lebanon has essentially become a client state of Syria.

ALGERIAN TRAGEDY

The FLN ruled Algeria as a one-party state from 1962 to 1989, during which time it adhered to socialistic economic policies, and was a key member of the non-aligned movement. The country experienced immediate internal problems stemming from the FLN's policies, Ben Bella's ruling style, and the brain drain of French technicians who went back to France. Serious Kabyle Berber uprisings had to be crushed by the army in 1963–1964, and Muhammad Khider absconded with $12 million worth of party funds after quarrels with Ben Bella (whose purges of party ranks caused a great deal of anxiety among FLN veterans). Thousands of *Harkis* were killed, and many others were deprived of their property, while the remnant *colon* community saw a substantial loss of property as it was confiscated by the state.[23] The *colons* were also barred from certain occupations and were not free to travel. Most of their churches were taken over by the state and transformed into mosques.

With the departure of French technicians, Algeria sought and received technicians and aid from the Soviet Union (causing anxiety in NATO).[24] Ben Bella actually sought to get what he could from each side of the Cold War conflict. He visited U.S. president Kennedy, then stopped in Cuba to see Castro, making sure to make public statements there critical of "American imperialism."[25] The Algerians were active at the 1964 non-aligned conference in Cairo, and then hosted a 1965 anticolonial conference in Algeria. The conference was complicated by the poorly timed overthrow of Ben Bella by Defense Minister Houari Boumedienne (Ben Bella was held under house arrest for fourteen years).[26] Boumedienne ruled until his death in 1978, and the army took over from the party as the country's primary source of power. He made the country lean more toward socialist economics. Strategic interests, including oil development and trade considerations, however, kept Algeria connected to France. De Gaulle's secretary of state for foreign affairs, Jean de Broglie, commented in 1964 that it was France's goal to keep Algeria from going communist, and to use that country as "the 'narrow door' through which we are penetrating the Third World."[27]

Boumedienne's successor was the more liberal Colonel Chadli Benjadid, who ended some of the more repressive policies of his predecessors, and released Ahmed Ben Bella.[28] An Islamic revival occurred in Algeria in the mid-1980s, and Muslim militants began criticizing the secular nature of the government.[29] Huge protests and riots by the Muslim militants wracked the country in 1985 and 1988. Changes in the Soviet Union under Gorbachev and the end of the Warsaw Pact in 1989 accelerated a shift away from socialist practices in Algeria and elsewhere. In response to internal and external factors, Benjadid allowed a referendum in February 1989, which accepted a new constitution. The constitution essentially ended one-party rule by the FLN, and forced the army to remove itself from the political arena. Other political parties soon emerged, whose operatives were already functioning clandestinely.[30]

The most important of these was the *Front Islamique du Salut* (FIS), established in 1989 by Abassi Madani. The FIS won a number of municipal and provincial elections in 1990.[31] Its goal was to establish the *sharia* throughout Algeria, and general sentiment was so sympathetic that it won by a large margin in 1991 in the first free national elections for the Algerian Assembly. The FIS won 188 seats, while the FLN won only fifteen seats. Benjadid, however, was overthrown by the army, and the results were overturned. The army set up a military government composed of a shadowy oligarchy called *Le Pouvoir*. Leadership of this government passed to Muhammad Boudiaff in 1991, then to Ali Kafi, and in 1994, to General Liamine Zeroual.[32] Huge FIS-inspired protests occurred late in 1991, and the government banned the party. An FIS military force, called the Islamic Salvation Army, established itself on the western and eastern edges of the country.

At around this time a much more dangerous organization emerged called the *Groupe Islamique Armeé* (GIA).[33] Founded by Mansouri Miliani, the GIA's goal was, like the FIS, the establishment of the *sharia* in Algeria. Its tactics, however, have differed from those of the FIS in the more extensive use of violence to achieve its goal.[34] *Colon* residents (including monks and priests) and visiting European workers have been traditional targets of GIA assassins. Another primary group of GIA victims has been Algerian Muslims regarded as Westernizers, including journalists, educators, and entertainers. The GIA has recruited heavily among Kabyle Berbers for members. The organization has been especially strong in northern areas around Algiers, not in the oil and gas regions far in the south. The GIA's activities have included kidnappings, torture, carbombings, and throat-slittings. The worst atrocities have occurred during Ramadan (November–December).

The vast majority of the GIA's victims have been ordinary Algerians whom it has regarded as loyal to the military government or the FIS. There are two strains of GIA thought—one wants to work for revolution in the wider world (the *Salafists*), and the other advocates revolution in Algeria only (the *Djazarists*). The two branches have quarreled violently over their rival visions. Altogether, there may be 10,000 members in the organization. In ten years (1992–2002), the GIA has killed about 100,000 victims. There has been an appearance of a strange collusion between the GIA and the army, as there have been many stories of the army sealing off an area and the GIA being allowed to commit mass murder. The secular military government has received the sympathy of Western powers as a consequence of the rise of Islamic radicalism, and some have speculated that the Algerian government has allowed some of the GIA's activities to occur for international advantage. The government severed relations with Iran and Sudan in 1993, claiming that those countries supported the GIA.[35]

In 1993 the GIA issued a statement that it wanted to rid the country of foreigners, and some eighteen Westerners were killed from October to December. Among the atrocities in 1994 were the killing of two French Catholic priests in Algiers in May, and five French Embassy workers in Algiers in August. In December the GIA hijacked an Air France flight to Algiers. The hijackers threatened to blow up the plane over Paris, and flew to Marseilles (home to a huge Muslim population). The fifty-four-hour siege began on Christmas Eve, and three hostages were murdered before a French anti-terror squad stormed the plane in Marseilles on December 26 (killing the four hijackers). The next day, the GIA killed four more priests in Algeria in revenge for the deaths of the hijackers. A dozen more Europeans were killed in Algeria in 1995, including two nuns killed in their Algiers convent, pipeline workers killed at their work site, and *colon* couples walking in public parks.

The 1995 elections in which General Zeroual was elected president were boycotted by the FIS. The GIA had no interest in elections of any sort. In March 1996 seven French monks were kidnapped in Medea, and held for over a month by the GIA, who offered to trade them for GIA operatives being held in French prisons. They were killed by the GIA after the French government refused to negotiate. On August 1, the French Catholic Archbishop of Oran and his chauffeur were blown up after he had met with the French foreign minister. Fearing the negative implications from such blatant images of jihad against resident Christians, General Zeroual banned all parties based on religion that December. The pace of GIA murder of ordinary Algerians intensified in 1997. On August 29, ninety-eight were killed in Rais, south of Algiers; on September 23, eighty-five were killed and sixty-seven wounded at Baraki, also near Algiers.

The GIA declared the *sharia* mandatory in the Algiers casbah in September, banning music and smoking, and declaring that women were not allowed in public without a related male escort present. The government tried to prevent the GIA from administering its brand of punishment. That fall, the government announced a cease-fire with the FIS and its Islamic Salvation Army, which contest had been a much lower-intensity conflict than that with the GIA. But it had no impact on the activities of the GIA except perhaps in intensifying the pace of murder. During Ramadan, some 400 ordinary Algerians were killed in a wave of GIA car-bombings and shootings in Algiers. General Zeroual tired of the conflict, and announced in 1998 that he would retire nineteen months before the end of his five-year term, and allow a new democratic election. In Ramadan 1998, 1,600 Algerians were killed by the GIA, 1,100 of whom were killed in the Relizane region, 150 miles southwest of Algiers.

The presidential election in April 1999 was won by Foreign Minister Abd al-Aziz Bouteflika, who was supported by the army. There were widespread allegations of fraud. Only 400 Algerians were killed in Ramadan 1999, a sign to many observers that the GIA may have begun losing its ability to conduct its operations on as large a scale as in previous years. The situation in Algeria is far from resolved, as the GIA still continues to commit murders. But GIA members are active elsewhere, in other radical Muslim groups, including Osama Bin Laden's *al-Qa'ida* organization. Algeria remains a country gripped by terror. France has supported the military regimes that have held power since the 1980s. France has been Algeria's largest trading partner for much of the period since independence, and French technicians have returned to the country. For these reasons, the GIA has targeted France for terrorism. France's commitment to its former Islamic empire has drawn it into a conflict with radical Muslims, which the French Right has equated with the battles of Charles Martel and St. Louis of centuries earlier.

FRANCE AS A NEW BATTLEGROUND

Today there are 14 million Muslims in Western Europe as a whole, many of whom are second- or third-generation immigrants of Arab, Turkish, or South Asian origin. France has a Muslim population of between 4 million and 5 million, out of 58 million French citizens total. France experienced an influx of Muslim industrial labor during World War I, particularly into Paris, Lille, and Marseilles. Substantial suburban enclaves of poor Arab Muslims from Algeria emerged. St.-Denis, for example, is 25 percent Muslim today. The immigrants typically sent money home to family members, but remained at their European destination. Algerian political groups recruited in these suburban enclaves and fostered there a political consciousness connected to Algerian domestic developments.

In the late 1950s, France became a battefield as inter-Algerian violence spilled over into pockets of immigrants located in French cities. In 1957 alone, some 4,000 Algerians were killed in struggles between the FLN and the MLA (Messali Hajj's leftist organization). As France's situation in Algeria deteriorated, there were more instances of domestic backlash directed against the Algerian immigrants in the country. When a curfew was imposed on Algerian neighborhoods in Paris by Police Prefect Maurice Papon on October 17, 1961, Muslim demonstrations and rioting occurred. This in turn brought on a severe police response, in which 200 Algerian immigrants were killed. After Algerian independence, some of the important *Harkis* managed to flee to France, and from time to time FLN defectors arrived in France, as well.

Anti-immigrant sentiment coalesced into a right-wing political movement in the 1970s. A deputy named Jean-Marie Le Pen, who had been critical of de Gaulle's handling of the Algerian situation, formed an ultra-nationalist, anti-immigration party called the Front National (FN). By the 1980s, the FN won a significant share of seats in the National Assembly (almost 10 percent in 1986 elections), and took about one-third of the votes in many local elections, particularly in areas of the country where the Muslim immigrant population is high. Le Pen was elected to the European Parliament in 1984, and 4 million Frenchmen voted for him in his unsuccessful 1988 bid for the presidency. A 1973 novel by Jean Raspail called *Le Camp des Saints* (The Camp of Saints) reflected popular fears of an immigrant invasion, and the idea that it was cultural suicide for Europe to open its doors to large numbers of Third World immigrants (particularly as Europeans had lately been compelled to flee their colonies in the Third World). The book was harshly criticized (especially by the pro-immigration Left), but it sold enormously well nonetheless. Mainstream French authors were also beginning to regard Islam as a threat to the Western world. *Le Monde*'s long-time Cairo correspondent, Jean-Pierre Peroncel-Hugoz, wrote an important critique of the treatment of Christians in the Islamic world in a 1983 book called *Le radeau de Mahomet* (The Raft of Muhammad), which shaped French opinion.

The Iranian Revolution (1979) contributed to the resurgence of radical anti-Western Islamic movements around the world in the 1980s, and to fears of recruitment of immigrant Muslims into radical Islamic groups. Daniel Pipes has suggested that perhaps 9 percent of French Muslims held views consistent with radical Islam in the 1980s. When President Mitterand decided to change France's liberal immigration policies in the mid-1980s, some cyincs believed he was caving in to the anti-immigrant fears of the FN rather than responding to economic crises affecting the country, as he explained.[36] France was also affected by the Salman Rushdie affair of 1988–1989. Rushdie's novel *The Satanic Verses* caused a furor in the Islamic world, as many traditionalist-minded Muslims argued that it defamed the Prophet Muhammad and needed to be banned. Extremist Muslim clerics in Iran declared Rushdie (a South Asian Muslim who was a British subject) to be a heretic.

The Iranian *Ayatullahs* offered a reward for Rushdie's murder, and threatened the Western companies that published the book. *Ayatullah* Rafsanjani said Britain, Germany, France, and the United States in particular were trying to discredit Islam by allowing the book's publication.[37]

Among the first organized Muslim protests against the book was that outside the French Embassy in the Philippines. Some of the Islamic governments that made possession of the book illegal included the former French colonies of Mali and the Comoros. The original French company that was planning to publish the book, Presses de la Cité, decided at the last minute not to publish it, allegedly at the suggestion of Interior Minister Pierre Joxe.[38] French record stores around the same time pulled a recording by singer Veronique Sanson called "Allah," about religious tolerance, because the singer and some stores had received death threats from radical Muslims.[39]

The year 1989 saw the emergence of what came to be called the "Scarf Controversy." Lasting until 1994, this was a series of thirteen incidents in which young female Muslims got into legal trouble for wearing the *hijab*, the traditional Muslim woman's head scarf, to public schools in France. The National Assembly took up the issue of whether wearing the scarf was legally acceptable, as Christians could not wear the Crucifix and Jews could not wear the Star of David to school, according to French law. The first case in 1989 involved three young teenage girls (two Moroccans and one Tunisian) who were expelled by the principal of Creil Junior High School for refusing his demand to stop wearing the Muslim scarf in accordance with the existing laws requiring secularization of the French public educational system.[40] Here, curiously, French leftist organizations declared against "diversity" because of the alleged need to keep French public schools entirely secular. The FN agreed, but for different reasons. In November 1989, Education Minister Lionel Jospin and Prime Minister Michel Rocard said the Creil students could not wear the scarf, then reversed their position, nervous of a potential political and religious backlash by Muslims.[41] The dozen other incidents (some seemingly designed to provoke) finally resulted in a definitive decision in September 1994, by Education Minister François Bayrou to ban the wearing of the scarf.[42]

The Chanel fashion company found itself embroiled in a controversy with Muslims in January 1994. German designer Karl Lagerfeld used calligraphy he saw on the Taj Mahal (which he said he took to be love poetry) and used it, embroidered in gray pearls, on a black bustier he made for Chanel. The problem was that the pearls spelled out a Qur'anic verse, and the model who wore the bustier at a fashion show (Claudia Schiffer) received death threats over the garment. Muslims in Indonesia made the first protest, at the German Embassy in Jakarta. Chanel's chairman, Claude Eliette, met with a French Muslim leader, Dalil Boubakeur, and promised to burn the three bustiers, and issued a public appeal to all photographers and television crews "to return their films or pledge to destroy them."[43]

Another cultural problem emerged in France in October 1997, when actress and animal rights activist Brigitte Bardot criticized the Muslim ritual slaughter of sheep at the end of Ramadan. The actress was actually taken to court to face charges of defamation. She was found guilty of inciting "racial violence," and was forced to pay a fine in the tens of thousands of francs (several thousand dollars). Bardot made the same criticisms and went to court again in 1998 and 2000, with the same results. Seemingly angered at the turn of events, she has also written, *a la Raspail*, in not so warm terms of the Muslim immigrants flowing into France.

As GIA attacks intensified against the military dictatorship in Algeria, which regime was supported by France, France itself became a primary target for GIA operatives. The Air France hijacking in December 1994 demonstrated that the GIA was changing its tactics. In 1995 a series of bomb attacks were launched in France by the GIA that killed eight and wounded 150. The seeming failure of the Socialist party leadership to handle the terrorism paved the way for the long-serving (1977–1995) Gaullist mayor of Paris, Jacques Chirac, to be elected president of France in May 1995. Chirac had learned some Arabic when he was younger and had personal ties with Iraqi dictator Saddam Hussein in the 1970s. His foreign minister, Alain Juppé, worked to end the ongoing embargo on Iraq stemming from the time of the Persian Gulf War (1991). Several French oil firms are known to have an interest in developing oil pipelines in Iraq. Chirac's regime also has undertaken to make some contacts with the FIS in order to try to marginalize the GIA in Algeria, and it has supported Palestinian rights in Israel.

The domestic French Islamic terror problem intensified in 1996 with the emergence of the "Roubaix Gang."[44] Consisting of several dozen individuals, the gang's members included both Muslim immigrants and ethnic French converts to Islam, some of whom had assisted Muslims in Bosnia and trained there. One of the gang's leaders was Fateh Kamel, an Algerian with Canadian citizenship, who had an expertise in document forgery. The gang conducted a series of bank robberies in the Lille region in 1996 to fund radical Islamic activities (including making false identity documents and purchasing weapons for terrorism). The gang had been thought to be only a group of common criminals, but the true nature of the organization became apparent when the police arrested members for failed car-bomb explosions intended to disrupt the G-7 Summit in Lille in 1996. In late March there was a wild car chase and shootout to arrest some Roubaix Gang leaders including Omar Zemmiri (arrested in Belgium) and Hocine Benadaoui (arrested in France).[45] Another Roubaix leader, Mouloud Boughalene, was arrested in Bosnia. The investigation revealed that many Roubaix operatives had trained in Bosnia, and that Kamel had visited Osama Bin Laden in Afghanistan. Kamel also visited a petty criminal named Ahmed Ressam in Montreal, Canada, a man who subsequently was arrested trying to smuggle explosives into Seattle from Canada to disrupt millennium celebrations in the United States. In the end, Kamel and twenty-three of his colleagues were convicted in 2001 of terrorist activities, but proving direct connections with Bin Laden's *al-Qa'ida* proved elusive. Of course, it was only after the 1998 U.S. Embassy bombings in East Africa that Bin Laden came to be regarded as the kind of serious threat to Western countries that he is now known to have been since the mid-1990s.

French intelligence learned a great deal by infiltration, and their domestic strategic threat assessments were more accurate in many respects than those in many other Western countries. French intelligence agents uncovered a GIA plot in May 1998 to blow up the World Cup soccer tournament, then about to begin in France.[46] Fifty-three Muslim extremists associated with the GIA faction led by Hassan Hattab (men of French, Algerian, Tunisian, and Moroccan extraction) were arrested, and an incriminating computer and video were confiscated. By this time, many overseas GIA operatives were beginning to work for *al-Qa'ida*.

The September 11, 2001, attacks on the World Trade Center and the Pentagon by *al-Qa'ida* suicide attackers opened a new era of international cooperation against Islamic terrorism. In the subsequent American and Afghan warlord operation to drive the Taliban and *al-Qa'ida* from Afghanistan, a document surfaced called the "Manual of Afghan Jihad," which listed the Eiffel Tower as a legitimate terror target, being a site of "sentimental value." *Al-Qa'ida's* goal has been to force America to stop supporting Israel and withdraw its forces from Saudi Arabia, but France might be targeted as an American ally. In the operations against the Taliban and *al-Qa'ida*, some sixty Foreign Legionnaires participated in the restoration of the Mazar-i-Sharif airfield in late November 2001.

On September 21, 2001, just ten days after the horrendous *al-Qa'ida* suicide attacks on New York City and Washington, D.C., an AZF Petrochemical plant blew up in Toulouse in what originally was thought to be a chemical accident, killing twenty-nine and injuring 1,170. Subsequent investigations revealed the explosion to be the work of a Tunisian with French citizenship named Hassan Jandoubi, who had been hired a short time before the blast and had quarreled with fellow workers at the plant who had displayed the American flag in sympathy with the September 11 disasters. Jandoubi was found dead at the scene wearing the kind of garb that French police described as those of "kamikaze fundamentalists."[47] The blast caused a great deal of damage to the neighborhood, including a nearby facility that produces fuel for Arianespace, the French rocket company. An ammonia cloud caused schools and hospitals to be evacuated, and the Toulouse Open tennis tournament was canceled.

The arrest of Djamel Beghal (an Algerian with French citizenship) in Dubai in July 2001, for using a false passport led to the uncovering of an *al-Qa'ida* plot to blow up the American Embassy in Paris.[48] An *al-Qa'ida* plot to blow up historic Strasbourg Cathedral was also uncovered in 2001. This plot was intended to be the work of an Algerian *al-Qa'ida* faction called *Miliani* (named after GIA founder Mansouri Miliani) whose leader, Muhammad Bensakhria, had trained in Afghanistan and was arrested in Alicante, Spain.[49] Strasbourg had been the scene of a bitter controversy over plans to construct a huge mosque with funds from foreign Islamic governments, which the FN had loudly protested against (and had printed posters of a minaret attached to the cathedral, with the words: "Une mosquée centrale a Strasbourg? Non, c'est Non!"). The cathedral was a symbol of French national pride, the kind of target *al-Qa'ida* preferred to strike. Arrests in the Strasbourg case linked European *al-Qa'ida* operatives with a Moroccan holding French citizenship, Zacharias Moussaoui, who was subsequently been accused of collusion in the September 11 terror attacks (he was to have commandeered a fourth plane to fly into an American target).

Despite the fact of increased Franco-American cooperation in the struggle against *al-Qa'ida*, Chirac's foreign minister, Hubert Vedrine, expressed his dissatisfaction in February 2002 over what he termed the American tendency to simplify the issues involved in combating terrorism, especially America's support for Israel's hard-line approach to the Palestinians.

He believes that such policies cause even more problems by further antagonizing Muslims against the West. This is a critical concern for a country that is very much on the front line in the recent struggles between radical Islam and the West. France will remain on that front line due to its unique history and paternalistic tendencies toward its former empire, and due to the legacy of years of liberal immigration policies that have brought inhabitants of the former empire into French cities.

CONCLUSION

France's history of extensive contacts with Islam and Muslim populations at home and abroad have conditioned French foreign and domestic policies. France has maintained a presence in certain strategic areas of its former empire, including Chad and Djibouti, and has sent Legionnaires into foreign operations to assert France's interests in the face of ever-more complicated politics and economics—successfully in Chad, unsuccessfully in Lebanon. Since the end of the empire, a succession of French leaders (from de Gaulle to Chirac) have sought to exercise an influence in the former empire in a variety of ways, including such different endeavors as providing economic development assistance and defense assistance to sub-Saharan African countries, to the post-FLN military leaders of Algeria, and to the uneasy Maronite-Muslim coalition government in Lebanon.

Today, France finds itself increasingly pressed between the extreme policies of the GIA and *al-Qa'ida*, on the one hand, and the FN, on the other. France's Muslim minority may become endangered by a domestic backlash if the FN grows and the activities of the GIA and *al-Qa'ida* are not curbed from within the Muslim community itself. That French intelligence on radical Islamic groups is regarded as a step ahead of many other Western nations is the consequence of significantly greater contacts with Muslims over a longer period of time than that experienced by most other Western nations—the legacy of French Orientalists, and of Charles Martel, St. Louis, and Napoleon, as much as the existence of a French Islamic Empire that lasted for over a century.

Documents

I. AL-MAQQARI ON THE ITINERARY OF THE EIGHTH-CENTURY MUSLIM INVASIONS OF THE FRANKISH KINGDOM

One of the most geographically detailed Arabic sources for the early Muslim activity in France is the North African author al-Maqqari (d. 1631), who preserved parts of earlier works that are apparently no longer extant. One of the authors whose work was preserved by al-Maqqari is Ibn Hayyan (d. 1076). Not possessing an accurate chronology of the eighth-century events when he wrote in the sixteenth and seventeenth centuries, al-Maqqari blended together events from earlier activities of Tariq Ibn Ziyad and Musa Ibn Nusayr, who established Umayyad authority in al-Andalus, with those of Andalusi amirs al-Samh lbn Malik al-Khawlani, 'Anbasah Ibn Suhaym al-Kalbi, and Yusuf Ibn 'Abd al-Rahman, each of whom invaded Frankish realms in the 720s and 730s. The chronology can be superimposed onto the itinerary by examining the dates of the Muslim raids on individual monasteries, churches, and towns mentioned in the Frankish sources. Translation from the Arabic text in al-Maqqari (F. Dozy, G. Dugat, L. Krehl, and W. Wright, eds.), *Analectes sur l'histoire et la littérature des Arabes d'Espagne,* 2 vols. (Amsterdam: Oriental Press, 1967), 173.

The Muslims passed into Ifranja, and they conquered, plundered, established themselves, overwhelmed [their enemies], and pressed on until they arrived ultimately at the Wadi Rudanah (Rhône River). This was the most distant trace of the Arabs and their farthest foothold in the land of the barbarians. Detachments and raiding parties of Tariq had subjugated the country of 'Ifiranja, and the two cities of Barshaluna (Barcelona) and 'Arbuna (Narbonne) were seized, as was the rock of 'Abinyun (Avignon) and the fortress of Ludhun (Lyon) on the Wadi Rudanah.

II. DIFFERING ACCOUNTS OF THE BATTLE OF TOURS (732)

The Catholic monks of the Frankish realm recorded the local history of their monasteries and the historical events from elsewhere of which they may have heard. Some of them employed a common *corpus* of material for certain events, whose ultimate origins are only imprecisely known. Arabic historians, meanwhile, attempted to create universal histories based on earlier source material. The earliest Arabic account was written by Ibn 'Abd al-Hakam (d. 871) in the ninth century. The greatest Arabic annalistic historian was the Iraqi writer 'Izz al-Din Ibn al-Athir (d. 1234). One of the more widely recorded Christian-Muslim encounters of the eighth century was the battle fought between the Merovingian Frankish *Major Domus* Charles Martel and the Umayyad amir of al-Andalus, 'Abd ar-Rahman al-Ghafiqi, somewhere between Tours and Poitiers. Later historians magnified the importance of the Frankish victory to a titanic struggle between East and West, while more recent revisionist historians have seemingly overreacted, by relegating the battle to the realm of virtual insignificance. The Latin chronicles were compiled in the *Monumenta Germaniae Historica [MGH] Scriptores*, vol. I, G. H. Pertz, ed. (Hanover: Monumenta Germaniae Historica, 1826)—*Annals of St. Amand*, p. 8; *Annales Petaviani*, p 9; *Annals of Lorsch*, p. 24. The version of Ibn 'Abd al-Hakam is from *Futuh Misr*, ed. C. C. Torrey (New Haven: Yale University Press, 1922), 216–217. The excerpt from Ibn al-Athir is from 'Izz al-Din Ibn al-Athir, *al-Kamil fi 't-Tarikh*, vol. 5 (Beirut: Dar Sader and Dar Beyrouth, 1965), 174. Translations mine. The passage by Edward Gibbon is from *The Decline and Fall of the Roman Empire*, vol. 6, ed. J. B. Bury (New York: AMS Press, 1974), 16.

A. Latin Chronicles

1. **Annals of St. Amand,** *sub anno* 732:
Charles fought a battle against the Saracens in the month of October.
2. **Annales Petaviani,** *sub anno* 732:
Charles fought a battle against the Saracens in the month of October on a saturday.
3. **Annals of Lorsch,** *sub anno* 732:
Charles fought against Saracens on a saturday near Poitiers.

B. Arabic Chronicles

1. Ibn 'Abd al-Hakam, **Futuh Misr:**

Ubayda [had] appointed 'Abd ar-Rahman 'Abd Allah al-Akki as governor of al-Andalus. 'Abd ar-Rahman was a virtuous man, and hence he undertook a military expedition to 'Ifranja. They [the Franks] are the most distant enemy of [the Muslims of] al-Andalus. 'Abd ar-Rahman took a great deal of booty and he gained a victory over them. He obtained much gem-encrusted gold, covered with pearls, rubies, chrysolite, and he commanded that it be broken up. He sent out one-fifth of it [to 'Ubayda] and divided [the rest] among the Muslims who were with him. When news of this reached 'Ubayda, he was greatly angered. He sent a message to 'Abd ar-Rahman, demanding that he arrange to come to him. 'Abd ar-Rahman then sent a message to 'Ubayda, saying that "until the sky and the Earth are joined, the Merciful One would make the devout ones among them go out [to do battle with the infidels]." Then he led another military expedition against the Franks. He and all of his companions were martyred. His death, Yahya tells us, occurred in the year 115 A.H.

2. Ibn al-Athir, **al-Kamil fi't-Ta'rikh:**

Mention of the death of 'Abd ar-Rahman, Amir of al-Andalus and the Government of 'Abd al-Malik Ibn Qatan:

In this year, and it was the year 113... 'Ubayda appointed 'Abd ar-Rahman Ibn 'Abd Allah al-Ghafiqi as governor of al-Andalus. He undertook a military expedition to 'Ifranja, and he penetrated deeply into the land of Franks. He took a great deal of booty, and he obtained much gem-encrusted gold, covered with pearls, rubies, and emeralds. He broke it up and divided it among the people. News of this reached 'Ubayda and he was greatly angered. He sent a message to 'Abd ar-Rahman and chastised him. 'Abd ar-Rahman responded, and he was a virtuous man: "Until the sky and the Earth were joined, Allah would make the devout ones go out [to do battle with the infidels]." He then went out, leading a military expedition to the land of the Franks in this year. It is said that this was in the year 114 A.H., and this is the correct year; he and those who were with him died as martyrs for the faith.

C. Edward Gibbon, The Decline and Fall of the Roman Empire:

A victorious line of march had been prolonged above a thousand miles from the rock of Gibraltar to the bank of the Loire; the repetition of an equal space would have carried the Saracens to the confines of Poland and the Highlands of Scotland; the Rhine is not more impassable than the Nile or Euphrates, and the Arabian fleet might have sailed without a naval combat into the mouth of the Thames. Perhaps the interpretation of the Koran would now be taught in the schools of Oxford, and her pupils might demonstrate to a circumcised people the sanctity and truth of the revelation of Muhammad.

III. THE CRUSADES

The medieval Latin Christian struggle against Islam manifested itself in a series of overseas campaigns to Palestine, Egypt, and Tunisia in what originally was conceived of as a kind of armed pilgrimage, and later, as a formal venture known as a

crusade. Lasting from 1095 to 1270, eight distinct large expeditions (and many unenu-
merated smaller ones) were international undertakings whose purpose was to regain
the sites associated with the life of Christ and transform them again into Christian
lands. European—mainly French—colonization occurred within the crusader states,
and for almost 200 years, the crusaders held territory in the eastern Mediterranean,
which they called *Outremer* (the land beyond the sea). Reproduced here are: (1) the
initial call for crusaders by Pope Urban II in 1095 from among French knights, as
described by Robert the Monk; (2) an account of the perils of crusading, by Jean de
Joinville, who was captured in Egypt on the Fifth Crusade with St. Louis, April 1250;
(3) a description of the demise of the crusader states by Sir Stephen Runciman.
Urban's appeal was translated by Dana C. Munro, and comes from his volume
titled *Urban and the Crusaders* (Philadelphia: University of Pennsylvania, 1895),
5–8; Joinville's account was translated by M. R. B. Shaw in *Joinville and Villehardouin: Chronicles of the Crusades* (Harmondsworth, Middlesex, UK: Penguin,
1977), 242–243; Runciman's narrative is from the third volume of *A History of the
Crusades, the Kingdom of Acre and the Later Crusades* (New York: Harper and Row,
1967), 423.

A. Robert the Monk, Urban's Appeal for Crusaders:

Oh, race of Franks, race from across the mountains, race chosen and beloved by
God—as shines forth in very many of your works—set apart from all nations by
the situation of your country, as well as by your catholic faith and the honor of the
holy church! To you our discourse is addressed and for you our exhortation is
intended. We wish you to know what a grievous cause has led us to your country,
what peril threatening you and all the faithful has brought us. From the confines
of Jerusalem and the city of Constantinople a horrible tale has gone forth and very
frequently has been brought to our ears, namely, that a race from the kingdom of
the Persians, an accursed race, a race utterly alienated from God, a generation for-
sooth which has not directed its heart and has not entrusted its spirit to God, has
invaded the lands of those Christians and has depopulated them by the sword, pil-
lage and fire; it has led away a part of the captives into its own country, and a part
it has destroyed by cruel tortures; it has either entirely destroyed the churches of
God or appropriated them for the rites of its own religion.... The kingdom of the
Greeks is now dismembered by them and deprived of territory so vast in extent
that it can not be traversed in a march of two months. On whom therefore is the
labor of avenging these wrongs and of recovering this territory incumbent, if not
upon you? You, upon whom above other nations God has conferred remarkable
glory in arms, great courage, bodily activity, and strength to humble the hairy
scalp of those who resist you. Let the deeds of your ancestors move you and incite
your minds to manly achievements; the glory and greatness of king Charles the
Great, and of his son Louis, and of your other kings, who have destroyed the king-
doms of the pagans, and have extended in these lands the territory of the holy
church. Let the holy sepulchre of the Lord our Savior, which is possessed by

unclean nations, especially incite you, and the holy places which are now treated with ignominy and irreverently polluted with their filthiness. Oh, most valiant soldiers and descendants of invincible ancestors, be not degenerate, but recall the valor of your progenitors.

B. Jean de Joinville, on the perils of crusading in Egypt, from *La Vie de Saint Louis:*

After our sailors had brought us out of the creek into which they had taken us, we saw two small ships (which the king had given us to shelter our sick) flying towards Damietta. Then the wind had begun to blow so strongly from the north, that, in spite of the current, we could make no headway. Alongside both banks of the [Nile] river were a great number of small craft belonging to those of our people who had not been able to get down the stream, and had consequently been stopped and captured by the Saracens. These wretches were killing our men and flinging their bodies into the water, and dragging chests and baggage out of the boats they had taken. The mounted Saracens on the bank shot arrows at us because we refused to go over to them. My men had given me a jousting hauberk to put on, to prevent my being wounded by the shafts that kept falling into our boat.... [W]e saw four of the sultan's galleys coming towards us, with a good thousand men aboard. So I called my knights and the rest of my men together and asked them which they would prefer to surrender to the sultan's galleys or to the Saracens on shore. We all agreed that we would rather surrender to the sultan's galleys, because in that way we should remain together, than yield ourselves to the enemy on land, who would separate us, and sell us to the Bedouins.

C. Stephen Runciman, on the demise of the crusader states, *A History of the Crusades:*

For some months the Sultan's troops marched up and down the coast-lands, carefully destroying anything that might be of value to the Franks should they ever attempt another landing. Orchards were cut down, irrigation-systems put out of order. The only castles that were left standing were those that were back from the coast, like Mount Pilgrim at Tripoli, and Marqab on its high mountain. Along the sea there was desolation. The peasants of those once-rich farms saw their steads destroyed and sought refuge in the mountains. Those of Frankish origin hastened to merge themselves with the natives; and the native Christians were treated little better than slaves. The old easy tolerance of Islam was gone. Embittered by the long religious wars, the victors had no mercy for the infidel.

IV. NAPOLEON IN EGYPT

The impetus for Napoleon's campaign in Egypt in 1798 derived from the evolving Franco-British rivalry, rather than from a spirit of crusade. His attitudes toward

Islam were shaped by a tolerance born of the Enlightenment, and by an interest in winning the Egyptians over to the French side against Britain. His occupation forces defeated superior Mamluk and Turkish forces (honing the skills of his officers who would win him an empire in Europe), and held out for two years, even after British ships sank the French fleet in the Battle of the Nile. During that time, Western influences seeped into Egyptian society, including the printing press and newspapers, while French Orientalists like Champollion would soon decipher the mysteries of hieroglyphics from the Rosetta Stone, which was found by Napoleon's soldiers. Below is an excerpt from Napoleon's proclamation to his troops before Alexandria, translated by J. Christopher Herold, in *Bonaparte in Egypt* (New York: Harper and Row, 1962), 56.

The Mamluk beys, who exclusively favor English trade, who have oppressed our merchants with vexations, and who are tyrannizing over the unhappy people of the Nile valley, will cease to exist in a few days after our landing. The people with whom we shall live are Mohammedans. Their chief creed is this: "There is no God but God, and Muhammad is His prophet." Do not contradict them. Act toward them as in the past you have acted toward the Jews and the Italians. Respect their muftis and imams, as you have respected the rabbis and the bishops. Show the same tolerance toward the ceremonies prescribed by the Koran and toward the mosques as you have shown toward convents and synagogues, toward the religions of Moses and Jesus Christ. The Roman legions used to protect all religions.... The first city we shall see was built by Alexander. At every step we shall find traces of deeds worthy of being emulated by the French.

V. BOURMONT'S ULTIMATUM TO THE DEY OF ALGIERS

Count Louis de Bourmount (1773–1846) commanded the French forces that defeated the dey of Algiers in 1830. He had previously served under Napoleon and Louis XVIII, and became a marshal of France in the Bourbon Restoration. In the summer of 1830 he led a brilliant campaign against the Turkish forces in Algeria, which culminated in the surrender of the dey and his men. Reprinted here is Bourmont's ultimatum to the dey on July 4, 1830, which the dey accepted. It is reprinted from Barton Perceval, *Algiers, with Notices of the Neighboring States of Barbary* vol. 1 (London: 1835), Whittaker and Company 119–120.

Ultimatum to the Dey of Algiers:

1. The fort of the Kassaubah, with all the other forts dependent on Algiers, and the harbour, shall be placed in the hands of the French troops the 5th of July, at 10 o'clock, A.M.
2. The general-in-chief of the French army ensures the Dey of Algiers personal liberty, and all his private property.

3. The Dey shall be free to retire with his family and wealth wherever he pleases. While he remains at Algiers he and his family shall be under the protection of the commander-in-chief. A guard shall insure his safety, and that of his family.

4. The same advantages, and same protection are assured to all the soldiers of the militia.

5. The exercise of the Mohammedan religion shall remain free; the liberty of the inhabitants of all classes, their religion, property, commerce, and industry shall receive no injury; their women shall be respected: the general takes this on his own responsibility.

6. The ratification of this convention to be made before 10 A.M., on the 5th of July, and the French troops immediately after to take possession of the Kassaubah, and other forts.

VI. GUIZOT ON ALGERIA: 'ABD AL-QADIR, BUGEAUD, AND THE DUC D'AUMALE

François Guizot (1787–1874) was one of nineteenth-century France's leading statesmen, and one of the most important supporters of the "Citizen-King" Louis Philippe. Born to a Protestant family in Nîmes, Guizot became first, a deputy, then minister of public instruction (1833–1837), then prime minister, 1847–1848. After the definitive overthrow of the Bourbons in 1848, Guizot spent the rest of his life writing history and his memoirs. The following extract is from his *History of France,* trans. Robert Black (New York, The Cooperative Publication Society, 1869), 358–360.

Guns lost their dominion when, on the 18th March, 1845, the treaty between France and the Emperor of Morocco was signed. Abd el-Kader, nevertheless, still continued to infest our frontiers, and frequently made sudden attempts to surprise our soldiers, assisted by a wide-spread conspiracy of the Arabian chiefs. One of the insurrections in the Dahra tribes induced a struggle with a tribe till then unsubdued; and on the Mohammedans taking refuge in a cave when pursued by Colonel Pelissier, he summoned them several times to come forth, promising them their liberty if they delivered up their arms and horses. The Arabs refusing, the colonel had bundles of wood heaped up at the entrance of the cavern, and threatened to set fire to them. The Arabs fired upon our soldiers from within the cavern; the flames rose, and most of the obstinate wretches perished, choked by the smoke. In this deplorable alternative of the necessities of war, which put in the balance humanity towards the enemy and the safety of the soldiers whom he was commanding, Colonel Pelissier (after, Marshal Duc de Malakoff) acted as Ludlow did in Ireland against the peasants in revolt, as Napoleon did at Austerlitz against the Russian battalions when crowded on the ice, which he broke under their feet by cannon-shot. This act of Pelissier was fiercely attacked by the journals of the opposition. Guizot alone defended him. Marshal Bugeaud was greatly offended, thinking that his attempts at military colonization were not sufficiently encouraged; and without being authorized, addressed a circular to the chiefs of the Algerian corps, ordering the application of his views. The government's embarrassment in Algeria was increased by their authority being thus perpetually harassed. Bugeaud had already several times announced his intention to retire, but the renewal of hostilities with the Arabs, and the distinction of the campaign in the plains of the Mitidja against the insurrection excited by Abd el-Kader, delayed the accomplishment of this resolution. Marshal Soult, now old and weak, withdrew from the practical direction of affairs, soon to rest altogether with the title of Marshal-General of France, which had been borne only by Turenne, Villars, and Saxe. General Molines St. Yon, who succeeded him as war minister, drew up a scheme for military colonization which confirmed Bugeaud's views, though the latter considered it weak and colorless. The chamber objected to the proposal, and the ministry, in accordance with the decision of a special committee rejected it. Marshal Bugeaud immediately resigned.

The king had long thought of placing one of his sons at the head of the government of Algeria. The Duc d'Aumale served there with distinction, and Bugeaud wrote, "I wish to be replaced here by a prince, not in the interests of the constitutional monarchy, but those of the matter in hand. He will be granted what would be refused to me. The Duc d'Aumale is, and will daily more and more be, a man of ability. I shall leave him, I trust, the office in good working order; but there will still be much to do for a long time. It is a labor of giants and of ages." On the 11th September, 1847, the Duc d'Aumale was appointed Governor of Algeria, as the most natural successor to Marshal Bugeaud, and best fitted to exercise upon the army there, as well as the native races, a happy and powerful influence. Only a few months, however, were to elapse before the tempest of new revolutions tore him away from a life and duty that were dear to him. Before that sad day the young prince had at last forced Abd el-Kader to his last entrenchments, compelling from the hero of that religious and national resistance a submission which he was no longer able to refuse. In spite of several further attempts at insurrection, the conquest of Algeria was finally completed in February, 1848.

It was no doubt to our success in Africa and the prudent firmness of our attitude that we must attribute the development of our influence with the Mohammedans. From 1845 to 1847 the representatives of the great Mussulman powers flocked to Paris—the Morocco ambassador, Sidi-ben-Achache; Ibrahim Pacha, eldest son of Mehemet Ali; the Bey of Tunis; and the envoy from the Shah of Persia. Turkey had at last agreed to give the various races of Lebanon the natural chiefs whom they demanded, especially the Druses and Maronites. In spite of the opposition of the Pachas and their slow compliance, the European diplomatic demands obtained a certain amount of satisfaction. From 1845 to 1848 the state of the Syrian Christians was sensibly improved, and gave them hopes of a happier future. The same protection over the Christian populations extended throughout the Ottoman Empire. By a convention of 21st March, 1844, the lives of Christian converts who had been seized with remorse and abjured Islam were assured. France's influence had now regained in the east much of her ancient empire.

VII. NINETEENTH-CENTURY JUSTIFICATIONS OF EMPIRE

Jules Ferry (1832–1893) was one of France's leading statesmen in the nineteenth century. An anti-clerical left-wing politician, he reorganized the French educational system as minister of education, and then served as prime minister twice (1880–1881 and 1883–1885). In that capacity, Ferry was the French Left's leading proponent of empire. Following is an excerpt from a speech made by Ferry to the Chamber of Deputies in 1883 on the necessity of empire, from George B. Kirsch, Frederick M. Schweitzer, Wolodymyr Stojko, George L. Mahoney, *The West in Global Context* (Upper Saddle River, NJ: Prentice-Hall, 1997), 214–215. Gabriel Charmes (1850–1886) was an important pro-colonial journalist who wrote frequently of the empire in the *Journal des Debats,* edited at one time by his brother Francis. Charmes spent nine years traveling throughout the Middle East, spending time in Constantinople, Syria, Egypt, and Morocco, covering stories that he believed French readers needed to know, and making impassioned appeals for the expansion of French influence abroad. The excerpted passage is from the *Journal des Debats* (October 19, 1880), in Agnes Murphy, R-S.C.J., *The Ideology of French Imperialism, 1871–1881* (New York: Howard Fertig, 1968), 188–189. General Thomas Robert Bugeaud de la Piconnerie (1784–1849) was instrumental in the conquest of Algeria, and served as the colony's governor-general from 1840 to 1847. He had served in Napoleon's Imperial Guard, and remained an influential figure in France upon his return from Algeria. Following is an excerpt from a letter that he wrote to General Charon, dated September 4, 1848, in which he stresses the need to colonize Algeria with Frenchmen, excerpted from Paul H. Beik, *Louis Philippe and the July Monarchy* (Princeton: D. Van Nostrand Company, 1965), 162. General Louis H. G. Lyautey (1854–1934) was one of France's most distinguished soldiers of his day. He served with distinction in Indochina, Madagascar, and Algeria before being appointed France's first resident-general for the Protectorate of Morocco in 1912. He was an ardent imperialist, and excerpted here are some of his comments on the state of affairs in Morocco a year after his appointment, from David Thomson, ed., *France: Empire and Republic, 1850–1940, Historical Documents* (New York: Walker and Company, 1968), 314.

A. Jules Ferry, Speech before the Chamber of Deputies:

We say then, that all the portions of the colonial domain, its least shreds, must be sacred to us, first, because it is a legacy from the past, and next, because it is a reserve for the future. Must the Republic have an ephemeral policy, a shortsighted policy, preoccupied only with living from day to day? Must it not, like every other government, consider from a somewhat higher point of view, the future generations which are confided to it, the future of this great democracy of labor, industry, and trade, whose care is entrusted to it?

So you, gentlemen, who have regard for this future, who truly recognize that it belongs to those who work for it, and who are courageous, cast your eyes on the map of the world, and see with what watchfulness, with what eagerness, the great nations who are your friends or your rivals are reserving outlets for themselves. It is not a question of the future of tomorrow, but the future of 50 years or 100 years, of the future of even the Fatherland, of what will be the inheritance of our children.

B. Gabriel Charmes, in *Journal des Debats:*

If we leave the Oriental question to be resolved without us and against us, if we neglect to save our rights and those of our allies, if we abandon to European rivals those beautiful countries where our influence was formerly so preponderant, it would not only be our national prestige which would be injured, but our material prosperity of which we are so proud and which has sometimes consoled us in our misfortunes.

On that day when we shall no longer be in the Orient, and when other great European powers will be there, all will be at an end for our commerce in the Mediterranean, for our future in Asia, for the traffic of our southern ports. One of the most fruitful sources of our national wealth will be dried up.

C. General Thomas R. Bugeaud, Letter to General Charon:

I see with pleasure that at last public opinion is won over to an idea that I have set forth for some time, that of sending to Algeria the overflow of the population of our cities, and even transported convicts. This would with a single blow attain several great ends: 1. rid France of a persistently troublemaking element; 2. fulfill for a great number of proletarians a part of the absurd promises that the February Revolution made to them; 3. people the colony.

This population will be far from the equal of my military colonists; but in the present state of France, it is necessary to give up this excellent element; it is absolutely urgent to resign oneself, and at any cost, to establish in Africa those most excellent proletarians whose heads have been stuffed with the most disastrous ideas for them and for us.

D. General Louis H. G. Lyautey, Morocco in 1913:

Algeria took fifty years to conquer and pacify. It is only two years since we came out of the narrow limits of Chaouia to go to Fez. It is one year since I took command, and I would just ask you to look at the map to realize the advance in pacified territories. I have not asked for any reinforcements since the month of September, 1912. I know that there are none to send. I am faced with a country and a population of at least four times what we found on our arriving in Algeria, but fanatical in quite a different way, united, well-armed, and sustained by strange incitements which we never came across during the conquest of Algeria. I am well aware that the European situation does not allow any more troops to be sent, and I said from the start that France must at least give me money to compensate for the men she cannot give.

VIII. CROMER ON THE ANGLO-FRENCH RIVALRY IN THE MIDDLE EAST

Evelyn Baring (1841–1917), first Earl of Cromer, was one of the most prominent British colonial officials of his day. He served as commissioner of the Egyptian Public Debt Office, finance minister in India, and finally as the consul-general of Egypt (1883–1907). His 1908 book, *Modern Egypt*, serves as an important contemporary explanation of European imperialism in the late nineteenth and early twentieth centuries. The following excerpts are from vol. 2 of *Modern Egypt* (New York: Macmillan, 1908), pp 236–243 and 388–393, in which Cromer discussed (1) his perceptions of the differences between French and British imperialism in the Middle East, and (2) the Anglo-French Agreement of 1904 (the *Entente Cordiale*), in which the French agreed to continuing British influence in Egypt in return for British support for French influence in Morocco.

A. Differences between the British and French Imperial Styles in the Orient

For half a century prior to the British occupation, therefore, during which time the British Government were wholly inactive in respect to Egyptian education, no effort was spared to propagate a knowledge of French in Egypt. The agents for the accomplishment of this object have been mainly Catholic priests. The great apostle of anti-clericalism in France, M. Gambetta, was careful to explain that his anti-clerical ideas were only intended for home consumption; they were not meant for export. The French Republic claims to be the defender of the Catholic Church in the East, and is very sensitive of its right to do so if in any way questioned. A Republican Government and their agents, be they never so anti-clerical at home, are fully alive to the advantages of taking clericalism by the hand abroad as a useful instrument to further their political aims.

Apart, however, from any consequences resulting from the action taken either by Mehemet Ali or by the French Government, it is to be observed that French civilisation possesses a special degree of attraction, not only to the Asiatic, but also to the European races of the Levant. This point is one of considerable importance, for amongst the obstacles which have stood in the way of the British reformer in Egypt, none is more noteworthy than that both Europeanised Egyptians and Levantines are impregnated with French rather than with English habits of thought.

The reasons why French civilisation presents a special degree of attraction to Asiatics and Levantes are plain. It is, as a matter of fact, more attractive than the civilisations of England and Germany, and, moreover, it is more easy of imitation. Compare the undemonstrative, shy Englishman, with his social exclusiveness and insular habits, with the vivacious and cosmopolitan Frenchman, who does not know what the word shyness means, and who in ten minutes is apparently on terms of intimate friendship with any casual acquaintance he may chance to make. The semi-educated Oriental does not recognise that the former has, at all events, the merit of sincerity, whilst the latter is often merely acting a part.[1] He looks coldly on the Englishman, and rushes into the arms of the Frenchman.

Look, again, to the relative intellectual attractions which the two Western races present. The Englishman is a follower of Bacon without knowing it. Inductive philosophy has become part of his nature. He instinctively rejects *a priori* reasoning. He will laboriously collect a number of facts before arriving at any conclusion, and, when he has collected his facts, he will limit his conclusion to the precise point which is proved. Compare this frame of mind with that of the quick-witted Frenchman, who, on the most slender basis of fact, will advance some sweeping generalisation with an assurance untempered by any shadow of doubt as to its correctness. Can it be any matter for surprise that the Egyptian, with his light intellectual ballast, fails to see that some fallacy often lies at the bottom of the Frenchman's reasoning, or that he prefers the rather superficial brilliancy of the Frenchman to the plodding, unattractive industry of the Englishman or the German? Look again, at the theoretical perfection of French administrative systems, at their elaborate detail, and at the provision which is apparently made to meet every possible contingency which may arise. Compare these features with the Englishman's practical systems, which lay down rules as to a few main points, and leave a mass of detail to individual discretion. The half-educated Egyptian naturally prefers the Frenchman's system, for it is to all outward appearances more perfect and more easy of application. He fails, moreover, to see that the Englishman desires to elaborate a system which will suit the facts with which he has to deal, whereas the main objection to applying French administrative procedures to Egypt is that the facts have but too often to conform to the ready-made system. From whatever point of view the subject be regarded, the same contrast will be found. On the one side, is a damsel possessing attractive, albeit somewhat artificial charms; on the other side, is a sober, elderly matron of perhaps somewhat greater moral worth, but of less pleasing outward appearance. The Egyptian, in the heyday of his political and intellectual youth, naturally smiled on the attractive damsel, and turned his back on the excellent but somewhat ill-favoured matron.

In some respects it is, for his own sake, greatly to be regretted that he did so. What the Egyptian most of all requires is, not so much that his mind should be trained, as that his character should be formed. It is certain that a very high tone of morality pervades those admirable educational institutions which spring, Pallas-like, from the fertile brain of the Vatican, and most of which, in Egypt, are under French control. It is also certain that those who base their opinion of French character and morals on the light French literature of the day are wholly in error. I believe that in no country are the domestic virtues more generally cherished than in France. It has, however, to be remembered[1] that the Oriental has a remarkable capacity for assimilating to himself the worst and rejecting the best arts of any European civilisation with which he may be brought in contact. It is not from the best, but rather from the least admirable traits in the French character that those young Egyptians, who have been brought under French influences, have generally drawn their moral inspirations.

It is not to be supposed that the educated Egyptian fails to note the defects of his European monitors, be they French or English. He often sees those defects clearly enough, and the result not unfrequently is that, even though he may himself become partially Europeanised, he will despise European civilisation. In what respect, he says to himself, are we Egyptians morally inferior to our teachers? We may be deceitful, untruthful, and unchaste, but we are not one whit worse than those whom we are told to regard as the ultimate product of European civilisation.[2] The result is that the Europeanised Egyptian often returns to Egypt in order to become, both by precept and example, an apostle of anti-European ideas. The conservatism of older Moslems, who regard him as a living warning that they should beware of European civilisation, becomes stereotyped on observing his behaviour and on hearing his language; whilst he himself, in spite of his partial Europeanisation, will, with an inconsistency which would be strange were we not dealing with the "Land of Paradox," hate the Europeans quite as much as the less educated sections of his own countrymen.

The question of the effect of European, and notably French education on the rising generation of Egyptians has to be considered from another point of view. The tendency of every Egyptian official is to shirk responsibility. He thinks less of what should be done than of acting in such a manner that no personal blame can be attached to himself. This habit of thought makes the Egyptian official instinctively shrink from the British system of administration, for under that system much is left to the discretion of the individual, who is, therefore, obliged to think for himself. He flies for refuge to the French system, and there he finds administrative procedures prescribed which exactly suit his character and habits of thought. He finds that provision is apparently made for everything, to the most minute detail, in a series of elaborate codes. Entrenched behind these codes, the Europeanised Egyptian is, to his joy, relieved in a great degree from the necessity of thinking for himself. Some emergency may, indeed, occur which requires prompt action and the exercise of common sense. The Europeanised Egyptian, however, but too often does not recognise emergencies, and he spurns common sense. He refers to some article in his regulations, and maintains that he cannot depart from the provisions of that article by one hair's-breadth. The result may be disastrous, but he is indifferent as to the result; for, having conformed strictly to his orders, he cannot be blamed by his superiors. The Egyptian official was always predisposed to be an automaton.[1] Once Europeanised—more especially if he be Gallicised—his automatic rigidity becomes more wooden than it was before.

It can scarcely be doubted that, from this point of view, French training has done little to rectify the defects of the Egyptian national character. In everything, it has tended to stereotype the Egyptian predisposition to look to the letter which killeth, and neglect the spirit which giveth life.

Scores of cases could be mentioned illustrative of the tendency to which allusion is here made. One or two instances will, however, suffice.

A case occurred of a stationmaster declining to send a fire-engine by a train which was about to start, in order to help in putting down a serious fire. He pointed with inexorable logic to the regulations, which did not permit trucks being attached to that particular train. No exception was to be found in the code, with which he had been furnished, to meet the case of a burning town to which a fire-engine had to be despatched. Again, at one time it was the practice, if an accident occurred in the streets, not to transport the individual who had been injured at once to the hospital, but to leave him lying on the ground, whatever might be his condition, until the proper official had arrived to make a "Process-verbal" of the facts connected with the accident. On one occasion, a doctor was sent to examine into the condition of a stationmaster, supposed to be insane. On entering the room, he was attacked and nearly strangled by the madman. He was able, after a sharp struggle, to call on two orderlies, who had been present all the time, to seize the man. They saluted and did so. On being asked why they had not interfered sooner, they replied that they had received no orders to that effect. Without doubt, they considered that the struggle on the floor, which they had witnessed, was part of some strange European process, with which they were unfamiliar, for dealing with insane stationmasters.[1]

I may mention that a subordinate Egyptian official, notably a policeman, regards the preparation of a "Process-verbal" as a proceeding of peculiar sanctity. It matters little what the document contains. Provided he can get a "Process-verbal" prepared in due form, the Egyptian official considers that he is free from responsibility, and he is, therefore, happy. Otherwise, he feels that a certain amount of personal responsibility weighs upon him, and he is miserable. This plethora of "Process-verbaux" has done a good deal to nip in the bud any feeble tendencies towards individualism which might otherwise have been developed.

In a word, the French bureaucratic and legal systems, although there is much to be said in their favour when they are carried into execution by a highly civilised and intelligent race such as the French, are little adapted to the formation of either competent officials or useful citizens in a country such as Egypt.

Such, therefore, is the Europeanised Egyptian. His intellectual qualities have, of late years, certainly been developed. His moral attributes have generally been little, if at all, improved by contact with Europe. The old orthodox Moslem is bound hand and foot by ancient custom based on his religion. The Europeanised Egyptian is often bound almost as fast by a set of rigid formulae, which he mistakes for the substance, whereas they are in reality but some fortuitous incidents of European civilisation.

B. THE ANGLO-FRENCH AGREEMENT OF 1904

For some years subsequent to the Wolff negotiations, no attempt was made to deal with the larger aspects of the Egyptian Question. Whenever the British Government were reproached by the French, or by British partisans of evacuation, with not having fulfilled their pledge to evacuate, the reply persistently given, by both

Conservative and Liberal statesmen, was that England's work in Egypt was not yet completed. This reply, though regarded by some as a mere subterfuge, was perfectly true; yet it did not convey the whole truth. It encouraged the inference that England's work would be completed at some period, which would not be very remote, whereas not one of the British statesmen who gave the reply had any precise idea as to whether the period would be remote or proximate. The better was his aquaintance with the facts, the stronger would his conviction be that the period would be remote, even to the extent of giving a distinctly permanent character to the occupation, which was originally intended to be temporary.

For more than twenty years, therefore, politicians, whether professional or amateur, French or English, wandered aimlessly in a labyrinth to which there was no clue. They sought for the solution of a question which was in reality insoluble on any basis which had, during that period, been formulated. Eventually, Englishmen relaxed their attempts to make a pyramid stand on its apex; whilst Frenchmen gradually recognised two facts. One was that the British occupation of Egypt was beneficial rather than hurtful to the material interests of France, whilst general French political interests suffered from the prolonged estrangement of the two countries, which was caused by the Egyptian Question. The other was that, unless the evacuation of Egypt was to be made a *casus belli* with England, the British view of the facts had to be accepted.

An English politician, writing in 1844, had said: "It is impossible for any statesman who carries his views forward a few years not to see that there must be eventually a contest among European Powers for the possession of Egypt."[1]

That contest, if it ever came, could only be between England and France. It was the business of diplomacy to be on the watch for any opportunity to settle the question, and thus avoid any such calamity as that predicted by Lord Ellenborough.

The main facts connected with the Egyptian Question were in reality very simple.

It was certain that, in the early days of the occupation, the British Government stated publicly their desire to withdraw the British garrison, so soon as circumstances admitted of the adoption of such a course.

It was equally certain to all who considered the subject impartially, and with a full knowledge of the circumstances, that the British Government could not, with a due regard to all the interests involved, carry out their declared intention.

Gradually, the truth of this latter statement came to be generally recognised, and when once it was recognised, all that was required to set diplomatic action in movement was an opportunity for negotiating with a fair prospect of success.

Such an opportunity occurred in 1904. The visits of King Edward VII to Paris, and of the President of the French Republic to London, prepared the public opinion of both countries for a general settlement of all outstanding differences. Moreover, at this moment the affairs of Morocco acquired some prominence.

That State had been for some while past traversing the various stages on the road to ruin, which would appear to be normal in the case of Oriental countries. The final stage had nearly been reached. The exercise of unbridled personal power by the ruler of the State led to misgovernment, culminating in revolution. European intervention had become inevitable. The only practical question at issue was to decide on the nationality of the Europeans who were to intervene.

The choice practically lay between three nations, Spain, England, and France.

Spain, still staggering under the effects of a disastrous war with America, was manifestly incapable of assuming the task of regenerator.

England was unwilling to add to her already heavy burden of world-wide responsibilities.

The duty of dealing with Morocco devolved, therefore, naturally on France.[1] But, in order that the task should be taken in hand with a fair prospect of success, the goodwill of England was necessary. What, therefore, could be more natural than to barter British support in Morocco for French support in Egypt?

Negotiations on this basis were commenced in the summer of 1903, with the result that, on April 8, 1904, three Conventions were signed by Lord Lansdowne, who then presided over the British Foreign Office, and by M. Cambon, the French Ambassador in London.

Two of these Conventions dealt with the affairs of Newfoundland, Nigeria, Siam, Madagascar, and the New Hebrides. The consideration of these questions lies outside the scope of the present work.

As regards Egypt, it has been already explained that the Egyptian Government acquired financial liberty, and also that the British Government recognised the Suez Canal Convention of 1888. Further, a "Declaration" made on April 8, 1904, contained the following very important provision:—

"His Britannic Majesty's Government declare that they have no intention of altering the political status of Egypt.

"The Government of the French Republic, for their part, declare that they will not obstruct the action of Great Britain in that country by asking that a limit of time be fixed for the British Occupation or in any other manner."

In other words, the occupation was recognised, and the British Government were left a far freer hand than formerly to deal with Egyptian affairs.

The Governments of Germany, Austria, and Italy subsequently adhered to this declaration.

Thus, the "Egyptian Question," in the sense in which that phrase had heretofore been used, was partially settled. It is rare that an arrangement of this kind is of a nature to give satisfaction to all those who are directly or indirectly concerned. Such, however, was the case as regards the Anglo-French Agreement.

As to the advantages which are likely to accrue to the residents in Egypt, both European and Egyptian, there cannot be a shadow of doubt. Apart from the fact that the financial restrictions, which by a change of circumstances had become obsolete and unnecessary, have been removed, it is to be observed that Egyptian progress will now, it may be hoped, continue to advance without being hampered by that somewhat acute stage of international rivalry which has been productive of so much harm in the past.

Both England and France gained in the removal of a difference of opinion which had for long embittered the relations of two nations whose common interest it is to strengthen the bonds of close friendship.

England gained by obtaining a practically valid sanction to a position which was previously, to some extent, irregular. I had for long been convinced that the early withdrawal of the British garrison from Egypt was quite impossible, but I never regarded lightly the non-fulfilment of the engagement to withdraw. Neither did I ever think that a good deal of provocation in local matters constituted a sufficient plea to justify the annulment of that engagement. It is a distinct advantage for a nation, which is bound to a scrupulous respect of international obligations by every consideration of public morality and self-interest, that it can no longer be accused of any apparent disregard of those obligations.

France also gained. The large French interests at stake in Egypt are secured by specific engagements, and are still more amply secured by the traditional character of British predominance, wherever it has been acquired. On the other hand, any apparent loss of French political influence in Egypt received compensation elsewhere.

Lastly, the civilised world—whose principal interest I conceive to be the maintenance of peace—gained by the re-establishment of very friendly relations between two of the most important members of the European family.

Such, therefore, is the view I venture to submit of this very important and auspicious transaction. I began my connection with Egypt twenty-eight years previous to the signature of the Anglo-French Agreement, when England and France moved hand in hand together in that country. I rejoice that my connection lasted long enough to enable me to see the friendly relations of the past re-established after an interlude of misunderstanding which was detrimental alike to British, French, and Egyptian interests.

A further Egyptian Question remains behind. It consists in gradually adapting the institutions of the country to the growing needs of the population. Possibly, time will also solve that problem, but, unless disaster is to ensue, it must be a long time.

IX. THE ALGECIRAS CONVENTION

The *Algeciras Convention* was the document signed in 1906, in which the Great Powers (Germany, Austria-Hungary, Belgium, Spain, the United States, France, Britain, Italy, Morocco, the Netherlands, Portugal, Russia, and Sweden) determined the fate of Morocco. Moroccan interests, however, were largely ignored. Germany had tried to prevent the further expansion of French imperial influence in 1905, when France began pressing for the creation of a protectorate in Morocco. Kaiser Wilhelm himself visited Tangier to make the point that Morocco could not become just another segment of France's imperial realm. Spain also claimed dominance in Morocco, and Germany supported Spain's claim, while Britain backed France's claim there as a consequence of the *Entente Cordiale*. In the end, both France and Spain gained spheres of control in Morocco as a consequence of the Algeciras Convention (with France having the largest portion), but most Moroccans were not happy. The Westernizing Sultan 'Abd al-Aziz, who agreed to the treaty, was overthrown by his brother 'Abd al-Hafiz in 1908, and France expended much money and manpower in subduing the protectorate through the 1920s.

Algeciras, April 7, 1906

In the Name of Almighty God.
    His Majesty the Emperor of Germany, King of Prussia, in the name of the German Empire; His Majesty the Emperor of Austria, King of Bohemia, etc., and Apostolic King of Hungary; His Majesty the King of the Belgians; His Majesty the King of Spain; the President of the United States of America; the President of the French Republic; His Majesty the King of the United Kingdom of Great Britain and Ireland, and of the British Dominions beyond the Seas, Emperor of India, etc.; His Majesty the King of Italy; His Majesty the Sultan of Morocco; Her Majesty the Queen of the Netherlands; His Majesty the King of Portugal and of the Algarves, etc., etc., etc.; His Majesty the Emperor of All the Russias; His Majesty the King of Sweden:
    Inspired by the interest attaching itself to the reign of order, peace, and prosperity in Morocco, and recognizing that the attainment thereof can only be effected by means of the introduction of reforms based upon the triple principle of the sovereignty and independence of His Majesty the Sultan, the integrity of his domains, and economic liberty without any inequality, have resolved, upon the invitation of His Shereefian Majesty, to call together a conference at Algeciras for the purpose of arriving at an understanding upon the said reforms, as well as examining the means for obtaining the resources necessary for their application, and have appointed as their delegates plenipotentiary the following:

    His Majesty the Emperor of Germany, King of Prussia, in the name of the German Empire: Mr. Joseph de Radowitz, His Ambassador Extraordinary and Plenipotentiary to His Catholic Majesty, and Christian, Count of Tattenbach, His Envoy Extraordinary and Minister Plenipotentiary to His Very Faithful Majesty.
    His Majesty the Emperor of Austria, King of Bohemia, etc., and Apostolic King of Hungary: Rudolph, Count of Welsersheimb, His Ambassador Extraordinary

and Plenipotentiary to His Catholic Majesty, and Leopold, Count Bolesta-Koziebrodzki, His Envoy Extraordinary and Minister Plenipotentiary to Morocco.

His Majesty the King of the Belgians: Maurice, Baron Joostens, His Envoy Extraordinary and Minister Plenipotentiary to his Catholic Majesty, and Conrad, Count of Buisseret Steenbecque de Blarenghem, His Envoy Extraordinary and Minister Plenipotentiary to Morocco.

His Majesty the King of Spain: Don Juan Manuel Sanchez y Gutierrez de Castro, Duke of Almodovar del Rio, His Minister of State, and Don Juan Perez-Caballero y Ferrer, His Envoy Extraordinary and Minister Plenipotentiary to His Majesty the King of the Belgians.

The President of the United States of America: Mr. Henry White, Ambassador Extraordinary and Plenipotentiary of the United States of America to His Majesty the King of Italy, and Mr. Samuel R. Gummere, Envoy Extraordinary and Minister Plenipotentiary of the United States of America to Morocco.

The President of the French Republic: Mr. Paul Revoil, Ambassador Extraordinary and Plenipotentiary of the French Republic to the Swiss Confederation, and Mr. Eugene Regnault, Minister Plenipotentiary.

His Majesty the King of the United Kingdom of Great Britain and Ireland, and of the British Dominions beyond the Seas, Emperor of India: Sir Arthur Nicolson, His Ambassador Extraordinary and Plenipotentiary to His Majesty the Emperor of All the Russias.

His Majesty the King of Italy: Emile, Marquis Visconti Venosta, Knight of the Order of the Very Holy Annunciation, and Mr. Giulio Malmusi, His Envoy Extraordinary and Minister Plenipotentiary to Morocco.

His Majesty the Sultan of Morocco: El Hadj Mohammed Ben-el Arbi Ettorres, His Delegate at Tangier and Ambassador Extraordinary, El Hadj Mohammed Ben Abdesselam El Mokri, His Minister of Expenses, El Hadj Mohammed Es-Seffar, and Sid Abderrhaman Bennis.

Her Majesty the Queen of the Netherlands: Jonkheer Hannibal Testa, Her Envoy Extraordinary and Minister Plenipotentiary to His Catholic Majesty.

His Majesty the King of Portugal and of the Algarves, etc., etc., etc.: Anthony, Count of Tovar, His Envoy Extraordinary and Minister Plenipotentiary to His Catholic Majesty, and Francis Robert, Count of Martens Ferrao, Peer of the Kingdom, His Envoy Extraordinary and Minister Plenipotentiary to Morocco.

His Majesty the Emperor of All the Russias: Arthur, Count Cassini, His Ambassador Extraordinary and Plenipotentiary to His Catholic Majesty, and Mr. Basile de Bacheracht, His Minister to Morocco.

His Majesty the King of Sweden: Mr. Robert Sager, His Envoy Extraordinary and Minister Plenipotentiary to His Catholic Majesty and His Very Faithful Majesty.

Who, furnished with full powers, which were found in good and due form, have, in conformity with the programme upon which His Shereefian Majesty and the powers have agreed, successively discussed and adopted:

I. A declaration relative to the organization of the police.
II. A regulation concerning the detection and repression of the contraband of arms.
III. An act of concession for a Moroccan State Bank.
IV. A declaration concerning a better return of taxes, and the creation of new revenues.

V. A regulation concerning the customs of the Empire and the repression of fraud and smuggling.

VI. A declaration relative to public services and public works.

VII. General provisions.

And having decided that these different documents might usefully be coordinated in a single instrument, they have united them in a general act composed of the following articles:

CHAPTER I.

Declaration relative to the organization of the police.

I.

The conference summoned by His Majesty the Sultan to pronounce on the measures necessary to organize the police declares that the following provisions should be made:

II.

The police shall be under the sovereign authority of His Majesty the Sultan. It shall be recruited by the Maghzen from Moorish Mohammedans, commanded by Moorish Kaids, and distributed in the eight ports open to commerce.

III.

In order to aid the Sultan in the organization of this police, Spanish officers and noncommissioned officers as instructors, and French officers and noncommissioned officers as instructors, shall be placed at His disposal by their respective Governments, which shall submit their designation to the approval of His Shereefian Majesty. A contract drawn between the Maghzen and these instructors, in conformity to the regulation provided by article IV, shall determine the conditions of their engagement and fix their pay, which must not be less than double of the pay corresponding to the rank of each officer or noncommissioned officer. In addition they will be allowed living expenses, varying according to their residence. Proper lodgings will be placed at their disposal by the Maghzen, which will likewise supply them with their horses and the necessary fodder.

The Governments having jurisdiction over the instructors reserve the right to recall them and replace them by others, accepted and engaged under the same conditions.

IV.

These officers and noncommissioned officers for a period of five years, to date from the ratification of the act of the conference, shall give their service to the organization of a body of Shereefian police. They shall assure instruction and discipline in conformity with the regulations to be drawn up in respect thereto. They shall also see that the men enlisted are fit for military service. In a general way they shall supervise the administration of the soldiers and superintend the payment of their salary, which shall be effected by the "Amin," assisted by the accounting officer instructor. They shall extend to the Moorish authorities invested with the command of these bodies their technical aid in the exercise of the said command.

The regulations to assure the recruital, discipline, instruction, and administration of the bodies of police shall be established by mutual agreement between the Shereefian Minister of War or his delegate, the inspector provided by article VII, and the highest ranking French and Spanish instructors.

The regulations shall be submitted to the Diplomatic Body at Tangier, which will formulate its opinion within a month's time. After that period the regulations shall be enforced.

V.

The total strength of the police shall not be more than 2,500 men, nor less than 2,000. It shall be distributed, according to the importance of the ports, in groups varying between 150 and 600 men. The number of Spanish and French officers shall be between sixteen and twenty; of Spanish and French noncommissioned officers, between thirty and forty.

VI.

The funds necessary to maintain and pay soldiers and officers and noncommissioned officer instructors shall be advanced by the State Bank to the Shereefian Treasury within the limits of the annual budget assigned to the police, which shall not exceed two million and a half pesetas for an effective strength of two thousand five hundred men.

VII.

During the same period of five years a general inspection shall be made into the working of the police. Such inspection shall be intrusted by His Shereefian Majesty to a superior officer of the Swiss army, who will be submitted to His approval by the Swiss Federal Government. This officer will be styled Inspector-General and reside at Tangier.

He shall inspect at least once a year the different bodies of the police, and after such inspection he shall draw up a report which he will address to the Maghzen.

In addition to such regular reports, he will, if he regards it as necessary, draw up special reports with reference to the working of the police.

Without directly intervening either in the command or the instruction, the Inspector-General will ascertain the results obtained by the Shereefian police, as regards the maintenance of order and security in the places where this police shall have been established.

VIII.

A copy of the reports and communications made to the Maghzen by the Inspector-General, with reference to his mission, shall at the same time be transmitted to the Dean of the Diplomatic Body at Tangier, in order that the Diplomatic Body be enabled to satisfy itself that the Shereefian police acts in conformity to the decisions taken by the conference, and to see whether it guarantees effectively, and in conformity with the treaties, the security of person and property of foreign citizens, subjects, and proteges, as well as that of commercial transactions.

IX.

In the case of complaints filed with the Diplomatic Body by the legation concerned, the Diplomatic Body may, upon notice given to the representative of the Sultan, direct the Inspector-General to investigate and report for all available purposes in the matter of such complaints.

X.

The Inspector-General shall receive an annual salary of 25,000 francs. In addition, he will be allowed 6,000 francs for the expenses of his tours. The Maghzen will place at his disposal a suitable residence and will look after the maintenance of his horses.

XI.

The material conditions of his engagement and of his establishment, as provided by article X, shall be the subject of a contract drawn up between him and the Maghzen. A copy of this contract shall be communicated to the Diplomatic Body.

XII.

The staff of instructors of the Shereefian police (officers and noncommissioned officers) shall be Spanish at Tetuan, mixed at Tangier, Spanish at Larache, French at Rabat, mixed at Casablanca, and French in the other three ports.

CHAPTER II.

Regulations concerning the detection and repression of the contraband of arms.

XIII.

Throughout the Shereefian Empire, except in the cases specified by articles XIV and XV, the importation and sale is forbidden of arms of war, parts of guns, ammunition of any nature, loaded or unloaded, powder, saltpeter, gun cotton, nitroglycerin, and all compositions destined exclusively for the manufacture of ammunition.

XIV.

Such explosives as are necessary for industry and public works may, however, be introduced. A regulation drawn up in the manner indicated by article XVIII shall determine the conditions under which their importation may be effected.

XV.

The arms, parts of guns, and ammunition intended for the troops of His Shereefian Majesty will be admitted after the fulfillment of the following formalities:

A declaration signed by the Moorish Minister of War, describing the number and nature of such articles ordered abroad, must be presented to the legation of the country of their origin, whose visa shall be affixed thereto.

The passage through the customs of the cases and packages containing the arms and munitions, delivered at the order of the Moorish Government, shall be effected upon the presentation:

1) Of the aforesaid declaration.

2) Of the invoice indicating the number and weight of the packages and the number and kind of the arms and munitions contained therein. This document must be visaed by the legation of the country of their origin, which will mark on the back the successive amounts previously passed through the customs. This visa will be refused when the order shall have been entirely delivered.

XVI.

The importation of sporting and high-priced arms, parts of guns, cartridges loaded and unloaded, is likewise forbidden. It may none the less be authorized—

1. For the strictly personal requirements of the importer;

2. For supplying the gunshops authorized by article XVIII.

XVII.

Sporting and high-priced arms and the ammunition for the same will be admitted for the strictly personal requirements of the importer on presentation of a permit issued by the representative of the Maghzen at Tangier. If the importer is a foreigner, this permit will only be granted at the request of his legation.

With respect to ammunition for sporting purposes, each permit shall allow a maximum of a thousand cartridges or the supplies necessary for the manufacture of a thousand cartridges. The permit shall only be issued to those who have never been sentenced for any offense.

XVIII.

The trade in sporting and high-priced arms, not rifles, of foreign manufacture, as well as of the ammunition appertaining to the same, shall be regulated, as soon as circumstances permit, by a Shereefian decision made in conformity with the advice of a majority of the Diplomatic Body at Tangier. This shall be the case, as well, with decisions intended to suspend or restrict the exercise of such trade.

Only such persons as have secured a special and temporary license from the Moorish Government shall be allowed to open and operate retail shops for the sale of sporting guns and ammunition. This license shall only be given at the written request of the applicant, indorsed by his legation.

Regulations drawn up in the manner indicated by the first paragraph of this article shall determine the number of such retail shops which may be opened at Tangier and, if occasion arises, in the ports that may be later designated. They shall fix the formalities to be imposed on the importation of explosives intended for industry and public works, of arms and ammunition intended to supply such shops, as well as the maximum quantity of stock that can be kept.

In case of the violation of the regulating ordinances, the license may be temporarily or permanently withdrawn without prejudice to other penalties incurred by the offenders.

XIX.

Every introduction of, or attempt to introduce, the prohibited merchandise shall make it liable to confiscation, and further to the punishments and fines mentioned below, which shall be pronounced by the competent jurisdiction.

XX.

The introduction or attempt to introduce in a port open to commerce, or through a custom-house, shall be punished:

1. By a fine of from 500 to 2,000 pesetas and an additional fine equal to three times the value of the imported merchandise;

2. By imprisonment of from five days to a year, or else by only one of these two punishments.

XXI.

The introduction or attempt to introduce outside a port open to commerce or a custom-house shall be punished:

1. By a fine of from 1,000 to 5,000 pesetas and an additional fine equal to three times the value of the imported merchandise;

2. By imprisonment of from three months to two years, or else by only one of these two punishments.

XXII.

The fraudulent sale, the receiving and peddling, of merchandise prohibited by the present regulations shall be punished according to the penalties specified in article XX.

XXIII.

The accomplices in the offenses set forth in articles XX, XXI, and XXII shall be liable to the same penalties as the principals. The elements determining complicity shall be adjudged according to the laws of the court in charge of the case.

XXIV.

When there is good reason to suppose that a vessel anchored in a port open to commerce carries guns, ammunition, or other prohibited merchandise, with a view of introducing the same into Morocco, the officers of the Shereefian customs shall so inform the competent consular authority, in order that the latter may carry out, in company with a delegate of the Shereefian customs, such investigations, verifications, or searches as may be judged necessary.

XXV.

In the case of the introduction or the attempted introduction by sea of prohibited merchandise outside of a port open to commerce, the Moorish customs authorities may bring the vessel to the nearest port, to be turned over to the consular authority, who shall have the right to seize it and continue such seizure until payment of the fines decreed. The vessel may, however, be released at any period of the trial, provided that the judicial proceedings shall not be impeded thereby, on the deposit made with the consular authority of the maximum of the fine, or else under responsible bail accepted by the customs.

XXVI.

The Maghzen may retain the confiscated merchandise either for its own use, if able to utilize it, on condition that the subjects of the Empire shall not be able to get possession of it, or it shall dispose of it abroad. The conveyances of the same on shore may be confiscated and shall be sold for the profit of the Shereefian Treasury.

XXVII.

The sale of arms condemned by the Moorish Government shall be prohibited throughout the Shereefian Empire.

XXVIII.

Rewards taken out of the amount of the fines levied are to be given to the informants who have been instrumental in discovering forbidden merchandise and to the agents who have effected its seizure. Such rewards shall be assigned after deducting, if necessary, the costs of the trial, one-third to be distributed by the customs among the informants, one-third to the officers who seized the merchandise, and one-third to the Moroccan Treasury.

If the seizure has been effected without the intervention of an informer one-half of the fines shall go to the officer making the seizure and the other half to the Shereefian Treaty.

XXIX.

The Moorish customs authorities shall notify directly the diplomatic or consular agents of any violations of this regulation committed by those under their jurisdiction, in order that the same may be prosecuted before the proper jurisdiction.

Similar violations committed by Moorish subjects shall be submitted directly by the customs to the Shereefian authority.

A delegate of the customs shall be assigned to follow the procedure of cases pending before the different jurisdictions.

XXX.

In the region bordering on Algeria, the enforcement of the regulations on the contraband of arms shall be the exclusive concern of France and Morocco.

Similarly, the enforcement of the regulation on the contraband of arms in the Riff and in general in the regions bordering on the Spanish possessions shall be the exclusive concern of Spain and Morocco.

CHAPTER III.

Act of concession for a State Bank.

XXXI.

A bank shall be established in Morocco under the name of the "State Bank of Morocco," to exercise the following specified rights, which are granted to it by His Majesty the Sultan for a period of forty years, to date from the ratification of this act.

XXXII.

The Bank, which will have power to carry on all transactions entering into the operations of a bank, shall have the exclusive privilege of issuing notes to bearer, payable on presentation and receivable for public dues throughout the Moorish Empire.

The Bank shall maintain for a period of two years, to date from its going into operation, cash on hand at least equal to half its notes in circulation, and equal to at least one-third after the expiration of said period of two years. At least one-third of such cash on hand is to be gold bullion or gold coin.

XXXIII.

The Bank shall, to the exclusion of every other bank or establishment of credit, discharge the duty of disbursing treasurer of the Empire. To this end the Moorish Government shall take all necessary measures to deposit in the Bank the proceeds of the customs revenues, exclusive of the part thereof applied to the loan of 1904, and such other revenues as it may designate.

With reference to the special tax established in order to carry out certain public works, the Moorish Government must have the same deposited in the Bank, as well as the revenues it may later pledge for its loans, the Bank being especially charged with the payments thereon, except, however, in the case of the loan of 1904, which is governed by special contract.

XXXIV.

The Bank shall be the financial agent of the Government both within and without the Empire, without prejudice to the Government's right to apply to other banking houses or establishments of credit for its public loans. The Bank, however, shall enjoy, in regard to such loans, a right of preference, other conditions being equal, over any banking or credit establishment.

For Treasury notes or other short-term notes which the Moorish Government may wish to negotiate without making it a public issue, the Bank shall, however, be charged, to the exclusion of every other establishment, with negotiating the same for the account of the Moorish Government, either in Morocco or abroad.

XXXV.

The Bank shall make advances to the Moroccan Government on account current up to a million francs, chargeable against Treasury receipts.

The Bank shall likewise open a credit account for the Government for the period of ten years, to date from its establishment, such account not to exceed two-thirds of its initial capital.

This credit account shall be distributed over several years and employed primarily for the expenses of establishing and maintaining the bodies of police, organized in conformity to the decisions adopted by the conference, and secondarily for the expenses of such works of public interest as might not be charged to the special fund as provided for by the following article:

The maximum rate for these two advances will be 7 per cent, bank commission included, and the Bank may ask the Government to give as security an equal amount in Treasury notes.

If before the expiration of the said term of ten years the Moorish Government should contract a loan, the Bank would have the right to obtain the immediate reimbursement of its advances made in accordance with the second paragraph of the present article.

XXXVI.

The proceeds of the special tax (articles XXXIII and LXVI) shall form a special fund for which the Bank shall keep a separate account. This fund shall be employed in conformity to the regulations adopted by the conference.

In the case of its insufficiency, and chargeable to later receipts, the Bank may open a special credit for such fund, the amount of which should not exceed the total of the receipts for the previous year.

The conditions of the rate and commission shall be the same as those established by the preceding article for advances to the Treasury on account current.

XXXVII.

The Bank shall take such measures as it may deem conducive to a sounder monetary situation in Morocco. Spanish currency shall continue to be permitted to circulate as legal tender.

In consequence, the Bank shall have the exclusive charge of purchasing precious metals, of striking and melting coins, as well as of all its other monetary operations for the account and profit of the Moorish Government.

XXXVIII.

The home office of the Bank shall be at Tangier, but it shall establish branches and agencies in the principal cities of Morocco or in any other place it may deem expedient.

XXXIX.

The land necessary for the establishment of the Bank, as well as its branches and agencies in Morocco, shall be placed gratuitously at its disposal by the Government, and at the expiration of the concession the Government shall retake possession of it and reimburse the Bank for the cost of building these establishments. The Bank shall further be authorized to purchase such houses and land as it may require for the same purpose.

XL.

The Shereefian Government shall insure and be responsible for the safety and protection of the Bank, its branches and agencies. To this end it shall place an adequate guard at the disposal of each establishment in every city.

XLI.

The Bank, its branches and agencies, shall be exempt from all imposts or dues, ordinary or extraordinary, existing or to be created. The same exemption shall be extended to real estate devoted to its use, and to the certificates and coupons of its shares and to its notes. The importation and exportation of metals and coins intended for banking operations shall be authorized and exempted from every tax.

XLII.

The Shereefian Government shall exercise its high supervision over the Bank by a High Commissioner, whom it shall appoint after a previous agreement with the Bank's Board of Directors.

This High Commissioner shall have the right to examine into the management of the Bank. He shall supervise the issuance of bank notes and shall see that the provisions of the concession are strictly observed.

The High Commissioner shall sign every note or affix thereto his seal. He shall be charged with the supervision of the relations between the Bank and the Imperial Treasury.

He shall take no part in the administration or transaction of the banking business, but he shall always have the right to attend the meetings of the Censors.

The Shereefian Government shall appoint one or two deputy commissioners, who shall be especially charged with the supervision of the financial transactions of the Treasury with the Bank.

XLIII.

A set of rules defining the relations of the Bank and of the Moorish Government shall be framed by the special committee provided for in article LVII and approved by the Censors.

XLIV.

The Bank, organized with the approval of the Government of His Shereefian Majesty in the form of a corporation, shall be governed by the French law relative thereto.

XLV.

Actions instituted in Morocco by the Bank shall be brought before the Consular Court of the defendant or before the jurisdiction of Morocco, in accordance with the rules of competence established by the Shereefian treaties and firmans.

Actions instituted in Morocco against the Bank shall be brought before a special tribunal consisting of three consular magistrates and two associates. The Diplomatic Body shall, each year, arrange the list of magistrates, associates, and substitutes.

This tribunal shall apply to such cases the rules of law, procedure, and competence established by the French legislation in commercial matters. Appeals from judgments pronounced by this tribunal shall be taken to the Federal Court of Lausanne, whose decision shall be final.

XLVI.

In case of dispute over the clauses of the concession or litigation arising between the Moorish Government and the Bank, the difference shall be referred, without appeal or recourse, to the Federal Court of Lausanne.

All disputes arising between the shareholders and the Bank in regard to the enforcement of the by-laws or by reason of the corporate business shall likewise be referred, without appeal or recourse, to the same court.

XLVII.

The by-laws of the Bank shall be framed on the following bases by a special committee provided for in article LVII. They shall be approved by the Censors and ratified by the General Assembly of Shareholders.

XLVIII.

The General Constituent Assembly of the corporation shall fix the place where the meetings of the shareholders and the sessions of the Board of Directors shall be held; the latter, however, shall have the faculty of meeting at any other city if it deems it expedient.

The office of the manager of the Bank shall be at Tangier.

XLIX.

The Bank shall be administered by a Board of Directors consisting of as many members as there are parts in the initial capital.

The Directors shall have the most extensive powers for the administration and management of the corporation; they shall especially appoint the managers, assistant managers, and members of the commission indicated in article LIV, as well as the managers of branches and agencies.

The employees of the company shall be recruited so far as possible from among the citizens, subjects, or proteges of the several powers which have taken part in subscribing the capital.

L.

The Directors, who shall be appointed by the General Assembly of Shareholders, shall be nominated by the groups subscribing the capital.

The first Board shall remain five years in office. At the expiration of this period, there shall be a renewal at the rate of three members annually. The order of outgoing Directors shall be determined by lot; they may be reelected.

On the constitution of the corporation, each subscribing group shall have the right to nominate as many directors as it shall have subscribed entire parts, but such groups shall not be compelled to select candidates of their own nationality.

The subscribing groups shall not retain their right of nominating directors when the latter are superseded or reelected, unless they can prove that they still have in their possession at least one-half the share conferring that right upon them.

In a case where, by reason of these provisions, a subscribing group should be no longer in a position to nominate a director, the General Assembly of Shareholders shall make a direct nomination.

LI.

Each of the following institutions: the Bank of the German Empire, the Bank of England, the Bank of Spain, and the Bank of France, shall, with their Government's approval, appoint a Censor for the State Bank of Morocco.

The Censors shall remain in office four years. The outgoing Censors may be reappointed.

In the case of death or resignation the institution which had appointed the former incumbent shall fill the vacancy, but only for the unexpired term of the vacated office.

LII.

The Censors who shall exercise their mandate by virtue of this act of the Signatory Powers shall, in the interests of the latter, see that the Bank is efficiently operated and insure the strict observance of the clauses of the concession and of the statutes. They shall see that the regulations governing the issuance of notes are precisely fulfilled, and shall supervise the operations tending to put the monetary situation on a sound basis, but they shall never, under any pretext, interfere in the conduct of business or in the internal administration of the Bank.

Each of the Censors shall be empowered to examine at all times the Bank accounts, and to call for information either from the Board of Directors or the manager's office with regard to the management of the Bank, and attend the meetings of the Board of Directors, but only in an advisory capacity.

The four Censors shall meet at Tangier in the discharge of their duties at least once every two years, at a time to be fixed by them. Other meetings at Tangier or elsewhere may take place if three of the Censors should demand it.

The four Censors shall draw up in common accord an annual report, which shall be annexed to that of the Board of Directors. The Board of Directors shall transmit without delay a copy of such report to each of the Governments signatory to the act of the conference.

LIII.

The Censors' emoluments and traveling expenses shall be fixed by the committee on by-laws. They shall be paid directly by the banks charged with their nomination, and the amount reimbursed to these institutions by the State Bank of Morocco.

LIV.

To assist the manager's office a committee shall be established at Tangier, the members of which shall be chosen by the Board of Directors, without distinction of nationality, from among the notables residing at Tangier and holding shares of the Bank.

This committee, which shall be presided over by one of the managers or assistant managers, shall give its advice on questions of discounts and opening of credit accounts.

It shall transmit a monthly report on these various subjects to the Board of Directors.

LV.

The capital, of which the amount shall be fixed by the special committee designated in article LVII, shall be not less than fifteen million francs nor more than twenty million francs, and shall be of gold coin, and the shares thereof, of the value of five hundred francs each, shall be inscribed with the various gold coinages at a fixed rate of exchange, as determined by the by-laws.

The said capital may thereafter be increased at one or more times by a decision of the General Assembly of Shareholders.

The subscription to the increased capital shall be reserved for all shareholders, without distinction of groups, in proportion to their individual holdings.

LVI.

The initial capital of the Bank shall be divided into as many equal parts as there are participants among the powers represented at the conference.

To this end, each power shall designate a bank which shall exercise either for itself or for a group of banks the above-specified right of subscription, as well as the right of nomination of the Directors, as provided in article L. Any bank selected as head of a group may, with its Government's authorization, be superseded by another bank of the same country.

States wishing to avail themselves of their rights of subscription must notify such intention to the Royal Government of Spain within a period of four weeks from the signature of this act by the representatives of the powers.

Two parts, however, equal to those reserved to each of the subscribing groups, shall be assigned to the *consortium* of banks signatory of the contract of June 12, 1904, in compensation for the cession which shall be made by the *consortium* to the State Bank of Morocco:

1) Of the rights specified in article XXXIII of the contract;

2) Of the right inscribed in article XXXII (paragraph 2) of the contract concerning the available balance of the customs receipts, with the express reservation of the general preferential right to the aggregate proceeds of customs granted to bondholders by article XI of the same contract.

LVII.

Within a period of three weeks from the time of closing the subscriptions, notified by the Royal Government of Spain to the powers interested, a special committee composed of delegates appointed by the subscribing groups, as provided in article L for the appointment of Directors, shall meet with a view to elaborating the by-laws of the Bank.

The General Constituent Assembly shall meet two months after the ratification of this act.

The functions of such special committee shall cease upon the organization of the corporation.

The special committee shall fix the place of its meetings.

LVIII.

No modification shall be made in the by-laws except on the motion of the Board of Directors and with the advice and consent of the Censors and the Imperial High Commissioner.

Such modifications must be voted by a three-quarters majority, either present or represented, of the General Assembly of Shareholders.

CHAPTER IV.

A declaration concerning a better return of taxes, and the creation of new revenues.

LIX.

As soon as the *tertib* shall have been put into regular operation with regard to Moorish subjects, the representatives of the powers at Tangier shall subject their citizens, subjects, and proteges in the Empire to the application thereof. But it is understood that this tax shall not be applied to foreign subjects except—

1) Under the conditions stipulated by the regulation of the Diplomatic Body at Tangier on November 24, 1903;

2) At places where it shall effectively be collected from Moorish subjects.

The consular authorities shall retain a certain percentage of the receipts of the taxes they collect from those subject to their jurisdiction to cover the cost of tax bills and collection.

The rate of such percentage shall be fixed by mutual agreement between the Maghzen and the Diplomatic Body at Tangier.

LX.

In accordance with the right granted by article XI of the Madrid Convention, foreigners shall have the right to acquire property throughout the Shereefian Empire, and His Majesty the Sultan shall issue to his administrative and judicial officers such instructions as may be necessary for them not to refuse the registration of deeds without lawful cause. Subsequent transfers, either by deeds between living parties or by death, shall continue without hindrance.

In the ports open to commerce and within a radius of ten kilometers around such ports, His Majesty the Sultan, generally and without it being necessary henceforth for foreign subjects to obtain a special permission for each purchase of property, now grants the consent required by article XI of the Madrid Convention.

At Ksar el Kebir, Arzila, Azemour, and eventually in other towns of the coast or the interior, the general authorization stated above is likewise granted to foreigners, but only for purchasers within a radius of two kilometers around those towns.

Wherever foreigners may have acquired property they will be permitted to erect buildings in compliance with regulations and usage.

Before authorizing the execution of deeds for transferring property, the Cadi will have to satisfy himself of the validity of the title in conformity to the Mohammedan law.

The Maghzen shall designate in each city and district specified in this article the Cadi who shall have charge of such verification.

LXI.

With a view to creating new resources for the Maghzen, the conference recognizes in principle that a tax may be established on city buildings.

A part of the receipts thus realized shall be set aside for the requirements of municipal streets and hygiene, and generally for the expense of improvement and conservation of the cities,

The tax is due from the Moorish or foreign owner, without distinction, but the tenant or the holder of the key shall be responsible to the Moorish Treasury.

Regulations issued jointly by the Shereefian Government and the Diplomatic Body at Tangier shall establish the rate, its method of collection and application, and shall determine the quota of revenue thus created which shall be devoted to the expense of improvement and conservation of the cities.

At Tangier this quota shall be turned over to the International Sanitary Council, which shall decide as to its use until the creation of a municipal organization.

LXII.

His Shereefian Majesty having decided in 1901 that the Moorish officials who collect the agricultural taxes should no longer receive either the "sokhra" or the "mouna," the conference is of the opinion that this rule should be made general, so far as is possible.

LXIII.

The Shereefian delegates have stated that *habou* property, or certain State property, notably buildings of the Maghzen, occupied at a rental of 6 per cent, are held by persons subject to foreign jurisdiction without regular title or by virtue of contracts subject to revision. The conference, desirous of remedying this state of affairs, charges the Diplomatic Body at Tangier to solve these two questions equitably, in accord with the special commissioner whom His Shereefian Majesty may be pleased to designate to that effect.

LXIV.

The conference takes formal note of the proposition formulated by the Shereefian delegates on the subject of taxes to be created on certain trades, industries, and professions.

If as the result of the collection of such taxes from Moorish subjects the Diplomatic Body at Tangier should deem it advisable to extend the same to those under foreign jurisdiction, it is hereby specified that the said taxes shall be exclusively municipal.

LXV.

The conference adheres to the proposition proposed by the Moorish delegation to create, with the assistance of the Diplomatic Body—

1) A stamp tax on contracts and notarial acts brought before "adouls."

2) A maximum transfer tax of 2 per cent on sales of real estate.

3) A statistical and weighing tax of a maximum of 1 per cent *ad valorem* on merchandise transported by coasting vessels.

4) A passport fee to be collected from Moorish subjects.

5) Eventually, wharfage and light-house dues, the proceeds of which shall be devoted to harbor improvement.

LXVI.

Merchandise of foreign origin shall temporarily be subject on entry into Morocco to special taxes amounting to 2 1/2 per cent *ad valorem.* The whole proceeds of this special tax shall form a special fund, which shall be devoted to the execution of and expenses connected with public works for the development of navigation and the general trade of the Shereefian Empire.

The programme of works and their order of priority shall be determined jointly by the Shereefian Government and the Diplomatic Body of Tangier.

The surveys, estimates, plans, and specifications appertaining thereto shall be made by a competent engineer, appointed by the Shereefian Government jointly with the Diplomatic Body. This engineer may, if necessary, be assisted by one or more assistant engineers. Their salaries shall be charged to the special fund.

The special fund will be deposited with the State Bank of Morocco, which is to keep its accounts.

Public contracts shall be awarded in the form and under the general terms prescribed by the regulations that the Diplomatic Body at Tangier is charged to frame, together with the representative of his Shereefian Majesty.

The board of awards shall consist of one representative of the Shereefian Government, of five delegates of the Diplomatic Body, and of the engineer.

The award shall be given in favor of the bidder who, in conformity with the specifications, may submit the bid offering the most advantageous general terms.

As for the sums yielded by the special tax and collected at the customs-houses, in the districts specified in article CIII of the Customs Regulations, their expenditure will be determined upon by the Maghzen, with the consent of the neighboring power, in accordance with the clauses of this article.

LXVII.

The conference, without detriment to the observations offered upon this point, expresses the wish that the export duties on the following merchandise be reduced as follows:

Per cent

Chick-peas 20

Corn 20

Barley 50

Wheat 34

LXVIII.

His Shereefian Majesty will consent to increase from six to ten thousand the number of head of cattle of the bovine species which each power shall have the right to export from Morocco. Such exportation may be effected through any customhouse. If by misfortune there should be a scarcity of cattle in any particular district His Shereefian Majesty shall have the right to temporarily forbid the exportation of cattle through the port or ports of that district. Such measure shall not exceed two years; nor shall it be applied at the same time to all the ports of the Empire.

It is further understood that the preceding provisions do not modify the other conditions for the exportation of cattle as fixed by previous firmans.

The conference expresses the additional wish that a veterinary inspection be organized as soon as possible at the seaports.

LXIX.

In accordance with the previous decisions of His Shereefian Majesty, and notably the decision of September 28th, 1901, the transportation is allowed by coasting vessels, between all ports of the Empire, of cereals, grains, vegetables, fruits, eggs, poultry, and in general of merchandise and animals of every kind, of Moroccan origin or not; except horses, donkeys, and camels, for which a special permit from the Maghzen will be necessary. Such coasting trade may be carried on by vessels of every nationality without such articles being subjected to payment of the export duties, but subject to the special taxes and regulations relative thereto.

LXX.

The rate of sojourn and anchorage dues levied on ships in Moorish ports being fixed by treaties with certain powers, the said powers are disposed to consent to a revision of such dues.

The Diplomatic Body at Tangier is therefore charged to effect an agreement with the Maghzen on the terms of such revision, which can not, however, take place until after the improvement of the ports.

LXXI.

The customs storage dues shall be collected in all Moorish ports where there are adequate warehouses, in conformity to the regulations existing or to be adopted in regard thereto by the Government of His Shereefian Majesty in accord with the Diplomatic Body at Tangier.

LXXII.

Opium and kiff will continue to be a monopoly of the Shereefian Government. The importation of opium specially intended for medicinal purposes will, however, be allowed by special permit issued by the Maghzen at the request of the legation, the physician, or apothecary importing the same. The Shereefian Government and the Diplomatic Body shall jointly determine the maximum quantity which may be thus introduced.

LXXIII.

The representatives of the powers take note of the Shereefian Government's intention to extend to tobacco of all kinds the monopoly existing in the case of snuff. They reserve the right of their citizens, subjects, and proteges to be duly indemnified for damages which the said monopoly may cause such of them as carry on a tobacco business established under the present system. In case no amicable agreement shall be reached, the damages shall be fixed by experts designated by the Maghzen and the Diplomatic Body, in conformity with the provisions governing expropriation for public purposes.

LXXIV.

The principle of awarding contracts on bids without preference of nationality shall be applied to the farming of the monopoly of opium and kiff. The same rule would apply to the tobacco monopoly, if created.

LXXV.

If the occasion should arise to modify any of the provisions of this declaration, the Maghzen and the Diplomatic Body at Tangier shall reach an understanding on this point.

LXXVI.

In all the cases provided for by the present declaration where the Diplomatic Body shall be called upon to intervene, except in what concerns articles LXIV, LXX, and LXXV, the decision shall be reached by a majority of the votes.

CHAPTER V.

A regulation concerning the customs of the Empire and the repression of fraud and smuggling.

LXXVII.

Every captain of a merchantman coming from a foreign or a Moorish port shall, within twenty-four hours after having been granted free pratique in any of the ports of the Empire, deposit at the customs an exact copy of his manifest, signed by him and certified to by the vessel's consignee. He shall furthermore, if required to do so, produce before the customs authorities the original of his manifest.

The customs shall have power to station one or more watchmen on board to prevent illicit trade.

LXXVIII.

The following are exempt from depositing the manifest:

1. Men-of-war or ships chartered for the account of a power.

2. Boats belonging to private individuals for their personal use and never carrying any merchandise.

3. Boats or craft used for shore fisheries.

4. Yachts intended only as pleasure boats and registered as such at their home ports.

5. Ships especially charged with laying down and repairing telegraphic cables.

6. Boats exclusively used in life-saving service.

7. Hospital ships.

8. Training ships of the merchant marine not engaged in commercial operations.

LXXIX.

The manifest deposited at the customs shall state the nature and origin of the cargo, with the marks and numbers of the cases, bales, bundles, casks, etc.

LXXX.

If there is serious reason to suspect the accuracy of the manifest, or in case the captain of the ship should refuse to allow the visit and verifications of customs officers, the case shall be brought to the attention of the proper consular authority, in order that the latter, in company with a delegate of the Shereefian customs, shall undertake the investigations, visits, and verifications that he may judge necessary.

LXXXI.

If after twenty-four hours, as stated in article LXXVII, the captain has not deposited his manifest, he shall incur, unless the delay be a case of *vis major*, a fine of 150 pesetas for each day's delay: provided, however, that the fine shall not exceed 500 pesetas. If the captain has fraudulently presented an inaccurate or incomplete manifest, he shall be personally condemned to pay a sum equal to the value of the merchandise for which he has failed to produce the manifest, and a fine of from 500 to 1000 pesetas, and the vessel and merchandise shall be further liable to seizure by consular authority as security for such fine.

LXXXII.

Any person about to pass through the customs merchandise imported or intended for exportation shall file in the custom-house a detailed statement setting forth the nature, quality, weight, number, measurement, and value of the merchandise, as well as the nature, marks, and numbers of the packages containing the same.

LXXXIII.

If there should be found at the time of the visit fewer packages or less merchandise than declared, the declarant, unless able to prove that he has acted in good faith shall pay double duties for the missing merchandise, and the merchandise presented shall be retained in the customs as security for such double duty. If, on the contrary, there should be found at the time of the visit an excess of packages, or quantity, or weight of the merchandise, this excess shall be seized and confiscated for the benefit of the Maghzen, unless the person making the declaration can prove his good faith.

LXXXIV.

If the declaration should be found inaccurate as to kind or quality, and the declarant is unable to prove his good faith, the merchandise wrongly declared shall be seized and confiscated by the proper authority for the benefit of the Maghzen.

LXXXV.

If the declaration should be found inaccurate as to the declared value, and the declarant should be unable to prove his good faith, the customs may either levy the duty in kind, then and there, or, if the merchandise is indivisible, take the said merchandise by at once paying to the declarant its declared value, plus 5 per cent.

LXXXVI.

If the declaration should be found false as to the nature of the merchandise the latter shall be considered as not having been declared, and the offense shall fall under articles LXXXVIII and XC hereinbelow, and shall be punished by the penalties provided for in the said articles.

LXXXVII.

The smuggling, flagrant or attempted, in or out of the country, by land or by sea, of merchandise subject to duty shall be punishable by confiscation of the merchandise, without prejudice to the penalties and fines hereinbelow, which shall be imposed by the proper jurisdiction. In addition, the conveyances on shore shall be seized and confiscated when smuggled goods form the greater part of the load.

LXXXVIII.

The smuggling, flagrant or attempted, in or out of the country, through a port open to commerce or through a custom-house, shall be punished by a fine not to exceed triple the value of the merchandise so smuggled and by imprisonment of from five days to six months, or by only one of these penalties.

LXXXIX.

The smuggling, flagrant or attempted, in or out of the country, outside of a port open to commerce or of a custom-house, shall be punished by a fine of from 300 to 500 pesetas, and by an additional fine equal to three times the value of the merchandise, or by imprisonment of from a month to a year.

XC.

The accomplices in offenses as provided by articles LXXXVIII and LXXXIX shall be liable to the same penalties as the principals. The elements constituting complicity shall be adjudged according to the law of the tribunal in charge of the case.

XCI.

In the case of smuggling, flagrant or attempted, in or out of the country, by a vessel outside of a port open to commerce, the Moorish customs shall have the right to take such vessel to the nearest port, to be turned over to the consular authority, and the said authority may seize and detain the vessel until it shall have paid the amount of the penalties imposed. The vessel shall be released at any stage of the action, in so far as the preliminary judicial proceedings are not impeded thereby, upon deposit made with the consular authority of the maximum of the fine, or else under responsible bail accepted by the customs.

XCII.

The provisions of the preceding articles are also applicable to coasting vessels.

XCIII.

Such merchandise as is not subject to an export duty, shipped in a Moorish port to be transported by sea to some other port in the Empire, shall be accompanied by a certificate issued by the customs, under penalty of being subjected to the payment of import duties, and even of being confiscated, if not entered in the manifest.

XCIV.

The transportation by coasting vessels of products subject to export duties can only be effected by depositing at the custom-house of the port of departure the amount of export duties on such merchandise and taking receipt therefor.

This money shall be returned to the depositor by the custom-house where it was deposited, on production of a declaration on which the customs certify the arrival of such merchandise and of the receipt for the deposit of the amount of the duties. The documents proving the arrival of the merchandise shall be produced within three months from the time of shipment. After this term, unless the delay be a case of *vis major*, the amount deposited shall become the property of the Maghzen.

XCV.

The import and export duties shall be paid [in] cash at the custom-house where liquidation has been made. The *ad valorem* duties shall be liquidated according to the cash wholesale value of the merchandise delivered in the custom-house and free from customs duties and storage dues. Damages to the merchandise, if any, shall be taken into account in appraising the depreciation thereby caused. Merchandise can only be removed after the payment of customs duties and storage.

The holding of the goods or the collection of duty shall, in every case, be made the subject of a regular receipt delivered by the officer in charge.

XCVI.

The value of the chief articles of merchandise dutiable in the Moorish customs is to be appraised every year under the conditions specified in the foregoing article by a committee on customs valuations, meeting at Tangier, and consisting of—

1. Three members appointed by the Moorish Government.
2. Three members appointed by the Diplomatic Body at Tangier.
3. One delegate of the State Bank.
4. One agent of the delegation of the 5 per cent Moroccan loan of 1904.

This committee shall appoint from twelve to twenty honorary members resident in Morocco, whom it shall consult when called upon to determine the value, and whenever it may see fit. These honorary members shall be selected from the lists of notables drawn up in the case of foreign subjects by each legation, and in the case of Moors by the Sultan's representative. They shall be appointed as far as possible in proportion to the importance of the commerce of each nation.

The committee shall be appointed for the term of three years.

The schedule of values fixed by it shall serve as a basis for the appraisals which the administration of Moorish customs shall make in every custom-house. It shall be posted at all custom-houses and in the chanceries of the legations and consulates at Tangier.

The schedule may be revised at the end of six months in case of considerable changes in the values of certain articles.

XCVII.

A permanent committee, to be known as the "Committee of Customs," shall be organized at Tangier and appointed for a term of three years. It shall consist of a special commissioner of His Shereefian Majesty, of a member of the diplomatic or consular body appointed by the Diplomatic Body at Tangier, and of a delegate from the State Bank. It shall be empowered to add to its members, in an advisory capacity, one or more representatives of the customs service.

This committee shall exercise its high supervision over the customs service, and shall have the right to propose to His Shereefian Majesty such measures as are likely to effect improvement in the service and assure the regularity and supervision of operations and collections (landing, shipping, land transportation, handling, the incoming and outgoing of merchandise, storage, appraisal, liquidation and collection of duties). The creation of such a Committee of Customs shall in no way infringe [on] the rights stipulated in favor of the bondholders by articles XV and XVI in the loan contract of June 12th, 1904.

Instructions to be drawn up by the Committee of Customs and the services interested therein shall determine the details of the enforcement of article XCVI and of the present article. They shall be submitted to the advice and consent of the Diplomatic Body.

XCVIII.

In custom-houses where sufficient warehouses exist the customs service shall take charge of the disembarked merchandise as soon as it is turned over by the captain of the vessel to the officers in charge of the lighterage, who shall receipt therefor, and until such time as it shall have been regularly cleared from the customs. The customs service is responsible for injuries caused by loss of or damage to merchandise which may be imputed to [be] the fault or negligence of its officers. It is not responsible for damages resulting either from the natural decay of merchandise, or from too lengthy a storage in the warehouse, or from cases of *vis major*.

In custom-houses where there are not sufficient warehouses the agents of the Maghzen are required only to employ such means of preservation as may be at the disposal of the custom-house.

A revision of the storage regulations now in force shall be made under the direction of the Diplomatic Body, whose decisions shall be taken by a majority vote, in concert with the Shereefian Government.

XCIX.

Confiscated merchandise and conveyances shall be sold under direction of the customs service within eight days from the date of final judgment rendered by the competent tribunal.

C.

The net proceeds of the sale of confiscated merchandise and articles become the final property of the State; as to pecuniary fines and compromises thereof, the amount, after deduction of costs of all kinds, shall be divided between the Shereefian Treasury and those who have participated in the repression of fraud or smuggling:

One-third to be distributed by the customs among the informants,

One-third to the officers who have seized the goods,

One-third to the Moorish Treasury.

If the seizure has been made without the intervention of an informant, one-half the fine shall be awarded to the officers making the seizure and the other half to the Moorish Treasury.

CI.

The Moorish customs authorities shall directly inform the diplomatic or consular agents of any violations of this regulation, which may have been committed by those under their jurisdiction, in order that they may be prosecuted before the competent court.

Similar violations by Moorish subjects shall be brought directly by the customs before the Shereefian authority.

A delegate of the customs shall be charged to follow the legal proceedings in cases pending before the several jurisdictions.

CII.

Every confiscation, fine, or penalty must be imposed on foreigners by consular jurisdiction, and on Moorish subjects by Shereefian jurisdiction.

CIII.

In the region bordering on Algeria the enforcement of these regulations shall be the exclusive concern of France and Morocco.

The enforcement of these regulations in the Riff and in general in the regions bordering on the Spanish possessions shall likewise be the exclusive concern of Spain and Morocco.

CIV.

The provisions of the present regulations, other than those relating to penalties, may be revised by unanimous decision of the Diplomatic Body at Tangier and in accord with the Maghzen, at the expiration of a term of two years from the date of their taking effect.

CHAPTER VI.

A declaration relative to public services and public works.

CV.

With a view to assuring the application of the principle of economic liberty without any inequality, the Signatory Powers declare that none of the public services in the Shereefian Empire can be alienated for the advantage of private interests.

CVI.

In case the Shereefian Government should invoke the aid of foreign capital or foreign industry for the working of public services or for the operation of public works, roads, railways, ports, telegraphs, and other public works, the Signatory Powers reserve to themselves the right to see to it that the authority of the State over these great enterprises of general interest remains entire.

CVII.

The validity of the concessions which may be made under the terms of article CVI, as well as for Government supplies, shall, throughout the Shereefian Empire, be subordinated to the principle of public awards on proposals, without preference of nationality, whenever applicable under the rules followed in foreign laws.

CVIII.

As soon as the Shereefian Government shall have decided to invite proposals for execution of public works, it shall so inform the Diplomatic Body. It shall later communicate to it the plans, specifications, and all documents annexed to the call for proposals, in order to enable the nationals of all the Signatory Powers to form a clear idea of the contemplated works and compete for the same. A sufficient term for this shall be specified in the call for proposals.

CIX.

The specifications shall not contain, either directly or indirectly, any condition or provision which may be prejudicial to free competition and which may give advantage to competitors of one nationality over those of another nationality.

CX.

The contracts shall be awarded in the form and according to the general conditions prescribed by the regulations which the Shereefian Government shall draw up with the assistance of the Diplomatic Body.

The contracts shall be awarded by the Shereefian Government to the bidder who, while conforming himself to the specifications, shall have submitted the bid fulfilling the most advantageous general conditions.

CXI.

The rules of articles CVI to CX shall be applied to concessions for working cork forests, in accordance with the customary provisions in foreign laws.

CXII.

The Shereefian firman shall determine the conditions of the concessions and the working of mines and quarries. In the composition of this firman the Shereefian Government shall be guided by foreign laws relating to such matters.

CXIII.

If in the cases mentioned in articles CVI to CXII it should become necessary to occupy certain property, its expropriation may be effected by previous payment of a fair indemnity, in conformity to the following rules:

CXIV.

Expropriation can only be effected on the ground of public utility and when necessity for the same shall have been ascertained by any administrative investigation, the formalities of which shall be determined by Shereefian regulations drawn up with the assistance of the Diplomatic Body.

CXV.

If the property holders are Moorish subjects, His Shereefian Majesty shall take the necessary measures, that no hindrance shall impede the execution of works that he shall have declared to be of public utility.

CXVI.

If the owners are foreigners the method of expropriation shall be as follows:

In case of disagreement between the competent administration and the owner of the property to be expropriated, the indemnity shall be fixed by a special jury, or, if the occasion arises, by arbitration.

CXVII.

This jury shall be composed of six expert appraisers, three to be selected by the owner, three by the administration desiring to expropriate. A majority vote shall rule.

If there be no majority, the owner and the administration shall each appoint an arbitrator, and the two arbitrators shall name an umpire.

In case no agreement can be reached in selecting an umpire he shall be appointed by the Diplomatic Body at Tangier.

CXVIII.

The arbitrators shall be selected from a list drawn up at the beginning of each year by the Diplomatic Body, and they shall be selected, as far as possible, from experts not living within the district in which the work is to be carried out.

CXIX.

The owner may appeal from the arbitrators' decision to a competent jurisdiction, and in accordance with the rules set for arbitration cases by the law of the country to which he belongs.

CHAPTER VII.

General provisions.

CXX.

With a view to harmonizing its legislation, if the occasion arises, with the engagements contracted under the present General Act, each of the Signatory Powers engages to take the necessary steps leading to the enactment of such legislation as may be necessary so far as it is concerned.

CXXI.

The present General Act shall be ratified according to the constitutional laws of each state. The ratifications shall be deposited at Madrid as soon as practicable, and at the latest by December thirty-first, one thousand nine hundred and six.

A *procès verbal* shall be made of such deposit and a certified copy sent to each of the Signatory Powers through the diplomatic channel.

CXXII.

The present General Act shall enter into effect as soon as all the ratifications shall have been deposited, and at the latest on December thirty-first, one thousand nine hundred and six.

In case the special legislative measures which may be necessary in certain countries to insure the application to their nationals living in Morocco of certain stipulations of this present General Act shall not have been enacted by the date fixed for ratification, these stipulations shall only become applicable in respect to them after the legislative measures above referred to shall have been promulgated.

CXXIII and last.

All treaties, conventions, and arrangements of the Signatory Powers with Morocco remain in force. It is understood, however, that in case of conflict between their provisions and those of the present General Act, the stipulations of the latter shall prevail.

In faith whereof the Delegates Plenipotentiary have signed the present General Act and have affixed their seals thereto.

Done at Algeciras this seventh day of April, one thousand nine hundred and six, in a single copy, which shall remain deposited in the archives of the Government of His Catholic Majesty, and of which certified copies shall be transmitted through the diplomatic channel to the Signatory Powers.

For Germany:	(L.S.) JOSEPH DE RADOWITZ
	(L.S.) TATTENBACH
For Austria-Hungary:	(L.S.) WELSERSHEIMB
	(L.S.) BOLESTA-KOZIEBRODZKI
For Belgium:	(L.S.) JOOSTENS
	(L.S.) COMTE CONRAD DE BUISSERET
For Spain:	(L.S.) EL DUQUE DE ALMODOVAR DEL RIO
	(L.S.) J. PEREZ-CABALLERO

For the United States of America, with reservation of the declaration made in the plenary session of the conference on April 7, 1906:

	(L.S.) HENRY WHITE
	(L.S.) SAMUEL R. GUMMERE
For France:	(L.S.) REVOIL
	(L.S.) REGNAULT
For Great Britain:	(L.S.) A. NICOLSON
For Italy:	(L.S.) VISCONTI VENOSTA
	(L.S.) G. MALMUSI

For Morocco:

For the Netherlands:	(L.S.) H. TESTA
For Portugal:	(L.S.) CONDE DE TOVAR
	(L.S.) CONDE DE MARTENS FERRAO
For Russia:	(L.S.) CASSINI
	(L.S.) BASILE DE BACHERACHT
For Sweden:	(L.S.) ROBERT SAGAR

Additional Protocol.

On the point of signing the General Act of the Conference of Algeciras, the delegates of Germany, Austria-Hungary, Belgium, Spain, the United States of America, France, Great Britain, Italy, the Netherlands, Portugal, Russia, and Sweden,

Taking into account the declaration of the delegates of Morocco that they were not, for the present, in position to affix their signatures thereto, they being unable, owing to the distance, to receive an early reply from His Shereefian Majesty concerning the points in regard to which they deemed it their duty to refer to Him,

Reciprocally engage, by virtue of their respective full powers, to unite their efforts towards the ratification of the said General Act in its entirety by His Shereefian Majesty and towards the simultaneous enforcement of the reforms therein provided which are interdependent.

They therefore agree to charge His Excellency Mr. Malmusi, Minister of Italy to Morocco and Dean of the Diplomatic Corps at Tangier, to take the necessary steps to that end by calling the attention of His Majesty the Sultan to the great advantages that His Empire would derive from the stipulations adopted at the conference by the unanimous action of the Signatory Powers.

The adhesion given by His Shereefian Majesty to the General Act of the Conference of Algeciras shall be communicated through the Government of His Catholic Majesty to the Governments of the other Signatory Powers. This adhesion shall have the same force as if the delegates of Morocco had affixed their signatures to the General Act and will take the place of ratification by His Shereefian Majesty.

In witness whereof, the delegates of Germany, Austria-Hungary, Belgium, Spain, the United States of America, France, Great Britain, Italy, the Netherlands, Portugal, Russia, and Sweden have signed the present additional protocol and affixed their seals thereto.

Done at Algeciras on the seventh day of April, one thousand nine hundred and six, in a single copy, which shall remain filed in the archives of the Government of His Catholic Majesty, and of which certified copies shall be delivered to the Signatory Powers through the diplomatic channel.

For Germany:	(L.S.) JOSEPH DE RADOWITZ
	(L.S.) TATTENBACH
For Austria-Hungary:	(L.S.) WELSERSHEIMB
	(L.S.) BOLESTA-KOZIEBRODZKI

For Belgium:	(L.S.) JOOSTENS
	(L.S.) COMTE CONRAD DE BUISSERET
For Spain:	(L.S.) EL DUQUE DE ALMODOVAR DEL RIO
	(L.S.) J. PEREZ-CABALLERO

For the United States of America, with reservation of the declaration made in the plenary session of the conference on April 7, 1906:

	(L.S.) HENRY WHITE
	(L.S.) SAMUEL R. GUMMERE
For France:	(L.S.) REVOIL
	(L.S.) REGNAULT
For Great Britain:	(L.S.) A. NICOLSON
For Italy:	(L.S.) VISCONTI VENOSTA
	(L.S.) G. MALMUSI
For Morocco:	
For the Netherlands:	(L.S.) H. TESTA
For Portugal:	(L.S.) CONDE DE TOVAR
	(L.S.) CONDE DE MARTENS FERRAO
For Russia:	(L.S.) CASSINI
	(L.S.) BASILE DE BACHERACHT
For Sweden:	(L.S.) ROBERT SAGER

The said General Act and Additional Protocol were signed by the plenipotentiaries of the United States of America under reservation of the following declaration:

"The Government of the United States of America, having no political interest in Morocco and no desire or purpose having animated it to take part in this conference other than to secure for all peoples the widest equality of trade and privilege with Morocco and to facilitate the institution of reforms in that country tending to insure complete cordiality of intercourse without and stability of administration within for the common good, declares that, in acquiescing in the regulations and declarations of the conference, in becoming a signatory to the General Act of Algeciras and to the Additional Protocol, subject to ratification according to constitutional procedure, and in accepting the application of those regulations and declarations to American citizens and interests in Morocco, it does so without assuming obligations or responsibility for the enforcement thereof."

[In Executive Session, Senate of the United States]

Resolved (two-thirds of the Senators present concurring therein). That the Senate advise and consent to the ratification of the general act and an additional protocol, signed on April 7, 1906, by the delegates of the powers represented at the conference which met at Algeciras, Spain, to consider Moroccan affairs.

Resolved further, That the Senate, as a part of this act of ratification, understands that the participation of the United States in the Algeciras conference and in the formation and adoption of the general act and protocol which resulted therefrom, was with the sole purpose of preserving and increasing its commerce in Morocco, the protection as to life, liberty, and property of its citizens residing or traveling therein, and of aiding by its friendly offices and efforts, in removing friction and controversy which seemed to menace the peace between powers signatory with the United States to the treaty of 1880, all of which are on terms of amity with this Government; and without purpose to depart from the traditional American foreign policy which forbids participation by the United States in the settlement of political questions which are entirely European in their scope.]

X. THE SYKES-PICOT AGREEMENT

In May 1916, the French and British agreed to a secret partition of the Arab areas of the Ottoman Empire in the *Sykes-Picot Agreement.* The negotiators were François Georges-Picot, French hgh commissioner in the Levant, and Sir Mark Sykes of the British Foreign Office. Pre-Soviet Russia was involved in negotiations, and Britain wanted Japan to be notified of the agreement, as well. The agreement established the territorial interests of France and Britain in the Arab Middle East (these stated interests became the basis for the future League of Nations mandates in the Middle East given to France and Britain, with some modifications). Soviet leaders disclosed the treaty to the Turks (who then informed the Arabs), causing a great stir during the later stages of the war, considering that the Allies had been working with the Arabs against the Central Powers in the Middle East, and that the British had already given tacit approval for Arab independence. France had been investing in Lebanon since the second half of the nineteenth century, indicating an ongoing interest in the old lands of *Outremer.*

1. Sir Edward Grey to Paul Cambon, 15 May 1916

I shall have the honour to reply fully in a further note to your Excellency's note of the 9th instant, relative to the creation of an Arab State, but I should meanwhile be grateful if your Excellency could assure me that in those regions which, under the conditions recorded in that communication, become entirely French, or in which French interests are recognised as predominant, any existing British concessions, rights of navigation or development, and the rights and privileges of any British religious, scholastic, or medical institutions will be maintained.

His Majesty's Government are, of course, ready to give a reciprocal assurance in regard to the British area.

2. Sir Edward Grey to Paul Cambon, 16 May 1916

I have the honour to acknowledge the receipt of your Excellency's note of the 9th instant, stating that the French Government accept the limits of a future Arab State, or Confederation of States, and of those parts of Syria where French interests predominate, together with certain conditions attached thereto, such as they result from recent discussions in London and Petrograd on the subject.

I have the honour to inform your Excellency in reply that the acceptance of the whole project, as it now stands, will involve the abdication of considerable British interests, but, since His Majesty's Government recognise the advantage to the general cause of the Allies entailed in producing a more favourable internal political situation in Turkey, they are ready to accept the arrangement now arrived at, provided that the co-operation of the Arabs is secured, and that the Arabs fulfil the conditions and obtain the towns of Homs, Hama, Damascus, and Aleppo.

It is accordingly understood between the French and British Governments

1. That France and Great Britain are prepared to recognize and protect an independent Arab State or a Confederation of Arab States in the areas (A) and (B) marked on the annexed map, under the suzerainty of an Arab chief. That in area (A) France, and in area (B) Great Britain, shall have priority of right of enterprise and local loans. That in area (A) France, and in area (B) Great Britain, shall alone supply advisers or foreign functionaries at the request of the Arab State or Confederation of Arab States.

2. That in the blue area France, and in the red area Great Britain, shall be allowed to establish such direct or indirect administration or control as they desire and as they may think fit to arrange with the Arab State or Confederation of Arab States.

3. That in the brown area there shall be established an international administration, the form of which is to be decided upon after consultation with Russia, and subsequently in consultation with the other Allies, and the representatives of the Shereef of Mecca.

4. That Great Britain be accorded (1) the ports of Haifa and Acre, (2) guarantee of a given supply of water from the Tigris and Euphrates in area (A) for area (B). His Majesty's Government, on their part, undertake that they will at no time enter into negotiations for the cession of Cyprus to any third Power without the previous consent of the French Government.

5. That Alexandretta shall be a free port as regards the trade of the British Empire, and that there shall be no discrimination in port charges or facilities as regards British shipping and British goods; that there shall be freedom of transit for British goods through Alexandretta and by railway through the blue area, whether those goods are intended for or originate in the red area, or (B) area, or area (A); and there shall be no discrimination, direct or indirect against British goods on any railway or against British goods or ships at any port serving the areas mentioned.

That Haifa shall be a free port as regards the trade of France, her dominions and protectorates, and there shall be no discrimination in port charges or facilities as regards French shipping and French goods. There shall be freedom of transit for

French goods through Haifa and by the British railway through the brown area, whether those goods are intended for or originate in the blue area, area (A), or area (B), and there shall be no discrimination, direct or indirect, against French goods on any railway, or against French goods or ships at any port serving the areas mentioned.

6. That in area (A) the Baghdad Railway shall not be extended southwards beyond Mosul, and in area (B) northwards beyond Samarra, until a railway connecting Baghdad with Aleppo via the Euphrates Valley has been completed, and then only with the concurrence of the two Governments.

7. That Great Britain has the right to build, administer, and be sole owner of a railway connecting Haifa with area (B), and shall have a perpetual right to transport troops along such a line at all times.

It is to be understood by both Governments that this railway is to facilitate the connexion of Baghdad with Haifa by rail, and it is further understood that, if the engineering difficulties and expense entailed by keeping this connecting line in the brown area only make the project unfeasible, that the French Government shall be prepared to consider that the line in question may also traverse the polygon Banias-Keis Marib-Salkhab Tell Otsda-Mesmie before reaching area (B).

8. For a period of twenty years the existing Turkish customs tariff shall remain in force throughout the whole of the blue and red areas, as well as in areas (A) and (B), and no increase in the rates of duty or conversion from *ad valorem* to specific rates shall be made except by agreement between the two Powers. There shall be no interior customs barriers between any of the above-mentioned areas. The customs duties leviable on goods destined for the interior shall be collected at the port of entry and handed over to the administration of the area of destination.

9. It shall be agreed that the French Government will at no time enter into any negotiations for the cession of their rights and will not cede such rights in the blue area to any third Power, except the Arab State or Confederation of Arab States without the previous agreement of His Majesty's Government, who, on their part, will give a similar undertaking to the French Government regarding the red area.

10. The British and French Governments, as the protectors of the Arab State, shall agree that they will not themselves acquire and will not consent to a third Power acquiring territorial possessions in the Arabian peninsula, nor consent to a third Power installing a naval base either on the east coast, or on the islands, of the Red Sea. This, however, shall not prevent such adjustment of the Aden frontier as may be necessary in consequence of recent Turkish aggression.

11. The negotiations with the Arabs as to the boundaries of the Arab State or Confederation of Arab States shall be continued through the same channel as heretofore on behalf of the two Powers.

12. It is agreed that measures to control the importation of arms into the Arab territories will be considered by the two Governments.

I have further the honour to state that in order to make the agreement complete, His Majesty's Government are proposing to the Russian Government to exchange notes analogous to those exchanged by the latter and your Excellency's Government on the 26th April last. Copies of these notes will be communicated to your Excellency as soon as exchanged.

I would also venture to remind your Excellency that the conclusion of the present agreement raises, for practical consideration, the question of the claims of Italy to a share in any partition or rearrangement of Turkey in Asia, as formulated in article 9 of the agreement of the 26th April, 1915, between Italy and the Allies.

His Majesty's Government further consider that the Japanese Government should be informed of the arrangement now concluded.

XI. THE KING-CRANE COMMISSION

The King-Crane Commission was sent by U.S. president Woodrow Wilson to tour some of the provinces of the Ottoman Empire in Asia Minor and in the Arab lands in the summer of 1919, in order to ascertain the sentiments of the population. Originally, Wilson envisioned French and British participation in the commission, but the French refused to participate, and the British planned originally to join, but declined in the end, leaving only Americans to the task. Neither France nor Britain felt it was in their interests to gather such information under American auspices. The commission was led by Henry C. King (president of Oberlin College) and Chicago businessman Charles R. Crane, and also included Oberlin history professor Albert R. Lybyer and Oberlin alumnus Donald M. Brodie. They met with groups and individuals throughout Syria and Lebanon, and compiled substantial documentation of the will and interests of various religious and tribal groups in the region. Their final report was presented to President Wilson and the Peace Commission, but was ignored at the Paris Peace Conference. The report was not published until 1947. Included here is an extract from the section on Lebanon, which describes the sentiments of the pro-French Maronite community.

The French policy of "colonization" shows its fruits in many inhabitants of this area, as well as of Beirut and other parts of Syria, who feel that they know French better than Arabic, and who are apt to hold themselves as of a distinctly higher order of civilization than the people of the interior. It is among these that the idea of a complete political separation of the Lebanese area from the rest of Syria has taken root. The propinquity of this area led the Turkish government to be lenient and favorable to Christians and others in adjacent regions, so that no very sharp line of difference of prosperity is visible. Nevertheless the appeal of lighter taxes and military service, greater security and opportunities for office-holding has an effect upon Christians in neighboring areas, so that many of them incline toward a Greater Lebanon under a permanent French mandate. But there is a considerable party, even among the pro-French, who are opposed to becoming a part of France. This is in fact the official Maronite position. Any revision of the situation should not diminish the security of the inhabitants of the Lebanon, but should raise the rest of Syria to a like security. This can be provided for in a United Syria by a sufficient measure of local autonomy. Care should be taken to avoid leaving this portion of the country in a position of perpetual special privilege, in which the common burdens would rest more heavily on other areas.

XII. CLEMENCEAU ON THE TURKISH EMPIRE

Georges Clemenceau (1841–1929) trained as a medical doctor, and worked as a journalist and educator (spending some time in the United States during the reign of Napoleon III, to whom he was opposed). He became the staunchly republican mayor of Montmartre in 1869, and was elected to the Chamber of Deputies in 1876. He became a senator in 1906, and served as prime minister twice—1906–1909 and 1917–1920. His political bravado gave rise to the nickname of "the Tiger." His diplomacy dominated the Paris Peace Conference, which concluded World War I. Following is an excerpt from Clemenceau's remarks on the Ottoman Turks, and the need to roll back Turkish influence on the conclusion of World War I, from Harry N. Howard, *The Partition of Turkey: A Diplomatic History, 1913–1923* (New York: Howard Fertig, 1966), 237.

There is no case to be found either in Europe or in Asia or Africa, in which the establishment of Turkish rule in any country has not been followed by a diminution of material prosperity, and a fall in the level of culture; nor is there any case to be found in which the withdrawal of Turkish rule has not been followed by a growth in material prosperity and a rise in the level of culture. Neither among the Christians of Europe nor among the Moslems of Syria, Arabia and Africa has the Turk done other than destroy wherever he has conquered; never has he shown himself able to develop in peace what he has won by war.

XIII. THE ESTABLISHMENT OF THE MANDATES

After having supported the Allied cause against the Turks in World War I, the Arabs were disappointed by the outcome of the peace negotiations that provided not for their independence, but for French and British mandatory rule over many Arab lands. The Arabian peninsula alone was independent. French mandatory rule was established in Syria and Lebanon, while British mandatory rule was established in Iraq, Kuwait, and Palestine. The goal of mandatory rule was for French and British officials to guide the native populations toward independence, but French politicians found it difficult to surrender their Middle Eastern domains until forced to do so by the circumstances of World War II. Following is the League of Nations mandate for Syria and Lebanon (July 24, 1922), from the *League of Nations Official Journal* (August 1922): 1013–1017.

The Council of the League of Nations,

Whereas the Principal Allied Powers have agreed that the territory of Syria and the Lebanon, which formerly belonged to the Turkish Empire, shall, within such boundaries as may be fixed by the said Powers, be entrusted to a Mandatory charged with the duty of rendering administrative advice and assistance to the population, in accordance with the provisions of Article 22 (paragraph 4) of the Covenant of the League of Nations; and

Whereas the Principal Allied Powers have decided that the mandate for the territory referred to above should be conferred on the Government of the French Republic, which has accepted it; and

Whereas the terms of this mandate, which are defined in the articles below, have also been accepted by the Government of the French Republic and submitted to the Council of the League for approval; and

Whereas the Government of the French Republic has undertaken to exercise this mandate on behalf of the League of Nations, in conformity with the following provisions; and

Whereas by the aforementioned Article 22 (paragraph 8), it is provided that the degree of authority, control or administration to be exercised by the Mandatory, not having been previously agreed upon by the members of the League, shall be explicitly defined by the Council of the League of Nations;

Confirming the same mandate, defines its terms as follows:
Article I: The Mandatory shall frame, within a period of three years from the coming into force of this mandate, an organic law for Syria and the Lebanon.

This organic law shall be framed in agreement with the native authorities and shall take into account the rights, interests and wishes of all the population inhabiting the said territory. The Mandatory shall further enact measures to facilitate the progressive development of Syria and the Lebanon as independent states. Pending the coming into effect of the organic law, the Government of Syria and the Lebanon shall be conducted in accordance with the spirit of this mandate.

The Mandatory shall, as far as circumstances permit, encourage local autonomy.
Article 2: The Mandatory may maintain its troops in the said territory for its defence. It shall further be empowered, until the entry into force of the organic law and the re-establishment of public security, to organise such local militia as may be necessary for the defence of the territory and to employ this militia for defence and also for the maintenance of order. These local forces may only be recruited from the inhabitants of the said territory.

The said militia shall thereafter be under the local authorities, subject to the authority and the control which the Mandatory shall therefore retain over these forces. It shall not be used for purposes other than those above specified save with the consent of the Mandatory.

Nothing shall preclude Syria and the Lebanon from contributing to the cost of the maintenance of the forces of the Mandatory stationed in the territory.

The Mandatory shall at all times possess the right to make use of the ports, railways and means of communication of Syria and the Lebanon for the passage of its troops and of all materials, supplies and fuel.

Article 3: The Mandatory shall be entrusted with the exclusive control of the foreign relations of Syria and the Lebanon and with the right to issue exequaturs to the consuls appointed by foreign Powers. Nationals of Syria and the Lebanon living outside the limits of the territory shall be under the diplomatic and consular protection of the Mandatory.

Article 4: The Mandatory shall be responsible for seeing that no part of the territory of Syria and the Lebanon is ceded or leased or in any way placed under the control of a foreign Power.

Article 5: The privileges and immunities of foreigners, including the benefits of consular jurisdiction and protection as formerly enjoyed by capitulation or usage in the Ottoman Empire, shall not be applicable in Syria and the Lebanon. Foreign consular tribunals shall, however, continue to perform their duties until the coming into force of the new legal organisation provided for in Article 6.

Unless the Powers whose nationals enjoyed the aforementioned privileges and immunities on August 1st, 1914, shall have previously renounced the right to their re-establishment, or shall have agreed to their non-application during a specified period, these privileges and immunities shall at the expiration of the mandate be immediately re-established in their entirety or with such modifications as may have been agreed upon between the Powers concerned.

Article 6: The Mandatory shall establish in Syria and the Lebanon a judicial system which shall ensure to natives as well as to foreigners a complete guarantee of their rights.

Respect for the personal status of the various peoples and for their religious interests shall be fully guaranteed. In particular, the control and administration of Wakfs shall be exercised in complete accordance with religious law and the dispositions of the founders.

Article 7: Pending the conclusion of special extradition agreements, the extradition treaties at present in force between foreign Powers and the Mandatory shall apply within the territory of Syria and the Lebanon.

Article 8: The Mandatory shall ensure to all complete freedom of conscience and the free exercise of all forms of worship which are consonant with public order and morality. No discrimination of any kind shall be made between the inhabitants of Syria and the Lebanon on the ground of differences in race, religion or language.

The Mandatory shall encourage public instruction, which shall be given through the medium of the native languages in use in the territory of Syria and the Lebanon.

The right of each community to maintain its own schools for the instruction and education of its own members in its own language, while conforming to such requirements of a general nature as the administration may impose, shall not be denied or impaired.

Article 9: The Mandatory shall refrain from all interference in the administration of the Councils of management (Conseils de fabrique) or in the management of religious communities and sacred shrines belonging to the various religions, the immunity of which has been expressly guaranteed.

Article 10: The supervision exercised by the Mandatory over the religious missions in Syria and the Lebanon shall be limited to the maintenance of public order and good government; the activities of these religious missions shall in no way be restricted, nor shall their members be subjected to any restrictive measures on the ground of nationality, provided that their activities are confined to the domain of religion.

The religious missions may also concern themselves with education and relief, subject to the general right of regulation and control by the Mandatory or the local government, in regard to education, public instruction and charitable relief.

Article 11: The Mandatory shall see that there is no discrimination in Syria or the Lebanon against the nationals, including societies and associations, of any State Member of the League of Nations as compared with its own nationals, including societies and associations, or with the nationals of any other foreign State in matters concerning taxation or commerce, the exercise of professions or industries, or navigation, or in the treatment of ships or aircraft. Similarly, there shall be no discrimination in Syria or the Lebanon against goods originating in or destined for any of the said States; there shall be freedom of transit, under equitable conditions, across the said territory.

Subject to the above, the Mandatory may impose or cause to be imposed by the local governments such taxes and customs duties as it may consider necessary. The Mandatory, or the local governments acting under its advice, may also conclude on grounds of contiguity any special customs arrangements with an adjoining country.

The Mandatory may take or cause to be taken, subject to the provisions of paragraph I of this article, such steps as it may think best to ensure the development of the natural resources of the said territory and to safeguard the interests of the local population.

Concessions for the development of these natural resources shall be granted without distinction of nationality between the nationals of all States Members of the League of Nations, but on condition that they do not infringe upon the authority of the local government. Concessions in the nature of a general monopoly shall not be granted. This clause shall in no way limit the right of the Mandatory to create monopolies of a purely fiscal character in the interest of the territory of Syria and the Lebanon, and with a view to assuring to the territory the fiscal resources which would appear best adapted to the local needs, or, in certain cases, with a view to developing the natural resources either directly by the State or through an organisation under its control, provided that this does not involve either directly or indirectly the creation of a monopoly of the natural resources in favour of the Mandatory or its nationals, nor involve any preferential treatment which would be incompatible with the economic, commercial and industrial equality guaranteed above.

Article 12: The Mandatory shall adhere, on behalf of Syria and the Lebanon, to any general international agreements already existing, or which may be concluded hereafter with the approval of the League of Nations, in respect of the following: the slave trade, the traffic in drugs, the traffic in arms and ammunition, commercial equality, freedom of transit and navigation, aerial navigation, postal, telegraphic or wireless communications, and measures for the protection of literature, art or industries.

Article 13: The Mandatory shall secure the adhesion of Syria and the Lebanon, so far as social, religious and other conditions permit, to such measures of common utility as may be adopted by the League of Nations for preventing and combating disease, including diseases of animals and plants.

Article 14: The Mandatory shall draw up and put into force within twelve months from this date a law of antiquities in conformity with the following provisions. This law shall ensure equality of treatment in the matter of excavations and archaeological research to the nationals of all States Members of the League of Nations.

(1) "Antiquity" means any construction or any product of human activity earlier than the year 1700 A.D.

(2) The law for the protection of antiquities shall proceed by encouragement rather than by threat.

Any person who, having discovered an antiquity without being furnished with the authorisation referred to in paragraph 5, reports the same to an official of the competent Department shall be rewarded according to the value of the discovery.

(3) No antiquity may be disposed of except to the competent Department, unless this Department renounces the acquisition of any such antiquity. No antiquity may leave the country without an export licence from the said Department.

(4) Any person who maliciously or negligently destroys or damages an antiquity shall be liable to a penalty to be fixed.

(5) No clearing of ground or digging with the object of finding antiquities shall be permitted, under penalty of fine, except to persons authorised by the competent Department.

(6) Equitable terms shall be fixed for expropriation, temporary or permanent, of lands which might be of historical or archaeological interest.

(7) Authorisation to excavate shall only be granted to persons who show sufficient guarantees of archaeological experience. The Mandatory shall not, in granting these authorisations, act in such a way as to exclude scholars of any nation without good grounds.

(8) The proceeds of excavations may be divided between the excavator and the competent department in a proportion fixed by that department. If division seems impossible for scientific reasons, the excavator shall receive a fair indemnity in lieu of a part of the find.

Article 15: Upon the coming into force of the organic law referred to in Article I, an arrangement shall be made between the Mandatory and the local governments for reimbursement by the latter of all expenses incurred by the Mandatory in organising the administration, developing local resources, and carrying out permanent public works, of which the country retains the benefit. Such arrangement shall be communicated to the Council of the League of Nations.

Article 16: French and Arabic shall be the official languages of Syria and the Lebanon.

Article 17: The Mandatory shall make to the Council of the League of Nations an annual report to the satisfaction of the Council as to the measures taken during the year to carry out the provisions of this mandate. Copies of all laws and regulations promulgated during the year shall be attached to the said report.

Article 18: The consent of the Council of the League of Nations is required for any modification of the terms of this mandate.

Article 19: On the termination of the mandate, the Council of the League of Nations shall use its influence to safeguard for the future the fulfilment by the Government of Syria and the Lebanon of the financial obligations, including pensions and allowances, regularly assumed by the administration of Syria or of the Lebanon during the period of the mandate.

Article 20: The Mandatory agrees that, if any dispute whatever should arise between the Mandatory and another Member of the League of Nations relating to the interpretation or the application of the provisions of the mandate, such dispute, if it cannot be settled by negotiation, shall be submitted to the Permanent Court of International Justice provided for by Article 14 of the Covenant of the League of Nations.

The present instrument shall be deposited in original in the archives of the League of Nations and certified copies shall be forwarded by the Secretary-General of the League of Nations to all members of the League.

Done at London on the twenty-fourth day of July, one thousand nine hundred and twenty-two.

XIV. THE INDEPENDENCE OF MOROCCO

The Franco-Moroccan Joint Declaration signed in Paris on March 2, 1956, provided independence for the Kingdom of Morocco after fifty years as a protectorate within the French Empire. The document concluded the experiment of French rule in Morocco that had started with the Algeciras Convention of 1906. The document is from the Embassy of France Press and Information Service.

FRANCE-MOROCCO
JOINT DECLARATION
Signed at Paris, March 2, 1956

The Government of the French Republic and His Majesty Mohammed V, Sultan of Morocco, hereby solemnly state their determination to make fully operative the Declaration of La Celle-Saint-Cloud of November 6, 1955.

They note that, in view of Morocco's advance along the road to progress, the Treaty of Fez of March 30, 1912, is no longer consistent—with the requirements of modern life and can no longer govern Franco-Moroccan relations.

Consequently, the Government of the French Republic hereby solemnly confirms its recognition of the independence of Morocco—which implies in particular the right to a diplomacy and an army—as well as its determination to respect, and to see to it that others respect, the integrity of Moroccan territory, as guaranteed by international treaties.

The government of the French Republic and His Majesty Mohammed V, Sultan of Morocco, hereby declare that the purpose of the negotiations which have just opened in Paris between Morocco and France, as equal and sovereign States, is to conclude new agreements which will define the interdependence of the two countries in the fields where they have common interests, will thus organize their cooperation on a basis of liberty and equality, especially in matters of defense, foreign relations, economy and culture, and will guarantee the rights and liberties of French persons settled in Morocco and of Moroccans settled in France, with due respect for the sovereignty of the two States.

The Government of the French Republic and His Majesty Mohammed V, Sultan of Morocco, hereby agree that, pending the entry into force of these agreements, the new relations between France and Morocco, shall be founded on the provisions of the annexed Protocol to the present Declaration.

Done at Paris, in two original copies,
on March 2, 1956
(Signed) CHRISTIAN PINEAU,
EMBAREK BEKKAI

ANNEXED PROTOCOL

I.-The legislative power shall be exercised as a sovereign right by His Majesty the Sultan. The representative of France shall be advised of draft dahirs and decrees: during the transitional period, he shall have the right to submit observations on these texts when they concern the interests of France, French nationals or foreigners.

II.-His Majesty Mohammed V, Sultan of Morocco, shall have at his disposal a national army. France will render assistance to Morocco in the constitution of that army. The present status of the French army in Morocco shall remain unchanged, during the transitional period.

III.-Those administrative powers which up until now have been reserved shall be transferred in a manner to be determined by common agreement.
The Moroccan Government shall be represented, with a deliberative voice, on the Committee of the Franc Area, the central organ determining the monetary policy of the Franc Area as a whole.

Furthermore, the guarantees enjoyed by French civil servants and Government employees serving in Morocco shall be continued.

IV.-The representative of the French Republic in Morocco shall have the title of High Commissioner of France.

Done at Paris in two original copies, on March 2, 1966.
(Signed) CHRISTIAN PINEAU, EMBAREK BEKKAI

XV. THE ÉVIAN ACCORDS (1962)

The Évian Accords ended 132 years of French rule in Algeria. Algeria had been the first area of the Islamic world conquered by France in the modern period, and it was the centerpiece of the French Empire, with a million European colonists residing there. After a revolution and civil war lasting eight years, de Gaulle decided to jettison this last major portion of the French Empire. The accords officially ended the war between the French Army and the FLN Muslim revolutionaries on terms favorable to the FLN, granting independence to Algeria and acknowledging an FLN-dominated state (one-party rule in Algeria would last almost three decades). After the withdrawal of French armed forces and the evacuation of most of the European colonists, many of the provisions of the accords were abandoned by the FLN government within the first year of independence.

ÉVIAN DECLARATIONS
ÉVIAN-LES-BAINES
(MARCH 18, 1962)

CEASE-FIRE AGREEMENT IN ALGERIA

Article 1.

Military operations and all armed action throughout the Algerian territory will be brought to an end on March 19, 1962 at 12 o'clock noon.

Article 2.

The two parties pledge themselves to prohibit any recourse to acts of collective or individual violence.
    Any action of a clandestine nature and in violation of public order must cease.

Article 3.

The combatant forces of the National Liberation Front in existence on the day of the cease-fire will be stationed within areas corresponding to their current location. Individual movements by members of these forces outside of the area where they are stationed shall be made without arms.

Article 4.

The French forces stationed on the frontiers will not withdraw before the proclamation of the results of self-determination.

Article 5.

The stationing plans of the French army in Algeria will provide for measures necessary to avoid any contact between the forces.

Article 6.

For the purpose of settling problems relative to the application of the cease-fire, a joint Cease-Fire Commission shall be created.

Article 7.

The Commission will propose the measures to be taken at the request of the two parties, notably concerning:

—The solution of incidents that have been noted, after having proceeded to a documented inquiry;

—The resolution of difficulties that it would be impossible to settle on a local basis.

Article 8.

Each of the two parties is represented on this Commission by a field-grade officer and a maximum of ten members, including secretarial personnel.

Article 9.

The seat of the joint Cease-Fire Commission shall be fixed at Rocher-Noir.

Article 10.

In the departments, the joint Cease-Fire Commission will be represented, if the necessities so indicate, by local commissions composed of two members for each of the parties, which will function according to the same principles.

Article 11.

All prisoners taken during combat that are being held by each of the parties at the time of the entry into effect of the cease-fire shall be freed; they shall be returned within twenty days from the date of the cease-fire to the authorities designated for that purpose.

The two parties will inform the International Committee of the Red Cross of the place of internment of their prisoners and of all measures taken toward their liberation.

GENERAL DECLARATION, MARCH 19, 1962

The French people, by the referendum of January 8, 1961, recognized the right of the Algerians to choose by means of a consultation of direct and universal suffrage their political destiny in relation to the French Republic.

The negotiations that took place at Évian from March 7 to March 18, 1962, between the Government of the French Republic and the F.L.N. [Algerian National Liberation Front] reached the following conclusions:

A cease-fire is concluded. Military operations and the armed struggle will come to an end on March 19 throughout the Algerian territory.

The guarantees relative to the application of self-determination and the organization of public powers in Algeria during the transition period have been defined in common agreement.

The formation, after self-determination, of an independent and sovereign state appearing to conform to the realities of the Algerian situation, and in these conditions, cooperation between France and Algeria corresponding to the interests of the two countries, the French Government considers, together with the F.L.N., that the solution of the independence of Algeria in cooperation with France is the one which corresponds to this situation.

The Government and the F.L.N. have therefore defined this solution, in common agreement, in the declarations which will be submitted to the approval of the electors at the time of the self-determination vote.

CHAPTER I. *Organization of Public Powers During the Transition Period and Self-Determination Guarantees*

A.

The self-determination consultation will permit the electors to make known whether they want Algeria to be independent and in that case whether they want France and Algeria to cooperate in the conditions defined by the present declarations.

B.

This consultation will take place throughout the Algerian territory, that is to say, in the fifteen following departments: Algiers, Batna, Bône, Constantine, Medea, Mostaganem, Oases, Oran, Orleansville, Saida, Saoura, Setif, Tiaret, Tizi-Ouzou, Tlemcen.

The results of the different voting offices will be totaled and proclaimed for the whole territory.

C.

The freedom and the genuineness of the consultation will be guaranteed in conformity with the regulations fixing the conditions for the self-determination consultation.

D.

Until self-determination has been realized, the organization of public powers in Algeria will be established in accordance with the regulations which accompany the present declaration.

A Provisional Executive and a court of public law and order shall be set up. The French Republic shall be represented in Algeria by a High Commissioner. These institutions, in particular the Provisional Executive, will be installed as soon as the cease-fire comes into force.

E.

The High Commissioner will be the custodian of the powers of the Republic in Algeria, in particular in matters of defense, security and the maintenance of law and order in the last resort.

F.

The Provisional Executive will, in particular, be responsible for:

—Assuring the conduct of Algeria's own public affairs. It will direct the administration of Algeria and will have the task of admitting Algerians to positions in the various branches of this administration;
—Maintaining public law and order. For this purpose, it will have police services and a security force under its authority;
—Preparing and implementing self-determination.

G.

The court of public law and order will consist of an equal number of European and Moslem judges.

H.

The full exercise of individual and public liberties will be reestablished within the shortest possible time.

I.

The F.L.N. will be considered a legal political body.

J.

Persons interned both in France and Algeria will be released within a maximum period of twenty days from the date of the cease-fire.

K.

An amnesty will be proclaimed immediately. Detained persons will be released.

L.

Persons in refuge abroad will be able to return to Algeria. Commissions sitting in Morocco and Tunisia will facilitate this return.

Persons who have been relocated will be able to return to their regular place of residence. The Provisional Executive will take the first social, economic and other measures aimed at assuring the return of these people to a normal life.

M.

The self-determination vote will take place within a period of not less than three months and not exceeding six months. The date will be fixed on proposal of the Provisional Executive within the two months following its installation.

CHAPTER II. Independence and Cooperation

If the solution of independence and cooperation is adopted, the contents of the present declarations will be binding on the Algerian State.

A. INDEPENDENCE OF ALGERIA

I.

The Algerian State will exercise its full and complete sovereignty both internally and externally. This sovereignty will be exercised in all spheres, in particular in defense and foreign affairs.

The Algerian State will freely establish its own institutions and will choose the political and social regime which it deems to be most in conformity with its interests. On the international level, it will define and implement in full sovereignty the policy of its choice.

The Algerian State will subscribe unreservedly to the Universal Declaration of Human Rights and will base its institutions on democratic principles and on equality of political rights between all citizens without discrimination of race, origin or religion. It will, in particular, apply guarantees recognized for citizens of French civil status.

II.

Individual Rights and Liberties and Their Guarantees.
1. *Common provisions.*

No one shall be subject to police or legal measures, to disciplinary sanctions or to any discrimination on account of:

—Opinions expressed at the time of events that occurred in Algeria before the day of the self-determination vote;

—Acts committed at the time of these same events before the day of the cease-fire proclamation.

No Algerian shall be forced to leave Algerian territory or be prevented from leaving it.

2. *Provisions concerning French citizens of ordinary civil status.*

a) Within the framework of Algerian legislation on nationality, the legal situation of French citizens of ordinary civil status shall be regulated according to the following principles:

For a period of three years from the day of self-determination, French citizens of ordinary civil status:

—Born in Algeria and giving proof of ten years of permanent and regular residence on Algerian territory on the day of self-determination;
—Or giving proof of ten years of permanent and regular residence on Algerian territory on the day of self-determination and whose father or mother was born in Algeria and fulfills or could have fulfilled the conditions for exercising civil rights;
—Or giving proof of twenty years of permanent and regular residence on Algerian territory on the day of self-determination, Will enjoy, by right, Algerian civil rights and will be considered therefore as French nationals exercising Algerian civil rights,

French nationals exercising Algerian civil rights cannot simultaneously exercise French civil rights.

At the end of the above-mentioned three-year period, they shall acquire Algerian nationality by an application for registration or confirmation of their registration on the voters' lists. Failing this application, they shall enjoy the benefits of a resident aliens convention.

b) In order to assure, during a three-year period, to French nationals exercising Algerian civil rights, and at the end of this period, in a permanent way, to Algerians of French civil status, the protection of their person and their property and their normal participation in Algerian life, the following measures are provided for:

They will have a just and genuine part in public affairs. In the assemblies, their representation shall correspond to their actual numbers. In the various branches of the civil service, they will be assured of fair participation.

Their participation in the municipal life of Algiers and Oran will be the subject of special provisions.

Their property rights will be respected. No dispossession measures will be taken against them without their being granted fair compensation previously agreed upon.

They will receive guarantees appropriate to their cultural, linguistic and religious particularities. They will retain their personal status, which will be respected and enforced by Algerian courts comprised of magistrates of the same status. They will use the French language within the assemblies and in their relations with the public authorities.

An association for the safeguard of their rights will contribute to the protection of the rights which are guaranteed to them.

A Court of Guarantees, an institution of internal Algerian law, will be responsible for seeing that these rights are respected.

B. COOPERATION BETWEEN FRANCE AND ALGERIA

The relations between the two countries will be founded, in mutual respect of their independence, on the reciprocal exchange of benefits and the interests of the two parties.

Algeria shall guarantee the interests of France and the rights acquired by individuals and legal entities under the conditions fixed by the present declarations. In exchange, France will grant Algeria her technical and cultural assistance and will contribute privileged financial aid for its economic and social development.

1) For a period of three years, which may be renewed, France's aid will be fixed in conditions comparable to and at a level equivalent to those of the programs now under way.

Having in mind respect for Algeria's independence with regard to commerce and customs, the two countries will determine the different fields in which commercial exchanges will benefit from preferential treatment.

Algeria will belong to the franc area. It will have its own monetary unit and its own currency assets. Freedom of transfers will exist between France and Algeria under conditions compatible with the economic and social development of Algeria.

2) In the existing Departments of the Oases and of the Saoura, the development of the wealth of the subsoil will be carried out according to the following principles:

a) French-Algerian cooperation will be ensured by a technical body for Saharan cooperation. This body will be composed of equal numbers from both sides. Its role will be, in particular, to develop the infrastructure necessary for the exploitation of the subsoil, to give advice on draft bills and regulations relative to mining, to examine requests concerning the granting of mining titles. The Algerian State will issue the mining titles and will enact mining legislation in full sovereignty;

b) French interests will be assured in particular by:

—The exercise, in accordance with the regulations of the Saharan petroleum code, such as it exists at present, of the rights attached to mining titles granted by France;
—Preference being given, in the case of equal offers, in the granting of new mining titles, to French companies, in accordance with the terms and conditions provided for in Algerian mining legislation;
—Payment in French francs for Saharan hydrocarbons up to the amount of the supply needs of France and other countries of the franc area.

3) France and Algeria will develop their cultural relations. Each of the countries shall be able to set up on the territory of the other a University and Cultural Bureau whose establishments will be open to all.

France will lend her aid in the training of Algerian technicians. French personnel, in particular teachers and technicians, will be placed at the disposal of the Algerian Government by agreement between the two countries.

CHAPTER III. Settlement of Military Questions

If the solution of the independence of Algeria and of cooperation between Algeria and France is adopted, military questions will be settled according to the following principles:

—The French forces, whose numbers will gradually be reduced as of the cease-fire, will be withdrawn from the frontiers of Algeria when self-determination is realized. Their total force will be reduced to 80,000 men within a period of 12 months from the time of self-determination. The repatriation of these forces will have to be completed by the end of a second twenty-four-month period. Military installations will be correspondingly evacuated;
—Algeria shall lease to France the use of the Mers-el-Kabir base for a fifteen-year period, which may be renewed by agreement between the two countries;
—Algeria shall also grant France the use of a number of military airfields, the terrains, sites and installations necessary to her.

CHAPTER IV. Settlement of Litigation

France and Algeria will resolve differences that may arise between them by means of peaceful settlement. They will have recourse either to conciliation or to arbitration. Failing agreement by these procedures, each of the two States shall be able to have recourse directly to the International Court of Justice.

CHAPTER V. *Consequences of Self-Determination*

Upon the official announcement provided for in Article 27 of the statutes of self-determination, the instruments corresponding to these results will be drawn up. If the solution of independence and cooperation is adopted:

—The independence of Algeria will immediately be recognized by France;
—The transfer of jurisdiction will be realized forthwith;
—The regulations set forth in the present general declaration and declarations accompanying it will come into force at the same time.

The Provisional Executive will organize, within three weeks, elections for the designation of the Algerian National Assembly, to which it will hand over its powers.

DECLARATION OF GUARANTEES

PART ONE. *General Provisions*

1. *Personal safety.*

No one may be harassed, sought after, prosecuted, convicted or be subject to penal sentence, disciplinary sanction or any discrimination whatsoever, for acts committed in connection with political events that occurred in Algeria before the day of the proclamation of the cease-fire.

No one may be harassed, sought after, prosecuted, convicted or be subject to penal sentence, disciplinary sanction or any discrimination whatsoever, for words or opinions expressed in connection with political events that occurred in Algeria before the day of the voting on self-determination.

2. *Freedom of movement between Algeria and France.*

Barring a court ruling, any Algerian holding an identity card shall have freedom of movement between Algeria and France.

Algerians leaving Algerian territory with the intention of establishing themselves in another country may take their personal property outside Algeria.
They may, without restriction, dispose of their real estate and transfer the capital derived therefrom under the conditions provided for by the Declaration of Principles Concerning Economic and Financial Cooperation. Their pension rights shall be respected under the conditions provided for in this same declaration.

PART TWO

CHAPTER I. *Exercise of Algerian Civil Rights*

Within the framework of Algerian legislation on nationality, the legal situation of French citizens of ordinary civil status shall be regulated in accordance with the following principles:

For a period of three years from the day of self-determination, French citizens of ordinary civil status:

—Born in Algeria and giving proof of ten years of permanent and regular residence on Algerian territory on the day of self-determination;
—Or giving proof of ten years of permanent and regular residence on Algerian territory on the day of self-determination, and whose father or mother was born in Algeria and fulfills or could have fulfilled the conditions for exercising civil rights;
—Or giving proof of twenty years of permanent and regular residence on Algerian territory on the day of self-determination,

Will enjoy, by right, Algerian civil rights and will be considered therefore as French nationals exercising Algerian civil rights.

French nationals exercising Algerian civil rights cannot simultaneously exercise French civil rights.

At the end of the above-mentioned three-year period, they shall acquire Algerian nationality by an application for registration or confirmation of their registration on the voters' lists. Failing this application, they shall enjoy the benefits of a resident aliens convention.

CHAPTER II. Protection of the Rights and Liberties of Algerian Citizens of Ordinary Civil Status

In order to assure to Algerians of ordinary civil status the protection of their person and their property and their harmonious participation in Algerian life, the measures enumerated in the present chapter are provided.

French nationals exercising Algerian civil rights under the conditions provided for in Chapter I hereinabove shall benefit from these same measures.

1) Algerians of ordinary civil status shall enjoy the same treatment and the same guarantees in law and in fact as other Algerians.

They shall be subject to the same duties and to the same obligations.

2) The rights and liberties defined by the Universal Declaration of Human Rights shall be guaranteed to Algerians of ordinary civil status. In particular, no discriminatory measures may be taken against them on account of their language, their culture, their religion, or their personal status. These characteristic features shall be recognized and must be respected.

3) Algerians of ordinary civil status shall for five years be exempt from military service.

4) Algerians of ordinary civil status shall have a just part in the conduct of public affairs, both as concerns the general affairs of Algeria and those of local communities, public establishments and public enterprises.

Within the framework of a single electoral college common to all Algerians, Algerians of ordinary civil status shall enjoy the right to vote and to be elected to office.

5) Algerians of ordinary civil status shall be justly and genuinely represented in all the assemblies of a political, administrative, economic, social and cultural nature.

a) In the assemblies of a political nature and in the assemblies of an administrative nature (regional, general and municipal councils), their representation may not be less than their number in relation to the population. To this end, in each election district, a certain number of seats to be filled will be reserved—according to the proportion of Algerians of ordinary civil status in this district—for Algerian candidates of this status, regardless of what voting method is selected.

b) In the assemblies of an economic, social and cultural nature, their representation must take into account their moral and material interests.

6) a) The representation of Algerians of ordinary civil status in the municipal assemblies will be proportionate to their number in the district under consideration.

b) In all communes where there are more than 50 Algerians of ordinary civil status and where these persons, notwithstanding the application of the provisions of Article 5 hereinabove, shall not be represented in the municipal assembly, a special assistant shall be appointed who will be called upon to sit in this assembly with an advisory voice.

At the end of the municipal elections, the Algerian candidate of ordinary civil status who receives the greatest number of votes shall be proclaimed special assistant.

c) Without prejudice to the principles convened upon in paragraph a) hereinabove, during the four years that will follow the vote on self-determination, the cities of Algiers and Oran will be administered by municipal councils, whose president or vice president will be chosen from Algerians of ordinary civil status.
During this same period, the cities of Algiers and Oran shall be divided into municipal districts whose number will be not less than 10 for Algiers and not less than 6 for Oran.

In the districts where the proportion of Algerians of ordinary civil status exceeds 50 per cent, the authority placed at the head of the district shall belong to this category of citizens.

7) A just proportion of Algerians of ordinary civil status will be assured in the various branches of the civil service.

8) Algerians of ordinary civil status shall have the right to exercise their non-Koranic personal status until the promulgation in Algeria of a civil code, in the drafting of which they will take part.

9) Without prejudice to the guarantees established by the regulations relative to the participation of Algerians of ordinary civil status in the civil service, the following specific guarantees shall be provided in judicial matters with regard to the composition of the Algerian judiciary body:

A. Whatever may be the future organization of the judiciary in Algeria, it will in all cases include, as regards Algerians of ordinary civil status:
—A two-level court system, applying to examining courts as well;
—A jury in criminal matters;
—Traditional means of appeal: to the Court of Cassation and petition for mercy.

B. In addition, throughout Algeria:

a) All civil and criminal courts before which an Algerian of ordinary civil status must appear will necessarily comprise an Algerian judge of the same status.
Moreover, if the tribunal entertaining jurisdiction includes a jury, one-third of the jurors will be Algerians of ordinary civil status;

b) In all criminal courts under a single judge before which an Algerian of ordinary civil status shall appear and in which the judge is not an Algerian of the same status, the single judge will be assisted by an assessor who will be chosen from Algerians of ordinary civil status and will have an advisory voice;

c) All litigation concerned exclusively with the personal status of Algerians of ordinary civil status will be brought before a court comprising a majority of judges having this status;

d) In all courts in which the presence of one or several judges of ordinary civil status is required, these judges may be replaced by French judges detailed for the purpose of technical cooperation.

10) Algeria shall guarantee freedom of conscience and the freedom of the Catholic, Protestant and Jewish faiths. It shall assure to these faiths freedom of organization, practice and instruction as well as the inviolability of their places of worship.

11) a) Official texts shall be published or made known in the French language at the same time as in the national language. The French language shall be used in relations between the Algerian public services and Algerians of ordinary civil status. The latter shall have the right to use the French language notably in political, administrative and judicial matters.

b) Algerians of ordinary civil status shall be free to choose between the various educational establishments and types of education.

c) Algerians of ordinary civil status, as all other Algerians, shall be free to open and to operate educational establishments.

d) Algerians of ordinary civil status will be able to attend the French sections that Algeria will organize in its educational establishments of all kinds in conformity with the provisions of the Declaration of Principles Concerning Cultural Cooperation.

e) The part allotted by Algerian radio and television to broadcasts in the French language must correspond to the importance that is acknowledged to this language.

12) There will be no discrimination established with regard to property belonging to Algerians of ordinary civil status, in particular with regard to requisitioning, nationalization, agrarian reform and taxation. All dispossession measures will be subject to fair compensation previously agreed upon.

13) Algeria will not establish any discrimination with regard to access to employment. There will be no restrictions established on access to any profession, save requirements of competence.

14) Freedom of association and freedom to belong to labor unions shall be guaranteed. Algerians of ordinary civil status shall have the right to create associations and labor unions and to belong to the associations and labor unions of their choice.

CHAPTER III. Association for the Safeguard of Rights

Algerians of ordinary civil status shall belong, until the statutes come into force, to an association for the safeguard of their rights recognized as serving the public interest and governed by Algerian law.

The purpose of the Association shall be:
—To go to law, including before the Court of Guarantees, in order to defend the individual rights of Algerians of ordinary civil status, in particular the rights enumerated in the present declaration;
—To intervene before the public authorities;
—To administer cultural and welfare establishments.

The Association shall be directed, until the approval of its statutes by the competent Algerian authorities, by a managing board of nine members, one third to be named by representatives of religious and intellectual activities, one third by the magistrature and one third by members of the bar.

The managing board shall be assisted by a secretariat responsible to it; it may open offices in various localities.

The Association shall not be either a political party or group. It shall not concur in the expression of the vote.

The Association will be constituted as soon as the present declaration enters into force.

CHAPTER IV. *Court of Guarantees*

Litigation shall be referred, upon the request of any interested Algerian party, to the Court of Guarantees.

This Court shall be composed of:
—Four Algerian magistrates, of whom two shall be of ordinary civil status, appointed by the Algerian Government;
—A presiding magistrate appointed by the Algerian Government on the proposal of the four magistrates.

The Court may validly deliberate when a minimum of three out of five members are present.

It may order inquiries to be held.

It may repeal any regulatory text or individual decision that is contrary to the Declaration of Guarantees.

It may decide on any measures of compensation.

Its decisions shall be final.

PART THREE. *French Persons Residing in Algeria as Aliens*

French persons, with the exceptions of those who shall enjoy Algerian civil rights, will be protected by a resident aliens convention in conformity with the following principles:

1) French nationals will be able to enter and leave Algeria provided they hold either a French national identity card or a French passport that is valid.
They will be able to move freely in Algeria and to establish their residence in the place of their choice.

French nationals residing in Algeria who will leave Algerian territory with a view toward establishing themselves in another country may take their personal property, dispose of their real estate and transfer their capital, under the conditions provided for in Section III of the Declaration of Principles Concerning Economic and Financial Cooperation and to retain the right to pension allowances acquired in Algeria, under the conditions provided for in the Declaration of Principles Concerning Economic and Financial Cooperation.

2) French nationals on Algerian territory will be entitled to equal treatment with nationals with regard to:

—The enjoyment of civil rights in general;
—Free access to all professions along with the rights necessary to practice them effectively, in particular that of conducting and establishing businesses;
—The benefits of relief and social security legislation;
—The right to acquire and to dispose of the ownership of all personal property and real estate, the right to administer it and the right to have use of it; subject to the provisions concerning agrarian reform.

3) a) French nationals on Algerian territory will enjoy all the liberties set forth in the Universal Declaration of Human Rights.

b) French persons shall have the right to use the French language in all their relations with the courts and the public authorities.

c) French persons may open and operate private educational and research establishments in Algeria, in conformity with the provisions in the Declaration of Principles Concerning Cultural Cooperation.

d) Algeria shall open its educational establishments to French persons. The latter may request to pursue the education offered in the sections provided for in the Declaration of Principles Concerning Cultural Matters.

4) The persons, property and interests of French nationals will be placed under the protection of laws, which will be substantiated by free access to the courts. They will be exempt from depositing in advance security for costs or damages.

5) No arbitrary or discriminatory measures will be taken against the vested property, interests and rights of French nationals. No one may be deprived of his rights, without fair compensation previously agreed upon.

6) The personal status of French nationals, including the inheritance system, will be governed by French law.

7) Algerian legislation will eventually determine the civil and political rights granted to French nationals on Algerian territory as well as the conditions of their admission to public office.

8) French nationals may participate within the framework of Algerian legislation in the activities of labor unions, associations for the protection of professional rights and organizations representing economic interests.

9) Civil and trading companies established under French law whose head office is in France and which have or will have economic activity in Algeria will enjoy on Algerian territory all the rights, defined by the present text, to which a legal entity is entitled.

10) French nationals will be able to obtain on Algerian territory administrative concessions, authorizations and permissions and will be allowed to make public contracts under the same conditions as Algerian nationals.

11) French nationals on Algerian territory may not be subject to duties, taxes or levies, under whatever denomination, different from those collected from Algerian nationals.

12) Subsequent provisions will be made with a view to curbing fiscal evasion and avoiding double taxation. French nationals will benefit on Algerian territory, under the same conditions as Algerian nationals, from all provisions making the State or public organizations responsible for compensation of damages suffered by persons or property.

13) No deportation measures against a French national deemed to be dangerous to the public order will be effected without the French Government having been informed beforehand. Except for absolute emergencies, ascertained by a decision, stating the grounds on which it rests, a sufficient time period will be allowed to the person concerned to settle his or her pressing affairs.

His or her property and interests will be safeguarded, under the responsibility of Algeria.

14) Supplementary provisions will be the subject of a subsequent agreement.

DECLARATION OF PRINCIPLES CONCERNING ECONOMIC AND FINANCIAL COOPERATION

Cooperation between France and Algeria in economic and financial matters shall be founded on a contractual basis in accordance with the following principles:

1) Algeria shall guarantee French interests and the vested rights of individuals and legal entities;

2) France shall undertake in return to grant Algeria her technical and cultural assistance and to make to its economic and social development a preferential contribution that is justified by the extent of French interests existing in Algeria;

3) In the framework of these reciprocal commitments, France and Algeria will maintain privileged relations, particularly as regards trade and currency.

TITLE I. *French Contribution to the Economic and Social Development of Algeria*

Article 1.

In order to make a lasting contribution to the continuity of the economic and social development of Algeria, France will continue her technical assistance and preferential financial aid. For an initial period of three years, renewable, this aid will be fixed in conditions comparable to and at a level equivalent to those of programs now under way.

Article 2.

French financial and technical aid will apply notably to the study, execution or financing of the public or private investment projects presented by the competent Algerian authorities; to the training of Algerian cadres and technicians; and to the assignment of French technicians. It will also apply to the transitional measures to be taken to facilitate the resumption of work by the regrouped populations.

The aid may take the form, as the case may be, of allowances in kind, loans, contributions or participations.

Article 3.

The competent Algerian and French authorities will act in concert to ensure the full effectiveness of the aid and its allocation to the purposes for which it was granted.

Article 4.

The terms and conditions of cooperation in administrative, technical and cultural matters shall be the subject of special provisions.

TITLE II. *Trade*

Article 5.

Within the framework of the principle of Algeria's independence with regard to trade and customs, trade with France, founded on the basis of the reciprocity of benefits and interests of the two parties, will be covered by a special statute corresponding to the terms of cooperation between the two countries.

Article 6.

This statute will specify:
—The institution of preferential tariffs or the absence of duties;
—Marketing facilities on French territory for Algerian surplus production, through the organization of markets for certain products, especially with regard to price conditions;
—Restrictions on the free movement of goods, justified in particular by the development of the national economy, the protection of public health and the suppression of fraud;
—Provisions for air and sea navigation between the two countries with a view to fostering the development and full use of the two flags.

Article 7.

Algerian nationals residing in France, particularly workers, will have the same rights as French nationals, with the exception of political rights.

TITLE III. *Monetary Relations*

Article 8.

Algeria will belong to the franc area. Its relations with this area will in addition be defined contractually on the basis of the principles laid down in Articles 9, 10 and 11 hereinafter.

Article 9.

Transactions related to conversion of Algerian currency into French currency and vice versa, and transfers between the two countries, shall be made on the basis of official parities recognized by the International Monetary Fund.

Article 10.

Transfers to France will be free. The total volume and rate of operations must nevertheless take into account the essential requirements of the economic and social development of Algeria, as well as Algeria's total receipts in francs, drawn notably from the financial aid granted by France.

For the application of these principles and with a view to protecting Algeria from the effects of speculation, France and Algeria will act in concert in a joint commission comprising the monetary authorities of the two countries.

Article 11.

The agreements concerning monetary cooperation between France and Algeria will notably specify:
—The terms and conditions of transferring the privilege of issue; the conditions for the exercise of this privilege during the period that will precede the establishment of the Algerian Bank of Issue; and the facilities necessary for the functioning of this Bank;
—The relations between this Bank of Issue and the Bank of France as regards the conditions of Algeria's participation in the currency pool; the individualization and the initial foreign currency drawing rights; the granting of contingent additional currency allocations; the regulations covering Algerian assets in French francs corresponding to the right to draw on foreign currency; and the possibilities of overdraft in French francs;
—The conditions for the establishment of common regulations with regard to transactions negotiated in currencies other than those of the franc area.

TITLE IV. *Guarantees of Vested Rights and Previous Commitments*

Article 12.

Algeria will ensure without any discrimination the free and peaceful enjoyment of patrimonial rights acquired on its territory before self-determination. No one will be deprived of these rights without fair compensation previously agreed upon.

Article 13.

Within the framework of agrarian reform, France will grant Algeria specific aid with a view to the repurchase in whole or in part of property rights held by French nationals.

On the basis of a repurchase plan drawn up by the competent Algerian authorities, the terms and conditions of this aid will be determined by agreement between the two countries, so as to reconcile the execution of the Algerian social and economic policy with the normal spreading out of the financial assistance provided by France.

Article 14.

Algeria shall confirm all the rights attached to mining or transport titles granted by the French Republic for the exploration, exploitation or transport of liquid or gaseous hydrocarbons and other mineral substances of the thirteen northern Algerian departments; the regulations governing these titles will continue to be the series of provisions applicable on the date of the cease-fire.

The present article shall concern all the mining or transport titles issued by France before self-determination; after the cease-fire, however, there will be no issue of new exclusive permits for research in areas that have not as yet been allocated, unless the areas in question have been put up for new bidding by a notification published prior to this date in the "Journal Official" of the French Republic.

Article 15.

Vested rights obtaining on the date of self-determination, with regard to retirement or invalidity pensions secured from Algerian organizations, shall be guaranteed.

These organizations will continue to ensure the payment of retirement or invalidity pensions; their final takeover as well as the terms and conditions of their ultimate repurchase will be determined by common agreement between the Algerian and the French authorities.

Retirement or invalidity pension rights obtained from French organizations shall be guaranteed.

Article 16.

Algeria will facilitate the payment of pensions owed by France to veterans and retired persons. It will authorize the competent French services to pursue the exercise of their activities on Algerian territory with regard to payments and the care and treatment of the disabled.

Article 17.

Algeria shall guarantee to French companies established on its territory, as well as to companies in which the majority of the capital is held by French individuals or French legal entities, the normal exercise of their activities in conditions excluding any discrimination to their detriment.

Article 18.

Algeria shall assume the obligations and enjoy the rights contracted in its name or in that of Algerian public establishments by the competent French authorities.

Article 19.

Public real estate in Algeria will be transferred to the Algerian State, excepting, with the agreement of the Algerian authorities, the premises deemed necessary for the normal functioning of temporary or permanent French services.

Public establishments of the State or companies belonging to the State and responsible for the administration of Algerian public services will be transferred to Algeria. This transfer will concern patrimonial funds allotted to the administration of these public services as well as to the liabilities pertaining thereto. Special agreements will determine the conditions in which these transfers will be carried out.

Article 20.

Barring a future agreement between France and Algeria, the credits and debts drawn up in francs, existing on the date of self-determination, between individuals or legal entities in public or private law, shall be considered payable in the currency of the place where the contract was concluded.

DECLARATION OF PRINCIPLES ON COOPERATION FOR THE EXPLOITATION OF THE WEALTH OF THE SAHARAN SUBSOIL

1) Within the framework of Algerian sovereignty, Algeria and France shall undertake to cooperate with each other to ensure the continuity of efforts for the exploitation of the wealth of the Saharan subsoil;

2) Algeria shall inherit from France her rights, prerogatives and obligations, as a public power granting concessions in the Sahara for the application of the mining and petroleum legislation, taking into account the provisions under Title III of the present declaration;

3) Algeria and France shall undertake, each on its own behalf, to observe the principles of cooperation set forth hereinabove and to respect and ensure respect of the application of the provisions hereinafter:

TITLE I. *Liquid and Gaseous Hydrocarbons*

A. GUARANTEE OF VESTED RIGHTS AND OF THEIR PROLONGATION

Par. I.—Algeria shall confirm all the rights attached to the mining and transport titles granted by the French Republic in pursuance of the Saharan petroleum code.

The present paragraph shall apply to all the mining and transport titles granted by France before self-determination; after the cease-fire, however, there will be no issue of new exclusive permits for exploration in areas that have not as yet been allocated, unless the areas in question have been put up for new bidding by a notification published prior to this date in the "Journal Officiel" of the French Republic.

a) The term "mining and transport titles" must be understood to mean primarily:
1. Prospecting authorizations;
2. Exclusive exploration permits, known as H permits;
3. Temporary exploitation authorizations;
4. Exploitation concessions and their corresponding covenants;
5. Approvals of equipment projects for the transportation of hydrocarbons and the corresponding transportation authorizations.

b) The term "Saharan petroleum code" must be understood to mean the series of provisions of all kinds applicable, at the time of the cease-fire, to the exploration, exploitation and transportation of hydrocarbons produced in the departments of the Oases and the Saoura and in particular to the transportation of these hydrocarbons to the terminal points on the coast.

Par. 2—The rights and obligations of the persons holding the mining and transport titles referred to in Par. 1 above and of the individuals or legal entities which are associated with them in protocols, agreements or contracts, approved by the French Republic, are those defined by the Saharan petroleum code and by the present provisions.

Par. 3—The right of the holder of mining titles and his associates to transport or arrange for the transportation by pipelines, under normal economic conditions, of his production of liquid or gaseous hydrocarbons to the points where they are refined or loaded and to see that they are exported is applicable, with regard to the determination of the layout of the pipelines, in accordance with the recommendations of the "Agency." (See Title III.)

Par. 4—The right of the concessionary and of his associates, within the framework of their own commercial organization or the organization of their choice, to sell and dispose freely of the production, i.e., to sell, trade or use it in Algeria or for export, shall apply provided that the requirements of Algerian domestic consumption and local refining have been met.

Par. 5—The rates of exchange and the currency parities applicable to all commercial or financial transactions must be in accordance with the official parities recognized by the International Monetary Fund.

Par. 6—The provisions of the present title shall be applicable without distinction to all persons holding mining or transport titles and to their associates, whatever the legal nature, origin or distribution of their capital and irrespective of any condition of nationality of the persons or of the locality of the head office.

Par. 7—Algeria will refrain from any measure likely to make more costly or stand in the way of the exercise of the rights guaranteed above, taking into account normal economic conditions. It will not infringe upon the rights and interests of the stockholders, shareholders or creditors of persons holding mining or transport titles, of their associates, or of enterprises acting for their account.

B. GUARANTEES FOR THE FUTURE (NEW MINING OR TRANSPORT TITLES)

Par. 8—During a period of six years, dating from the entry into force of the present provisions, Algeria will give preference to French companies with regard to research and exploitation permits in the case of equal offers for areas that have not as yet been allocated or have again become available. The applicable regulations will be those defined by existing Algerian legislation, French companies, however, remaining subject to the Saharan petroleum code referred to in Par. I hereinabove, as regards mining titles covered by the guarantee of vested rights.

The term "French companies," as it is used in the present paragraph, must be understood to mean those companies whose control is in fact assured by French individuals or legal entities.

Par. 9—Algeria shall refrain from any discriminatory measures to the detriment of French companies and their associates in the exploration, exploitation or transportation of liquid or gaseous hydrocarbons.

C. COMMON PROVISIONS

Par. 10—Purchasing and sales transactions for the export of hydrocarbons from the Sahara, intended directly or through technical exchange for the supply of France and the other countries of the franc area, shall be settled in French francs.

The export of Saharan hydrocarbons outside the franc area shall carry the right for Algeria to draw on foreign currency, up to the amount of the net profit in currency resulting from these transactions; the agreements on monetary cooperation, referred to in Article I i of the Declaration of Principles on Economic and Financial

Cooperation, will specify the practical terms and conditions for the application of this principle.

TITLE II. *Other Mineral Substances*

Par. 11—Algeria shall confirm all the rights attached to the mining titles granted by the French Republic for mineral substances other than hydrocarbons; the regulations governing these titles will remain those of the series of provisions applicable on the date of the cease-fire.

The present paragraph shall apply to all mining titles granted by France before self-determination; after the cease-fire, however, there will be no issue of new exclusive permits for research in areas that have not as yet been allocated, unless the areas in question have been put up for new bidding by a notification published prior to this date in the "Journal Officiel" of the French Republic.

Par. 12—French companies may submit claims for new permits and concessions under the same conditions as other companies; they will enjoy treatment as favorable as that accorded to the latter companies for the exercise of the rights deriving from these mining titles.

TITLE III. *The Technical Agency for the Exploitation of the Wealth of the Saharan Subsoil*

Par. 13—The rational exploitation of the wealth of the Saharan subsoil shall be entrusted, under the conditions defined in the following paragraphs, to a Franco-Algerian technical agency, hereinafter called the "Agency."

Par. 14—Algeria and France shall be the joint founders of the Agency which will be set up as soon as the present declarations of principles enter into effect.

The Agency shall be administered by a board to be composed of an equal number of representatives from the two founder countries. Each of the members of the board, including the chairman, shall have one vote.

The board shall deliberate on all the activities of the Agency. Decisions concerning the following shall be taken by means of a two-thirds majority:

—The appointment of the chairman and of the director general;

—The estimated expenditures referred to in Par. 16 hereinafter. Other decisions shall be taken by an absolute majority vote.

The chairman of the board and the director general must be chosen so that one is of Algerian nationality and the other of French nationality.
The board shall determine the respective competences of the chairman and of the director general.

Par. 15—The Agency shall have legal status and financial autonomy. It shall have at its disposal administrative and technical services, with priority being given in the composition of these services to the founder countries.

Par. 16—The Agency shall be responsible for promoting the rational exploitation of the wealth of the subsoil; in this respect, it shall in particular be responsible for the development and maintenance of the infrastructure necessary for mining activities.

To this end, the Agency shall each year draw up a draft program of expenditures, studies, maintenance of equipment and new investments, which it shall submit for approval to the two founder countries.

Par. 17—The role of the Agency in mining matters shall be defined as follows:
i) Texts of a legislative or regulatory nature concerning mining or petroleum regulations shall be enacted by Algeria on recommendation of the Agency;

2) The Agency shall examine the applications for mining titles and the rights deriving from these titles. Algeria shall decide upon the proposals of the Agency and shall grant mining titles;

3) The Agency shall assure the administrative supervision of companies holding permits or concessions.

Par. 18—The expenditures of the Agency shall include: expenditures;
—Expenditures for the maintenance of existing facilities and equipment;
—Expenditures for new equipment.

The resources of the Agency shall be provided by contributions by the member States determined in proportion to the number of votes which they hold on the board.

However, for a three-year period dating from self-determination, which period may eventually be renewed, these resources will be supplemented by an additional contribution by Algeria which will be not less than 12% of the receipts from petroleum taxation.

TITLE IV. *Arbitration*

Notwithstanding any provisions to the contrary, all litigation or disputes between the public authorities and the holders of rights guaranteed by Title I-A hereinabove shall be dealt with, in the first and last resort, by an international court of arbitration whose organization and functioning will be based on the following principles:

—Each of the parties shall appoint an arbitrator and the two arbitrators will nominate a third arbitrator who will preside over the court of arbitration; failing agree-

ment on the nomination of this arbitrator, the President of the International Court of Justice will be asked to make this appointment at the request of the first mover;
—The court of arbitration shall pronounce judgment by a majority vote;
—Recourse to this court shall constitute a stay;
—Sentence shall be enforceable on the territory of both parties without proceedings to enforce judgment in the other country; it shall be recognized as lawfully enforceable outside these territories during the three days following pronouncement of judgment.

DECLARATION OF PRINCIPLES CONCERNING CULTURAL COOPERATION

TITLE 1. *Cooperation*

Article 1.

France shall undertake, to the best of her ability, to place at the disposal of Algeria the necessary means for helping it to develop education, vocational training and scientific research in Algeria.

Within the framework of cultural, scientific and technical assistance, France will place at the disposal of Algeria—for purposes of education, control of studies, organization of examinations and competitive examinations, the functioning of the administrative services, and research—the teaching personnel, technicians, specialists and research workers which it may need.

This personnel will have all the facilities and moral guarantees necessary for the fulfillment of its task; it will be governed by the provisions of the Declaration of Principles on Technical Cooperation.

Article 2.

Each of the two countries may set up on the territory of the other educational establishments and university institutes in which instruction will be given in accordance with its own programs, schedules and teaching methods and will be sanctioned by their own diplomas—admission to these schools will be open to nationals of both countries.

France will retain a certain number of educational establishments in Algeria. The list of buildings and the conditions of their distribution between France and Algeria will be the subject of a special agreement.

The programs in these establishments will include the teaching of the Arabic language in Algeria and of the French language in France. The terms and conditions of control by the country in which the establishment is located will be the subject of a special agreement.

The setting up of an educational establishment in one or the other country will be subject to prior notification, enabling the authorities of either country to set forth their observations and suggestions in order to reach as great a degree of agreement as possible on the terms and conditions of setting up the establishment in question.

The establishments opened by each country will be attached to a university and cultural bureau.

Each country will facilitate in every respect the task of the services and persons responsible for the administration and control of the establishments of the other country functioning on its territory.

Article 3.

Each country will open its public educational establishments to pupils and students of the other country.

In localities where the number of pupils warrants such a measure, each country will organize, within its own school establishments, sections in which instruction will be given in accordance with the programs, schedules and methods practiced in the public educational system of the other country.

Article 4.

France will place at the disposal of Algeria the necessary means for helping it to develop its higher education and scientific research and to provide in these domains education of a quality equivalent to the corresponding education provided by French universities.

In the Algerian universities, Algeria will organize, to the best of its abilities, instruction in basic subjects commonly provided in French universities, under similar conditions with respect to programs, length of study and examinations.

Article 5.

The degrees and teaching diplomas granted in Algeria and in France, under the same conditions with respect to programs, length of study and examinations, shall be valid by right in both countries.

The equivalence of grades and diplomas granted in Algeria and in France under different conditions with respect to programs, length of study or examinations, will be determined by means of special agreements.

Article 6.

Nationals of each of the two countries, individuals or legal entities may open private educational establishments on the territory of the other country, subject to the observation of the laws and regulations concerning public order, morality, hygiene, conditions regarding diplomas and any other conditions that might be agreed upon by common accord.

Article 7.

Each country will facilitate the access of nationals of the other country to the educational and research establishments under its authority, by the organization of training courses and all other suitable means, and by the granting of scholarships or research fellowships or of loans on trust, which will be granted to the persons concerned through the intermediary of the authorities of their own country, after consultation between the responsible authorities of both countries.

Article 8.

Each of the two countries will ensure on its territory to the members of the teaching profession, in both public and private schools, of the other country the respect of academic freedom and traditional immunities of educational institutions.

TITLE II. *Cultural Exchanges*

Article 9.

Each of the two countries will facilitate the entry, circulation and distribution on its territory of all the instruments of expression of thought originating in the other country.

Article 10.

Each of the two countries will encourage on its territory the study of the language, history and civilization of the other country, facilitate the work undertaken in this field and the cultural activities organized by the other country.

Article 11.

The terms and conditions of technical assistance to be furnished by France to Algeria with regard to radio, television and motion pictures will be settled at a future date by common agreement.

TITLE III.

Article 12.

The aid provided for with respect to economic and financial cooperation shall be applicable to the areas referred to in the present declaration.

Notes

Series Foreword

1. Haynes Johnson, *The Best of Times: The Boom and Bust Years of America Before Everything Changed* (New York: A James H. Silberman Book, Harcourt, Inc., 2001), p. 3.

2. Eric Hobsbawm, *The Age of Extremes: A History of the World, 1917–1991* (New York: Pantheon, 1994).

3. Giovanni Arrighi, *The Long Twentieth Century: Money, Power, and the Origins of Our Times* (London: Verso, 1994).

Chapter 1

1. For al-Andalus, see in particular Évariste Lévi-Provençal, *Histoire de l'Espagne musulmane*, 3 vols. (Paris: Maisonneuve et Larose, 1950–1953); Hugh Kennedy, *Muslim Spain and Portugal: A Political History of al-Andalus* (London: Longman, 1996); W. Montgomery Watt and Pierre Cachia, *A History of Islamic Spain* (Edinburgh: University of Edinburgh Press, 1977); Thomas F. Glick, *Islamic and Christian Spain in the Middle Ages* (Princeton, NJ: Princeton University Press, 1979).

2. For the Muslim operations in this area, see Lévi-Provençal, *Histoire de l'Espagne musulmane*, vol. 1; for discussion of the motives for the Muslim drive into Septimania, see Michel Rouche, "Les Aquitains, ont-ils trahi avant la bataille de Poitiers?" *Le Moyen Âge* lxxiv, no. 1 (1968): 5–26; and William E. Watson, "The Battle of Tours-Poitiers Revisited," *Providence: Studies in Western Civilization* 1, no. 2 (Fall 1993): 51–68.

3. On this mosque, see Jean Lacam, "Vestiges de l'Occupation arabe en Narbonnaise," *Cahiers Archéologique* viii (1956): 93–115.

4. Jean Lacam, *Les Sarrazins dans le haut moyen âge français* (Paris: Maisonneuve et Larose, 1965), 87–88, 98.

5. Michel Rouche, "Les Aquitains"; more fully in his *L'Aquitaine des Visigoths aux Arabes, 418–781; naissance d'une region* (Paris: Éditions de L'École des Hauts Études en Sciences Sociales, 1979).

6. Maurice Mercier and André Seguin, *Charles Martel et la Bataille de Poitiers* (Paris: P. Geuthner, 1944); Ernest Mercier, "La bataille de Poitiers et les vraies causes du recul de l'invasion arabe," *Revue Historique* 7 (May, Aug. 1878): 1–13; Watson, "The Battle of Tours-Poitiers Revisited."

7. This was in the *Chronicle of Fredegar*. See Watson, "The Battle of Tours-Poitiers Revisited," 51.

8. François Guizot and Madame Guizot de Witt, (Robert Black, trans.), *History of France*, vol. 1 (New York: The Cooperative Publication Society, 1869), 154.

9. For a translation, see Dorothy L. Sayers, *The Song of Roland* (Harmondsworth, Middlesex, UK: Penguin, 1957).

10. See Richard Hodges and David Whitehouse, *Mohammed, Charlemagne, and the Origins of Europe* (Ithaca, NY: Cornell University Press, 1982).

11. Philippe Sénac, "Contribution a l'Étude des incursions musulmanes dans l'Occident chrétien: la localisation du Gabal al-Qilal," *Revue de l'Occident musulman et de la Méditerraneén* 31 (1981): 7–14.

12. P.-A. Amargier, "La capture de Saint Maieul de Cluny et l'expulsion des Sarrasins de Provence," *Revue Bénédictine* 73 (1963): 316–323.

13. Philippe Sénac, *Provence et Piraterie Sarrasine* (Paris: Maissoneuve et Larose, 1982).

14. Bernard Lewis, *The Muslim Discovery of Europe* (New York: W. W. Norton, 1982).

15. Norman Daniel, *Islam and the West: The Making of an Image* (Edinburgh: Edinburgh University Press, 1980), see especially pp. 229–241.

16. Daniel, *Islam and the West*, 58–61, for Western criticisms of the Qur'an; also James J. Kritzek, *Peter the Venerable and Islam* (Princeton, NJ: Princeton University Press, 1964).

17. James A. Bellamy, "Arabic Names in the *Chanson de Roland:* Saracen Gods, Frankish Swords, Roland's Horse, and the Olifant," *Journal of the American Orientalist Society* 107 (1987).

18. Benjamin Z. Kedar, *Crusade and Mission: European Approaches toward the Muslims* (Princeton, NJ: Princeton University Press, 1984), 55.

19. Daniel, *Islam and the West*, 113.

20. See Edward Peters's introduction in *The First Crusade* (Philadelphia: University of Pennsylvania Press, 1971).

21. Joshua Prawer, *The Crusaders' Kingdom: European Colonialism in the Middle Ages* (New York: Praeger, 1972).

22. Ibid.; see also Joshua Prawer, *Crusader Institutions* (Oxford: Clarendon Press, 1980); Jonathan Riley-Smith, *The Feudal Nobility and the Kingdom of Jerusalem, 1174–1277* (London: Macmillan, 1973).

23. See document III A, Robert the Monk, Urban's Appeal for Crusaders.

24. Louise Riley-Smith and Jonathan Riley-Smith, eds., *The Crusades: Idea and Reality* (London: Edward Arnold, 1981), contains documents discussing this and the transition of the knights to crusaders.

25. Among the standard works, see in particular, Kenneth M. Setton, ed., *A History of the Crusades*, 2 vols. (Philadelphia: University of Pennsylvania Press,

1955–1962)—the series was extended into several more volumes covering the later crusades by the University of Wisconsin Press; Stephen Runciman, *A History of the Crusades*, 3 vols. (New York: Harper and Row, 1967); a good one-volume history with an ample bibliography is Jonathan Riley-Smith, *The Crusades: A Short History* (New Haven, CT: Yale University Press, 1987).

26. See the documents in Peters, *The First Crusade*, for contemporary descriptions of the operations.

27. For the military infrastructure of the crusader states, see R. C. Smail, *Crusading Warfare, 1097–1193* (Cambridge: Cambridge University Press, 1956).

28. For interesting case studies, see Hans Eberhard Mayer, "The Origins of the Lordships of Ramla and Lydda in the Latin Kingdom of Jerusalem," *Speculum* 60, no. 3 (July 1985): 537–552.

29. Peters, *The First Crusade*, 220.

30. Jonathan Riley-Smith, *The Knights of St. John in Jerusalem and Cyprus, c. 1050–1310* (New York: St. Martin's, 1967).

31. See the essays in A. T. Luttrell, *The Hospitallers in Cyprus, Rhodes, Greece and the West (1291–1440)* (London: Variorum, 1978).

32. For Arab accounts, see Francesco Gabrieli, *Arab Historians of the Crusades* (Berkeley: University of California Press, 1984); Amin Maalouf, *The Crusades through Arab Eyes* (London: Al Saqi Books, 1984).

33. William C. Jordan, *Louis IX and the Challenge of Crusade: A Study in Rulership* (Princeton, NJ: Princeton University Press, 1979).

34. See document III B, Jean de Joinville, on the perils of crusading, from La Vie de Saint Louis; M. R. B. Shaw, trans., *Chronicles of the Crusaders: Joinville and Villehardouin* (Harmondsworth, Middlesex, UK: Penguin, 1963).

35. Riley-Smith, *The Crusades: A Short History*, 175.

36. See document III C, Stephen Runciman, on the demise of the crusader states, A History of the Crusades; Stephen Runciman, *A History of the Crusades*, vol. 3, *The Kingdom of Acre and the Later Crusades* (New York: Harper and Row, 1967), 423.

37. See Luttrell, *The Hospitallers*, for many of these activities.

38. See Nicolas Vatin, *Sultan Djem: un prince ottoman dans l'Europe du xve siecle d'après deux sources contemporaines* (Ankara: Imprimerie de la Société turque d'histoire, 1997).

39. Ion Ursu, *La Politique orientale de François Ier (1515–1547)* (Paris: H. Champion, 1908).

40. Michel Géoris, *François Ier: le Magnifique* (Paris: Éditions France-Empire, 1998); André Clot, *Suleiman the Magnificent* (New York: New Amsterdam, 1992).

41. Stanford J. Shaw, *A History of the Ottoman Empire and Modern Turkey*, vol. 1 (New York: Cambridge University Press, 1976–1977), 97–98.

42. Ibid.

43. François A. M. A. Mignet, *Rivalité de François Ier et Charles-Quint* (Paris: Didier, 1875).

44. Shaw, *A History of the Ottoman Empire and Modern Turkey*, vol. 1, 182, 189.

45. Ibid., vol. 1, 177.

46. See, for example, Maurice Ashley, *Louis XIV and the Greatness of France* (New York: Free Press, 1946), 103–104; John B. Wolf, *Louis XIV* (New York: Norton, 1968), 414–416.

47. Franco Cardini, *Europe and Islam* (Oxford and Malden, MA: Blackwell, 2001), 179–180, for one of the most recent discussions.

48. For the operations of Napoleon in Egypt and his wider ambitions in the Middle East, see in particular Christopher J. Herold, *Bonaparte in Egypt* (New York: Harper and Row, 1962).

49. Herold, *Bonaparte in Egypt*, 47.

50. Ibid., 56.

51. Ibid., 69.

52. Ibid., 183–186.

53. For the Napoleonic forces in Alexandria, see ibid., 71–81.

54. Ibid., 292–294.

55. Ibid., 294–295.

56. Ibid., 318–319.

57. Ibid., 369–370; see also the comments of M. M. Knight, "French Colonial Policy—The Decline of Association," *Journal of Modern History* 5, no. 2 (June 1933): 213; for the Muslim perspective, see Sheikh al-Jabarti (Shmuel Moreh, trans.), *Napoleon in Egypt: Al-Jabarti's Chronicle of the French Occupation* (Princeton, NJ: Markus Wiener, 1993).

58. Herold, *Bonaparte in Egypt*, 373–374.

59. Ibid., 186.

Chapter 2

1. Stephen Clissold, *The Barbary Slaves* (London: P. Elek, 1977), 17–25.

2. Ibid., 64–67.

3. Ibid., 12–16, 107–108.

4. Ibid., 156.

5. Guillaume Berthier de Sauvigny, (Lynn M. Case, trans.), *The Bourbon Restoration* (Philadelphia: University of Pennsylvania Press, 1966), 434–435; Edward Behr, *The Algerian Problem* (New York: Norton, 1962), 16; Clissold, *Barbary Slaves*, 163; Carl Brockelmann (Joel Carmichael and Moshe Perlmann, trans.), *History of the Islamic Peoples* (London: Routledge and Kegan Paul, 1980), 397; David Prochaska, *Making Algeria French: Colonialism in Bône, 1870–1920* (Cambridge: Cambridge University Press, 1994), 62.

6. De Sauvigny, *Bourbon Restoration*, 435; Behr, *The Algerian Problem*, 16; Clissold, *Barbary Slaves*, 163–164; Brockelmann, *History of the Islamic Peoples*, 397.

7. De Sauvigny, *Bourbon Restoration*, 435.

8. Ibid., 435; Brockelmann, *History of the Islamic Peoples*, 397.

9. De Sauvigny, *Bourbon Restoration*, 436.

10. Ibid., 435–436.

11. Ibid., 437.

12. Ibid.

13. Ibid., 437–438.

14. Ibid., 438; see also document V, Bourmont to the dey of Algiers.

15. Ibid., 438–439.

16. Ibid., 439.

17. Ibid.

18. Bruno Étienne, *Abdelkader* (Paris: Hachette, 1994), 118–121.

19. Behr, *The Algerian Problem*, 19–20.

20. Ibid.

21. On 'Abd al-Qadir's proclamation of jihad, see Étienne, *Abdelkader*, 122–126; Julia A. Clancy-Smith, *Rebel and Saint: Muslim Notables, Popular Protest, Colonial Encounters: Algeria and Tunisia, 1800–1904* (Berkeley: University of California Press, 1994), 71–72, 78; Behr, *The Algerian Problem*, 18.

22. See Raphael Danzinger, *Abd al-Qadir and the Algerians* (New York: Holmes and Meier, 1977).

23. Brockelmann, *History of the Islamic Peoples*, 398.

24. Ibid.

25. Ibid., 399.

26. For Bugeaud's own thoughts on the conquest and the military needs of the occupation, see Thomas R. Bugeaud, *L'Algérie: des moyens de conserver et d'utiliser cette conquete* (Paris: Dentu, 1842). See Behr's assessment of Bugeaud in *The Algerian Problem*, 20–22.

27. Étienne, *Abdelkader*, 170–173.

28. Brockelmann, *History of the Islamic Peoples*, 399.

29. Paul H. Beik, *Louis Philippe and the July Monarchy* (Princeton, NJ: D. Van Nostrand Company, 1965), 82; Clancey-Smith, *Rebel and Saint*, 75.

30. Beik, *Louis Philippe*, 82–83; Guizot, *History of France*, vol. 8, 356.

31. Brockelmann, *History of the Islamic Peoples*, 399–400.

32. Ibid., 400.

33. Guizot, *History of France*, vol. 8, 356–358; Beik, *Louis Philippe*, 83.

34. Beik, *Louis Philippe*, 83.

35. Étienne, *Abdelkader*, 202–212.

36. Brockelmann, *History of the Islamic Peoples*, 400–401; Guizot, *History of France*, vol. 8, 359.

37. Cited in Neville Barbour, "Algeria," in Colin Legum, ed., *Africa: A Handbook to the Continent* (New York: Praeger, 1967), 8.

38. Ibid., 7.

39. David Prochaska, *Making Algeria French: Colonialism in Bône, 1870–1920* (Cambridge: Cambridge University Press, 1994), 6–11, 124–125, 153–158; Guy Chapman, *The Third Republic of France: The First Phase, 1871–1894* (New York: St. Martin's, 1962), 248–249.

40. Guizot, *History of France*, vol. 8, 378; Beik, *Louis Philippe*, 103–105; Philip Guedella, *The Second Empire* (Garden City, NY: Garden City Publishing Company, 1922), 153.

41. On the idea of the Arab Kingdom, see Étienne, *Abdelkader*, 283–306; Beik, *Louis Philippe*, 248.

42. Clancy-Smith, *Rebel and Saint*, 231–253; Brockelmann, *History of the Islamic Peoples*, 401.

43. Brockelmann, *History of the Islamic Peoples*.

44. For the details of the revolts of the 1870s and 1880s, and the imperial government's policies regarding forest lands, see Charles-Robert Ageron, *Les Algériens musulmans et la France (1870–1919)*, vol. 1 (Paris: Presses Universitaires de France, 1968), 56–66, 103–128.

45. Cited in Barbour, "Algeria," 10.

46. Brockelmann, *History of the Islamic Peoples*, 401–402; Behr, *The Algerian Problem*, 24.

47. Clancy-Smith, *Rebel and Saint*, 94–95.

48. See the comments of Brockelmann, *History of the Islamic Peoples*, 402; Behr, *The Algerian Problem*, 24.

49. For a definitive account of the Legion, see Douglas Porch, *The French Foreign Legion: A Complete History of the Legendary Fighting Force* (New York: HarperCollins, 1992).

50. Thomas F. Power, *Jules Ferry and the Renaissance of French Imperialism* (New York: Octagon Books, 1966), 54–55.

51. Ibid.

52. Daniel Levering Lewis, *The Race to Fashoda: European Colonialism and African Resistance in the Scramble for Africa* (New York: Weidenfeld and Nicolson, 1987), 80.

53. William L. Langer, "The European Powers and the French Occupation of Tunis, 1878–1881, I," *American Historical Review* 31, no. 1 (Oct. 1925): 55–79.

54. Lewis, *The Race to Fashoda*, 84.

55. Douglas Porch, *The Conquest of the Sahara* (New York: Knopf, 1984), 128, 208–221, 225–227, 234–247.

56. J. D. Fage, *An Introduction to the History of West Africa* (Cambridge: Cambridge University Press, 1962), 67–68.

57. Ibid., 143.

58. Lewis, *The Race to Fashoda*, 80.

59. M. M. Knight, "French Colonial Policy," 208–209.

60. Agnes Murphy, R.S.C.J., *The Ideology of French Imperialism, 1871–1881* (New York: Howard Fertig, 1968), 176–191.

61. Fage, *West Africa*, 148–149; Thomas Pakenham, *The Scramble for Africa, 1871–1912* (New York: Random House, 1991), 166–170.

62. Pakenham, *Scramble for Africa*, 166–167.

63. Ibid., 172–177.

64. Fage, *West Africa*, 154–156.

65. Ibid., 156.

66. Ibid., 150–154.

67. Pakenham, *Scramble for Africa*, 368–369.

68. Lewis, *The Race to Fashoda*, 77–78.

69. Ibid., 79.

70. Ibid.

71. Ibid., 81–83; Norman Dwight Harris, "French Colonial Expansion in West Africa, the Sudan, and the Sahara," *The American Political Science Review* 5, no. 3 (Aug. 1911): 371.

72. Mark I. Cohen and Lorna Hahn, *Morocco: Old Land, New Nation* (New York: Praeger, 1966), 14–17.

73. For these developments, see Lord Cromer, *Modern Egypt*, vol. 1 (New York: Macmillan, 1908).

74. Philip Ziegler, *Omdurman* (New York: Knopf, 1974).

75. Lewis, *The Race to Fashoda*, 88–89.

76. Ibid., 88.

77. Ibid., 91.

78. Ibid., 158.

79. For Marchand's route, see ibid., 175–185, 209–220; for his arrival, see ibid., 219–220.

80. Ibid., 80.

81. See Ziegler, *Omdurman*, passim.

82. Ibid., 230; Philip Warner, *Kitchener: The Man behind the Legend* (New York: Athaneum, 1986), 101–104.

83. Warner, *Kitchener*, 102.

84. Charles Downer Hazen, *Europe since 1815* (New York: Henry Holt and Company, 1910), 358–364.

85. Cohen and Hahn, *Morocco: Old Land, New Nation*, 19–20.

86. Ibid., 19.

87. See document IX, The Algeciras Convention; see also Editorial Comment, "General Act of the International Conference of Algeciras, Signed April 7, 1906," *American Journal of International Law* 1, no. 1 (Jan. 1907): 47–78; "The Algeciras Conference," *American Journal of International Law* 1, no. 1 (Jan.–Apr. 1907): 138–140.

88. Cohen and Hahn, *Morocco: Old Land, New Nation*, 20.

89. Ibid., 21.

90. David Thomson, ed., *France: Empire and Republic, 1850–1940, Historical Documents* (New York: Walker and Company, 1968), 314; Cohen and Hahn, *Morocco: Old Land, New Nation*, 34–36.

91. "Treaty of November 27, 1912, between France and Spain Concerning Morocco," *American Journal of International Law* 7, no. 2 (Apr. 1913): 81–99.

92. Cohen and Hahn, *Morocco: Old Land, New Nation*, 35.

93. The only exception were the Chams of Cambodia, a few tens of thousands strong, whose ancestors migrated from Indonesia to Vietnam (Danang) in the medieval period, and subsequently migrated to Cambodia in 1720. Cambodia became a protectorate of France in 1862, at the request of the Cambodian king, who feared a Thai conquest.

Chapter 3

1. E. Lamy, *La France du Levant* (Paris: Plon-Nourrit et cie, 1900); René Ristelhueber, *Traditions françaises au Liban* (Paris: F. Alcan, 1918).

2. See Alexander W. Kinglake, *The Invasion of the Crimea*, vol. 1 (London: William Blackwood and Sons, 1885), 43–50.

3. M. S. Anderson, *The Eastern Question, 1774–1923* (New York: St. Martin's, 1966), 114–117; Hazen, *Europe since 1815*, 612.

4. See Guizot, *History of France*, vol. 8, 263–264.

5. Hazen, *Europe since 1815*, 609–610; Len Ortzen, *Guns at Sea: The World's Great Naval Battles* (New York: Galahad, 1976), 75–82.

6. Ortzen, *Guns at Sea*; see his battle plan, 81.

7. Hazen, *Europe since 1815*, 611.

8. General Sir Edward Hamley, *The War in the Crimea* (New York: Charles Scribner's Sons, 1891); see also the background in Guizot, *History of France*, vol. 8, 323–344.

9. Guizot, *History of France*, vol. 8, 324; Anderson, *The Eastern Question*, 84–86.

10. Guizot, *History of France*, vol. 8, 344; Anderson, *The Eastern Question*, 106–107.

11. Kinglake, *Invasion of the Crimea*, vol. 1, 43–50; see also Charles A. Frazee, *Catholics and Sultans: The Church and the Ottoman Empire, 1453–1923* (New York: Cambridge University Press, 1983); Anderson, *The Eastern Question*, 114–117, 120–122.

12. Anderson, *The Eastern Question*, 117.

13. Ibid., 124–125.

14. Ibid., 129–131.

15. In addition to Kinglake and Hamley, see also Robert B. Edgerton, *Death or Glory: The Legacy of the Crimean War* (Boulder, CO: Westview Press, 2000); Trevor Royle, *Crimea: The Great Crimean War, 1854–1856* (New York: St. Martin's, 2000); Hazen, *Europe since 1815*, 611–616; Anderson, *The Eastern Question*, 133–135.

16. Leila Tarazi Fawaz, *An Occasion for War: Civil Conflict in Lebanon and Damascus in 1860* (Berkeley: University of California Press, 1995); Ussama Samir Makdisi, *The Culture of Sectarianism: Community, History and Violence in Nineteenth–Century Ottoman Lebanon* (Berkeley: University of California Press, 2000); Dick Douwes, *The Ottomans in Syria: A History of Justice and Oppression* (London: Tauris, 2000).

17. Engin Akarli, *The Long Peace: Ottoman Lebanon, 1861–1920* (Berkeley: University of California Press, 1993).

18. Stephen Hemsley Longrigg, *Syria and Lebanon under French Mandate* (Beirut: Librarie du Liban, 1968), 42.

19. Andre Autheman, *La Banque imperiale ottomane* (Paris: Ministere de l'économie et des finances, 1996).

20. Longrigg, *Syria and Lebanon*, 19, 42.

21. Ibid., 42.

22. Ibid., 42–43.

23. Ibid., 43.

24. See Albert Hourani, *Islam in European Thought* (New York and Cambridge: Cambridge University Press, 1991).

25. Hourani, *Islam in European Thought*, 35; Edward Said, *Orientalism* (New York: Vintage, 1979), 63.

26. Said, *Orientalism*, 123–130; Hourani, *Islam in European Thought*, 32–35.

27. Said, *Orientalism*, 123–124; Hourani, *Islam in European Thought*, 32.

28. Said, *Orientalism*, 124.

29. Ibid., 124.

30. Ibid.

31. Hourani, *Islam in European Thought*, 33.

32. Said, *Orientalism*, 63.

33. Lewis, *The Race to Fashoda*, 74.

34. Hourani, *Islam in European Thought*, 118–119; Said, *Orientalism*, 263–274.

35. Hourani, *Islam in European Thought*, 119–120.

36. Ibid., 120.

37. Ibid., 125; Said, *Orientalism*, 268–269.

38. Louis Massignon, *Mission en Mesopotamie (1907–1908)*, 2 vols. (Cairo: Institut français d'archaéolgie orientale, 1910–1912).

39. Colonel Thomas Edward Lawrence, *The Seven Pillars of Wisdom* (London: J. Cape, 1935).

40. Hourani, *Islam in European Thought*, 119.

41. Ibid., 118–119.

42. Ibid., 119.

43. Bernard G. Baker, *The Passing of the Turkish Empire in Europe* (Philadelphia: Lippincott, 1913); Stephen P. H. Duggan, *The Eastern Question: A Study in Diplomacy* (New York: Columbia University Press, 1902); Thomas E. Holland, *The European Concert in the Eastern Question: A Collection of Treaties and Other Public Acts* (Aalen: Scientia Verlag, 1979); Hazen, *Europe since 1815*, 617–644.

44. David Stevenson, *French War Aims against Germany, 1914–1919* (Oxford: Clarendon Press, 1982).

45. Anderson, *The Eastern Question*, 261–286.

46. Christopher M. Andrew and Alexander S. Kanya-Forstner, *France Overseas: The Great War and the Climax of French Imperial Expansion* (Stanford, CA: Stanford University Press, 1981).

47. See document VIII, Cromer on the Anglo-French Rivalry in the Middle East.

48. Joachim Remak, *The Origins of World War One, 1871–1914* (Hinsdale, IL: Dryden Press, 1967); on the annexation of Bosnia, see Hazen, *Europe since 1815*, 639.

49. Joachim Remak, *Sarajevo: The Study of a Political Murder* (New York: Criterion Books, 1959).

50. Steven Miller, Sean M. Lynn-Jones, and Stephen Van Evera, eds., *Military Strategy and the Origins of the First World War* (Princeton, NJ: Princeton University Press, 1991).

51. Ahmet Emin Yalman, *Turkey in the World War* (New Haven, CT: Yale University Press, 1930).

52. Harry N. Howard, *The Partition of Turkey: A Diplomatic History, 1913–1923* (New York: Howard Fertig, 1966), 125.

53. Ibid., 122–125.

54. Anderson, *The Eastern Question*, 324–325.

55. Ibid., 325.

56. Ibid.

57. Ibid., 325–326.

58. Longrigg, *Syria and Lebanon*, 53.

59. Howard, *Partition of Turkey*, 188; Longrigg, *Syria and Lebanon*, 53.

60. Longrigg, *Syria and Lebanon*, 53.

61. Ibid.

62. Ibid., 61–63; George Antonius, *The Arab Awakening* (London: Hamish Hamilton, 1961), 227–235.

63. Longrigg, *Syria and Lebanon*, 65–66; Peter Mansfield, *The Ottoman Empire and Its Successors* (New York: St. Martin's, 1973), 45–46; Antonius, *Arab Awakening*, 227–229, 237–239.

64. Longrigg, *Syria and Lebanon*, 61.

65. Ibid., 65.

66. Ibid., 61.

67. Ibid., 54–55.

68. Ibid., 50–54; Antonius, *Arab Awakening*, 158–159, 164–165.

69. Howard, *Partition of Turkey*, 188.

70. Longrigg, *Syria and Lebanon*, 54–55; Mansfield, *Ottoman Empire*, 39–40; Antonius, *Arab Awakening*, 163–185.

71. Longrigg, *Syria and Lebanon*, 55.

72. Mansfield, *Ottoman Empire*, 41; Howard, *Partition of Turkey*, 189–190.

73. Antonius, *Arab Awakening*, 419.

74. Longrigg, *Syria and Lebanon*, 51.

75. Ibid., 55.

76. Ibid., 56 (and map on 57); Howard, *Partition of Turkey*, 185–186; Antonius, *Arab Awakening*, 245–253.

77. Longrigg, *Syria and Lebanon*, 58–59; Howard, *Partition of Turkey*, 185.

78. See maps in Antonius, *Arab Awakening*, 248; Longrigg, *Syria and Lebanon*, 57.

79. Antonius, *Arab Awakening*, 428–429.

80. Howard, *Partition of Turkey*, 190–191.

81. Mansfield, *Ottoman Empire*, 45; Longrigg, *Syria and Lebanon*, 59.

82. Longrigg, *Syria and Lebanon*, 48–49; Antonius, *Arab Awakening*, 240–242.

83. Elizabeth Thompson, *Colonial Citizens: Republican Rights, Paternal Privilege, and Gender in French Syria and Lebanon* (New York: Columbia University Press, 2000), 22.

84. Howard, *Partition of Turkey*, 188; Longrigg, *Syria and Lebanon*, 77.

85. Thompson, *Colonial Citizens*, 22.

86. Mansfield, *Ottoman Empire*, 47–48; Longrigg, *Syria and Lebanon*, 59–60; Antonius, *Arab Awakening*, 262–267.

87. Neville J. Mandel, *The Arabs and Zionism before World War I* (Berkeley: University of California Press, 1976), 9–15.

88. Ibid.

89. Myron J. Echenberg, *Colonial Conscripts: The Tirailleurs Senegalais in French West Africa, 1857–1960* (Portsmouth, UK: Heinemann, 1990).

90. James J. Cooke, "Paul Azan and *L'Armeé Indigène Nord-Africaine*," *Military Affairs* 45, no. 3 (Oct. 1981): 135.

91. Ibid.

92. Ibid.

93. Ibid., 135–136.

94. Antonius, *Arab Awakening*, 208–210, 240.

95. Longrigg, *Syria and Lebanon*, 65.

96. Howard, *Partition of Turkey*, 224.

97. Longrigg, *Syria and Lebanon*, 66–68; Mansfield, *Ottoman Empire*, 46.

98. Longrigg, *Syria and Lebanon*, 67.

99. Ibid., 67.

100. Ibid., 63–64.

101. Ibid., 66.

102. On Wilson's interest in the Middle East, see Howard, *Partition of Turkey*, 213, 230.

103. Antonius, *Arab Awakening*, 435–436; Howard, *Partition of Turkey*, 210–211; Mansfield, *Ottoman Empire*, 47.

104. Howard, *Partition of Turkey*, 212.

105. Longrigg, *Syria and Lebanon*, 86 n. 2; Anderson, *The Eastern Question*, 377.

106. Howard, *Partition of Turkey*, 230; Longrigg, *Syria and Lebanon*, 88–93.

107. Harry N. Howard, *The King-Crane Commission* (Beirut: Khayat's, 1963).

108. See document XI, The King-Crane Commission; for the text in an online version, see A. J. Plotke, Ph.D., "The Great War Primary Document Archive," ^http://library.byu.edu/rdh/wwI/1919/kingcrane.html&

109. Longrigg, *Syria and Lebanon*, 374.

110. Zeine N. Zeine, *The Struggle for Arab Independence: Western Diplomacy and the Rise and Fall of Faisal's Kingdom in Syria* (Delmar: Caravan Books, 1977).

111. Longrigg, *Syria and Lebanon*, 103.

112. Mansfield, *Ottoman Empire*, 54.

113. Capitaine G. Carbillet, *Au Djebel Druse* (Paris: Éditions Argo, 1929); Longrigg, *Syria and Lebanon*, 153.

114. Cited in Barbour, "Algeria," 5.

Chapter 4

1. See the comments of Edward Peter Fitzgerald regarding the empire after World War II, and the legacy of the Third Republic in "Did France's Colonial Empire Make Economic Sense? A Perspective from the Postwar Decade, 1946–1956," *Journal of Economic History* 48, no. 2 (June 1988): 373.

2. Ibid., 373–376.

3. Ibid., 384.

4. Martin Evans, "Projecting a Greater France," *History Today* 50, no. 2 (Feb. 2000): 18–25.

5. Ibid.

6. Gwendolyn Wright, "Tradition in the Service of Modernity: Architecture and Urbanism in French Colonial Policy, 1900–1930," *Journal of Modern History* 59, no. 2 (June 1987): 291.

7. Michael Greenhalgh, "The New Centurions: French Reliance on the Roman Past during the Conquest of Algeria," *War and Society* 16, no. 1 (1998): 1–28.

8. Mansfield, *Ottoman Empire*, 55, 73.

9. Howard, *Partition of Turkey*, 242–249; Anderson, *The Eastern Question*, 363–364.

10. Howard, *Partition of Turkey*, 254–256.

11. Ibid., 277–314.

12. Majid Khadduri, "The Alexandretta Dispute," *American Journal of International Law* 39, no. 3 (July 1945): 406–425.

13. Mansfield, *Ottoman Empire*, 75.

14. Longrigg, *Syria and Lebanon*, 82, 94, 96–101.

15. Ibid., 115, 138.

16. Thompson, *Colonial Citizens*, 42.

17. Longrigg, *Syria and Lebanon*, 115.

18. Thompson, *Colonial Citizens*, 60.

19. Longrigg, *Syria and Lebanon*, 127–128.

20. Ibid., 147.

21. Ibid., 82.

22. Thompson, *Colonial Citizens*, 62.

23. Ibid.

24. See David Prochaska, *Making Algeria French: Colonialism in Bône, 1870–1920* (Cambridge: Cambridge University Press, 1994), 7–25. I have relied heavily on Prochaska's study of Bône here, as it offers abundant illustrations of the French imperial takeover in Algeria.

25. Ibid., 18, 85–88, 147–152.

26. Ibid., 63–64.

27. Ibid., 77–78.

28. Ibid.

29. Ibid., 88–89.

30. Ibid., 80–83.

31. Ibid., 71–76.

32. Ibid., 65.

33. Ibid., 66, 70.

34. Ibid., 70–71.

35. Ibid., 66–67.

36. Ibid., 78–79.

37. Ibid., 78.

38. Ibid., 82–83.

39. Ibid., 83–85.

40. Ibid., 85.

41. Ibid.

42. Ibid., 106–110.

43. Ibid., 105–106.

44. Longrigg, *Syria and Lebanon*, 121. I have relied heavily on Longrigg in this section, as he was a contemporary British military observer of many of the major events in the period of the mandates.

45. Ibid., 152.

46. Ibid.

47. Ibid., 153.

48. Ibid., 154.

49. Ibid., 153–157.

50. Ibid., 157.

51. Ibid., 134–135.

52. Thompson, *Colonial Citizens*, passim.

53. Longrigg, *Syria and Lebanon*, 148–149.

54. Ibid., 149–150.

55. Ibid., 150.

56. Ibid., 160, 163, 169–170.

57. Ibid., 170.

58. Ibid.

59. Ibid.

60. Ibid., 201.

61. Ibid., 203.

62. On Barakat, see ibid., 129, 151, 173, 183.

63. Ibid., 176–177.

64. Ibid., 183.

65. Ibid., 184–185.

66. Ibid., 188.

67. Ibid., 191.

68. Ibid., 192–193.

69. Ibid., 194.

70. Ibid., 195.

71. Ibid., 196.

72. See Porch, *Conquest of the Sahara*, for French expansion into the Lake Chad region, 198–207, Timbuktu, 143; and the "southern approaches," 126–146.

73. David Robinson, *Paths of Accommodation: Muslim Societies and French Colonial Authorities in Senegal and Mauritania, 1880–1920* (Athens: Ohio University Press, 2000); William F. S. Miles, *Hausaland Divided: Colonialism and Independence in Nigeria and Niger* (Ithaca, NY: Cornell University Press, 1994).

74. Melvin E. Page, ed., *Africa and the First World War* (New York: St. Martin's, 1987); Brian K. Digre, *Imperialism's New Clothes: The Repartition of Tropical Africa, 1914–1919* (New York: P. Lang, 1990).

75. Ian Gleeson, *The Unknown Force; Black, Indian, and Coloured Soldiers through the World Wars* (Rivonia: Ashanti Publishers, 1994).

76. A. J. Christopher, *Colonial Africa* (London: Croom and Helm, 1984), 36–37.

77. Ibid., 37.

78. See Catherine Coquery-Vidrovitch, "French Colonization in Africa to 1920: Administrative and Economic Development," in L. H. Gann and Peter Duignan, eds., *Colonialism in Africa, 1870–1960*, vol. 1 (Cambridge, UK: Cambridge University Press, 1969), 165–198.

Chapter 5

1. Longrigg, *Syria and Lebanon*, 217.

2. Ibid., 216–217.

3. Ibid., 217–218.

4. Ibid., 218.

5. Ibid., 218–224.

6. Ibid., 225–229; see the recent work of Richard Haddad, *Les Phalanges libanaises* (Beirut: Édition Charlemagne, 1993).

7. Ibid., 225–226.

8. Robert O. Paxon, *Vichy France: Old Guard and New Order, 1940–1944* (New York: Columbia University Press, 2001); Robert Aron, *The Vichy Regime, 1940–1944* (London: Putnam, 1958); Michele Cointet, *Vichy et le fascisme: les hommes, les structures et les pouvoirs* (Brussels: Éditions Complexe, 1987); Marc Ferro, *Pétain* (Paris: Fayard, 1987); Geoffrey Warner, *Pierre Laval and the Eclipse of France* (New York: Macmillan, 1968); Jean-Pierre Azima, *Vichy, 1940–1944* (Paris: Perrin, 1997); Jacques LeGroignec, *Pétain et les Allemands* (Paris: Nouvelles Éditions latines, 1997); Charles de Gaulle (Richard Howard, trans.), *The Complete War Memoirs of Charles de Gaulle* (New York: Da Capo Press, 1988).

9. John Keegan, *The Waffen SS: The Asphalt Soldiers* (New York: Ballantine, 1970), 96–99, 129.

10. Longrigg, *Syria and Lebanon*, 233. For documents of the war in the mandates, see Walter L. Browne, ed., *Documents on the French Mandate and World War II, 1936–1943* (Salisbury, NC: Documentary Publishers, 1977).

11. Longrigg, *Syria and Lebanon*, 236.

12. Ibid., 237.

13. Ibid., 294.

14. Ibid., 296–297.

15. Ibid., 299.

16. For Dentz, see André Charles Victor Laffargue, *Le Général Dentz (Paris 1940–Syrie 1941)* (Paris: Iles d'or, 1954).

17. Winston L. S. Churchill, *Memoirs of the Second World War*, ab. ed. (Boston: Houghton Mifflin, 1991), 450.

18. Longrigg, *Syria and Lebanon*, 304; Churchill, *Memoirs*, 452–453.

19. Longrigg, *Syria and Lebanon*, 304–305.

20. Corelli Barnett, *The Desert Generals* (Bloomington: Indiana University Press, 1983); Churchill, *Memoirs*, 450–460.

21. See Harold E. Raugh, *Wavell in the Middle East, 1939–1941: A Study in Generalship* (New York: Macmillan, 1993).

22. For this critical action and the British counter-thrust, see Michael Carver, *Tobruk* (London: Batsford, 1964).

23. From among the many works on Montgomery, see Ronald Lewin, *Montgomery as Military Commander* (London: Batsford, 1971).

24. Churchill, *Memoirs*, 453.

25. On Catroux, see Henri Lerner, *Catroux* (Paris: Albin Michel, 1990); see also Catroux's own memoirs, *Dans la Bataille de Méditerraneé* (Paris: René Julliard, 1949).

26. Churchill, *Memoirs*, 453–454; see also the recent work of A. B. B. Gaunson, *The Anglo-French Clash in Lebanon and Syria, 1940–45* (New York: St. Martin's, 1987).

27. Longrigg, *Syria and Lebanon*, 308.

28. Ibid., 310.

29. Ibid., 311–312.

30. Ibid., 313.

31. Ibid.

32. See Longrigg's comments, ibid., 314–316.

33. Ibid., 315.

34. Vincent Jones, *Operation Torch: Anglo-American Invasion of North Africa* (New York: Ballantine, 1972), 16–25.

35. Ibid., 28–29.

36. David Rolf, *The Bloody Road to Tunis: Destruction of Axis Forces in North Africa, November 1942–May 1943* (Mechanicsburg, PA: Stackpole Press, 2001).

37. George E. Melton, *Darlan: Admiral and Statesman of France, 1881–1942* (Westport, CT: Praeger, 1998).

38. Anthony Verrier, *Assassination in Algiers: Churchill, Roosevelt, De Gaulle and the Murder of Admiral Darlan* (New York: Norton, 1990).

39. Elmar Krautkramer (Wanda Vulliez, trans.), *Vichy-Alger, 1940–1942* (Paris: Économica, 1992).

40. Martin W. Wilmington, *The Middle East Supply Centre* (Albany: SUNY Press, 1971).

41. Longrigg, *Syria and Lebanon*, 322.

42. Ibid., 323.

43. Ibid., 326–327.

44. Ibid., 328–333.

45. Ibid., 329.

46. Majid Khadduri, "The Franco-Lebanese Dispute and the Crisis of November, 1943," *American Journal of International Law* 38, no. 4 (Oct. 1944): 601–620.

47. Longrigg, *Syria and Lebanon*, 333.

48. Ibid., 342; see also Philip S. Khoury, *Syria and the French Mandate: The Politics of Arab Nationalism, 1920–1945* (Princeton, NJ: Princeton University Press, 1990).

49. The Senegalese were particularly despised. See ibid., 347–348.

50. This remarkable scenario is described in ibid., 349.

51. Longrigg, ibid, 355

Chapter 6

1. See John Keegan, *Six Armies in Normandy* (New York: Viking, 1983).

2. Ibid., 289–290.

3. Ibid., 290–291.

4. Geoffrey Warner, *Pierre Laval and the Eclipse of France* (New York: Macmillan, 1968).

5. Charles Williams, *The Last Great Frenchman: A Life of General De Gaulle* (New York: Wiley, 1997).

6. For Bourguiba, see Sophie Bessis, *Bourguiba*, vol. 1 (Paris: Groupe jeune Afrique, 1988); Bernard Cohen, *Habib Bourguiba: Le pouvoir d'un seul* (Paris: Flammarion, 1986).

7. Rolf, *The Bloody Road to Tunis.*

8. J. D. Hargreaves, *Decolonization in Africa* (London: Longman, 1988), 150.

9. Martin Thomas, *The French North African Crisis: Colonial Breakdown and Anglo-French Relations, 1945–62* (New York: St. Martin's, 2000), 40–41.

10. Ibid., 40.

11. Herbert Tint, *French Foreign Policy since the Second World War* (London: Weidenfeld and Nicolson, 1972), 192.

12. Samya El Machat, *La Tunisie, les chemins vers independence, 1945–1956* (Paris: Éditions L'Harmattan, 1992).

13. Irwin M. Wall, *France, the United States and the Algerian War* (Berkeley: University of California Press, 2001), 99–133.

14. Thomas, *The French North African Crisis*, 186; Nicole Grimaud, "La crise de Bizerte," *Revue d'Histoire Diplomatique* 110 (1996): 328–340.

15. For Tunisia since independence, see Clement Henry Moore, *Tunisia since Independence: The Dynamics of One-Party Government* (Westport, CT: Greenwood Press, 1982).

16. Cohen-Hahn, *Morocco: Old Land, New Nation*, 34. For the patterns of resistance in the period before the establishment of the French protectorate, see Edmund Burke III, "Pan-Islam and Moroccan Resistance to French Colonial Penetration, 1900–1912," *Journal of African History* 13 (1972): 97–118; and more fully, in idem., *Prelude to Protectorate in Morocco: Precolonial Protest and Resistance, 1860–1912* (Chicago: University of Chicago Press, 1976).

17. See Moshe Gershovich, *French Military Rule in Morocco: Colonialism and Its Consequences* (London: F. Cass, 2000).

18. Cohen-Hahn, *Morocco: Old Land, New Nation*, 25.

19. Ibid., 43.

20. Ibid., 42.

21. Ibid., 36–38.

22. Ibid., 24–25, 38.

23. Ibid., 38–39.

24. Ibid., 45–46.

25. Ibid., 46–47.

26. Ibid., 49–50.

27. Ibid., 53–54.

28. Thomas, *The French North African Crisis*, 53; Cohen-Hahn, *Morocco: Old Land, New Nation*, 53–54.

29. Cohen-Hahn, *Morocco: Old Land, New Nation*, 50–77, passim.

30. Ibid., 56–60, 66, 69.

31. Thomas, *The French North African Crisis*, 61; Cohen-Hahn, *Morocco: Old Land, New Nation*, 58–59.

32. Thomas, *The French North African Crisis*, 62; Cohen-Hahn, *Morocco: Old Land, New Nation*, 65–66.

33. Thomas, *The French North African Crisis*, 63; Cohen-Hahn, *Morocco: Old Land, New Nation*, 69.

34. Cohen-Hahn, *Morocco: Old Land, New Nation*, 60.

35. Ibid., 72–74, 185.

36. Matthew Connelly, "Taking Off the Cold War Lens: Visions of North-South Conflict during the Algerian War for Independence," *American Historical Review* 105, no. 3 (June 2000): 756–757.

37. Cohen-Hahn, *Morocco: Old Land, New Nation*, 74.

38. Ibid., 75–77.

39. Thomas, *The French North African Crisis*, 63; Cohen-Hahn, *Morocco: Old Land, New Nation*, 70–74.

40. See document XIV, The Independence of Morocco (1956).

41. For a discussion of the differences in meaning to each side, see Thomas, *The French North African Crisis*, passim.

42. The transition was not easy, however, as there was significant violence perpetrated against those accused of collaborating with the French. See Cohen-Hahn, *Morocco: Old Land, New Nation*, 77–86.

43. Ibid., 86–90.

44. Ibid., 91–92.

45. Discussed in Matthew Connelly, "The French-American Conflict over North Africa and the Fall of the Fourth Republic," *Revue française d'Histoire d'Outre-Mer* 84, no. 315 (1997): 9–27.

46. Thomas, *The French North African Crisis*, 93, notes that there was an "undue comparison between the Viet Minh and the FLN"; see also the words of Jacques Massu on the subject of arriving in Algeria after service in Vietnam in Massu, *La Vrai Bataille d'Alger* (Paris: Plon, 1971), 53–55.

47. Martin Walker, *The Cold War: A History* (New York: Henry Holt, 1995), 50–53.

48. Walker, *The Cold War*, 57; David Rees, *The Age of Containment* (New York: St. Martin's, 1968), 28–29.

49. Rees, *Age of Containment*, 30.

50. Discussed in Thomas, *The French North African Crisis*, 158.

51. Rees, *The Age of Containment*, 37–51.

52. Walker, *The Cold War*, 73–77.

53. Ibid., 60–63.

54. For the changes in the U.S. position, see Walker, *The Cold War*, 94–95; Connelly, "Taking Off the Cold War Lens," 754.

55. Thomas, *The French North African Crisis*, 90.

56. Connelly, "Taking Off the Cold War Lens," 758–759.

57. Irwin M. Wall, *France, the United States and the Algerian War* (Berkeley: University of California Press, 2001), 32–66.

58. Keith Kyle, *Suez* (New York: St. Martin's, 1992); Albert Hourani, "The Middle East and the Crisis of 1956," *St. Antony's Papers, no. 4 Middle Eastern Affairs One* (London: Chatto and Windus, 1958), 9–42.

59. Thomas, *The French North African Crisis*, 111.

60. Ibid., 126.

61. Wall, *France, the United States and the Algerian War*, 57.

62. For French views of British actions, see Thomas, *The French North African Crisis*, 127.

63. Ibid., 176–177.

64. Ibid., 128.

65. For these missions, see ibid., passim.

66. Ibid., 197.

67. Tint, *French Foreign Policy*, 187–188; Fage, *Introduction to the History of West Africa*, 200; Hargreaves, *Decolonization in Africa*, 64–66, 78–80.

68. Hargreaves, *Decolonization in Africa*, 154.

69. Ibid., 149–156; Fage, *Introduction to the History of West Africa*, 210.

70. Lapido Adamolekun, *Sékou Touré's Guinea: An Experiment in Nation Building* (London: Methuen, 1976); Pierre Nandjui, *Houphouet-Boigny: l'homme de la France en Afrique* (Paris: L'Harmattan, 1995).

71. Fage, *Introduction to the History of West Africa*, 209.

72. Robert Theobald, ed., *The New Nations of West Africa* (New York: H. W. Wilson Co., 1960), 62; Hargreaves, *Decolonization in Africa*, 154; Fage, *Introduction to the History of West Africa*, 210.

73. Fage, *Introduction to the History of West Africa*, 210.

74. Tint, *French Foreign Policy*, 195; Fage, *Introduction to the History of West Africa*, 211.

75. Tint, *French Foreign Policy*, 199.

76. Ibid.

77. William J. Foltz, *From French West Africa to the Mali Federation* (New Haven, CT: Yale University Press, 1965).

Chapter 7

1. Thomas, *The French North African Crisis*, 14–15; Michael Kettle, *De Gaulle and Algeria, 1940–1960* (London: Quartet, 1993), 27–29.

2. Cooke, "L'Armeé Indigène," 134; Knight, "French Colonial Policy," 218.

3. Joan Gillespie, *Algeria: Rebellion and Revolution*. (New York: Praeger, 1960), 23.

4. Knight, "French Colonial Policy," 218–219; Bernard Droz and Evelyne Lever, *Histoire de la Guerre d'Algérie 1954–1962* (Paris: Éditions du Seuil, 1982), 27; Gillespie, *Algeria: Rebellion and Revolution*, 11, 24; Behr, *The Algerian Problem*, 37–38.

5. Knight, "French Colonial Policy," 219.

6. Evans, "Projecting a Greater France," passim.

7. Quoted in Alistair Horne, *A Savage War of Peace: Algeria 1954–1962* (London: Macmillan, 1977), 37.

8. Patricia M. Lorcin, *Imperial Identities: Stereotyping, Prejudice, and Race in Colonial Algeria* (New York: St. Martin's, 1995).

9. Droz and Lever, *Histoire de la Guerre*, 28.

10. Horne, *Savage War*, 38–43; Droz and Lever, *Histoire de la Guerre*, 27–28; Behr, *The Algerian Problem*, 45–47.

11. Gillespie, *Algeria: Rebellion and Revolution*, 40–44, 47–48.

12. Droz and Lever, *Histoire de la Guerre*, 28–29.

13. Ibid., 31; Horne, *Savage War*, 42.

14. Horne, *Savage War*, 42.

15. Droz and Lever, *Histoire de la Guerre*, 31–32; Gillespie, *Algeria: Rebellion and Revolution*, 58–59; Behr, *The Algerian Problem*, 52–53; Kettle, *De Gaulle and Algeria*, 29–30.

16. Anthony Clayton, "The Sétif Uprising of May 1945," *Small Wars and Insurgencies* 3, no. 1 (1992): 1–21; Horne, *Savage War*, 23–28; Droz and Lever, *Histoire de la Guerre*, 32; Thomas, *The French North African Crisis*, 16–17; Kettle, *De Gaulle and Algeria*, 30–31; Charles-Robert Ageron, "La survivence d'un mythe: la puissance par l'Empire colonial, 1944–1947," *Revue Française d'Histoire d'Outre-Mer* 72, no. 269 (1985): 387–405.

17. Droz and Lever, *Histoire de la Guerre*, 49; Gillespie, *Algeria: Rebellion and Revolution*, 103–104; Martha Crenshaw Hutchinson, *Revolutionary Terrorism. The FLN in Algeria, 1954–1962* (Stanford, CA: Hoover Institution Press, 1978).

18. James I. Lewis, "French Politics and the Algerian Statute of 1947," *Maghrib Review* 17, nos. 3–4 (1992): 146–172; Droz and Lever, *Histoire de le Guerre*, 33–35; Gillespie, *Algeria: Rebellion and Revolution*, 25–27, 70–87; Behr, *The Algerian Problem*, 38–39.

19. Thomas, *The French North African Crisis*, 3, and see his comments, 165–166.

20. Marcel-Edmond Naegelen, *Mission en Algérie* (Paris: Flammarion, 1962).

21. Droz and Lever, *Histoire de la Guerre*, 45–51, tables of elections, 1945–1954, on page 46.

22. Gillespie, *Algeria: Rebellion and Revolution*, 96–99.

23. Horne, *Savage War*, 406–407.

24. Thomas, *The French North African Crisis*, 81–94.

25. Droz and Lever, *Histoire de la Guerre*, 214–215; Gillespie, *Algeria: Rebellion and Revolution*, 100–101.

26. Horne, *Savage War*, 129–131; Behr, *The Algerian Problem*, 108–109.

27. Droz and Lever, *Histoire de la Guerre*, 81–83, 116–119; Horne, *Savage War*, 132–134, 138.

28. Frantz Fanon, *L'An V de la revolution algérienne. Sociologie d'une revolution* (Paris: Maspero, 1959); David Macey, *Frantz Fanon: A Biography* (New York: St. Martin's, 2001).

29. Albert Camus, *Chroniques algériennes (1939–1958)* (Paris: Gallimard, 1958); David Carroll, "Camus's Algeria: Birthrights, Colonial Injustice, the Fiction of a French-Algerian People," *Modern Language Notes* 112 (1997): 517–549; Horne, *Savage War*, 124–126; Droz and Lever, *Histoire de la Guerre*, 147–149.

30. Horne, *Savage War*, 128–131.

31. Connelly, "Taking Off the Cold War Lens."

32. Charles-Robert Ageron, "L'Opinion française devant la guerre d'Algérie," *Revue de la France d'Outre Mer* 231 (1976): 256–285; Jeffrey A. Lefebvre, "Kennedy's Algerian Dilemma: Containment, Alliance Politics and the 'Rebel Dialogue,'" *Middle Eastern Studies* 35, no. 2 (1999): 61–82.

33. Jacques Soustelle, *Aimeé et Souffrante Algérie* (Paris: Plon, 1956); Denis Rolland, "Jacques Soustelle, de l'éthnologie a la politique," *Revue d'Histoire moderne et contemporaine* 43, no. 1 (1996): 137–150; Droz and Lever, *Histoire de la Guerre*, 66–75.

34. See Connelly, "Taking Off the Cold War Lens."

35. Kettle, *De Gaulle and Algeria*, 47–48.

36. Droz and Lever, *Histoire de la Guerre*, 75–77; Horne, *Savage War*, 118–124; Behr, *The Algerian Problem*, 83–84.

37. Horne, *Savage War*, 126–127.

38. Droz and Lever, *Histoire de la Guerre*, 88–89; Horne, *Savage War*, 148–149; Alexander Harrison, *Challenging De Gaulle: The O.A.S. and the Counterrevolution in Algeria* (Westport, CT: Greenwood Press, 1989), 41.

39. Horne, *Savage War*, 150–151; Droz and Lever, *Histoire de la Guerre*, 87–90.

40. Ibid.

41. Horne, *Savage War*, 183–187; Droz and Lever, *Histoire de la Guerre*, 127–129; Behr, *The Algerian Problem*, 100–101.

42. Wall, *France, the United States and the Algerian War*, 50–56.

43. Horne, *Savage War*, 187; Droz and Lever, *Histoire de la Guerre*, 129; Behr, *The Algerian Problem*, 100.

44. Horne, *Savage War*, 180–181; Droz and Lever, *Histoire de la Guerre*, 136 n. 3.

45. Raoul Salan, *Mémoires: Fin d'un empire*, vol. III, *Algérie française*, and vol. IV, *Algérie, de Gaulle, et moi* (Paris: Presses de la Cité, 1972–1974); Horne, *Savage War*, 178–182.

46. Jacques Massu, *La Vrai Bataille d'Alger* (Paris: Plon, 1971); Horne, *Savage War*, 187–189.

47. Marcel Bigeard, *Pour une parcelle de gloire* (Paris: Plon, 1975); Horne, *Savage War*, 189–190; Droz and Lever, *Histoire de la Guerre*, 130–131.

48. Droz and Lever, *Histoire de la Guerre*, 98; Horne, *Savage War*, 181.

49. Horne, *Savage War*, 190–192.

50. Droz and Lever, *Histoire de la Guerre*, 130–131; Horne, *Savage War*, 209–211.

51. Gregor Mathias, *Les Sectiones administratives specialiseés en Algérie. Entre Ideal et realité (1955–1962)* (Paris: Éditions L'Harmattan, 1998); William B. Quandt, *Revolution and Political Leadership: Algeria, 1954–1968* (Cambridge, MA: MIT Press, 1969).

52. Droz and Lever, *Histoire de la Guerre*, 113; Wall, *France, the United States and the Algerian War*, 85–86.

53. Horne, *Savage War*, 249–250; Droz and Lever, *Histoire de la Guerre*, 166–167; Wall, *France, the United States and the Algerian War*, 99–133.

54. Horne, *Savage War*, 212–217; Kettle, *De Gaulle and Algeria*, 96–98.

55. Harrison, *Challenging De Gaulle*, 42.

56. Horne, *Savage War*, 283–287.

57. Ibid., 286–287; Droz and Lever, *Histoire de la Guerre*, 172–174; Kettle, *De Gaulle and Algeria*, 191–240.

58. Horne, *Savage War*, 289; Droz and Lever, *Histoire de la Guerre*, 174–175.

59. Droz and Lever, *Histoire de la Guerre*, 177–178; Horne, *Savage War*, 290–291; Kettle, *De Gaulle and Algeria*, 196.

60. Droz and Lever, *Histoire de la Guerre*, 177.

61. Ibid., 178–179; Horne, *Savage War*, 293–295.

62. Droz and Lever, *Histoire de la Guerre*, 179; Horne, *Savage War*, 294–295; Kettle, *De Gaulle and Algeria*, 217.

63. See Droz and Lever, *Histoire de la Guerre*, 183–184, for an interesting discussion of de Gaulle's motives.

64. Horne, *Savage War*, 301; Droz and Lever, *Histoire de la Guerre*, 189; Kettle, *De Gaulle and Algeria*, 238–239.

65. Horne, *Savage War*, 305–308, 340–342; Droz and Lever, *Histoire de la Guerre*, 197–198, 271–277; Behr, *The Algerian Problem*, 154; Kettle, *De Gaulle and Algeria*, 279–280.

66. Droz and Lever, *Histoire de la Guerre*, 213–214; Horne, *Savage War*, 315–317.

67. Horne, *Savage War*, 310; Droz and Lever, *Histoire de la Guerre*, 202–203.

68. Horne, *Savage War*, 332–333; Mohand Hamoumou, *Et ils sont devenus harkis* (Paris: Fayard, 1993), 91–113, 116.

69. Rita Maran, *Torture: The Role of Ideology in the French-Algerian War* (Westport, CT: Greenwood Press, 1989), 97–105.

70. Paul Aussaresses, *Services Speciaux: Algérie, 1955–1957* (Paris: Perrin, 2000); see also Erwan Bergot, *Le dossier rouge: services secrets contre FLN* (Paris: Grasset, 1976).

71. Horne, *Savage War*, 337–338; Henry Descombin, *Guerre d'Algérie 1959–60. Le Cinquieme Bureau ou 'Le theoreme du poisson'* (Paris: Éditions L'Harmattan, 1994); Michel Cornaton, *Les Camps de regroupement de la guerre d'Algérie* (Paris: Éditions L'Harmattan, 1998).

72. Cited in Horne, *Savage War*, 343.

73. French opinion changed, and de Gaulle recognized it. See Droz and Lever, *Histoire de la Guerre*, 277–285; Christopher Harrison, "French Attitudes to Empire and the Algerian War," *African Affairs* (1983): 75–95; Martin Evans, *The Memory of Resistance, French Opposition to the Algerian War (1954–1962)* (Oxford: Berg, 1997); Philip Dine, *Images of the Algerian War. French Fiction and Film, 1954–1992* (Oxford: Clarendon Press, 1994).

74. Cited in Horne, *Savage War*, 351–352.

75. Droz and Lever, *Histoire de la Guerre*, 232–234.

76. Ibid., 235–236.

77. Ibid., 237–243; Pierre Lagaillarde, *On a triché avec l'honneur* (Paris, La Table Ronde, 1960); Behr, *The Algerian Problem*, 165–176.

78. Droz and Lever, *Histoire de la Guerre*, 238–246; Horne, *Savage War*, 363–368.

79. Horne, *Savage War*, 369; Droz and Lever, *Histoire de la Guerre*, 244.

80. Droz and Lever, *Histoire de la Guerre*, 245–246; Horne, *Savage War*, 371.

81. Horne, *Savage War*, 371; Droz and Lever, *Histoire de la Guerre*, 252–253.

82. Horne, *Savage War*, 392; Droz and Lever, *Histoire de la Guerre*, 253–254.

83. Horne, *Savage War*, 394–397.

84. Ibid., 428–433; Droz and Lever, *Histoire de la Guerre*, 262–264.

85. Droz and Lever, *Histoire de la Guerre*, 278–279.

86. Ibid., 264; Horne, *Savage War*, 434–435.

87. Harrison, *Challenging De Gaulle*; Droz and Lever, *Histoire de la Guerre*, 284–285; Horne, *Savage War*, 440–441.

88. Horne, *Savage War*, 436–460; Droz and Lever, *Histoire de la Guerre*, 296–313.

89. Droz and Lever, *Histoire de la Guerre*, 306–307; Horne, *Savage War*, 453–454.

90. Horne, *Savage War*, 454.

91. Ibid.; Droz and Lever, *Histoire de la Guerre*, 306.

92. Droz and Lever, *Histoire de la Guerre*, 309; Horne, *Savage War*, 455.

93. Horne, *Savage War*, 458–460; Droz and Lever, *Histoire de la Guerre*, 308–313.

94. Horne, *Savage War*, 482–495; Droz and Lever, *Histoire de la Guerre*, 313–316; Harrison, *Challenging De Gaulle*, 78–98.

95. Horne, *Savage War*, 467–469; Jerome Helie, *Les Accords d'Évian. Histoire de la paix ratee en Algérie* (Paris: Olivier Orban, 1992).

96. Horne, *Savage War*, 515–518; Droz and Lever, *Histoire de la Guerre*, 326–333.

97. Horne, *Savage War*, 533.

Chapter 8

1. John K. Cooley, *Libyan Sandstorm* (New York: Holt, Rinehart, and Winston, 1982); Guy Arnold, *The Maverick State: Gaddafi and the New World Order* (London: Cassell, 1996); Jonathan Burman, *Qadhafi's Libya* (London: Zed Books, 1986).

2. Mansour O. El Khikia, *Libya's Qaddafi: The Politics of Contradiction* (Gainesville: University Press of Florida, 1998).

3. Sam C. Nolutshungu, *Limits of Anarchy: Intervention and State Formation in Chad* (Charlottesville: University Press of Virginia, 1996).

4. Cooley, *Libyan Sandstorm*, 204; Virginia Thompson and Richard Adloff, *Conflict in Chad* (Berkeley: University of California Press, 1981).

5. Cooley, *Libyan Sandstorm*.

6. Ibid., 206.

7. Ibid., 205–211.

8. Mario J. Azevedo, *Roots of Violence: A History of War in Chad* (London: Routledge, 1998).

9. Cooley, *Libyan Sandstorm*, 205.

10. "Exit Gadafi, Enter Mitterand," *Time Magazine*, Nov. 16, 1981, 50.

11. Cooley, *Libyan Sandstorm*, 206–207.

12. Mario J. Azevedo and Emmanuel U. Nnadozie, *Chad: A Nation in Search of Its Future* (Boulder, CO: Westview Press, 1998).

13. Kamal S. Salibi, *A House of Many Mansions: The History of Lebanon Reconsidered* (Berkeley: University of California Press, 1990).

14. Farid El Khazen, *The Breakdown of the State in Lebanon, 1967–1976* (Cambridge: Harvard University Press, 2000).

15. Daniel Pipes, *Greater Syria: The History of an Ambition* (New York: Oxford University Press, 1992).

16. Itamar Rabinovich, *The War for Lebanon, 1970–85* (Ithaca, NY: Cornell University Press, 1990); Dilip Hiro, *Holy Wars: The Rise of Islamic Fundamentalism* (New York: Routledge, 1989), 93–94.

17. Edgar O'Ballance, *Civil War in Lebanon, 1975–92* (New York: St. Martin's, 1998).

18. Ze'Ev Schiff and Ehud Ya'Ari, *Israel's Lebanon War* (New York: Simon and Schuster, 1984).

19. On the role of Assad, see Patrick Seale, *Asad: The Struggle for the Middle East* (Berkeley: University of California Press, 1988).

20. Eyal Zisser, *Lebanon: The Challenge of Independence* (London: Tauris, 2000).

21. "Jacques Chirac, 'Lebanese Reconstruction,'" *Presidents and Prime Ministers* 4, no. 5 (Nov./Dec. 1995): 28.

22. Sam Ghattas, "Lebanese Army Arrests Up to 250," Associated Press, Aug. 8, 2001, <http:member.compuserve.com/news/stor.jsp?floc=FF-APO-1107>

23. Edward A. Kolodziej, *French International Policy under De Gaulle and Pompidou* (Ithaca, NY: Cornell University Press, 1974), 471; Hamoumou, *Et ils sont devenus harkis*, 246–251.

24. Kolodziej, *French International Policy*, 463.

25. Ibid., 465.

26. Ibid.

27. Ibid., 464.

28. Michael Willis, *The Islamist Challenge in Algeria: A Political History* (New York: New York University Press, 1999), 95–99.

29. For potential external influences on the organization, see Willis *The Islamist Challenge*, 88–94.

30. Ibid., 101–102.

31. Ibid., 191–210, see also election tables on 393–394.

32. Ibid., 316–317.

33. Ibid., 279–281.

34. Ibid., 281–284.

35. I have reconstructed the sequence of events in this section from numerous print and online news stories from the *New York Times* and the *Philadelphia Inquirer.*

36. Peter Fysh and Jim Wolfreys, *The Politics of Racism in France* (New York: St. Martin's, 1998); Neil MacMaster, *Colonial Migrants and Racism: Algerians in France, 1900–62* (New York: St. Martin's, 1997).

37. Daniel Pipes, *The Rushdie Affair: The Novel, the Ayatollah, and the West* (New York: Birch Lane, 1990), 126.

38. Ibid., 168–169.

39. Ibid., 197.

40. Youssef M. Ibrahim, "Arab Girls' Veils at Issue in France," *New York Times*, Sun., Nov. 12, 1989, A5.

41. "France: Islamic Scarf OK in School," *Philadelphia Inquirer*, Tue., Nov. 28, 1989, D16.

42. "French Schools Ban Head Scarf," *Philadelphia Inquirer*, Sun., Sept. 11, 1994, A26.

43. Lee Yanowitch, "Chanel Design Angers French Muslims," *Philadelphia Inquirer*, Sun., Jan. 23, 1994, A18.

44. Bruce Crumley, "Fighting Terrorism: Lessons from France," Time.com, <http://www.time.com/time/nation/printout/0,8816,176139,00.html>

45. Peter Humi, "French Car Bomb Escapade Ends in Belgium," CNN.com, <http://www.europe.cnn.com/WORLD/9603/france_shootout/>

46. Ian Phillips, "Police Detain 88 Islamic Militants," *Philadelphia Inquirer*, Wed., May 27, 1998, A2.

47. "Anti-terror Probe into French Blast," CNN.com, Oct. 4, 2001, <http://cnn.worldnews.printthis.clickability.com/pt/printThis?clickmap>

48. "French Track Bin Laden Link as World Hunts Network," Reuters, <http://member.compuserve.com/news/story.jsp?floc=FF-PLS-PLS&id=60202>

49. "Bin Laden Associate Arrested in Spain," CNN.com, Feb. 9, 2002, <http://cnn.worldnews.printthis.clickability.com/pt/printThis?clickmap>

Documents

Document VIII

1. Shortly after the Franco-German War, in defending the French against General Blumenthal, I said, "You must admit, General, that the French are good

actors." The sturdy old Gallophobe replied, "It is the only thing they can do. They are always acting." I do not at all agree with the first part of the distinguished General's view. The French can do a great many things besides act well.

1. Vide ante, vol. i, p. 59.
2. The moral superiority of English over French training is recognised by the Egyptians themselves, and has at times been recognised by cultivated Frenchmen. Senior (Conversations, etc., vol. i, p. 213) relates the following conversation: "Hekekan. It is remarkable that all the Egyptians and Asiatics whom Mehemet Ali sent to England for education came back, like myself and young Stephan, Anglomaniacs, while all whom he sent to France returned disgusted with Europe....Clot (the founder of the Egyptian School of Medicine). "I have made the same remark....Our students see only bad company in Paris, and are disgusted with it. In London, they get if not into the fashionable world, at least, into a respectable world, infinitely superior in morals, knowledge, and intelligence to anything in the East."

1. It has been conclusively shown by Taine and others that many of the administrative methods generally practised on the continent of Europe are not, as is very commonly supposed, the result of the French Revolution, but that they existed—often under a different form—in pre-Revolutionary days. Similarly, the idea, which is somewhat prevalent, that the extreme formalism which characterises Egyptian official life is the result of contact with Europe, though it may be partially correct, does not convey the whole truth. Mr. St. John (Egypt and Mohammed Ali, vol. ii. p. 419) gives a remarkable instance of the extreme formalism with which Egyptian official work was conducted in his time.

1. These cases have already been cited in my Report for the year 1903 (Egypt, No. 1, of 1904, p. 78). An endless number of similar illustrations of the tendency to which allusion is made above might be given.

1. Letter from Lord Ellenborough, Sir Robert Peel, vol. iii, p. 259.

1. The difficulties which subsequently occurred between France and Germany, as also the proceedings of the Algeciras Conference, lie obviously outside the scope of this work. Moreover, those difficulties did not arise until a period subsequent to the signature of the Anglo-French Agreement of April 8, 1904.

Bibliography

THE ERA OF THE MUSLIM INVASIONS OF FRANCE

Al-Maqqari (R. Dozy, G. Dugat, L. Krehl, and W. Wright, eds.). *Analectes sur l'histoire et la littérature des Arabes d'Espagne.* 2 vols. Amsterdam: Oriental Press, 1967.

Amargier, P.-A. "La capture de Saint Maieul de Cluny et l'expulsion des Sarrasins de Provence." *Revue Bénédictine* 73 (1963): 316–323.

Bellamy, James A. "Arabic Names in the *Chanson de Roland:* Saracen Gods, Frankish Swords, Roland's Horse, and the Olifant." *Journal of the American Orientalist Society* 107 (1987).

Brockelmann, Carl (Joel Carmichael and Moshe Perlmann, trans.). *History of the Islamic Peoples.* London: Routledge and Kegan Paul, 1980.

Burns, Robert I., S.J. *The Crusader Kingdom of Valencia: Reconstruction of a Thirteenth–Century Frontier.* 2 vols. Cambridge: Cambridge University Press, 1967.

Daniel, Norman. *Islam and the West: The Making of an Image.* Edinburgh: Edinburgh University Press, 1980.

Glick, Thomas F. *Islamic and Christian Spain in the Middle Ages.* Princeton, NJ: Princeton University Press, 1979.

Hodges, Richard, and David Whitehouse. *Mohammed, Charlemagne, and the Origins of Europe.* Ithaca, NY: Cornell University Press, 1982.

Hourani, Albert. *A History of the Arab Peoples.* Cambridge, MA: The Belknap Press of Harvard University, 1991.

Ibn Abd al-Hakam (C. C. Torrey, ed.). *Futuh Misr.* New Haven CT: Yale University Press, 1922.

James, Edward. *The Origins of France: From Clovis to the Capetians, 500–1000.* New York: St. Martin's, 1982.

Kedar, Benjamin Z. *Crusade and Mission: European Approaches toward the Muslims.* Princeton, NJ: Princeton University Press, 1984.

Kennedy, Hugh. *Muslim Spain and Portugal: A Political History of al-Andalus*. London: Longman, 1996.

Kritzek, James J. *Peter the Venerable and Islam*. Princeton, NJ: Princeton University Press, 1964.

Lacam, Jean. *Les Sarrazins dans le haut moyen âge français*. Paris: Maisonneuve et Larose, 1965.

———."Vestiges de l'Occupation arabe en Narbonnaise," *Cahiers Archaéologique* viii (1956): 93–115.

Lévi-Provençal, Évariste. *Histoire de l'Espagne musulmane*. 3 vols. Paris: Maisonneuve et Larose, 1950–1953.

Levillain, Leon, and Charles Samaran. "Sur le lieu et la date de la bataille dite De Poitiers de 732." *Bibliothèque de l'École de Chartres* 99 (1938): 243–267.

Lewis, Bernard. *The Muslim Discovery of Europe*. New York: W. W. Norton, 1982.

Mercier, Ernest. "La bataille de Poitiers et les vraies causes du recul de l'invasion arabe." *Revue Historique* 7 (May, Aug. 1878): 1–13.

Mercier, Maurice, and André Seguin. *Charles Martel et la Bataille de Poitiers*. Paris: P. Geuthner, 1944.

Nykl, Alois R. *Hispano-Arabic Poetry and Its Relations with the Old Provencal Troubadours*. Baltimore: J. H. Furst, 1946.

O'Callaghan, Joseph F. *A History of Medieval Spain*. Ithaca, NY: Cornell University Press, 1983.

Pellat, Charles. *Études sur l'histoire socio-culturelle de l'Islam (VIIe–XVes.)* London: Variorum Reprints, 1976.

Reinaud, Joseph Toussaint. *Invasions des Sarrazins en France et de la France en Savoie, en Piemont et dans la Suisse*. Paris: Librarie "Orient," 1964.

Rouche, Michel. *L'Aquitaine des Visigoths aux Arabes, 418–781; naissance d'une region*. Paris: Éditions de L'École des Hauts Études en Sciences Sociales, 1979.

———. "Les Aquitaines, ont-ils trahi avant la bataille de Poitiers? *Le Moyen Âge* lxxiv, no. 1 (1968): 5–26.

Saunders, J. J. *A History of Medieval Islam*. London: Routledge and Kegan Paul, 1980.

Sayers, Dorothy L., trans. *The Song of Roland*. Hardmondsworth, Middlesex, UK: Penguin, 1957.

Semann, Khalil I. *Islam and the Medieval West: Aspects of Intercultural Relations*. Albany: SUNY Press, 1980.

Sénac, Philippe. *Provence et Piraterie Sarrasine*. Paris: Maissonneuve et Larose, 1982.

———. "Contribution a l'Étude des incursions musulmanes dans l'Occident chrétien: la localisation du Gabal al-Qilal." *Revue de l'Occident musulman et de la Méditerranée* 31 (1981): 7–14.

Visquis, Alain. "Presence sarrazine au rade d'Agay au xme siecle." *Rencontre D'Archaéologie Sous-Marine de Fréjus-Saint-Raphaèl*. Fréjus: Société d'archaéologie subaquatique, 1974, n. p.

Watson, William E. "The Battle of Tours-Poitiers Revisited." *Providence: Studies in Western Civilization* 1, no. 2 (Fall 1993): 51–68.

Watt, W. Montgomery, and Pierre Cachia. *A History of Islamic Spain*. Edinburgh: University of Edinburgh Press, 1977.

THE PERIOD OF THE CRUSADES

Donovan, Joseph P. *Pelagius and the Fifth Crusade.* New York: AMS Press, 1978.

Gabrieli, Francesco. *Arab Historians of the Crusades.* Berkeley: University of California Press, 1984.

Jordan, William C. *Louis IX and the Challenge of Crusade: A Study in Rulership.* Princeton, NJ: Princeton University Press, 1979.

Luttrell, A. T. *The Hospitallers in Cyprus, Rhodes, Greece and the West (1291–1440).* London: Variorum, 1978.

Maalouf, Amin. *The Crusades through Arab Eyes.* London: Al Saqi Books, 1984.

Mayer, Hans Eberhard. "The Origins of the Lordships of Ramla and Lydda in the Latin Kingdom of Jerusalem." *Speculum* 60, no. 3 (July 1985): 537–552.

Peters, Edward M. *Christian Society and the Crusades, 1198–1229.* Philadelphia: University of Pennsylvania Press, 1971.

———, ed. *The First Crusade.* Philadelphia: University of Pennsylvania Press, 1971.

Powell, James L. *Anatomy of a Crusade, 1213–1221.* Philadelphia: University of Pennsylvania Press, 1986.

Prawer, Joshua. *Crusader Institutions.* Oxford: Clarendon Press, 1980.

———. *The Crusaders' Kingdom: European Colonialism in the Middle Ages.* New York: Praeger, 1972.

Riley-Smith, Jonathan S. C. *The Crusades: A Short History.* New Haven, CT: Yale University Press, 1987.

———. *The Feudal Nobility and the Kingdom of Jerusalem. 1174–1277.* London: Macmillan, 1973.

———. *The Knights of St. John in Jerusalem and Cyprus, c. 1050–1310.* New York: St. Martin's, 1967.

Riley-Smith, Louise, and Jonathan Riley-Smith, eds. *The Crusades: Idea and Reality.* London: Edward Arnold, 1981.

Runciman, Steven. *A History of the Crusades.* vol. 3, *The Kingdom of Acre and the Later Crusades.* New York: Harper and Row, 1967.

Setton, Kenneth M. *Western Hostility to Islam and Prophecies of Turkish Doom.* Philadelphia: American Philosophical Society, 1992.

———., ed. *A History of the Crusades.* 2 vols. Philadelphia: University of Pennsylvania Press, 1955–1962.

Shaw, M. R. B, trans. *Chronicles of the Crusaders: Joinville and Villehardouin.* Harmondsworth, Middlesex, UK: Penguin, 1963.

Smail, R. C. *Crusading Warfare, 1097–1193.* Cambridge: Cambridge University Press, 1956.

THROUGH THE ERA OF NAPOLEON

Al-Jabarti, Sheikh (Shmuel Moreh, trans.). *Napoleon in Egypt: Al-Jabarti's Chronicle of the French Occupation.* Princeton, NJ: Markus Wiener, 1993.

Ashley, Maurice. *Louis XIV and the Greatness of France.* New York: Free Press, 1946.

Cardini, Franco. *Europe and Islam.* Oxford and Malden, MA: Blackwell, 2001.

Clissold, Stephen. *The Barbary Slaves*. London: P. Elek, 1977.

Clot, André. *Suleiman the Magnificent*. New York: New Amsterdam, 1992.

Géoris, Michel. *François Ier: le Magnifique*. Paris: Éditions France-Empire, 1998.

Herold, J. Christopher. *Bonaparte in Egypt*. New York: Harper and Row, 1962.

Keddie, Nikki R., ed. *Scholars, Saints, and Sufis: Muslim Religious Insitutions since 1500*. Berkeley: University of California Press, 1972.

Lamb, Harold. *Suleiman the Magnificent*. Garden City, NY: Doubleday, 1951.

Lokke, Carl Ludwig. "French Dreams of Colonial Empire under Directory and Consulate." *The Journal of Modern History* 2, no. 2 (June 1930): 237–250.

Masters, Bruce. *The Origins of Western Economic Dominance in the Middle East: Mercantilism and the Islamic Community in Aleppo, 1600–1750*. New York: New York University Press, 1988.

Mignet, François A. M. A. *Rivalité de François Ier et Charles-Quint*. Paris: Didier, 1875.

Ridley, Ronald T. *Napoleon's Proconsul in Egypt: The Life and Times of Bernardino Drovetti*. London: Rubicon Press, 1998.

Rule, John C., ed. *Louis XIV and the Craft of Kingship*. Columbus: Ohio State University Press, 1969.

Schwartz, Merlin L., trans. *Studies on Islam*. New York: Oxford University Press, 1981.

Shaw, Stanford J. *A History of the Ottoman Empire and Modern Turkey*. 2 vols. New York: Cambridge University Press, 1976–1977.

Thomson, Ann. *Barbary and Enlightenment: European Attitudes towards the Maghrib in the Eighteenth Century*. Leiden and New York: Brill, 1987.

Ursu, Ion. *La Politique orientale de François Ier (1515–1547)*. Paris: H. Champion, 1908.

Vatin, Nicolas. *Sultan Djem: un prince ottoman dans l'Europe du xve siecle d'après deux sources contemporaines*. Ankara: Imprimerie de la Société turque d'histoire, 1997.

Wilson, Arthur McCandless. *French Foreign Policy during the Administration of Cardinal Fleury, 1726–1743. A Study in Diplomacy and Commercial Development*. Cambridge: Harvard University Press, 1936.

Wolf, John B. *Louis XIV*. New York: Norton, 1968.

THE EMPIRE AND THE "EASTERN QUESTION" THROUGH WORLD WAR I

Akarli, Engin. *The Long Peace: Ottoman Lebanon, 1861–1920*. Berkeley: University of California Press, 1993.

Anderson, M. S. *The Eastern Question, 1774–1923*. New York: St. Martin's, 1966.

Andrew, Christopher M., and Alexander S. Kanya-Forstner. *France Overseas: The Great War and the Climax of French Imperial Expansion*. Stanford, CA: Stanford University Press, 1981.

Antonius, George. *The Arab Awakening*. London: Hamish Hamilton, 1961.

Autheman, Andre. *La Banque imperiale ottomane*. Paris: Ministere de l'économie et des finances, 1996.

Baker, Bernard G. *The Passing of the Turkish Empire in Europe.* Philadelphia: Lippincott, 1913.

Betts, Raymond F. *Assimilation and Association in French Colonial Theory, 1890–1914.* New York: Columbia University Press, 1961.

Carbillet, Capitaine G. *Au Djebel Druse.* Paris: Éditions Argo, 1929.

Carnegie Endowment for International Peace. *The Treaties of Peace, 1919–1923.* 2 vols. New York: Carnegie Endowment for International Peace, 1924.

Cromer, Lord. *Modern Egypt.* 2 vols. New York: Macmillan, 1908.

Douwes, Dick. *The Ottomans in Syria: A History of Justice and Oppression.* London: Tauris, 2000.

Duggan, Stephen P. H. *The Eastern Question: A Study in Diplomacy.* New York: Columbia University Press, 1902.

Edgerton, Robert B. *Death or Glory: The Legacy of the Crimean War.* Boulder, CO: Westview Press, 2000.

Fawaz, Leila Tarazi. *An Occasion for War: Civil Conflict in Lebanon and Damascus in 1860.* Berkeley: University of California Press, 1995.

Fisher, Alan W. *A Precarious Balance: Conflict, Trade, and Diplomacy on the Russian-Ottoman Frontier.* Istanbul: Isis, 1999.

Fitzgerald, Edward Peter. "France's Middle Eastern Ambitions, the Sykes-Picot Negotiations, and the Oil Fields of Mosul, 1915–1918." *The Journal of Modern History* 66, no. 4 (Dec. 1994): 697–725.

Frazee, Charles A. *Catholics and Sultans: The Church and the Ottoman Empire, 1453–1923.* New York: Cambridge University Press, 1983.

Gottlieb, W. W. *Studies in Secret Diplomacy during the First World War.* London: G. Allen and Unwin, 1957.

Hamley, General Sir Edward. *The War in the Crimea.* New York: Charles Scribner's Sons, 1891.

Hazen, Charles Downer. *Europe since 1815.* New York: Henry Holt and Company, 1910.

Holland, Thomas E. *The European Concert in the Eastern Question: A Collection of Treaties and Other Public Acts.* Aalen, Germany: Scientia Verlag, 1979.

Hourani, Albert. *Islam in European Thought.* New York and Cambridge: Cambridge University Press, 1991.

Kinglake, Alexander W. *The Invasion of the Crimea.* 2 vols. London: William Blackwood and Sons, 1885.

Lamy, E. *La France du Levant.* Paris: Plon-Nourrit et cie, 1900.

Lawrence, Colonel Thomas Edward. *The Seven Pillars of Wisdom.* London: J. Cape, 1935.

Makdisi, Ussama Samir. *The Culture of Sectarianism: Community, History and Violence in Nineteenth-Century Ottoman Lebanon.* Berkeley: University of California Press, 2000.

Mandel, Neville J. *The Arabs and Zionism before World War I.* Berkeley: University of California Press, 1976.

Mansfield, Peter. *The Ottoman Empire and Its Successors.* New York: St. Martin's, 1973.

Massignon, Louis. *Mission en Mesopotamie (1907–1908).* 2 vols. Cairo: Institut français d'archaéologie orientale, 1910–1912.

Miller, Geoffrey. *Straits: British Policy towards the Ottoman Empire and the Origins of the Dardanelles Campaign.* Hull: University of Hull Press, 1997.

Miller, Steven, Sean M. Lynn-Jones, and Stephen Van Evera, eds. *Military Strategy and the Origins of the First World War.* Princeton, NJ: Princeton University Press, 1991.

Murphy, Agnes, R.S.C.J. *The Ideology of French Imperialism, 1871–1881.* New York: Howard Fertig, 1968.

Ortzen, Len. *Guns at Sea: The World's Great Naval Battles.* New York: Galahad, 1976.

Power, Thomas F. *Jules Ferry and the Renaissance of French Imperialism.* New York: Octagon Books, 1966.

Remak, Joachim. *The First World War: Causes, Conflict, Consequences.* New York: Wiley, 1971.

———. *The Origins of World War One, 1871–1914.* Hinsdale, IL: Dryden Press, 1967.

———. *Sarajevo: The Study of a Political Murder.* New York: Criterion Books, 1959.

Richard, Henry. *La Syrie et la guerre.* Paris: Chapelot, 1916.

Ristelhueber, René. *Traditions françaises au Liban.* Paris: F. Alcan, 1918.

Roederer, Carl. *La Syrie et la France.* Paris: Berger-Levrault, 1917.

Royle, Trevor. *Crimea: The Great Crimean War, 1854–1856.* New York: St. Martin's, 2000.

Said, Edward. *Orientalism.* New York: Vintage, 1979.

Stevenson, David. *French War Aims against Germany, 1914–1919.* Oxford: Clarendon Press, 1982.

Yalman, Ahmet Emin. *Turkey in the World War.* New Haven, CT: Yale University Press, 1930.

ISLAMIC AFRICA THROUGH WORLD WAR II

Abun-Nasser, J. A. *A History of the Maghrib.* Cambridge: Cambridge University Press, 1971.

Ageron, Charles-Robert, "La survivence d'un mythe: la puissance par l'Empire colonial, 1944–1947." *Revue Française d'Histoire d'Outre-Mer* 72, no. 269 (1985): 387–405.

———. *France coloniale ou parti colonial?* Paris: Presses Universitaires de France, 1978.

———. *Politiques coloniales au Maghrib.* Paris: Presses Universitaires de France, 1973.

———. *Les Algériens musulmans et la France (1870–1919).* 2 vols. Paris: Presses Universitaires de France, 1968.

Aldrich, Robert. *Greater France. A History of French Overseas Expansion.* London: Macmillan, 1996.

"The Algeciras Conference." *American Journal of International Law* 1, no. 1 (Jan.–Apr. 1907): 138–140.

Andrew, Christopher. "The French Colonial Party: Its Composition, Aims, and Influence, 1885–1914." *Historical Journal* 14 (1971): 91–128.

Aron, Robert. *The Vichy Regime, 1940–1944.* London: Putnam, 1958.

Azima, Jean-Pierre. *Vichy, 1940–1944.* Paris: Perrin, 1997.

Beik, Paul H. *Louis Philippe and the July Monarchy.* Princeton, NJ: D. Van Nostrand Company, 1965.

Bernett, Corelli. *The Desert Generals.* Bloomington: Indiana University Press, 1983.

Berque, Jacques (trans. Jean Stewart). *French North Africa: The Maghrib between Two World Wars.* New York: Praeger, 1962.

Brown, Leon Carl. "The Many Faces of Colonial Rule in French North Africa." *Revue de l'Occident musulman et de la Méditeranée* 13–14 (1973): 171–191.

Brunschwig, Henri. *French Colonialism, 1871–1914: Myths and Realities.* London: Pall Mall, 1966.

Bugeaud, Thomas R. *L'Algérie: des moyens de conserver et d'utiliser cette conquete.* Paris: Dentu, 1842.

Burke, Edmund, III. *Prelude to Protectorate in Morocco: Precolonial Protest and Resistance, 1860–1912.* Chicago: University of Chicago Press, 1976.

———. "Pan-Islam and Moroccan Resistance to French Colonial Penetration, 1900–1912." *Journal of African History* 13 (1972): 97–118.

———. "Recent Books on Colonial Algerian History." *Middle Eastern Studies* 7 (1971): 241–250.

Carver, Michael. *Tobruk.* London: Batsford, 1964.

Chapman, Guy. *The Third Republic of France: The First Phase, 1871–1894.* New York: St. Martin's, 1962.

Christelow, Alan. "Ritual, Culture and Politics of Islamic Reformism in Algeria." *Middle Eastern Studies* 23, no. 3 (1987): 255–273.

———. *Muslim Law Courts and the French Colonial State in Algeria.* Princeton, NJ: Princeton University Press, 1985.

Christopher, A. J. *Colonial Africa.* London: Croom and Helm, 1984.

Churchill, Winston L. S. *Memoirs of the Second World War.* Ab. ed. Boston: Houghton Mifflin, 1991.

Clancy-Smith, Julia A. *Rebel and Saint: Muslim Notables, Popular Protest, Colonial Encounters: Algeria and Tunisia, 1800–1904.* Berkeley: University of California Press, 1994.

Clayton, Anthony. "The Sétif Uprising of May 1945." *Small Wars and Insurgencies* 3, no. 1 (1992): 1–21.

Cointet, Michele. *Vichy et le fascisme: les hommes, les structures et les pouvoirs.* Brussels: Éditions Complexe, 1987.

Collot, Claude. *Les Institutions de l'Algérie durant la periode coloniale (1830–1962).* Paris: Éditions du CNRS, 1987.

Conklin, Alice L. *A Mission to Civilize: The Republican Idea of Empire in France and West Africa, 1895–1930.* Stanford, CA: Stanford University Press, 1997.

Cooke, James J. "Paul Azan and *L'Armeé Indigène Nord-Africaine.*" *Military Affairs* 45, no. 3 (Oct. 1981): 133–138.

———. "Lyautey and Étienne: The Soldier and the Politician in the Penetration of Morocco." *Military Affairs* 36, no. 1 (Feb. 1972): 14–18.

Crummey, Donald, ed. *Banditry, Rebellion and Social Protest in Africa.* Portsmouth, UK: Heinemann, 1986.

Danzinger, Raphael. *Abd al-Qadir and the Algerians.* New York: Holmes and Meier, 1977.

De Gaulle, Charles (Richard Howard, trans.). *The Complete War Memoirs of Charles de Gaulle.* New York: Da Capo Press, 1988.

De Sauvigny, Guillaume Berthier (Lynn M. Case, trans.). *The Bourbon Restoration.* Philadelphia: University of Pennsylvania Press, 1966.

Digre, Brian K. *Imperialism's New Clothes: The Repartition of Tropical Africa, 1914–1919.* New York: P. Lang, 1990.

Echenberg, Myron J. *Colonial Conscripts: The Tirailleurs Senegalais in French West Africa, 1857–1960.* Portsmouth, UK: Heinemann, 1990.

El Qadery, Mustapha. "Les Berberes entre le mythe colonial et la negation nationale. Le cas du Maroc." *Revue d'Histoire Moderne et Contemporaine* 45, no. 2 (1998): 425–450.

Étienne, Bruno. *Abdelkader.* Paris: Hachette, 1994.

Evans, Martin. "Projecting a Great France." *History Today* 50, no. 2 (Feb., 2000): 18–25.

Fage, J. D. *An Introduction to the History of West Africa.* Cambridge, UK: Cambridge University Press, 1962.

Ferro, Marc. *Pétain.* Paris: Fayard, 1987.

Fetter, Bruce, ed. *Colonial Rule in Africa.* Madison: University of Wisconsin Press, 1969.

Gann, L. H., and Peter Duignan, eds. *Colonialism in Africa, 1870–1960.* 3 vols. Cambridge, UK: Cambridge University Press, 1969.

Gellner, Ernest, and Charles Micaud, eds. *Arabs and Berbers: From Tribe to Nation in North Africa.* Lexington, MA: D. C. Heath, 1972.

"General Act of the International Conference of Algeciras, Signed April 7, 1906." Editorial comment. *American Journal of International Law* 1, no. 1 (Jan. 1907): 47–78.

Gleeson, Ian. *The Unknown Force; Black, Indian, and Coloured Soldiers through the World Wars.* Rivonia, South Africa: Ashanti Publishers, 1994.

Guedella, Philip. *The Second Empire.* Garden City, NY: Garden City Publishing Company, 1922.

Guilhaume, Jean-François. *Les myths fondatuers de l'Algérie française.* Paris: Éditions L'Harmattan, 1992.

Guizot, François, and Madame Guizot de Witt (Robert Black, trans.). *History of France.* 8 vols. New York: The Cooperative Publication Society, 1869.

Harris, Norman Dwight. "French Colonial Expansion in West Africa, the Sudan, and the Sahara." *The American Political Science Review* 5, no. 3 (Aug. 1911): 353–373.

Jones, Vincent. *Operation Torch: Anglo-American Invasion of North Africa.* New York: Ballantine, 1972.

Keegan, John. *Six Armies in Normandy.* New York: Viking, 1983.

———. *The Waffen SS: The Asphalt Soldiers.* New York: Ballantine, 1970.

Knight, M. M. "French Colonial Policy—The Decline of Association." *Journal of Modern History* 5, no. 2 (June 1933): 208–224.

Krautkramer, Elmar (Wanda Vulliez, trans.). *Vichy-Alger, 1940–1942.* Paris: Économica, 1992.

Langer, William L. "The European Powers and the French Occupation of Tunis, 1878–1881, I." *American Historical Review.* 31, no. 1 Oct., 1925: 55–79.

Lawton, Frederick. *The Third French Republic.* Philadelphia: Lippincott, 1909.

Leconte, Daniel. *Les pieds noirs. Histoire et portrait d'une communauté.* Paris: Seuil, 1980.

LeGroignec, Jacques. *Pétain et De Gaulle*. Paris: Nouvelles Éditions latines, 1998.
——. *Pétain et les Allemands*. Paris: Nouvelles Éditions latines, 1997.
Lewin, Ronald. *Montgomery as Military Commander*. London: Batsford, 1971.
Lewis, Daniel Levering. *The Race to Fashoda: European Colonialism and African Resistance in the Scramble for Africa*. New York: Weidenfeld and Nicolson, 1987.
Lewis, I. M. *Islam in Tropical Africa*. Bloomington: International African Institute—Indiana University Press, 1980.
Lewis, Martin D. "One Hundred Million Frenchmen: The Assimilation Theory in French Colonial Policy." In Robert O. Collins, ed., *Historical Problems in Imperial Africa*, 140–153. Princeton, NJ: Markus Wiener, 1994.
Lorcin, Patricia M. *Imperial Identities: Stereotyping, Prejudice, and Race in Colonial Algeria*. New York: St. Martin's, 1995.
Melton: George E. *Darlan: Admiral and Statesman of France, 1881–1942*. Westport, CT: Praeger, 1998.
Miles, William F. S. *Hausaland Divided: Colonialism and Independence in Nigeria and Niger*. Ithaca, NY: Cornell University Press, 1994.
Page, Melvin E., ed. *Africa and the First World War*. New York: St. Martin's, 1987.
Pakenham, Thomas. *The Scramble for Africa, 1871–1912*. New York: Random House, 1991.
Paxon, Robert O. *Vichy France: Old Guard and New Order, 1940–1944*. New York: Columbia University Press, 2001.
Porch, Douglas. *The French Foreign Legion: A Complete History of the Legendary Fighting Force*. New York: HarperCollins, 1992.
——. *The Conquest of the Sahara*. New York: Knopf, 1984.
Prochaska, David. *Making Algeria French: Colonialism in Bône, 1870–1920*. Cambridge: Cambridge University Press, 1994.
——. "The Political Culture of Settler Colonialism in Algeria: Politics in Bône, 1870–1920." *Revue de l'Occident musulman et de la Méditerranée* 48–49 (1988): 293–311.
Raugh, Harold E. *Wavell in the Middle East, 1939–1941: A Study in Generalship*. New York: Macmillan, 1993.
Roberts, Richard. "French Colonialism, Imported Technology, and the Handicraft Textile Industry in the Western Sudan, 1898–1918." *Journal of Economic History* 47, no. 2 (June 1987): 461–472.
Robinson, David. *Paths of Accommodation: Muslim Societies and French Colonial Authorities in Senegal and Mauritania, 1880–1920*. Athens: Ohio University Press, 2000.
Rolf, David. *The Bloody Road to Tunis: Destruction of Axis Forces in North Africa, November 1942–May 1943*. Mechanicsburg, PA: Stackpole Press, 2001.
Tardieu, André. *La Conference d'Algeciras: histoire diplomatique de la crise Marocaine (15 janvier–7 avril 1906)*. Paris: Alcan, 1909.
Thomson, David, ed. *France: Empire and Republic, 1850–1940, Historical Documents*. New York: Walker and Company, 1968.
"Treaty of November 27, 1912, between France and Spain Concerning Morocco." Official documents. *American Journal of International Law* 7, no. 2 (Apr. 1913): 81–99.
Trimingham, J. Spencer. *Islam in West Africa*. Oxford: Clarendon Press, 1959.

Verrier, Anthony. *Assassination in Algiers: Churchill, Roosevelt, De Gaulle and the Murder of Admiral Darlan.* New York: Norton, 1990.

Warner, Geoffrey. *Pierre Laval and the Eclipse of France.* New York: Macmillan, 1968.

Warner, Philip. *Kitchener: The Man behind the Legend.* New York: Atheneum, 1986.

Wright, Gwendolyn. *The Politics of Design in French Colonial Urbanism.* Chicago: University of Chicago Press, 1991.

———. "Tradition in the Service of Modernity: Architecture and Urbanism in French Colonial Policy, 1900–1930." *Journal of Modern History* 59, no. 2 (June 1987): 291–316.

Ziegler, Philip. *Omdurman.* New York: Knopf, 1974.

THE MANDATES

Browne, Walter L., ed. *Documents on the French Mandate and World War II, 1936–1943.* Salisbury, NC: Documentary Publishers, 1977.

Catroux, General. *Dans la Bataille de Méditerranée.* Paris: René Julliard, 1949.

Cumming, Henry H. *Franco-British Rivalry in the Post-War Near East: The Decline of French Influence.* London: Oxford University Press, 1938.

Gaunson, A. B. B. *The Anglo-French Clash in Lebanon and Syria, 1940–45.* New York: St. Martin's, 1987.

Gelvin, James L. *Divided Loyalties: Nationalism and Mass Politics in Syria at the Close of Empire.* Berkeley: University of California Press, 1999.

Haddad, Richard. *Les Phalanges libanaises.* Beirut: Édition Charlemagne, 1993.

Harvey, John. *With the French Foreign Legion in Syria.* Mechanicsburg, PA: Stackpole Books, 1995.

Howard Harry N. *The Partition of Turkey: A Diplomatic History, 1913–1923.* New York: Howard Fertig, 1966.

———. *The King-Crane Commission.* Beirut: Khayat's, 1963.

Khadduri, Majid. "The Alexandretta Dispute." *American Journal of International Law* 39, no. 3 (July 1945): 406–425.

———. "The Franco-Lebanese Dispute and the Crisis of November, 1943." *American Journal of International Law* 38, no. 4 (Oct. 1944): 601–620.

Khoury, Philip S. "Continuity and Change in Syrian Political Life: The Nineteenth and Twentieth Centuries." *American Historical Review* 96, no. 5 (Dec. 1991): 1374–1395.

———. *Syria and the French Mandate: The Politics of Arab Nationalism, 1920–1945.* Princeton, NJ: Princeton University Press, 1990.

Laffargue, André Charles Victor. *Le Général Dentz (Paris 1940–Syrie 1941).* Paris: Iles d'or, 1954.

Lapierre, Jean. *Le Mandat français en Syrie.* Paris: Librarie du Recueil Sirey, 1936.

Lerner, Henri. *Catroux.* Paris: Albin Michel, 1990.

Longrigg, Stephen Hemsley. *Syria and Lebanon under French Mandate.* Beirut: Librarie du Liban, 1968.

Nevakivi, Jukka. *Britain, France, and the Arab Middle East, 1914–1920.* Leiden, The Netherlands: Brill, 1969.

Sorel, Jean Albert. *Le Mandat français et l'expansion économique de la Syrie et du Liban.* Paris: M. Giard, 1929.

Thompson, Elizabeth. *Colonial Citizens: Republican Rights, Paternal Privilege, and Gender in French Syria and Lebanon*. New York: Columbia University Press, 2000.

Wilmington, Martin W. *The Middle East Supply Centre*. Albany: SUNY Press, 1971.

Winder, R. Bayly, "Syrian Deputies and Cabinet Ministers, 1919–59," Vol. 16, no. 4 Part II. *Middle East Journal* Vol. 17, no. 1 and 2 (Winter 1963): 35–54.

————. "Syrian Deputies and Cabinet Ministers, 1919–59," Part I. *Middle East Journal* no. 16 (Autumn 1962): 407–429.

Zamir, Meir. *Lebanon's Quest: The Road to Statehood, 1926–1939*. London: Taurus, 2000: 335–364

Zeine, Zeine N. *The Struggle for Arab Independence: Western Diplomacy and the Rise and Fall of Faisal's Kingdom in Syria*. Delmar, NY: Caravan Books, 1977.

ISLAMIC AFRICA THROUGH INDEPENDENCE

Adamolekun, Lapido. *Sékou Touré's Guinea: An Experiment in Nation Building*. London: Methuen, 1976.

Ageron, Charles-Robert. "L'Opinion française devant la guerre d'Algérie." *Revue de la France d'Outre Mer* 231 (1976): 256–285.

Alleg, Henri, ed. *La Guerre d'Algérie*. 3 vols. Paris: Temps Actuels, 1981.

Anderson, Lisa. *The State and Social Transformation in Tunisia and Libya, 1830–1980*. Princeton, NJ: Princeton University Press, 1986.

Aussaresses, Paul. *Services Speciaux: Algérie, 1955–1957*. Paris: Perrin, 2000.

Barbour, Neville. "Algeria." In Colin Legum, ed., *Africa: A Handbook to the Continent*, 5–20. New York: Praeger, 1967.

Behr, Edward. *The Algerian Problem*. New York: Norton, 1962.

Bergot, Erwan. *Le dossier rouge: services secrets contre FLN*. Paris: Grasset, 1976.

Bessis, Sophie. *Bourguiba*. 2 vols. Paris: Groupe jeune Afrique, 1988–1989.

Bigeard, Marcel. *Pour une parcelle de gloire*. Paris: Plon, 1975.

Camus, Albert. *Chroniques algériennes (1939–1958)*. Paris: Gallimard, 1958.

Cannon, Cavendish W. "Status of Tangier." Official Documents. *American Journal of International Law* 51, no. 2 (Apr. 1957): 460–466.

Carroll, David. "Camus's Algeria: Birthrights, Colonial Injustice, the Fiction of a French-Algerian People." *Modern Language Notes* 112 (1997): 517–549.

Challe, Maurice. *Notre revolte*. Paris: Presses de la Cité, 1968.

Cohen, Bernard. *Habib Bourguiba: Le pouvoir d'un seul*. Paris: Flammarion, 1986.

Cohen, Mark L., and Lorna Hahn. *Morocco: Old Land, New Nation*. New York: Praeger, 1966.

Cohen-Solal, Annie. "Camus, Sartre, and the Algerian War." *Journal of European Studies* 28, no. 1 (1998): 43–50.

Cointet, Michele. *De Gaulle et l'Algérie française, 1958–1962*. Paris: Perrin, 1995.

Cornaton, Michel. *Les Camps de regroupement de la guerre d'Algérie*. Paris: Éditions L'Harmattan, 1998.

Cowan, L. Gray. "The New Face of Algeria: Part I." *Political Science Quarterly* 66, no. 3 (Sep. 1951): 340–365.

De Cock, Laurence. "La France et Bourguiba: 1945–1956." *Revue d'Histoire Diplomatique* 110 (1996): 255–264.

Descombin, Henry. *Guerre d'Algérie 1959–60. Le Cinquieme Bureau ou 'Le théorème du poisson.* Paris: Éditions L'Harmattan, 1994.

Dine, Philip. *Images of the Algerian War. French Fiction and Film, 1954–1992.* Oxford: Clarendon Press, 1994.

Droz, Bernard, and Evelyne Lever. *Histoire de la Guerre d'Algérie 1954–1962.* Paris: Éditions du Seuil, 1982.

El Machat, Samya. *La Tunisie, les chemins vers independence, 1945–1956.* Paris: Editions L'Harmattan, 1992.

El Tayeb, Salah el Din el Zein. "The Europeanized Algerians and the Emancipation of Algeria." *Middle Eastern Studies* 22, no. 2 (1986): 206–235.

Evans, Martin. *The Memory of Resistance. French Opposition to the Algerian War (1954–1962).* Oxford: Berg, 1997.

Fanon, Frantz. *L'An V de la revolution algérienne. Sociologie d'une revolution.* Paris: Maspero, 1959.

Foltz, William J. *From French West Africa to the Mali Federation.* New Haven, CT: Yale University Press, 1965.

Gadant, Monique. *Islam et Nationalisme en Algérie d'après 'El Moudjahid' organe central du FLN de 1956 a 1962.* Paris: Éditions L'Harmattan, 1988.

Gbagbo, Laurent. *La Côte d'Ivoire: economie et société a la veille de l'independence, 1940–1960.* Paris: L'Harmattan, 1982.

Gershovich, Moshe. *French Military Rule in Morocco: Colonialism and Its Consequences.* London: F. Cass, 2000.

Gillespie, Joan. *Algeria: Rebellion and Revolution.* New York: Praeger, 1960.

Gordon, David. *The Passing of French Algeria.* New York: Oxford University Press, 1966.

Greenhalgh, Michael. "The New Centurions: French Reliance on the Roman Past during the Conquest of Algeria." *War and Society* 16, no. 1 (1998): 1–28.

Grimaud, Nicole. "La crise de Bizerte." *Revue d'Histoire Diplomatique* 110 (1996): 328–340.

Hamoumou, Mohand. *Et ils sont devenus harkis.* Paris: Fayard, 1993.

Hargreaves, J. D. *Decolonization in Africa.* London: Longman, 1988.

Harrison, Alexander. *Challenging De Gaulle: The O.A.S. and the Counterrevolution in Algeria.* Westport, CT: Greenwood Press, 1989.

Harrison, Christopher. "French Attitudes to Empire and the Algerian War." *African Affairs* (1983): 75–95.

Helie, Jerome. *Les Accords d'Évian. Histoire de la paix ratée en Algérie.* Paris: Olivier Orban, 1992.

Hoffman, Stanley H. "The French Constitution of 1958: I. The Final Text and Its Prospects." *American Political Science Review* 53, no. 2 (June 1959): 332–357.

Hoisington, William. "Commerce and Conflict: French Businessmen in Morocco, 1952–1955." *Journal of Contemporary History* 9 (1974): 49–67.

Horne, Alistair. *A Savage War of Peace: Algeria 1954–1962.* London: Macmillan, 1977.

Hutchinson, Martha Crenshaw. *Revolutionary Terrorism. The FLN in Algeria, 1954–1962.* Stanford, CA: Hoover Institution Press, 1978.

Jouhaud, Edmond. *O mon pays perdu!* Paris: Fayard, 1969.

Kettle, Michael. *De Gaulle and Algeria, 1940–1960.* London: Quartet, 1993.

Lagaillarde, Pierre. *On a triché avec l'honneur.* Paris, La Table Ronde, 1960.

Le Goyet, Pierre. *La Guerre d'Algérie.* Paris: Perrin, 1989.

Lewis, James I. "French Politics and the Algerian Statute of 1947." *Maghrib Review* 17, nos. 3–4 (1992): 146–172.

Macey, David. *Frantz Fanon: A Biography.* New York: St. Martin's, 2001.

MacMaster, Neil. *Colonial Migrants and Racism: Algerians in France, 1900–62.* New York: St. Martin's, 1997.

Manning, Patrick. *Francophone Sub-Saharan Africa, 1880–1995.* New York: Cambridge University Press, 1999.

Maran, Rita. *Torture: The Role of Ideology in the French-Algerian War.* Westport, CT: Greenwood Press, 1989.

Massu, Jacques. *La Vrai Bataille d'Alger.* Paris: Plon, 1971.

Mathias, Gregor. *Les Sectiones administratives specialiseés en Algérie. Entre Ideal et realité (1955–1962).* Paris: Éditions L'Harmattan, 1998.

Naegelen, Marcel-Edmond. *Mission en Algérie.* Paris: Flammarion, 1962.

Nandjui, Pierre. *Houphouet-Boigny: l'homme de la France en Afrique.* Paris: L'Harmattan, 1995.

Quandt, William B. *Revolution and Political Leadership: Algeria, 1954–1968.* Cambridge, MA: MIT Press, 1969.

Rolland, Denis. "Jacques Soustelle, de l'éthnologie a la politique." *Revue d'Histoire moderne et contemporaine* 43, no. 1 (1996): 137–150.

Saint Verin, Robert (Virginia Thompson and Richard Adloff, trans.). *Djibouti: Pawn of the Horn of Africa.* Metuchen, NJ: Scarecrow Press, 1981.

Salan, Raoul. *Mémoires: Fin d'un empire.* T. III, *Algérie française.* T. IV, *Algérie, de Gaulle, et moi.* Paris: Presses de la Cité, 1972–1974.

Salem, Norma. *Habib Bourguiba, Islam and the Creation of Tunisia.* London: Croom Helm, 1984.

Shah-Kazemi, Reza, ed. *Algeria: Revolution Revisited.* New York: St. Martin's, 1998.

Smith, Tony. *The French Stake in Algeria, 1945–1962.* Ithaca, NY: Cornell University Press, 1978.

Soustelle, Jacques. *Aimeé et Souffrante Algérie.* Paris: Plon, 1956.

Theobald, Robert, ed. *The New Nations of West Africa.* New York: H. W. Wilson Co., 1960.

Thomas, Martin. *The French North African Crisis: Colonial Breakdown and Anglo-French Relations, 1945–62.* New York: St. Martin's, 2000.

Thompson, Virginia, and Richard Adloff. *Conflict in Chad.* Berkeley: University of California Press, 1981.

THE ERA OF THE COLD WAR

Connelly, Matthew, "Taking Off the Cold War Lens: Visions of North-South Conflict during the Algerian War for Independence." *American Historical Review* 105, no. 3 (June 2000): 739–769.

———. "The French-American Conflict over North Africa and the Fall of the Fourth Republic." *Revue française d'Histoire d'Outre-Mer* 84, no. 315 (1997): 9–27.

Fitzgerald, Edward Peter. "Did France's Colonial Empire Make Economic Sense? A Perspective from the Postwar Decade, 1946–1956." *Journal of Economic History* 48, no. 2 (June 1988): 373–385.

Harrison, Michael M. "Mitterand's France in the Atlantic System: A Foreign Policy of Accommodation." *Political Science Quarterly* 99, no. 2 (Summer 1984): 219–246.

Hourani, Albert. "The Middle East and the Crisis of 1956." In *St. Antony's Papers, no. 4 Middle Eastern Affairs One*, 9–42. London: Chatto and Windus, 1958.

Jasse, Richard L. "The Baghdad Pact: Cold War or Colonialism?" *Middle Eastern Studies* 27, no. 1 (1991): 140–156.

Kerekes, Tibor, ed. *The Arab Middle East and Muslim Africa*. New York: Praeger, 1961.

Kolodziej, Edward A. *French International Policy under De Gaulle and Pompidou*. Ithaca, NY: Cornell University Press, 1974.

Kyle, Keith. *Suez*. New York: St. Martin's, 1992.

Lefebvre, Jeffrey A. "Kennedy's Algerian Dilemma: Containment, Alliance Politics and the 'Rebel Dialogue.'" *Middle Eastern Studies* 35, no. 2 (1999): 61–82.

Rees, David. *The Age of Containment*. New York: St. Martin's, 1968.

Sanjian, Ara. "The Formulation of the Baghdad Pact." *Middle Eastern Studies* 33, no. 2 (1997): 226–266.

Tint, Herbert. *French Foreign Policy since the Second World War*. (London: Weidenfeld and Nicolson, 1972).

Walker, Martin. *The Cold War: A History*. New York: Henry Holt, 1995.

Wall, Irwin M. *France, the United States and the Algerian War*. Berkeley: University of California Press, 2001.

Williams, Charles. *The Last Great Frenchman: A Life of General De Gaulle* (New York: Wiley, 1997)

CONTEMPORARY PROBLEMS

Abraham, Antoine J. *The Lebanon War*. Westport, CT: Greenwood Press, 1996.

Al-Khalil, Samir. *Republic of Fear: The Inside Story of Saddam's Iraq*. New York: Pantheon, 1989.

Arnold, Guy. *The Maverick State: Gaddafi and the New World Order*. London: Cassell, 1996.

Azevedo, Mario J. *Roots of Violence: A History of War in Chad*. London: Routledge, 1998.

Azevedo, Mario J., and Emmanuel U. Nnadozie. *Chad: A Nation in Search of Its Future*. Boulder, CO: Westview Press, 1998.

Bodansky, Yossef. *Bin Laden: The Man Who Declared War on America*. Roseville, CA: Forum, 2001.

Burman, Jonathan. *Qadhafi's Libya*. London: Zed Books, 1986.

Ciment, James. *Algeria: The Fundamentalist Challenge*. New York: Facts on File, 1997.

Cooley, John K. *Libyan Sandstorm*. New York: Holt, Rinehart, and Winston, 1982.

Decalo, Samuel. *Historical Dictionary of Chad*. Lanham, MD: Scarecrow Press, 1997.

"The Devil behind the Scenes: The Rebels Declare Victory but Gaddafi May be the Real Winner." *Time Magazine*, Dec. 17, 1990, 40.

El Khazen, Farid. *The Breakdown of the State in Lebanon, 1967–1976*. Cambridge: Harvard University Press, 2000.

El Khikia, Mansour O. *Libya's Qaddafi: The Politics of Contradiction*. Gainesville: University Press of Florida, 1998.

"Exit Gadafi, Enter Mitterand." *Time Magazine*, Nov. 16, 1981, 50.

"France: Islamic Scarf OK in School." *Philadelphia Inquirer*, Tue., Nov. 28, 1989, D16.

"French Schools Ban Head Scarf." *Philadelphia Inquirer*, Sun., Sep. 11, 1994, A26.

Fysh, Peter, and Jim Wolfreys. *The Politics of Racism in France*. New York: St. Martin's, 1998.

Hiro, Dilip. *Holy Wars: The Rise of Islamic Fundamentalism*. New York: Routledge, 1989.

Ibrahim, Youssef M. "Arab Girls' Veils at Issue in France." *New York Times*, Sun., Nov. 12, 1989, A5.

Jacquard, Roland. *In the Name of Osama Bin Laden: Global Terrorism and the Bin Laden Brotherhood*. Durham, NC: Duke University Press, 2002.

"Jacques Chirac, 'Lebanese Reconstruction.'" *Presidents and Prime Ministers*. 4, no. 5 (Nov./Dec. 1995): 28.

Jansen, G. H. *Militant Islam*. New York: Harper and Row, 1979.

Kaplan, Robert D. *The Arabists: The Romance of an American Elite*. New York: Free Press, 1993.

Kifner, John. "In a Pinch, Qaddafi Can Rely Mostly on Himself." *New York Times*, Sun., Aug. 23, 1981, E1.

Mernissi, Fatima (Mary Jo Lakeland, trans.). *Islam and Democracy: Fear of the Modern World*. Reading, MA: Addison-Wesley, 1992.

Moore, Clement Henry. *Tunisia since Independence: The Dynamics of One-Party Government*. Westport, CT: Greenwood Press, 1982.

Nolutshungu, Sam C. *Limits of Anarchy: Intervention and State Formation in Chad*. Charlottesville: University Press of Virginia, 1996.

O'Ballance, Edgar. *Civil War in Lebanon, 1975–92*. New York: St. Martin's, 1998.

Phillips, Ian. "Police Detain 88 Islamic Militants." *Philadelphia Inquirer*, Wed., May 27, 1998, A2.

Pipes, Daniel. *The Hidden Hand: Middle East Fears of Conspiracy*. New York: St. Martin's, 1996.

———. *Greater Syria: The History of an Ambition*. New York: Oxford University Press, 1992.

———. *The Rushdie Affair: The Novel, the Ayatollah, and the West*. New York: Birch Lane, 1990.

Rabinovich, Itamar. *The War for Lebanon, 1970–85*. Ithaca, NY: Cornell University Press, 1990.

Salem, Eli Adib. *Violence and Diplomacy in Lebanon: The Troubled Years, 1982–1988*. London: Tauris, 1995.

Salibi, Kamal S. *A House of Many Mansions: The History of Lebanon Reconsidered*. Berkeley: University of California Press, 1990.

Schiff, Ze'Ev, and Ehud Ya'Ari. *Israel's Lebanon War*. New York: Simon and Schuster, 1984.

Seale, Patrick. *Asad: The Struggle for the Middle East*. Berkeley: University of California Press, 1988.

Shirley, Edward. "Is Iran's Present Algeria's Future?" *Foreign Affairs* 74, no. 3 (May/June 1995): 28–44.

Willis, Michael. *The Islamist Challenge in Algeria: A Political History.* New York: New York University Press, 1999.

Yanowitch, Lee. "Chanel Design Angers French Muslims." *Philadelphia Inquirer,* Sun. Jan. 23, 1994, A18.

Zisser, Eyal. *Lebanon: The Challenge of Independence.* London: Tauris, 2000.

Index

About the Author

WILLIAM E. WATSON is Associate Professor of History at Immaculata College. His research interests include cross-cultural contact and conflict. His previous publications include *Collapse of Communism in the Twentieth Century* (Greenwood, 1998).

Schmitt

St. Louis Community College
at Meramec
Library